THE QUOTIDIAN REVOLUTION

THE QUOTIDIAN REVOLUTION

Vernacularization, Religion,
and the Premodern Public Sphere in India

Christian Lee Novetzke

Columbia University Press
New York

Columbia University Press
Publishers Since 1893
New York   Chichester, West Sussex
cup.columbia.edu

Library of Congress Cataloging-in-Publication Data
Names: Novetzke, Christian Lee, 1969- author.
Title: The quotidian revolution : vernacularization, religion, and the
premodern public sphere in India / Christian Lee Novetzke.
Description: New York : Columbia University Press, 2016. |
Includes bibliographical references and index.
Identifiers: LCCN 2016012704| ISBN 9780231175807 (cloth : alk. paper) |
ISBN 9780231542418 (e-book)
Subjects: LCSH: Marathi literature—History and criticism. |
Marathi language—Social aspects—History. | Maharashtra (India)—History.
Classification: LCC PK2405 .N68 2016 | DDC 891.4/609—dc23
LC record available at https://lccn.loc.gov/2016012704

Columbia University Press books are printed on permanent
and durable acid-free paper.
Printed in the United States of America
c 10 9 8 7 6 5 4 3 2 1

COVER DESIGN: Milenda Nan Ok Lee
COVER PAINTING: Sudhir Waghmare, *New Modikhana*

To my parents

Mary E. Novetzke

William E. Novetzke

and

In memory of my father-in-law

Sharatkumar Kale (1940–2013)

Who waited for everyone

Contents

Preface
The Shape of the Book

This book is about the moment in recorded history when literary Marathi appeared in medieval India. Situated in Maharashtra of the thirteenth century, the book traces this history by examining Marathi inscriptions and the first two extant texts of Marathi literature, the *Līḷācaritra* (c. 1278 CE) and the *Jñāneśvarī* (c. 1290 CE). This study also explores the lives of the two key figures associated with those texts, Chakradhar (c. 1194 [1273 departure from Maharashtra]),[1] the founder of the Mahanubhav religion, and Jnandev (c. 1271 [1296 entombment]),[2] who later becomes a key figure of the Varkari religion. The book presents these figures and texts as emblems of the process of vernacularization in Maharashtra, using them to argue that through this process public culture was invested with the idioms of the "everyday" and the quotidian became valorized in public and political expression. Vernacularization was compelled by a critique of social inequity as a result of this emphasis on ordinary life. This critique of social inequity, and the literary sphere engendered by vernacularization, inaugurated the first trace of a nascent public sphere in the region.

The book is divided into three parts, each composed of either two or three chapters, bounded by an introduction and a conclusion. The introduction presents the book's key subjects and materials, and surveys the primary ideas, concepts, and debates the book engages. Part 1 provides a view of what I call the Yadava century, the period presided over by the Yadava dynasty in the region of Maharashtra from 1189 to 1317 CE. The primary textual and archival evidence for these three chapters is the Marathi inscriptional record of the Yadava state, as well as, secondarily, social, cultural, economic, and religious historical evidence that can be gleaned from the *Līḷācaritra* and the *Jñāneśvarī*.

Part 1 begins with chapter 1, which explores the sociopolitical world of the Yadava century that served as the context for Marathi literary vernacularization. The Yadavas, also called the Sevunas, were a non-Brahmin dynasty that helped stabilize their political territory by creating a clientelist Brahminic ecumene. Select members of that ecumene were awarded land and grants for temples, monasteries, and other institutions, given at the beneficence of the Yadava state as rewards for certain kinds of textual production and other services. The Brahminic ecumene of the Yadava century was primarily composed of Brahmin literary and ritual experts engaging in traditional Brahminic activities, though other high castes, such as Kayasthas and Guravs, also participated. The Yadavas, like many polities of the age, used these gifts of state to create distinct spheres of entitlements throughout their political geography. This nonthreatening, nonmilitarized Brahminic ecumene helped stabilize the political sphere in the Yadava century. As a system it served the political aims of the non-Brahmin Yadava state, displaying a downward flow of power from Kshatriya or "King" to Brahmin.

Chapter 2 uses the inscriptional record left by the Yadavas to counter a common assumption made by historians that Marathi vernacularization was underwritten by Yadava political support. I find no evidence for this widely held claim, but instead show how the inscriptional record and other aspects of the Yadava century suggest that the royal court, while it did not support Marathi literary production with official state funds, did appear to regard Marathi as a language of significant utility in accessing the vast quotidian "public" that surrounded and populated the Yadava realm. We will see that the indifference to Marathi displayed by the royal court and its Brahminic ecumene allowed greater freedom for new religious communities to adopt Marathi as a means to reach a nonelite population. At the same time, the social value of literacy, a feature of the Brahminic ecumene, led the Brahmin figures at the center of literary vernacularization (Chakradhar, the early Mahanubhavs, Jnandev) to compose a new literature in Marathi.

Chapter 3 provides a necessary prelude to the next two parts of the book through a survey of the social contexts and received biographies of

Chakradhar and Jnandev. This chapter supplies the remembered biographical data and likely public memory of Chakradhar and Jnandev that help shape the context of the four chapters that follow. The chapter also argues that meaning coheres around these received biographies in a way that stabilizes their "value" in a particular kind of spiritual economy of the age. The three chapters of part 1 thus provide a vision of the preconditions of vernacularization in medieval western India.

Part 2 focuses on the *Līḷācaritra*, using the text primarily as a historical archive for the cultural sphere in which vernacularization emerged and a nascent Marathi public sphere formed in the thirteenth century. Though the *Līḷācaritra* is the first instance we have of Marathi literature, what it records is its own prehistory—it details the conditions for its own creation. I consider the *Līḷācaritra* to be an example of something like historical literary realism as it seeks to convey a high level of historicity and real-life encounters, even while it is a text of *bhakti*, of religious devotion to Chakradhar. Indeed, the authors of the *Līḷācaritra* took great pains to precisely recall the life of Chakradhar by drawing on their immediate memories of his life and teachings. So attentive to historical correctness were the compilers of the *Līḷācaritra* that they present recollections of their leader that display not only his glorious traits, but his peculiarities as well. If part 1 of the book described the preconditions for the vernacular turn by portraying the cultural and political landscape of the Yadava century, then part 2 is configured as a study of the portrayal of vernacularization, the cultural memory of this moment, as preserved in the *Līḷācaritra*.

Chapter 4 observes the attention to historical detail in the *Līḷācaritra* and this allows us some access to the social conditions that were arrayed around vernacularization in the decades just before the full advent of Marathi literature. In the *Līḷācaritra*, we learn that the greatest site of contention for this evolving vernacular sphere was not the literary-political world but rather a contention with the gurus and godmen who competed in a religious market for followers and patronage, often around the social economies of temples. Chakradhar is not only emblematic of a religious innovator, but is one of the most radical of his age, for he promoted a new religion that rejected caste and gender difference in principle. Chapter 4 studies the cultural practices of caste and gender that pervaded everyday life in the mid-thirteenth century and were recorded by the early Mahanubhavs in the *Līḷācaritra*. If vernacularization directly engaged caste and gender differences at least rhetorically, then attention to these questions of social ethics is vital for understanding the cultural politics at work at the core of a new literary world in Marathi. I show how the early Mahanubhavs grappled with these social issues, both within their community and outside in the ordinary world.

Chapter 5 tracks how this rejection of social inequity inspired, or even compelled, the use of Marathi as the medium of communication for the early Mahanubhav community. I give several reasons for the use of Marathi to record the life of Chakradhar in the *Līḷācaritra*. In writing a historical text, the early Mahanubhavs wished to preserve the language their founder was remembered to have used, which was Marathi. This was a language understood as feminine and "imperfect" in the taxonomies of Sanskritic linguistic hierarchy, yet it perfectly suited his audience, especially the female followers whom the early Mahanubhavs wished not to alienate. The choice of Marathi for the preservation of the key text of the Mahanubhav religion was a practical one made around the ethical conviction to leave a text intelligible to the larger quotidian world that did not know Sanskrit. However, Chakradhar's ethical urge toward inclusiveness—of women, low castes, and those deemed "Untouchable"—led him afoul of the Brahminic elite of the Yadava century, according to the *Līḷācaritra*. His story ends with a purported public trial and his own exit from the region of Maharashtra and also from recorded human history.

The two chapters of part 2 demonstrate that the cultural origin of vernacularization was not at the nexus of literature and royal power. Instead, the materials examined here proclaim a desire to communicate as widely as possible the teachings of a new spiritual figure in the Yadava domains. The early Mahanubhavs created the first work of Marathi literature as an extension of the radical social ideals of their founder, not as a project to create a new literary idiom in Marathi.

Part 3 of the book turns to Jnandev and his *Jñāneśvarī*. The two chapters in this part of the book use the *Jñāneśvarī* to see how, in the contexts described in parts 1 and 2 of the book, a work arises in Marathi that evinces a high self-consciousness about its literary, religious, and social aims. In chapter 6 I discuss the rationale that Jnandev gives in his text for the innovative use of Marathi rather than Sanskrit as his medium. Contrary to the intentions of the Mahanubhavs, Jnandev takes the language Krishna is said to have spoken, which is Sanskrit, and shifts Krishna's religious and ethical message into a new linguistic medium, Marathi. Jnandev claims that he uses Marathi for the sake of "women, low castes, and others," which is the constituency he believes the *Bhagavad Gītā* also exists to serve. I take this social formulation of "women, low castes, and others" not only to indicate those who did not have access to Sanskrit but also as a phrase that points toward public culture in quotidian life. While it may seem like a description of the "downtrodden" it was in fact a description of the vast majority of the population.[3] Jnandev believed that the mission of the *Bhagavad Gītā* and of Krishna was to address all people, not just high-caste males. Transferring the salvational promise of the *Bhagavad Gītā* into everyday language furthered the *Bhagavad Gītā*'s own ethics according to Jnandev. He often imagines his text situated at the "crossroads" of towns and cities, that is, in the public square where the creation of the *Jñāneśvarī* is the re-creation of the social conditions for public expression itself. In this chapter I observe how the *Jñāneśvarī* serves as a manifesto for a very particular ethics around society and literature.

In chapter 7 I draw out the contours of this social ethics in the *Jñāneśvarī* by tracking the relationship between statements about social equality and idioms of social inequality that were endemic to thirteenth-century Marathi. I follow how the *Jñāneśvarī* rejects social distinction by recourse to "cosmic reality" where all social and physical differences are dissolved. This ethics of transcendence occurs primarily in the first nine chapters of the *Jñāneśvarī* and tracks a similar argument in the first nine chapters of the *Bhagavad Gītā*. However, in the latter half of the *Jñāneśvarī*, Jnandev draws in colloquial Marathi that reveals the quotidian social prejudices of his age, though they are not his own prejudices. The *Jñāneśvarī* reveals a paradox, for the radical nature of putting this classic Sanskrit text in Marathi for all to access also means importing the language, colloquialisms, idioms, and other registers of social inequity that mark all languages. Vernacularization, located within the field of everyday life, simultaneously presses for greater social equity and reinforces other means of social difference. The *Jñāneśvarī* both explicitly rejects caste and gender difference in the context of cosmic reality, yet also testifies to distinctions passively through the colloquial use of Marathi. Vernacularization thus reveals a dual function: to expand the scope of social access by valorizing everyday life, yet also to circumscribe such access by rehearsing the deeper habitus of social distinction in the quotidian world. The *Jñāneśvarī* reveals a sonic equality that existed in a world of deep social inequality.

The structure of these latter two parts of the book creates a mirrored dialectic. Part 2 moves from a discussion of an unequivocal social ethics of egalitarianism among the Mahanubhavs (chapter 4) to an ethical rationale for the use of Marathi and hence for the creation of literary Marathi (chapter 5). Part 3, conversely, begins with a discussion of an unequivocal valorization of a new literary Marathi sphere inaugurated by the *Jñāneśvarī* (chapter 6), but returns to the question of social ethics to find that a sonic equality precedes social equality in the early world of Marathi literary vernacularization (chapter 7).

The book's conclusion reflects on the quotidian politics of vernacularization in the centuries that followed the narrow band of decades that consumes the majority of the book. From the fourteenth century onward, Jnandev's sonic equality was transformed into a vision of social equality. His key hagiographer, the Marathi *sant* Namdev (1270–1350), is said to have composed sacred biographies in which Jnandev is portrayed in the company of low-caste people and women despite the fact that the *Jñāneśvarī* does not explicitly state that this social world surrounded Jnandev. This displays the vernacularization of Jnandev's public memory after his life, and thus the force of the "quotidian revolution" to draw its subjects into the gravity of its conceptualization of the "ordinary." Conversely, I discuss how the Mahanubhavs receded in the centuries after their founding, precisely because they increasingly rejected the quotidian world to become an ascetical sect, a kind of antivernacularization. The book ends with a reflection on how these ideas, formulated with materials from the thirteenth century, might accompany an analysis of the vernacularization of democracy and of the public sphere in India today.

I approach the subjects of this book with profound respect. My investigation of the lives of Chakradhar and Jnandev, of the *Līḷācaritra* and other Mahanubhav texts, and of the *Jñāneśvarī*; and my many conversations with Mahanubhavs, Varkaris, and other believers have only raised my already great admiration for the historical figures, religious traditions, and texts that are the subjects of this book. Over the last fifteen years, several scholarly works, some written by non-Indians, some by Indians, have generated anger, protests, legal challenges, censorship, and even violence in India.

Because of these reactions, I have felt compelled to clearly state my own position, or lack of a position, on several subjects in this book. These statements appear throughout, and they may confound or irritate a reader, particularly a non-Indian reader, who will perhaps see them as irrelevant. But I offer them to clearly mark my sincere desire to avoid causing offense to anyone. If anything I write here were to offend anyone who holds dear the subjects of this study, it would be entirely contrary to my intentions or sentiments, and it would represent a personal failing on my part, and a failing that would be wholly my own responsibility and no one else's.

Acknowledgments

A book is a ledger of debts. Were it not for the many people who advised, cajoled, interceded, corrected, debated, rejected, lobbied, encouraged, discouraged, joked, observed, and embraced, this book would not be. This is also true of my own career and my own scholarship, for beyond this or any one work. Such debts cannot be paid, much less adequately acknowledged, by the trite formula of an acknowledgments section. I ask all those thanked here, and those I could not thank (or forgot to thank—I'm getting old), to forgive me for not doing more.

At Columbia University Press, I have had the tremendous fortune to work with Wendy Lochner, an extraordinary editor. I am thankful to Christine Dunbar, Justine Evans, Zachary Friedman, Ben Kolstad, Milenda Lee, Susan Pensak, Robert Swanson, and others at the Press for their help and patience with me and this book. Rivka Israel's expert eyes have helped smooth my prose and sharpen its meaning. Mariam Sabri provided expert proofreading for the final text. My thanks to Sudhir Waghmare, wonderful artist and dear friend, who graciously offered the use of his painting of an everyday scene in New Modikhana, Pune, for my book cover.

A number of institutions and funding agencies support this work in various forms. I thank the American Institute of India Studies, the American Council of Learned Societies, the National Endowment for the Humanities, and the Fulbright-Nehru Program for vital support during research and writing. The University of Pennsylvania supported some of this work through research funding at a very early stage. The University Seminars Publication

Fund at Columbia University provided a generous subvention. My thanks to David Magier, Alice Newton, Robert Pollack, and Serinity Young.

My home institution, the Jackson School of International Studies at the University of Washington, and in particular the programs in South Asia Studies, Comparative Religion, and Global Studies, have offered me not only financial support but an intense and diverse intellectual environment coupled with a level of collegiality that makes my life among my extraordinary colleagues at UW a sheer delight day after day. In particular, I would like to thank Ana Mari Cauce, Judy Howard, Reşat Kasaba, Priti Ramamurthy, Michael Shapiro, Bob Stacey, Jim Wellman, and Anand Yang for their support and for making leave and research possible. Among my wonderful colleagues at UW, several made particular efforts to read and comment on my work. My thanks to Jameel Ahmed, Sareeta Amrute, David Bachman, Deepa Banerjee, Paul Brass, Dan Chirot, Frank Conlon, Collett Cox, Sara Curran, Purnima Dhavan, Jennifer Dubrow, Avinash Gamre, Maria Elena Garcia, Reşat Kasaba, Sabine Lang, Tony Lucero, Sudhir Mahadevan, Joel Migdal, Shruti Patel, Heidi Pauwels, Robert Pekkanen, Saadia Pekkanen, Priti Ramamurthy, Cabeiri Robinson, Richard Salomon, Keith Snodgrass, Clark Sorenson, Nathalie Williams, and Anand Yang. I would also like to thank Dvorah Oppenheimer, Toni Read, Tamara Leonard, and Keith Snodgrass, who helped this book come into being through crucial support.

I have presented this work in several venues where I received very useful feedback: Stanford University, Columbia University (and the University Seminars), and Harvard University; the American Academy of Religion, the Association for Asian Studies, and the Annual South Asia Conference at the University of Wisconsin, Madison. Two workshops were especially important for the development of several parts of this book. I am thankful to Anne Monius, Jon Keune, and Gil Ben-Herut who invited me to a workshop at Harvard Divinity School, my old home, and my thanks to my colleagues at that workshop who offered excellent advice to me. In particular, I am grateful to V. Narayana Rao, Tony Stewart, as well as Anne, Jon, Gil, Jack Hawley, and others who attended this workshop. I also thank Srilata Raman for her invitation to a conference at Yale in the spring of 2015 in honor of Vasudha Dalmia. I received wonderful advice from several participants, especially Srilata, Vasudha, Phyllis Granoff, Kumkum Sangari, Adheesh Sathaye, Heidi Pauwels, Martin Fuchs, Katie Lofton, and Nikhil Govind.

A number of colleagues and friends have offered sage advice and interventions along the way. For these many kindnesses, insights, debates, and emendations, I thank Dean Accardi, Purushottam Agarwal, Daud Ali, Jeffrey Brackett, Allison Busch, Jae Chung, Paul Courtright, Kurush Dalal, Naisargi Dave, Don Davis, Richard Davis, Prachi Deshpande, Milind Dhere, Wendy Doniger, Irina Glushkova, Dan Gold, Thomas Blom Hansen, James Hare, Paul Harrison, Linda Hess, Dan Jasper, Suman Keshari, Jon Keune, Steven Lindquist, David Lorenzen, Tim Lubin, Philip Lutgendorf, James Mallinson, William Mazzarella, Farina Mir, Lisa Mitchell, Anne Murphy, Rosalind O'Hanlon, Andrew Ollett, Patrick Olivelle, Gail Omvedt, Shreeyash Palshikar, Laurie Patton, Sudhir Patwardhan, Andrea Pinkney, Seth Powell, Teena Purohit, Nate Roberts, Prerna Rotellu, Ram Rawat, Uzma Rizvi, Adheesh Sathaye, Lee Schlesinger, Anna Schultz, Svati Shah, Neelima Shukla-Bhatt, Shana Sippy, Drew Thomases, Anand Venkatkrishnan, Rupa Viswanath, the Waghmares, and Karin Zitzewitz. I wrote this book while writing another one with Andy Rotman and Will Elison. I thank them for covering for me as I switched back and forth, for reading parts of this book when I needed their *do-se-bhale-teen* support, and providing a constant and amiable refuge. Sumit Guha read the book and remained a constant interlocutor, and his work, a touchstone for excellence for me. I have a particular debt of gratitude to express to Jim Laine and Davesh Soneji for anonymous reasons. Shailendra Bhandare generously shared images of *gadhegal* and discussed them with me, for which I'm very thankful. And to Whitney Cox, who read this book and, in some cases, several parts of it several times, my thanks for critical insights that pushed this work to be far better than it would have been without him.

In India several people provided extremely valuable assistance. I thank Prashant Kothadiya, Ujwala Mehendale, Tukaram at the ACM Office, Professor Avinash Awalagaonkar, and Dr. Suman Belvalkar. The late Meera Kosambi was a delightful interlocutor, strong critic, and constant supporter. Dr. Sucheta Paranjape was my Marathi teacher when I first went to India in 1990, and I have been learning from her ever since. My gratitude to you, Sucheta, is immense. Mukund and Bharati were ideal neighbors, and their friendship made our stay in Pune a delight. Without Jennifer, none of this work could have been done; I thank her and her family. Gayatri Chatterjee's friendship and her intellectual spirit have made my life and work inestimably better, and this book bears the imprint of a thousand conversations on three continents with you, Gayatri. Sadly, I have left unnamed and unthanked several individuals and institutions in India that were vital to my work. I wish it were otherwise, but I cannot thank them, at their request.

In India and the U.S., I have had the good fortunate to discuss many of the subjects of this book with devotees of both Jnandev and Chakradhar, with Varkaris and Mahanubhavs. I make no pretense to a level of understanding of these texts that comes from the deep religious convictions possessed by my generous interlocutors. I appreciate their time in explaining these texts and ideas to me. Their faith is deeply moving and humbling, and I offer them my profound gratitude.

Among the many scholars to whom I owe thanks, I would like to single out a few people in particular whose work is central to my own in this book.

My studies of the Mahanubhavs, their texts, and of Chakradhar are possible solely because of the pioneering work of Anne Feldhaus. Anne's presence—through her brilliant books and articles and her generous advice along the way—was constant during the writing of this book. She read the final manuscript, making it stronger with many essential critiques and insights. And though Anne doesn't agree with all I've written here, I presented this book to her as one submits one's work to one's guru. Thank you, Anne.

This is a book that would not be possible without Sheldon Pollock's scholarship over the last several years, and I draw inspiration from the extraordinary depth and scope of his work. His intellectual curiosity knows no bounds. Shelly read parts of this manuscript and supported its publication, even though we disagree here and there. Yet, when I do disagree with him, it is with the greatest respect for a scholar I deeply admire.

A word of thanks to my teachers, particularly Rachel McDermott, Fran Pritchett, and Elizabeth Castelli. My formative time with them continues to shape my work.

To Jack Hawley, who has remained my adviser in several capacities for twenty years, who read this work in various forms, and who has carried on conversations with me about all aspects of my scholarship, even the most arcane, with a generosity and intellectual warmth that is singular—thank you Jack.

As the book went to press, I learned of the death of my teacher and friend, Eleanor Zelliot (1926–2016). Eleanor inspired my interest in issues of caste, gender, and social justice. I am forever grateful, dear Eleanor.

To my family, thanks seems too small a thing. India is a home to me because of my family and friends there. To the Paranjapes, Leles, Baiskars, and Kales I express my thanks for letting me into their family. This has been the best part of my "research." William Novetzke, Mary Novetzke, Danielle Greene, Dan Greene, Vidula Kale, Michael Coggins, Minal Kale, Stephen Pierson, and the beloved *bacche*: Jahnavi, Nishka, Meha, Bhairavi, Amanda, and Catherine: I am thankful for this lovely, warm, artifice we call family—it means everything to me.

I have special thanks to offer to my mother-in-law, Shobha Kale. She and I discussed and worked on almost all the translations in this book drawn from the *Jñāneśvarī* and many of the inscriptions as well. Though she's a "real doctor," not like me, she entered my world too, and allowed me to enter her world, particularly her reverence for the *Jñāneśvarī*, as well—and I think we not only produced some excellent translations but we had a great time doing it. I wish for all *jāvi* to have such luck!

To my children—Sahil and Siyona—you tolerated many times when I could not go for that bike ride, have that tickle fest or that dance party, read that story to you, or just contemplate the universe with you, as you two so love to do. Books make for bad Babas, and I know, sooner not later, I will have rather had all those moments with you, or even just a single one of them, than a hundred more books like this one.

My partner Sunila S. Kale read this book several times in many forms and endured endless conversations about it. But more than this, our constant conversation and my reading of her work is the strongest influence on my own. She's in every word here, even those words with which she disagrees. But more than this: she makes all the rest of it possible, this life of love and thought with her that I cherish.

Seattle, Washington

Note on Translation, Transliteration, and Abbreviations

This book relies on three primary sources: 1. inscriptions from the oldest layer of Marathi; 2. the *Līḷācaritra*; and 3. the *Jñāneśvarī*. My note here describes these sources, their editions, and choices I have made regarding these texts, which are the basis for my translations in this book.

The first text is the body of Marathi inscriptions from the eleventh century to the fourteenth century that I use primarily in chapters 1 and 2. My key source for these inscriptions is the *Prācīn Marāṭhī Korīv Lekha* or the *Old Marathi Inscriptions,* edited with extensive commentary by S. G. Tulpule in 1963. I abbreviate this text as PMKL and provide the corresponding inscription number, as given by Tulpule. Where I have used other sources, I have noted those in the accompanying backnotes.

The second text is the *Līḷācaritra*. I use the version edited by V. B. Kolte in 1978 and published by the State Government of Maharashtra. This is the most scholarly edited version of the *Līḷācaritra*, and though it has been the source of some public disputes since the 1980s (see the conclusion for more on this), I have chosen to use this text because it is edited and contains the largest selection of stories, drawn from a rich archive of manuscripts. Out of respect for all involved, I have not reproduced the episode that caused so much strife. An interested reader can easily find it on his or her own. I realize some Mahanubhavs may disagree with my choice to use this text, but I have tried to use it in such a way as to respect what I understand to be their protests and disagreements about this text and I carefully note those stories that some Mahanubhavs believe to be untrue.

These would include the story of Chakradhar's purported trial and well as his purported beheading, subjects discussed in chapters 3 and 5. I include them here because of what they reveal about the politics of vernacularization *as stories,* but I do not include them here as historical fact. In other words, *I do not claim that these stories are historically true. I do not claim that Chakradhar underwent a trial or was beheaded.*

Kolte's version of the *Līḷācaritra* is divided into the "The Initial Half" or "Pūrvārdha" and the "The Latter Half" or "Uttarārdha." See chapter 3 for the distinction between these two "chapters" in Chakradhar's life. In this book, I abbreviate references to the two parts of the *Līḷācaritra* as edited by Kolte by referring to the "Pūrvārdha" as LC-P and to the "Uttarārdha" as LC-U. In addition to Kolte's edition, H. N. Nene produced an edition of the *Līḷācaritra* in 1936, reprinted in 1954. S. G. Tulpule reedited Nene's edition beginning in 1964. If I make reference to either of these versions of the *Līḷācaritra,* I duly note that usage.

The third text is the *Jñāneśvarī,* edited by S. V. Dandekar et al. in 1963 and published by the government of Maharashtra. This is a reedited version of the *Jñāneśvarī* published by V. K. Rajwade in 1909. While there are many versions of the *Jñāneśvarī,* I have used Dandekar's edition, as I believe it to be the best scholarly edition. Where I have differed from his version, I have noted other sources. In the book I abbreviate this text with Jn followed by the chapter number and the verse number(s).

In addition, chapters 6 and 7 contain quotations from the *Bhagavad Gītā.* Rather than produce substandard translations of these Sanskrit verses myself, I have opted to use the excellent translation by Laurie Patton, published by Penguin Classics in 2008. I have not retained Patton's layout of the verses on the page, however. These citations are abbreviated as BG followed by the chapter and verse number(s).

I follow the conventions of Columbia University Press regarding transliteration and diacritics. People's titles, proper names, place names, or words of Indian origin now common in English have no diacritics. For non-English words used many times, I provide diacritics only in the glossary and without italicization after first use; words used once or infrequently have retained diacritics. I also retain diacritics in direct quotations from non-English sources. All non-English titles of literary works have diacritical marks. Contrary to the *Chicago Manual of Style* guidelines, I italicize all text titles, whether sacred or profane.

THE QUOTIDIAN REVOLUTION

Introduction

The Argument of the Book

Democracy depends on the belief of the people that there is some scope
left for collectively shaping a challenging future.
—JÜRGEN HABERMAS, "LEADERSHIP AND *LEITKULTUR*"

Imagine you are in India. The year is 1290 CE, in the month of May, and it is very hot. You and your husband work a parcel of land each, along with your children, but you won't begin work until the rains come, and you are eagerly awaiting the rains, by which you live. Near to your land is a monastery where learned Brahmins produce texts in a language you and your husband do not understand; people of your caste do not generally learn the language of the Brahmin scholars, even though you speak with them in the common language of the street and bazaar. A portion of your land's yearly yield goes to support that monastery, a portion goes to the local ruler, and a portion you may keep for your own use and trade. In the afternoon, when the sun is too strong to stay in the open sunshine, you join a group of others gathered near a temple where there is a large banyan tree that offers cool shade. A man is sitting under the tree, and you recognize him as a learned man and a Brahmin. He is giving a speech in the language of the field and the market, not the language of the monastery, and this surprises you. Though his language is different, his subjects are the same as the ones taken up in those realms of learning that are unintelligible and inaccessible to you. He is speaking the common language of the region, but his subject is extraordinar. He is talking about the salvation of your soul and the end to life's suffering. As you listen, you notice the monastery on the hill behind the tree, beyond the preacher, and it comes into a new focus in your eyes, as if it has moved closer to you.

This is a book about the cultural politics surrounding a momentous yet enigmatic period in Indian history. During the thirteenth century, western

India witnessed the emergence of literary Marathi, one of the key languages of India. For the first time in Indian history, Marathi took the shape of literature. It did so in relationship to high literary forms of Sanskrit, but also in relationship to the idioms, colloquialisms, and oral texts of the region in the local language of everyday life. I argue in this book that this new literary idiom led to the creation of a public discursive field where we find vibrant debates about the social inequities of language, caste, and gender. These debates, articulated in the words of the quotidian world, ostensibly opened up a sphere of ethical engagement across the social spectrum. It was by no means an equal sphere, however. And it was certainly not a democratic one. This is a time and a place far removed from modern liberalism, and certainly from what Elizabeth Povinelli and others have identified as the liberalism of "settler colonies."[1] But a public debate did emerge, and, restricted as it was, this debate was occasioned by several vectors of social difference and transformation. One vector was a critique of the social restrictions that surrounded the "cosmopolitan" language of Sanskrit. This was a world to which, in general, only high-caste males had access. Another vector involved the observation and discussion of the routine practices of social difference that make up the world of everyday life, everywhere and for everyone.

Across South Asia, before and after this period, many other regional languages developed literatures in a general band of time we can regard as the vernacular turn. This is a period spanning the fifth to the fifteenth centuries, and the history of each language presents its own unique set of conditions. In some cases, vernacularization happened first through the documentary and literary activities of royal courts.[2] In Maharashtra, however, the production of a new Marathi literature occurred in the field of everyday life, outside of the royal court of the Yadava dynasty (1183–1317 CE) and its reigning state ideology. Far from the courts and institutions that received royal patronage, this new literary world was produced at the crossroads of towns and cities, among networks of villages linked by trade and roving preachers, under trees, outside temples and monasteries, amid farms and homes.

The earliest Marathi materials are situated in what we would now call the field of "religion." These texts engaged with the salvation of the human soul as their primary object. In the service of this goal, these texts challenged social difference. Importantly, these early Marathi literary works were composed in the context of devotion or *bhakti*, a devotion to deities, exalted individuals, and even society itself. At the same time, the concerns of the mundane world were hardly muted. This new literature observed political machinations, theorized social difference, and generated new aesthetic norms. And the social space in which Marathi literature emerged, with its debates about social equality front and center, existed properly within the realm of the public, in the spaces in between the many social fields of privacy and privilege that mark the medieval era in India. I refer to this new stratum of social discourse—existing independently of courtly culture, political elites, religious institutions, or other exclusive structures—as a nascent public sphere.

Though this nascent public sphere bore the hallmarks of literary aesthetics it came into existence not primarily as a literary or aesthetic endeavor, as happened elsewhere. Rather, this new literature was propelled by an essential critique of cultural inequity in relationship to religious salvation, social divisions, and political life. Despite these avowedly critical stances, the remembered agents of vernacularization also reveal an ambivalence about the scope of change that vernacularization might bring to society. Though the immanent critique of social inequity posed a challenge to the normative social ethics of the age, in ways both explicit and implicit, the agents of vernacularization also curtailed the viable scope of social change. For example, the Mahanubhavs' salvational messages were broadcast widely through Chakradhar's tireless lectures and discourses, yet the radical egalitarianism of the community remained restricted to a closed sphere of initiates. And though Jnandev offered the possibility of hearing the salvational message of the *Bhagavad Gītā* in the language of everyday life and for everyone, he did not propose a radical social reorganization of society. Marathi literary vernacularization enters into a quotidian revolution, but contained within the revolutionary process are mechanisms of restraint and control. This is a revolution measured in centuries, not days or years, and it moves in line with the pace of everyday life: consistent, constant, but cautious of change too rapidly enacted.[3] Like the proverbial frog in a well, the quotidian revolution moves two steps forward and one step back.

To make the arguments of this book, I use as my historical archive the two oldest literary texts extant in Marathi. These texts self-consciously represented the "vernacular turn" and did so, in part, through a social critique. The first text is the *Līḷācaritra*, a prose collection of biographical vignettes said to have been composed in 1278 CE by the followers of Chakradhar (c. 1194 CE). Chakradhar was something like a spiritual entrepreneur or what I've called elsewhere a "venture spiritualist."[4] He gathered together a set of followers around an innovative spiritual social order and carved out a new economy of spirit and salvation. Chakradhar founded a group who called themselves the Mahanubhavs, "Those of the Great Experience." They were renunciates who held Chakradhar to be God and the world to be a snare of sensual pleasure. The second text is the *Jñāneśvarī*, a Marathi commentary and quasi translation of the famous Sanskrit text *Bhagavad Gītā* or "Song of God." The *Jñāneśvarī* is said to have been composed in 1290 CE by the Marathi *sant* Jnandev (c. 1271 CE),[5] also called Jnaneshwar, who was another spiritual innovator of the age. His innovation was to draw into Marathi one of the key texts of Sanskritic Hinduism and thereby reconfigure the cultural capital not only of the text but of Marathi itself. The *Jñāneśvarī*, though not the first work of Marathi literature we have, is often considered Marathi literature's founding text. This is because Jnandev supplied a moral core drawn from the Sanskritic world in a form intended to be intelligible to all people in the region. The *Jñāneśvarī* is therefore at the heart of the "imagined nation" of many Marathi speakers living in India and abroad today, just as Shakespeare's works may be for English speakers or Tagore for Bangla speakers (of all religions) across the globe.

From these two figures, Chakradhar and Jnandev, and the two texts, the *Līḷācaritra* and the *Jñāneśvarī*, I draw a genealogy of Marathi vernacularization. I see these texts not as points of origin, but as evidence of a process that was already well underway; the texts and their authors articulate the quotidian revolution rather than inaugurate it; they speak to a world of change already swirling around them.

I delve into these two works—and surrounding materials as well—to uncover how each text represented the impetus and ethics of its own creation as well as the social conditions in which each emerged. I show how the texts self-consciously address a collection of issues involving language, caste, and gender, but also how they restricted the inherent and explicit critiques therein. Part 1 of the book establishes a context for these texts by sketching an image of the social and political structures of the late Yadava society in which the two texts are said to have emerged. This engagement provides a social, political, historical, and cultural basis for the textual analysis that follows. I argue that this navigation of the tension between normative social ethics and prevailing everyday social norms engendered what we tend to identify as the key feature of vernacularization—literary production in a regional language invested with idioms and representations of power.[6] Power, however, in the context of Marathi vernacularization, was configured not at the apex of the royal court, but within the far more messy and contingent world of the ordinary. This is also a world notoriously occluded from historical sources. We will examine how common social mores were challenged by vernacularization, even while the prejudices and practices of the vernacular world turned upon its new literary idiom to control the very transformative forces they set in motion. *The Quotidian Revolution* is about this momentous time and the cultural politics that attended this change.

Terms and Concepts

This book draws upon a range of terms and ideas to help explain the vernacular literary turn in Marathi and its cultural significance, in the thirteenth century and later. These ideas include theories of vernacularization, everyday life, and the public sphere. In addition, I draw upon social phenomena that are stock features of scholarship on South Asia, yet remain highly contested and reconfigured concepts. Among such concepts, caste, gender, and religion are perhaps the most challenging. Here I briefly discuss what I mean when I use these ideas and terms, although the full expression of their meaning is in the body of the book itself in relation to the specific historical, social, and literary materials that I will discuss. The use of any critical keyword, especially a highly contested one, remains inherently incomplete. My aim is not to shut off other possible meanings and interpretations, but to orient the reader to my use of these keywords.

Vernacularization, Religion, and the Everyday

Fundamental to the story I want to tell is the concept of vernacularization. In particular, I want to highlight the distinction between an investment in a vernacular language as a public communicative medium, on the one hand, and the larger social process that infiltrates and influences this process, on the other. In a very general sense, vernacularization means the written, and later literary, use of a regional or "natural" language rooted in a given place, and the effect this use of language has had on a given culture and polity. It is not only language that is available for "vernacularization" but also other expressive idioms, like art, dance, music, and all other spheres of affect (gestures, clothing, etc.). Politics, courtly manners, and diplomacy all take on the valences of a vernacular character as well. Vernacularization is a kind of indigenizing of a broad range of discursive mediums across a semiotic landscape that includes literature, arts, architecture, politics, and so on.

In my engagement with vernacularization I draw on the exemplar provided by Sheldon Pollock's *The Language of the Gods in the World of Men*. Pollock refers to the mere written use of a regional language as "literization." This is distinct from the creation of a new literature in a language, with a system of aesthetical distinction, which he calls "literarization."[7] Pollock also situates these two processes, and particularly the latter one, in the second millennium CE, making of vernacularization a historical period as well. In common usage, then, vernacularization also refers to a period in time—apparently shared simultaneously between Europe and India, and elsewhere, from the fifth to the seventeenth centuries—that marked a transition from the use of a "cosmopolitan" language without a strong regional circumscription, such as Latin or Sanskrit, to the use of a regional language or a vernacular, such as English, French, Marathi, Kannada, or Bengali. In this way, vernacularization names a time period, an aesthetic, and a period of social change much as the terms *modern* and *postmodern* do today. Part of the brilliance of Pollock's work is to read vernacularization well beyond its literary context, rather as a force like modernity, a force invoking broad social and intellectual change.

According to Pollock, this transition is often registered in multiple domains, particularly in repositories of written records: royal courts, religious institutions, and elite literary worlds. As he incisively notes, vernacularization is almost always a display of "power" in some form or another. It may be the power of courts and empires to enunciate their dictates to their subjects and rivals or the power of religious leaders to express their texts and practices to their followers and distinguish themselves from contending traditions or the power of literary elites to recondition the aesthetics of literature and power within the literary field. Of course, the various spheres where literacy obtained (and more could be summoned) were not, and are not now, mutually exclusive. For this reason, Pollock succinctly summarized vernacularization as the "literary and political promotion of language" in multiple spheres at once.[8] He considers the process of vernacularization to be "a transformation in cultural practice, social-identity formation, and political order" that caused a change "by which the universalistic orders, formations, and practices of the preceding millennium were supplemented and gradually replaced by localized forms."[9] It follows that vernacularization is a process that displays the relationship between power, language, and place. Hence Pollock's study is fundamentally about the politics of language, literature, and imagining the world in which people live. Though Pollock does not use this term, I take the potent mix of power, language, and place to point toward a *public.*

Pollock situates vernacularization, in general in South Asia, within elite spheres of courts and other royal institutions. Yet this scope of power and the political is a point on which I differ from him. In his work *power* tends to connote the operational force of politics within the field of kingship, royalty, and courts. His empirical historiography amply shows the court to be a vital epicenter for the process of vernacularization. He makes this close association between power and royal courts through a distillation of the Sanskrit term *rajya,* which he glosses as "the state of being, or function of, a king."[10] As Pollock rightly displays, vernacularization as a literary process has a deep utility in the field of kingly power. It serves as a harbinger for "a new kind of vernacular political order" because geographic region is entirely intertwined with political power at the core of monarchy and all other governmental forms.[11] A political space is conditioned by power almost by a tautological definition of the latter—politics is power, as they say. Foucault's knowledge/power dialectic plays off of this common conceit. However, power here is not solely exercised by courts. There is a power exerted also by the force of public sentiment, even well before any modern notion of a liberal theory of politics. And the discursive recourse of this general public is its expressive idiom, its vernacular language, and, later, its literature. Where Pollock examines power configured by courts, I examine power configured by publics outside (though not exclusive of) the royal court, which, in the Marathi case, involves the field of religion.

In Pollock's commanding work, royal courts were a key location for the vernacular literary turn, particularly as a process that reconditioned the public discourse of kingship as well as the very nature of political thinking in South Asia. A central issue for Pollock in his study, as it relates to South Asia (he also discusses medieval Europe, amazingly), is to see how rajya exists in a dynamic relationship with changing fields of aesthetics or *kavya*. This latter term indicates "poetry and literary prose," but also signals the conventions of literary aesthetics that will link the "cosmopolitan" literature of Sanskrit to new literary work in regional languages in the vernacular millennium. One of the chief functions of vernacularization among the elite fields Pollock studies is the reinvention of aesthetic formulae perfected and commented upon in Sanskrit sources, which are then transposed into regional languages and deployed by royal courts.[12] For Pollock's purposes, a core subject of vernacularization is the way in which these two forces—rajya and kavya, kingship and poetics—interacted. This is where Pollock locates "power" in vernacularization, in the field of the royal court and its public expression of self and sovereignty, where language and power meet, molded into a new aesthetic of power in literature.

I share Pollock's conviction that vernacularization reveals a history of power. However, I seek to shift the base of what constitutes vernacularization by restricting my study to a far more modest terrain and time: the relatively small kingdom of the Yadavas in the latter half of the thirteenth century. Pollock comes to his study through an impulse to see the connection between the elite Sanskrit literary world of the first millennium CE—the "Sanskrit cosmopolis"—and the transformed world of the second millennium, when regional languages largely replace Sanskrit at the nexus of literature (kavya) and royal power (rajya). My study, by contrast, involves a far smaller unit of measure: not two millennia, but rather a single long century, and not the scope of South Asia (as well as Southeast Asia and Europe), but a relatively small region controlled by the Yadavas in that century. However, I seek to use this relatively limited historical and geographic case to rethink vernacularization in what I hope will be an expansive way, perhaps forming a heuristic to be applied to other parcels of time and place.

Another key distinction between my work and that of Pollock involves the perceived audience attending to the vernacular turn as well as the intentions of its agents. Pollock's study is, he admits, a study of "elites," but, as he perceptively points out, "if concentrating on elite representations means we miss the role of 'the people' in history, we do capture something of the ideas that ultimately transformed the people's world."[13] I agree with this position; yet examining vernacularization in Marathi-speaking contexts in the thirteenth century forces us to see that the world of elites—the masters of court, temple, monastery, and scholastic institutions—in general did not appear interested in Marathi as a literary language. As part 1 of the book will show, the Yadava court showed little interest in supporting Marathi as a literary medium. To locate the transformation of the people's world in western India through literary vernacularization, we must look outside of the elite sphere of the royal court that is the location of Pollock's study. In particular, we must enter into terrains that are in general "nonelite." By the use of this term, I do not mean to say that the agents of vernacularization were not themselves elites or the product of elite culture. Indeed, Jnandev, Chakradhar, and many of the early Mahanubhavs were elite high-caste males. This fact is essential to understanding the origins of a new Marathi literature in the thirteenth century. However, these figures opted out of, or rather ventured out from, the institutions of the elite to which they had access, even while they moved in elite circuits. And they did so with the expressed intention of reading a nonelite audience in the field of everyday life. That the agents of Marathi vernacularization occupied this dual position—emerging from inside elite spheres in the Yadava century but opting to circulate outside of them—is a sociopolitical dynamic that is at the core of what made a new vernacular literature possible. This was a world betwixt and between, to echo Victor Turner (and Albert Camus), a liminal social sphere where spiritual and social innovators made productive use of the heterogeneous space they occupied, where they could articulate disparate worlds. In this arena arose questions of caste and gender inequity, questions that did not appear to be salient within the elite worlds Pollock studied.[14]

As I hope to show, my impulse to focus on and theorize the quotidian is shaped by my materials. My two key literary sources are outside the purview of royal courts, high literary culture, temples, monasteries, and rarefied trading classes. Yet the quotidian is not the same as the demotic or subaltern, a point I emphasize here. I think of the quotidian as the space in which elite and nonelite meet, even if these meetings are mediated and inherently uneven. Yet it is not a space of uniform dominance, as a court or a highly stratified institution would be. And while the space of the quotidian is conditioned by the social rules of a place—largely signaled by the ideas of caste, class, and gender—the quotidian is also the place where these varying degrees of difference are negotiated and adjusted. It is the space of the "common" among classes, castes, genders, and religions. The materials examined in this book amply engage this space and the conflicts that arise in it. It is also therefore at times situated within something like the medieval English "commons," a space shared by agreement among parties with various needs, here configured as the bazaar, the meeting of the roads, under the shade of a tree—the spaces in between. The distinction I will draw instead juxtaposes such common spaces with what I would call the private spheres of the royal court or court-sanctioned institutions such as monasteries and temples. I contrast these private spaces with the general cultural sphere of the "public." I will say more about how I conceive of the public below, but here I only want to signal that the location of Marathi literary vernacularization is a process that occurs in public culture within the quotidian world. Seen from this vantage point, vernacularization advances across social contexts—courts, country, religion, economy, literature, and daily life—through a common mechanism rather than through political fiat.

With these ideas in mind, let me define vernacularization as *the strategic use of the topos of everyday life within a social, political, artistic, linguistic, and cultural process in which the quotidian ("ordinary," "everyday") expands at the center of a given region's public culture.* In this process the features of vernacularization identified by Pollock—the "literary and political promotion of language"—involve an engagement with "Place" that is not only geographic but deeply geocultural.[15] New vernacular expressive idioms grew from the public cultures of given regions. In other words, the common space was being represented discursively as a space of expressive language, of literature.

My reconfiguration of the idea of vernacularization owes a great deal to the highly innovative field of political anthropology. In particular, I draw inspiration from a vibrant strand of this subfield that explores the experience and transformation of democracy in contemporary India, often called the "vernacularization of democracy." While I make no claim that the thirteenth century reveals a democratic political liberalism of any kind similar to what we (heterogeneously and unevenly) experience in modernity, I am struck by the continuity between the emphasis on everyday life present in thirteenth-century Marathi literary work and the experience of democracy uncovered by political anthropologists. For example, in such political anthropology vernacularization is seen as the "deepening of democracy," a process in which political discourse grounds itself in a highly stylized "local" cultural sense that emphasizes and valorizes "the common" person and "everyday life." Emblematic of this work are the pioneering studies of Thomas Blom Hansen, whose political ethnographies in contemporary India, especially in Mumbai, register the "vernacularization of democratic discourses and procedures."[16] In particular, in his study of the Shiv Sena (a "nativist" regional political party of Maharashtra), Hansen finds that the vernacularization of politics indexes a belief in "the virtues of 'the ordinary.'"[17] The vernacularization of democracy, represented by the ascension of the Shiv Sena in the regional politics of Maharashtra, is viewed by advocates as a "triumph of the ordinary" itself.[18] Hansen shows how the originator of the Shiv Sena, the late Bal Thackeray, though himself a figure of the "political elite," expounds a "message of self-respect [that] feeds on elevating the lower castes and the 'ordinary.'"[19] Lucia Michelutti, following and expanding upon Hansen, sees vernacularization as "the ways in which values and practices of democracy become embedded in particular cultural and social practices, and in the process become entrenched in the consciousness of ordinary people."[20]

These ideas about how vernacularization recodes the political idioms of locality and place, and hence also of autochthony and authenticity, all calibrate to the "ordinary" in public culture. These insights resonate in this book, and I propose that one force propelling the changing political order in South Asia over the last seven hundred years is the expansion of the quotidian into the field of power. This is a process that was partly accomplished by the deployment of the trope of everyday life as a rhetorical device. Sometimes the speed of this force has been swift and momentous, as in India's constitutional enshrinement of universal suffrage in 1950, and at others almost imperceptibly slow. But I do argue that vernacularization is a force as evident in thirteenth-century Maharashtra as in twenty-first-century India.

The resonance between vernacular culture and everyday life is apparent as well in ethnographic and historical studies of highly localized religious practices of modern and contemporary India that also feed back upon political culture. For example, Joyce Flueckiger identifies a "vernacular Islam" constructed around a charismatic female healer in South India, which Flueckiger situates within the "public realm."[21] She identifies this realm with the term *chaurasta,* or "four roads," what she calls "a public social space."[22] We will see Flueckiger's *chaurasta* echoing from the thirteenth century when, in chapters 6 and 7, we find Jnandev locating the *Bhagavad Gītā* and his own commentary on that text at the *chauhata,* the "four corners," of the town square, that is, the market. In histories of vernacularization as a literary-linguistic phenomenon, the everyday remains a central concern. Farina Mir, in her study of the Punjabi *qissa* genre in colonial India, and particularly the Hir-Ranjha story, finds that "vernacular culture" exemplified by the *qissa* operated within "the practices of everyday life," and this genre helps us recover historical visions of those everyday practices.[23] In the anthropology of selfhood within South Asia, we have ample demonstrations of the way everyday life conditions social being as a process of the vernacularization of the self.[24] One might think of Anand Pandian's exploration of the *maṇatu* or "heart" in the cultivation of virtue, Valentine Daniel's study of the habitus of Tamil personhood drawn from everyday life, and Leela Prasad's ethnography of ethics and everyday life in Sringeri in Karnataka.[25] Ritu Birla's idea of the "vernacular capitalist" joined the modern capitalist networks of colonialism with the quotidian life forms of caste and kinship, which existed at the heart of "that everyday abstraction we now call 'the market' . . . a name for the colonial public."[26] The vernacular and the everyday are revealed in particular in India's many cinemas, as Sudhir Mahadevan has shown in his marvelous study of the bioscope and the "everyday" genealogy of India's photography-film nexus.[27] The list could go on, revealing that a turn toward "everyday life" is a burgeoning enterprise in South Asia studies and outside of it as well.[28] In art, one can see the intricate everyday scenes painted by Sudhir Patwardhan, or the everyday urban landscapes of New Modikhana, Pune, painted by Sudhir Waghmare, like the beautiful work of art on the cover of this book. In all of these cases, religion, language, state, court, selfhood, and literature intertwine, cohering around an articulation of the public perception of the quotidian as a central feature of vernacularization, whether of literature or politics or culture itself.

I should note again here that I do not claim that vernacularization (or religion or *bhakti* for that matter) in thirteenth-century India engenders modern Indian democracy—it does not. However, I am inspired by the connections that scholars of contemporary political anthropology and other subjects have drawn between vernacularization, everyday life, and political culture, revealing a consistent association with the valorization of the ordinary. At the same time, I do not believe that democracy, even in postcolonial contexts, can be reduced to the effects or aftereffects of colonialism or European hegemony. The modern world is no more sui generis in India or the rest of the postcolonial world than it was in Europe or America. Worlds of multiple modernities have multiple origins for their modernity. And so I do argue that woven into the heterogeneous braid of Indian modernity and democracy is the strand of thought and debate I examine in this book.

Given my emphasis on the quotidian, let me chart out here what I mean by this term and its several synonyms. I use the terms *quotidian, common, ordinary,* and *everyday* more or less interchangeably. While I am aware of the many shades of difference among these words, I tend to see them all within a semantic field similar to Charles Taylor's use of "ordinary life" as a way to describe a new location for cultural valuation and a new epicenter for cultural politics. Taylor locates this in late medieval Europe, from which emerged the building blocks of the modern secular age as he constructs it.[29] I adapt this usage to a very different time and context. In India during the Yadava century a new cultural politics surfaced, which revalued "the everyday" at the core of public culture, displacing the values of the literary cosmopolitan, for example, but also very mundane relations among people around caste, gender, and language. The emphasis on "ordinary life" is unmistakable in the materials I study in this book. I suggest that this new emphasis, represented through the power of literature, is part of the long history of India's present.

Similarly, I borrow from Michel de Certeau's ideas about "everyday life" as the cultural location where individuals, particularly nonelites, can slowly mold and reconstruct cultural conditions and the politics of their age, where they can resist or submit, according to their needs. In this context, I take inspiration in particular from de Certeau's idea that the realm of governmental power and elites is a world of "strategy." By this he names the state's power to create disciplinary systems by force—as simple as sidewalks or as complicated as penal codes and constitutions—that seek to channel the movements, actions, and thoughts of common people, of its citizenry (something akin to what Foucault has called "governmentality" and simply "discipline"). Conversely, people in everyday life respond with "tactics," according to de Certeau, to creatively rewire and alternatively use those channels—and this is often done beneath or beside the direct surveillance of the court, state, or elites.[30] Here de Certeau's idea about how "the governed" work with or even subvert the political society in which they belong dovetails with James Scott's ideas about the "weapons of the weak" or Partha Chatterjee's recent arguments about how "popular politics" represent a "politics of the governed."[31] Indeed, it is for "the governed," and not on behalf of the governing, that Marathi literary vernacularization claims to speak. Here is another close parallel with contemporary political conceits in India where the everyday person is valorized and "represented" through political systems. Similarly, those who govern did not inaugurate vernacularization in the Marathi context. As Ranajit Guha famously announced in the inaugural work of the Subaltern Studies Collective, "The politics of the people [is] . . . an autonomous domain."[32] I propose in this book to edge as close as possible to this imagined "politics of the people" and this "autonomous domain." And though I do not portray this domain as autonomous in fact, it also was not subsumed entirely by the political, social, or religious forces of power that usually animate the historiography of medieval India.

As we will see, neither Chakradhar nor Jnandev is part of any of the formal social structures of the Yadava century, such as the Yadava governmental structure or the many religious and literary institutions it supported. However, as male Brahmins of high pedigree (as I think Chakradhar was), they are no doubt elites. Yet they evince no "strategy" in de Certeau's conception of this idea, they have no access to "political power" to effect change through force; indeed, we will see stories of Chakradhar resisting and avoiding opportunities to tap into political power. Instead they both employ and engender a set of tactics—rhetorical and practical—that reformulate "the public square" through currents outside governmental forms, reconfigured in enduring literary monuments. Their lack of "will and power"—what de Certeau ascribes to those with "strategy"[33]—is partly indicated by the fact that the tactics they inaugurate set in motion processes these agents of vernacularization and their public memories ultimately cannot contain. The social critiques they propose are not confined to the intentions we might attribute to them through a reading of the materials left to us today. In other words, tactics will work upon tactics; both the Mahanubhav religion and Jnandev's pioneering text, not to mention his very biography, will go on being subjected to centuries of permutations and emendations by subsequent currents of vernacularization—a subject I touch upon in the conclusion.

And so we can add to these theories of everyday life the very power of the quotidian world to expand beyond the parameters of its inaugurators or champions. And sometimes, or perhaps always, this force will move social and cultural forms away from those original intentions. The politics of the people is, at least in this sense, not autonomous in that the public—past and present—folds back upon itself in a recursive fashion, a heterogeneous and changing set of social forces that cannot be described in the singular. Vernacularization, then, represents tactics that are endemic to its form and function, beyond the ability of its many agents to control; they are the maneuvers of everyday life.

If we consider vernacularization in relation to the topos of everyday life and, by extension, to an immanent critique of social difference, then this allows us to see that the process of vernacularization occurs long before vernacular literatures arise. It is deeply embedded in the discourse of the "cosmopolitan" itself contained in Sanskrit texts. The idea of a critique of social inequity, around caste and gender in particular, is a part of the textual histories of Jainism, Buddhism, and Hinduism and is present in epic literature (such as the *Mahābhārata* especially) and *purana* literature. Indeed, several key purana texts, though in Sanskrit, declare that they were composed for the benefit of "women, low castes, and others."[34] The *Mahābhārata* also states its inclusion of women, low castes, and others within the sphere of its imagined community of receivers. As we will see in relation to the *Bhagavad Gītā*, Jnandev will declare that the text was explicitly composed for women, low castes, and others (*strishudradika*),[35] yet it could not reach this audience until it was retold in a regional language. From another point of view, the very representation of languages other than Sanskrit in the Sanskritic world already displays an engagement with this nonelite world—for instance, the vast array of Prakrits of various sorts assigned to female and low-caste figures. Add to these textual and traditional forms the many collectivities of renunciates, *sadhus*, *sannyasis*, and others who, alone and in groups, renounced all social distinction and desire, hence disregarding caste difference and often forming new communities that are socially heterodox. The seeds of vernacularization were planted deeply within the soil of the Indian cosmopolitan long before the recorded era of literary vernacularization arose.

If we move away from the idea that vernacularization is about a literary endeavor, but instead see it as a more encompassing social endeavor that is marked by the strategic use of the topos of everyday life, then we can see the quotidian revolution to be an age-old process, inherent in the world of the Sanskrit cosmopolis over millennia.[36] In this way, we can notice that moments of literary vernacularization on the subcontinent are not ruptures but displays of the continuation of a very long process that I am calling a quotidian revolution. In other words, the strategic use of everyday life to critique social inequality did not originate in the thirteenth century. Instead, I am arguing that this was an ages-old critique that took a new form—a literary form in the Marathi vernacular; that it did so with the wind of a particular kind of historical critique at its back; and that this was a critique that the Brahmin males at the center of Marathi literary vernacularization seem to have known well.

As this is a book that also engages the academic study of "religion" in history, I must comment on Pollock's position on the association between "religion" and the history of vernacularization. If Pollock's work examined the language of the Gods in the world of men, this book explores the language of men (and women) in a world of Gods. Pollock argues in the introduction to his edited volume, *Literary Cultures in History*, that "religion . . . became and has remained virtually the single lens through which to view all texts and practices in the subcontinent, further distorting what little attention had been directed toward literary culture."[37] By "literary culture" here Pollock does not mean literature devoid of themes of a "religious" or mythological variety, but rather the productive center and impetus for this culture, which is the court and its literary aims. In other words, Pollock is well aware that religions produce literatures and condition the literary, but his point is something more. Pollock references one of the chief features of Orientalist scholarship that Said and others had also registered—the association of "religion" and religious thinking (often read as nonrational, affective thinking in general) with the non-West.[38] Yet Pollock's concern and corrective runs deeper. In the generally accepted history of vernacularization in the subcontinent, the role of a particular aspect of religion—devotionalism or *bhakti* expressed through song-poems and hagiography—had indeed come to stand not only as the sole representative of the earliest layers of literary vernacularization but also as the harbinger of vernacularization's apparent social ethics of equality.[39] Pollock ascribes this association between vernacularization and religion in particular to a new misconfiguration in scholarship, a "disciplinary bias toward religious studies" that eclipsed a clear vision of "the primary moments of vernacularization" in South Asia.[40] This leads Pollock to declare that "religion was largely irrelevant to the origins of South Asian vernacularization" because vernacularization was a "courtly project . . . largely unconcerned with religious differences."[41] However, where religion does enter the history of vernacularization, Pollock refers to this as a "second vernacular revolution,"[42] by which he means that the primary pivot of the vernacular turn occurred, by and large, outside the sphere of organized religion and its literature and very precisely in the worlds of the court and literary elite.

There is no doubt that Pollock's work further compels a corrective to any ahistorical, simplistic review of the history of vernacularization. I share his concern that "religion," and in particular *bhakti* or "devotionalism," too often functions as the epistemological limit point for all non-Western and premodern cultural contexts. Yet Pollock's work itself evinces a far more circumspect perspective than these statements on religion suggest. The primary empirical context for his argument is the field of Kannada vernacularization where early materials suggest the courtly origins of Kannada's vernacular turn.[43] Though Pollock gives us a sweeping statement about religion and vernacularization, he is too fine a scholar to let it remain vague. He does provide a more discrete list of the languages whose history conforms to the Kannada model. These are Assamese, Gujarati, Malayalam, and Telugu, which were "much more concerned with the terrestrial than with the transcendent."[44]

What about the remaining many languages of South Asia? The one literary history Pollock sets aside from his analysis as anomalous is Marathi. As he shows—and as this book concurs—he is entirely correct in seeing that Marathi literary vernacularization occurred almost entirely outside the sphere of the royal court, even while literization is evident only in the inscriptional record, which is common throughout South Asia.[45] In other words, it seems correct that the traces of literization are almost always confined to the production of courts or institutions supported by royal patronage. However, the first iterations of literarization, of new literatures in regional languages, show a greater variation, and the case of Marathi is emblematic of this variation. As chapters 1 and 2 will show, Marathi literization is recorded solely in inscriptions associated with royal courts, while Marathi literarization appears to flourish in the context of public culture and in the fields we refer to as "religion" and bhakti, and to do so relatively independent of the Yadava court. This means that though the royal court has a role to play in Marathi literarization, it is neither the epicenter of this process nor its driver. Instead the Yadava indifference, or rather benign ambivalence, toward Marathi literature allowed this new discursive world to grow relatively unimpeded.

Yet it seems to me that Marathi is not alone in this regard. There are other languages with literary histories in which it is not possible to distinguish the "terrestrial" from the "transcendent" in terms of influences or locations for vernacularization. This is true of Punjabi, for example, and particularly apparent in the genealogies of Tamil and Hindi/Urdu—arguably the largest and most influential literary languages of southern and northern India, respectively. As with Marathi, in the histories of vernacularization of these three languages, too, the "secular" and "sacred" cannot be bisected.[46] Even in the case of Kannada, D. R. Nagaraj—writing in Pollock's edited volume that explores the histories of particular literatures in South Asia—argues that the figures representing bhakti, such as the Virashaivas, rejected the court and temple cultures of their age. Hence they would have also rejected literacy and the elite aesthetics of literature. In other words, representatives of bhakti and "religion" excluded themselves *by design* from the field of "vernacularization" as Pollock traces it, an emergent elite literary aesthetic located in royal courts, or so Nagaraj argues is the case with Kannada.[47] If religion is irrelevant to literary vernacularization, it may be a result of the rejection of the royal court as literary epicenter by some religious figures. Thus, while Nagaraj does not appear to disagree with Pollock, he does seem to suggest that bhakti in particular was extremely important to the history of vernacularization in Kannada regardless of whether the first Kannada literary texts appeared at courts or elsewhere.

This suggests to us that the usual phenomenological content of the term *religion* is bifurcated. One the one hand, we have religion at its institutional level, the temple, and within a field of literary production of religious authority. On the other hand, we have religion a field filled by an engagement with everyday life, which may entail a rejection of the former idea of institutional-literary religion, or it may not. But the two designations of religion here are by no means cooperative spheres. They may be antagonists to one another, as in the case of Kannada, and perhaps in the case of Marathi too. To say vernacularization occurred outside the confines of "religion" collapses too many variables. Instead, in such cases (perhaps in a majority of cases in fact), we have a complicated mesh of elite royal courts, institutionalized religious culture, and an intermediary high literary sphere in which religion or bhakti is as vital as any other aspect of a given cultural sphere. In this way I do not disagree with Pollock's emphasis on politics, or even on courts, but rather with the way the term *religion* is forced to envelop fields that are, otherwise, in contention with one another. If a figure like Basava in the twelfth century sings songs about God but rejects God's temple, where can we locate the sole representative of "religion"?

As chapters 4 and 5 will show, Chakradhar was a figure around whom bhakti circulated, but a figure whose relationships with religious institutions—monasteries and sometimes temples—and with rival religious figures—monastery leaders and other popular religious figures—were regularly antagonistic. And chapters 6 and 7 will demonstrate that Jnandev rejected a world of elite Sanskrit learning such as the Vedas—surely a "religious" sphere—in order to transpose elite salvational possibilities to a quotidian religious field. And yet Pollock's corrective is, I hope, heeded in this book, for while "religion" may describe the social fields of Chakradhar, the early Mahanubhavs, and Jnandev and his text, I attempt to carefully delineate the specific scope of each figure, community, and text. If the process of vernacularization is fundamentally about expanding the sphere of everyday life and representing that expansion in expressive forms (literature, art, language, politics, etc.), then it is also about noticing difference and distinction in many areas of life experience.

Bhakti, Caste, and Gender

These forces of the social constructions of everyday life to which I allude, and which are taken up as primary subjects in the materials we will explore, centrally involve caste and gender. In the context of Marathi vernacularization, an explicit observation of and critique of inequities surrounding caste and gender in Yadava-era society will form a core subject. I appraise the form of a new literature—its aesthetics, for example—alongside its content, which in the case of new Marathi literature of the thirteenth century entails particular attention to inequities of caste and gender. I realize that for many readers an association among bhakti, vernacularization, and critiques of caste and gender will sound like old wine in a new skin.[48] This is just the sort of conflation and assumption that Pollock rightly seeks to contradict when he tells us that religion and bhakti were largely irrelevant in the primary history of vernacularization. Indeed, this is a point that has been made by other scholars as well, and I too have made such an argument around bhakti, challenging the idea that it represents a cohesive social movement across India or that its fundamental function is "social justice."[49] Instead, I have argued that bhakti primarily creates publics. In this process, caste and gender differences are sometimes a social problem and at other times an accepted aspect of the fabric of culture to be preserved and even honored. And though bhakti does not fully circumscribe the sphere we will engage in this book, it is central enough to warrant some discussion of its function here.

Jack Hawley, in his study of the history and historicity of "the *bhakti* movement," shows us how the modern idea of a bhakti movement as a reformist movement is especially indebted to Hindi scholarship of the modern period, deeply ensnared in the social and political vicissitudes surrounding the formulation of Indian nationalism.[50] Yet Hawley also shows us that the materials these modern scholars accessed from the vast sea of bhakti compositions did engage caste and gender inequity, along with a host of other issues including religious animosities between Hindus and Muslims. Hawley reveals that—from Maharashtra northward to the Hindi heartland—one can trace lines of interconnection among various bhakti groups over time and space, just as Pollock traces commonalities of cosmopolitan and vernacular socioliterary orders across South Asia and beyond. Hawley coins this interconnection the "*bhakti* network" as opposed to a bhakti movement. To argue that bhakti presented a uniform critique of the inequities of society, a social movement in short, and that this critique alone compelled vernacularization, would be a gross mischaracterization. But, as Hawley shows us, we can see multiple commonalities within the wide sphere of the bhakti network that have had a tremendous influence on Indian society for a millennium or more. And, as we will see in the pages that follow, Marathi vernacularization is unmistakably situated in relation to the sphere of bhakti in complex ways, though it is not circumscribed by it. In this realm of devotionalism, social inequity became a subject of public debate.

The material I study in this book forces my engagement with bhakti here. It will be apparent I hope that bhakti and social critique sit side by side in this case, as in many other cases documented throughout South Asia. As several scholars such as David Lorenzen and Jayant Lele have shown, bhakti often carries with it a social critique that seems linked to its theological and social form. It would be as wrong to say that bhakti is unequivocally and always a form of social protest as it would be to ignore the many examples of social protest enunciated in the language of bhakti.

Sanskrit writings during the Yadava period indicate that the royal court and other institutions were preoccupied with describing and regulating caste relations. In Marathi too, caste distinctions are a ubiquitous subject, as we will see. Two terms referring to caste were constant in public discourse in the thirteenth-century Maharashtra, both in Sanskrit and in the Marathi materials we will examine. These terms are *jati* and *varna* and, in addition, the words that designate a given jati or varna, both indicating practices of social distinction that,[51] in basic forms, likely existed in India for at least three millennia.[52] The process of social distinction can be tied to birth and regionalized occupation (jati) within a given political economy of space. Or the process can be broadened toward a traditional theory of social hierarchy (varna). The European term *caste* is a word I will use in this book at times to speak about jati and/or varna, though I will endeavor to make clear to the reader the referent in each case.[53] However, the use of this now English word since the eighteenth century in modern scholarship and in modern India evinces an entirely different history and practice— deeply embedded in colonial ethnology and postcolonial governance and politics. As Dirks and Cohn, in particular, have shown, political power conditions relationships and hierarchies between and among caste groups.[54] The romantic early British vision that somehow Brahmins controlled the mass of India's population by convincing them of the supremacy of their own ritual purity was entirely unraveled by the historical anthropology of caste and in the work of anthropologists like M. N. Srinivas.[55] I take this lesson about the interplay of political power and caste as fundamental to my analysis, but I also understand that caste mutates and fluctuates in meaning when in different contexts. For this reason, at many points in this book I will use *caste* to mean the collection of social practices and effects of varna and jati, but more often I will specify the terms used in the texts under study here. Both jati and varna appear in abundance in our materials, and so I should explain how I understand these words.

The term *jati* is an Indic word that essentially means "birth."[56] From this meaning, many other significations are derived, such as kind, genus, class, species, as well as natural disposition. For at least two millennia, the term *jati* has appeared in Sanskrit texts to indicate one's position in society by virtue of birth in a particular lineage, race, family, traditional occupation, region, language area, and so on.[57] In this latter usage, the former meanings are enfolded such that jati indicates one's "caste" as a feature of one's birth and, for women, marriage. This in turn implies various things about the person based on their jati in that jatis will often be described as bearing certain regular social, cultural, and even physical distinctions. In contrast to varna, the practice of jati in India is a social fundamental, shared by almost all Indians regardless of religion—that is, jati is common to Indian Christians, Muslims, Sikhs, and often Buddhists as well as Hindus. A jati can be as small as a few families in a given region or as large as a pan-Indian or even pan-religious designation.[58] Current estimates place the number of distinct jatis in India at around five thousand across regional, religious, and linguistic divides.[59]

However, jati, while it implies difference, does not suggest an absolute hierarchy or ritualistic distinction. Indeed, jati terms tend to indicate (if they indicate anything) associations with traditional occupation (mostly lost in modernity), region, and language. In other words, jati is often bounded by a regional political and social economy rather than an objective social hierarchy, as is sometimes assumed.[60] This is perhaps in part why jati survives independently of a given religion or region. In this book we will see many references to jati in the texts and contexts we examine. I think of jati in these contexts as *a social ontology*, a state of being that conforms to the social forces of a given region. But, as we will see, while jati was fixed, its cultural meaning was in constant negotiation: What was the distinction or character of a given jati? Was one jati more or less ritually pure than another? Which jatis needed to be rearticulated in new contexts? Such questions animated the cultural politics of the thirteenth century, as they do today.

Our second term indicated by caste is the Indic word *varna*. The essential meaning of this word is something like its cognates in English, "varnish" or "veneer." The word indicates a cover of some kind that projects an outward appearance or color; it is a broad type. The word is both older than jati and more embedded within what we might call Brahminic Hindu orthodoxy conveyed through Sanskrit texts, especially the Dharma Śāstra or "social science" texts of classical and medieval India. The word *varna* first appears in the oldest text of any sort for which we have a discernible record within the subcontinent, the *Rig Veda* (c. 1700 BCE). And it endures into the modern period.[61] The theory of varna is traditionally articulated as a fourfold division of society, but with emendation. These four aspects are typically expressed as: Brahmins or "ritualist scholars," Kshatriyas or "warrior-kings," Vaishyas or "merchants," and Shudras or "peasants." If jati indicates a social ontology, then we can think of varna as a kind of *social ideology*, a normative theory of social order itself.

The first three groups of the varna social ideology are often called "twice-born" or *dvija*, a reference to a "rebirth" ceremony in childhood, marking entry into the varna group. Twice-born varnas are often simply called "high castes" or, in contemporary nomenclature, "forward castes." The term *Shudra* appears to have remained its own category, differentiated from the other three by virtue of not being "twice-born." In common parlance today in India, groups associated with the varna of Shudra often adopt or are given the title "Other Backward Classes" or OBCs. This is a term that is used in the Indian Constitution, but one that does not reach its full definitional and ethnological-political power until the Mandal Commission Report of 1980 and the implementation of reservation policies for OBCs a decade later.

This fourfold division of *varna* probably became reified and theorized by the fifth century CE in a wide body of texts collectively known as Dharma Śāstra that examined the "science" (*shastra*) of "social-cosmic order" (*dharma*). As we will see, this genre of social thought was dominant in Yadava literary production in Sanskrit. It is in the context of the emergence of the science of dharma in the fifth century that we find the fullest articulation of the concept of "Untouchability," particularly in the codification called the Laws of Manu.[62] Though the rudiments of this idea are perhaps to be found in the Vedic identification of the *dāsa*, the "enemy" and "slave" of the Vedic Aryans, the concept as we know it today was formed fully, as a social theory, in this fifth-century context of Dharma Śāstra. The Laws of Manu has become emblematic of Brahminic social orthodoxy, an object about which leaders of the communities grouped under the term

"Untouchables," such as the Maharashtrian political leader B. R. Ambedkar, have vented their deep anger.[63] However, a large body of literature of social orthodoxy promoted the idea of Untouchability within the larger context of caste (as varna, jati, and gender).[64] This larger literary heritage of a Brahminic orthodoxy became the primary subject for the Sanskrit and court-literary spheres of the Yadava period in the thirteenth century.

In contemporary India, the practice of Untouchability is unconstitutional. Those jati groups that historically suffered the stigma of this social practice in India are designated "Scheduled Castes" in the Indian Constitution, which also grants them reservations in government jobs and education, along with historically disadvantaged tribal groups (called "Scheduled Tribes"). Most people associated with "Untouchable" jatis have adopted other terms for their status, such as Dalit ("downtrodden") or Harijan ("people of God") or have renamed their communities, such as Ravidasis, or have retained their jati titles, though having divested those titles of association with the practices of Untouchability. In this book, we will encounter several jati names conferred the varna status of Untouchable, and these will include the communities identified by the names Mahar, Chamar, Chambhar, and Mang, among others. I should note here that these names do not mean "Untouchable"; they are merely proper nouns that mark jati names. Rather this status is ascribed to (and through the centuries inflicted upon) the people born under this ontological sign.

As one can imagine, varna's fourfold division of human social order, particularly implying a broad sense of "occupation," has given rise to a number of analyses that compare this theoretical social structure to the modern idea of class.[65] However, the degree to which varna has ever dictated a uniform economic class or influenced governance or social order is uncertain even while these are clearly related forms of social distinction. In the material from the thirteenth century engaged in this book, varna will appear alongside jati. But, in contradistinction to jati, varna is cited as a social theory that embeds within it a latent and pernicious set of exclusionary principles. One of the key features of the reinterpretation of varna in the Dharma Śāstra literature was the idea that only men from the first three varnas—Brahmin, Kshatriya, and Vaishya—would be allowed to hear Sanskrit, much less learn it and use it. At the core of the cultural politics situated between language and caste in texts explored in this book is the idea that the exclusion of Shudras, Untouchables, and in many cases women, from the cultural sphere of Sanskrit is a social, and indeed cosmic, injustice. This injustice, as we will see with Jnandev, is tied to the idea that Sanskrit does contain a discourse of salvation that should be accessible to all people, the *Bhagavad Gītā* existing as a preeminent example. However, the critique Jnandev offers, we will notice, does not argue for the freedom of all people to learn Sanskrit or to participate in the "Sanskrit cosmopolis." Rather, he argues that all people should be allowed to access that salvational discourse contained in Sanskrit through translations into the languages of "Place," the *deshi*, which in this case, means Marathi. Jnandev's compassion is palpable and moving in his text, even while his primary concern is for the soul and salvation of his listeners, and less explicit attention is given to the social change this might bring. A more muddled and difficult task is to understand how this broad theory of cosmic justice plays out in the mundane social contexts of jati, varna, and especially of gender, and how the quotidian world might absorb and transform with the literarization of its primary linguistic core.

Caste is regularly a term used to enfold varna and jati into one another, but it often leaves aside the force of gender difference, even while gender and sex are at the very heart of both jati and varna as practices and concepts.[66] One commonality through all iterations of caste as a set of social practices—ancient to modern—is the importance of gender to its functioning. Caste and gender are at all times inseparable. The classical Dharma Śāstra literature infamously states that women are all born as Shudras and that a woman's varna is determined by the patriarchal matrix in which she lives, that is, an ontology that is always a question: who is your father, who is your husband, who is your son? A woman in this matrix is essentially without varna until it is granted to her by relationship with a man. And given that jati is based on birth (rather than the authorization of some dharma adjudicant), women are the ironic epicenter of the determination of jati—they literally engender jati, yet their own jati remains in flux in relation to men. As we will see in the materials to come, gender and caste are so intimately linked as to be in an shatterproof symbiosis. The materials I examine in this book amply show gender to be a central problem within the discourse around caste—jati and varna. While Sanskrit is made inaccessible to one of the four varnas, or to most of the numerous jatis of India, the simplest Rubicon is drawn by sex: almost all authors of Sanskrit texts or practitioners of Sanskrit rituals were (and are) men. And this is not by chance but by design.[67] So any discussion of caste that does not discuss gender is fundamentally incomplete. This is an idea clearly expressed in the materials examined in this book.

The critique of caste and gender encoded in the discursive field inaugurated by vernacularization places these critiques at the core of the new literary idioms of Marathi in the thirteenth century. Importantly, this new idiom of Marathi explicitly seeks to widen the social field that constitutes its audience. The materials we will study in this book conscientiously sought to expand the scope of debates about caste and gender to the majority of people who were subject to its rules, that is, to the general "public" of the Yadava century. Jnandev in the *Jñāneśvarī* will name this group "women, low castes, and others" (*strishudradika*) and the early Mahanubhavs will identify this same group through numerous stories from the life of Chakradhar and other figures. While this may seem a term that designates the "downtrodden" or dispossessed, in fact it designated, and continues to designate, the vast majority of the population of India.[68] It is a central contention of this book that this new literary idiom—replete with a debate about social order, everyday life, language, and literature (in short, cultural politics)—creates a rudimentary form of a premodern public sphere, which is one of the many genealogical precursors to the modern Indian public sphere. As we will see, the new literary world of Marathi came into being in the context of debates and challenges to prevailing social orders, not only those of the Sanskrit cosmopolis but also of conventions in the social fabric of everyday life. The vicissitudes of social difference along lines of caste and gender, akin to what Rupa Viswanath has evocatively called "everyday warfare," is a current of common and ordinary life that would form a natural core to a public debate about society.[69] And such a debate about society, equality, and humanity in public contexts is a hallmark of the modern public sphere in a modern liberal democracy. I argue here that one legacy of vernacularization is that social critique at least in part entered the public realm.

Publics, Public Culture, and Public Sphere

Some readers might find my engagement and arguments about a nascent public sphere to be a bridge too far. For such readers, my use of terms such as *public sphere* (not to mention *public* or *public culture* or even *state*) may be too anachronistic and inappropriate because the premodern world remains "inassimilable to the logic of the modern capitalist world order."[70] Yet my goal is to reach across territorial divides of time, place, and theory, to do what Whitney Cox describes as "controlled theoretical anachronism."[71] I adapt Cox's term, echoing an idea of Gayatri Spivak, to say that my goal is perhaps more like a *strategic anachronism*.[72] My use of the term *public sphere* here is meant to provoke an engagement *across* the normative rubrics of medieval and modern, Western and non-Western, divides rather strictly drawn in much scholarship on the public sphere, as I will note. In this sense, it is descriptive and heuristic, bearing some of the same characteristics as my use of *vernacularization* in the ways it is employed by contemporary political anthropologists and others who study the contemporary and modern periods. Because I am using the phrase *public sphere* in this way, I want clarify my usage.

One can scarcely invoke the term *public sphere* without reference to the pioneering work of the social philosopher Jürgen Habermas and his 1962 book *The Structural Transformation of the Public Sphere* (translated in 1989), among much other work. Habermas presented the public sphere as an emergent cultural form of the eighteenth century in Europe that prefigured a transition from a feudal order to liberal democracy by creating public venues within the new bourgeois class of educated citizens where critical debates on all matters—culture, politics, arts, government—could be discussed. For Habermas, the European public sphere grew from conversations by this class of people in cafés, public houses ("pubs" or bars), and public squares, transposed into the public media of periodicals, literature, pamphlets, and art.[73] Thus, for Habermas, the public sphere is a highly literate and literary one that implies an emphasis on education that marked, in part, the bourgeoisie, the emergent middle classes of Europe. This public conversation reconfigures the very nature of politics and government form. Yet the history of change that Habermas traces involves a set of conditions unique to Europe, in particular Europe as a global colonial power. These preconditions tend to revolve around a primary rationalization of the global economy that provided important networks of extrapolitical and rationalized communication. This is a very particular history—a European history—of what I consider to be a generalizable social form—a public sphere. My hope here is to tell a different story. Habermas, for all the qualifications and conditions he hangs upon his brilliant idea of a public sphere, provides us with really quite a simple definition. The public sphere, he says, is "a society critically engaged in public debate."[74] Or, as I have quoted him, democracy, with a vibrant public sphere at its core, allows "some scope . . . for collectively shaping a challenging future." A society engaged in debate, in public, and with a sight toward a collective future is the sense in which I import this term into my premodern, non-European context, and long before the rationalized market of colonialism would emerge. I will outline how I use the term *public sphere* in this book, but before one can speak of a public sphere, one must be able to identify the discursive existence of a public at all.

What is a public in my usage? I addressed this question at length in a previous work, and my use of the idea here conforms to my use of the term there and elsewhere.[75] By a public, here, I mean an open, social audience, one that attends to, but does not necessarily participate in, a capacious and circulating discourse within a given region, language, or other social context. This is a context of mutual intelligibility and access. Publics are constituted primarily by passive attention, and people often participate in them through consuming discourse and reflecting their engagement through affect. A public is defined by its open-ended address, available for attentive reception. A public is a social formation that is reflexive and organized by the circulation of a particular discourse of mutual concern.[76] A public can be of almost any size; it may be situated in a given historical time or geographic space, or it may be transregional and transhistorical. In most cases a public is maintained through media such as literacy, visual culture, art, or performance, though any medium for the circulation of ideas will do. And so a public is an open conversation. Indeed, a public often bears an idiosyncratic aesthetic, a way of imagining its particular "world" as well as a reflection of the world in which it is itself located, just as conversations have a flavor, a passion, and a context. However, participation in a public can be active or passive—it requires, as Michael Warner says, "mere attention" and so publics can include those who simply observe.[77] This will be an important point as we move through the socio-ethical universe of the thirteenth-century Marathi materials, for a promise of cosmic salvation is open to all in this context, but that promise does not extend fully to salvation from the vicissitudes of social segregation, preju-dice, and hierarchy. The cosmic salvation possible through a text like the *Jñāneśvarī* will be available by attentive listening alone, and so anyone who hears, regardless of caste, class, or gender, may benefit. A public, then, can cross social boundaries of caste, class, and gender, but it might not serve to unravel or even critique those boundaries in the process. In just this way, I have argued that bhakti, to give one example, has long existed as a "public," a social sphere of inclusion but not necessarily of social change, a sphere of critique but not necessarily of correction or coercion.

Public culture, in my usage, is the cultural expression of a given public. It is culture "out in the open," not the culture of private clubs, royal courts, selective organizations, institutions, guilds, or closed communities, or even of the home. Instead it names the culture surrounding and referencing the "common conversation" at the heart of any given public. The fact that "public culture" like "public memory" and just the term "public" itself comes to be associated with the efforts of modern governments to remember, represent, and control how they are viewed in the world is one very particular expression of the ways publics and public culture work. However, here, well before the modern liberal state, these terms cannot bear such significance. Yet the genealogy is clear, I think, and not necessarily too distant from our modern era. As the inscriptional record engaged in chapters 1 and 2 will show, the Yadava court and other governmental elites were quite eager to fend off the public that might threaten their reign, but also valorize that same public by associating themselves with it. The idea that governments, states, courts, and elites both fear the public and seek to be inserted in it, and even control its "conversation," is not alien to the thirteenth century, as we will see. The field of play among elites and non-elites, where the quotidian becomes the dominant trope of social, cultural, political, and aesthetic organization, is the field I would call a vernacular public culture.

Part 1 of this book seeks to establish the existence of a public around Marathi in the Yadava century. Parts 2 and 3 of this book explore how public culture was observed and targeted in the works of the early Mahanubhavs and in the *Jñāneśvarī*. In this sense, this book builds a heuristic model that suggests a rudimentary public sphere is possible only when founded upon a preexisting public and an attendant public culture. And in this way I am following in the wake of Habermas, who suggests much the same attends to the changes in the structure of the public sphere in Europe at its nascent stages. That said, I hope it is obvious to my reader that I do not aim to create a one-to-one correspondence with Habermas's history of the public sphere in Europe, but rather to note that something similar, though hardly the same, occurred in South Asia.

Habermas argued that the public sphere was not merely one of social critical interaction, but one conditioned by new rules of rational public discourse—a consubstantiation of a rationalized economy and a rationalized field of discourse. Hence, in Habermas's formulation, the public sphere is a rational sphere of public discourse that emerged *specifically* in Europe in the eighteenth century, borrowing the Greek and Roman ideals that were at the heart of the European Renaissance. This public sphere made possible liberal democratic participatory politics, and even though Habermas registers a decline of the public sphere's ability to affect governmental politics since the dawn of the twentieth century, most scholars in the Habermasian tradition still situate a rational public sphere at the core of liberal democracy as one of its unique features. The Habermasian public sphere is inherently modern, European, and Western in origin. Habermas is quite explicit on this point as he notes that the public sphere was a "child of the eighteenth century" that "cannot be abstracted from the unique developmental history of that 'civil society' . . . originating in the European High Middle Ages . . . nor can it be transferred, ideal-typically generalized, to any number of historical situations that represent formally similar constellations."[78] However, as with many great ideas, Habermas's innovative identification of the public sphere is an idea that grows beyond the intentions of its author or its author's prescriptive boundaries. To confine the idea of a public sphere to such a provincial realm would needlessly diminish its interest and power. Features of the concept, as Habermas identifies it, are apparent in other places and in much earlier times. And in those places and times we have the opportunity to fully expand upon Habermas's concept of a public sphere as a global historical phenomenon, but evincing a highly heterogeneous character grounded in the differences of time, culture, and especially place. In short, we can vernacularize Habermas's idea of a public sphere and see how it grows in other soils and other times.

In this work I follow scholars who seek to apply Habermas's ideas, in general, to contexts outside the scope of his original analysis, to abstract Habermas's idea of the public sphere from its "origins," restructure it as an ideal-typical generalization, and apply it to a very different historical situation: thirteenth-century Maharashtra and the history of India.[79] I will emend the conditions under which I use this term, but the general idea of a publicly accessible cultural field of discursive interaction in which social issues are critically engaged forms a core concept in this work. It is not my contention that the modern Indian public sphere is invented in thirteenth-century Maharashtra, however. This would be an untenable claim. Indeed, the modern Indian public sphere is more indebted to its counterpart in colonial-era Europe and America than to the period I study here. But I do hold that the genealogy of the Indian public sphere is not reducible solely to European historical shifts and models, to the effects of colonialism and Western modernity. Instead, the genealogy of the Indian public sphere is a complex braid of origins. Each vernacular turn in the many regions of India, as well as the grand Sanskrit cosmopolis, all form strands in that braid, and none should be ignored. In this sense, my book is about *a specific nascent public sphere* that relates to and flows into the modern one, joining many other streams of their own unique origin.

I will use terms like *nascent* and *rudimentary,* and so on, to qualify my use of *public sphere* because I am telling here the story of the thirteenth century to represent a social form that is similar to what we will find in modernity, but one that is indeed yet different and inchoate, far more restricted in circulation horizontally in space and vertically in terms of social stratification. While this may seem to imply a particular social evo-lutionary teleology, my hope is rather to show that the full promise of the social critique presented by the nascent public sphere of the thirteenth century was apparent to the agents and participants within the cultural forms I describe in this book. In other words, the vision of a more egali-tarian future, a future where public debate was more socially equitable and accessible, does appear to be present in the thirteenth century, even if within a highly restricted context.

I also do not think that a public sphere—European, modern, or otherwise—is conditioned by rationality. Habermas, drawing on Kant and Rawls, remains true to this central idea, or perhaps aesthetic, of modernity, that rationality is the core epistemology of the modern. Yet it is hard to observe any modern election in any liberal democracy today—leaving aside elections in illiberal "democracies"—and believe that "rationality" is the primary mode of politi-cal interaction, beyond all the other affective, personal, collective, or other affinities that motivate voters. Modernity is as whimsical as it is rational, and, to be sure, it is both. The idea that the political sphere anywhere at any time is primarily a rational sphere seems more normative than descriptive.[80]

Rationality may be the chief affect or aesthetic of public sphere discourse in modernity, but rationality itself is not descriptive of the public sphere in any context other than a purely idealistic one. People in the world debating with one another draw as much on emotion, "tradition," and idiosyncratic morality as they do on rational argumentation. I say this because I wish to avoid the old Orientalist conceit of a rational West and an irrational rest. This is not Habermas's conceit, and I do not impute it to him. But it is an idea that attends the concept of the public sphere, though not one I draw into this discussion or my use of the term. In this book I argue that the process of vernacularization in thirteenth-century Maharashtra created a social space for critical public debate in Marathi about society. However, this was a debate in which rationality shared space with the logic of the mystical cosmos and where emotional appeals for social inclusion met reasonable requests for cultural accommodation. I think that provincialized rationalism is very much apparent in the world we live in today as well.[81]

What we might take from Habermas's tracing of the "structural transformation" of the public sphere, of its decline and delimitation, is the idea that all public spheres are both socially capacious and restricted. The public sphere is a prescribed space even while it is a public one. If Habermas sees a "decline" in the publicality of the public sphere because of the power of late capital to control media, for example, we may also see restrictions placed around a public sphere as one formation of it emerges in Marathi in the thirteenth century. The expansion of the scope of the public sphere carrying the content of everyday life also brought with it limitations of social order, as we will see.

So let me say now what I have in mind regarding the use of the term *public sphere* in this book. I think of the public sphere as a common social space of discourse—filled by the literary, visual, affective, gestural, etc.—that is mutually intelligible to a given population (i.e., a regional-language population) and that has the potential to engage everyone and anyone. So far this is also what a public is. What distinguishes a public sphere from a mere public is that the population within a public sphere discusses matters of common interest, forming what Charles Taylor calls a "common mind" about such matters, a conversation "potentially engaging everyone," and this bears in some way on social order and usually on political order.[82] This is an important way in which I hope to retain the power of Habermas's original formulation: the public sphere is where discursive power is mediated between elites and the general "public." This common mind is not an agreement on those matters of common interest but an agreement on approach, subjects, and principles, the semiotic world that will now be shared between elites and everyone else. This process of agreement and disagreement within the context of decided upon principles and subjects is the scope of the political. However, the political is possible only within such an agreement. When we speak of a "political solution" to a problem, we generally mean one short of physical violence and war. The public sphere, in this sense, retains the character it has in Habermas's work, as a sphere for the negotiation of power in public.

To enter this sphere is to sublimate one's individual concerns, to make of oneself and one's needs a metonym for general wants and needs, to come to represent "society" as Habermas notes. Michael Warner calls this "the principle of negativity," to negate the particular and personal in favor of the social and collective. And it is this political process, this evolution of the "common mind" and critically engaged public debate that conditions the public sphere and allows the discursive negotiation of power to take place. I will argue that we see this principle of negativity at work when figures like Jnandev and Chakradhar—high-caste males who could have selected a far more routinized and privileged life as scholars of Sanskrit or overseers of temples, monasteries, or other endowed institutions—instead choose to inaugurate arguments that objectified their own caste and gender privilege, even while relying on that privilege. In other words, they "negated" one aspect of their social ontology to engage with another or perhaps the "Other," those not like them in the field of power.[83] A public sphere is created here at the confluence of a new expressive form—Marathi literature—with a particular (but not new) social critique around caste and gender.

This book joins several studies of the public sphere outside Europe, and specifically in India.[84] One can observe the superior work of Francesca Orsini on modern Hindi vernacular public spheres and on Marathi public spheres, the work of Milind Wakankar and Veena Naregal, who have already explored Habermas's ideas in comparable historical contexts.[85] Susanne and Lloyd Rudolph directly engage Habermas in a delightful study of Gandhi and civil society. In this work they adjust Habermas's original concept of the public sphere to observe Gandhi's central role in a nationalist and activist public in late colonial India.[86] Similar work on modern

Indian publics by Arjun Appadurai, Carol Breckenridge, Douglas Haynes, Sandria Freitag, Anne Hardgrove, and Keith Yandell and John Paul have explored ideas aligned to those expressed by Habermas.[87] Some work has skirted the edge of modernity and explicitly examined the public sphere in India, especially C. A. Bayly's studies of the Indian "ecumene" of the eighteenth century and Purushottam Agarwal's argument for a "bhakti public sphere" in early modern India.[88] Given Habermas's very specific interest in conditioning the public sphere as a literary field engaged by cultural elites in the discussion of critical questions in society, one could argue that a rather enormous body of scholarship engages "public spheres" in India across all time periods. Indeed, Pollock's epic exploration of cosmopolitan and vernacular literary change over two millennia, in this sense, is a study of a grand public sphere in literary history on a global scale.[89] It is an investigation of the discursive content of Sanskrit and languages of place that self-reflexively examines the very questions of the cosmopolitan and vernacular in a shared context. The concept of the "public sphere" has moved beyond the confines of its origins. In this work I try to follow others in expanding our use of the "public sphere" as a theoretical concept to new times and places. This is a time before modernity, before the technologies of mass media that extend from the printing press outward to our present that allow for a massive public sphere to emerge. But the core concept given to us by Habermas does endure here, the idea that the public sphere is a discursive field where power is mediated between elites and the quotidian, the "public" at large, where they engage in a critical debate about society, evincing an immanent hope for a better future.

The Quotidian Revolution has a simple thesis: that the primary driver of vernacularization is an engagement with the everyday life of a place, specially its language and other affective and expressive idioms. Vernacularization is *not* primarily about the creation of a new literature—this is a secondary effect. I argue that the emphasis on everyday life compels a cultural politics, and that politics, in turn, engages two of the most salient features of thirteenth-century life in Maharashtra, which are caste and gender. This inaugurates a "public" conversation about caste, gender, and other social inequities, even if it does not lead to resolutions.

The reason I argue that a nascent public sphere emerges as a result of the process of vernacularization is because what circulates around the contentions with this term are some of the very same questions of access, equality, progress, and humanity that seemed to compel the materials this book discusses. These are also subjects that continue to inspire societies on many levels today. It is my effort to resist the demarcation of a hermetically sealed field of the medieval, quarantined from the colonial or modern or postcolonial. We know well the differences among and between these historical eras, marked by political formations that no one can dismiss. But we know relatively less about what links and binds these eras, what flows through them and past them, into the future.[90] There is no time in the history of India that is not vital to its present, which is not linked to it inextricably and irrevocably. My goal in using a term like *public sphere* or *public* or even *state* (see chapter 1) will, I hope, press at the boundaries that divide the study of the premodern and the modern (themselves woefully inadequate terms of distinction).

I am also compelled by the important trade in terms that scholarship requires. We speak across time and space of gender, class, religion, and politics, sometimes in vague terms, but always with the hope that our vagaries can be planted in autochthonous soil. My goal is to make an argument about a term used across the humanities and social sciences, yet root this term in the empirical substance of the chapters that follow. Scholarship should always be about the details, certainly, but it should also venture into the general and abstract, for this is where "humanity" exists, if it exists anywhere. This is why any of us ever bother to speak over the differences of language, race, sex, nation, sexual orientation, religion, caste, class, time, and place. The public sphere is one good way of saying we all imagine ourselves to be an "Us" in the first place. And yes, there is the "Them" that presses upon social ethics. This book is about the experience of this tension, and a discussion about it, as well as visions for its resolution, in a place that seems far in the past but is perhaps as close to our present as anything could be.

PART ONE

CHAPTER ONE

The Yadava Century

Marathi literary vernacularization seems to have occurred during the rule of the Yadavas in the region of Maharashtra, which spans the long thirteenth century, roughly 1187–1317 CE. It is in this period under Yadava rule that the idea of Maharashtra as a geographic, political, and cultural region fully emerged and it is to this period that modern Maharashtra's origins are traced. As we will see here in chapter 1 and in the following chapter, in this period we have declarations of a new cultural configuration that links Marathi to this region through an ethnic identity formed around place and language, expressed through terms such as *marathe* and *Maharashtra*.[1] It is in the Yadava century that Marathi appears as a literary language and hence a linguistic-cultural zone, an epicenter for an enduring transformation and social organization over later centuries. To underscore the ligaments connecting past and present, it is the formulation of a social identity (aside from a political one) around language, region, and culture in the Yadava century that makes possible the linguistic subnationalism that led to the creation of the State of Maharashtra in postcolonial India in 1960.[2]

In the centuries between the Yadava era and the modern period, the memory of the dynasty continued to serve as a centering subject for a vision of a Marathi-speaking *rashtra* or "nation." The idea of the Yadava cohesion around language and region was rekindled to some degree under the rule of Shivaji (1674–1680 CE). When he rose to power and founded what would become the Maratha Empire, the Yadava blood in his veins, inherited from his mother Jijabai, was what many consider compelled Shivaji, in part, to return Maharashtra to the glories of its past in the thirteenth century, the period before the coming of political Islam to the region.[3] Thus, the Yadava century carries considerable historical baggage as the epicenter of the linguistic and cultural construction of Maharashtra itself, which makes a reexamination of this period valuable in its own right. And among the many factors that contribute to the weight borne by the Yadavas in Marathi and Indian nationalist historiography, the understanding that the Yadava century was coterminous with the literary vernacularization of Marathi is of key importance.

This chapter explores Yadava power, its sociopolitical dynamics, and the conditions created during Yadava rule that allowed literary vernacularization to flourish. It foregrounds the book's engagement with the literary vernacular turn in Maharashtra by providing an understanding of the political, social, linguistic, religious, and cultural conditions in which the *Līḷācaritra* and the *Jñāneśvarī* are believed to have been composed, and the period in which the two figures associated with these texts—Chakradhar and Jnandev—are remembered to have lived. While no Yadava court documents or other evidence corroborate the existence of either these figures or their texts in this period, the Yadava century is the context for their biographical and textual associations, both in historiography and in these texts themselves, which mention their time period and give historical details from their age. In other words, whether or not Jnandev and Chakradhar are historical personages (I think they are) and whether or not the texts associated with them were created in the late thirteenth century (I think they were), the public memory of these people and their associated texts so deeply imbricates them with the Yadava century that any study of them must engage this period and social context. As such, understanding the sociopolitical contours of the Yadava century is vital to any exploration of these figures, the texts associated with them, and the cultural conditions of Marathi vernacularization in general. I will present here a view of the spheres of power that defined the Yadava century and divide these into three heuristic though hardly hermetic categories: the Yadava political formation or "state"; the Brahminic ecumene supported by the Yadavas that supplied many of the luminaries of the age and populated the high ministerial ranks of the Yadava government; and the general public, including its public culture, that made up the vast experience of human life in this period. This is our first entry into the socio-political ecology of medieval public culture, and it is the overall goal of part 1 of the book to trace an image of this world. If chapter 1 examines the relations of court, Brahminic ecumene, and public culture in the Yadava period, chapter 2 delves into the inscriptional record of the period to search for the rudiments of the era's "public" along the fringes and between the lines of imperial edict. With these two contexts in place, chapter 3 fully introduces the two figures who serve as biographical metonyms for the book's subject—Chakradhar and Jnandev.

The Yadava "State"

What terms best describe the premodern corollaries to modern political formations like *state, government,* and *civil society*? Daud Ali has perceptively noted that too often the use of such terms in historiography signaled a pejorative assessment of early Indian political formations, especially around "the bourgeois concepts of 'state' and 'civil society' [which] were repeatedly counter-posed to the pomp and despotism of Indian potentates and the choking hold of the caste system" leading to the idea that "the 'state' in ancient India was a particularly debased form of monarchy, one steeped in sensuality and imagination [isolated] from 'society.'"[4] And yet these terms—*state, society, civil society,* etc.—are difficult to avoid when one enters into a discussion of a public sphere, even a nascent one, as I have in this book. And so these terms deserve some attention at the outset here in the context of the "strategic anachronism" of which I hope to make use.

Discussions of how best to describe the medieval "state" are vibrant and range from the heuristic deployment of this word in many historical studies to various proposals for a new set of terms,[5] such as the "segmentary state,"[6] or terms that eschew the word *state* entirely, such as Ronald Inden's idea of a "scale of lordship."[7] Daud Ali, in his study of courtly culture, follows Inden in proposing a "superordinate set of human relationships" that extended from well beyond the royal household "to revenue collectors and local lords" and others.[8] In contrast, Pollock crafts his own heuristic terminology to fill in for encumbered placeholders such as those cited in Hermann Kulke's 1995 survey of this concept in historiography, where Kulke invokes Habib's "medieval Indian system" and Stein's "medieval Indian social formation" as body-doubles for medieval *state.*[9] Pollock proposes the term *vernacular polity*,[10] a concept of the state that may take various forms and rearticulations, but that lurks in the shadows of all these reevaluations.

I see great benefit in the complications that surround the use of the term *state* for the study of a period that precedes the full force of the "state-effect," as Timothy Mitchell puts it, or the ways in which "the modern state" creates its own outward project, as Abrams has pointed out.[11] Yet this is a book not primarily concerned with the "state," or whatever term we might use. Indeed, the primary subjects of this book exist outside the medieval state or its vernacular polity and alongside the superordinate relations that compose "government." While this chapter, I hope, will show the contours of this hard-to-name political formation, the ultimate service of this examination is to see how vernacularization occurred outside "the state," and was not the effort of this particular "vernacular polity." And so when I refer to the Yadava "state," I mean the governmental structures and relations under the direct control of the Yadava court and its affiliates—that is, their network of government in its official capacities, which would include the machinations of the royal court, but also the military, general law-and-order structures directly under their control, and official state public displays and interactions. The vernacular polity here is particularly relevant when the state is represented in the vernacular, in Marathi. Much of the core material of this chapter and the next involves the polity expressing itself in Marathi, the "state" speaking the language of the "people," the "state-effect" produced by and through a vernacular language.

My "controlled theoretical anachronism" here is something to which I am committed only insofar as it helps explain a political-governmental terrain for which scholars of medieval India (and medieval elsewhere) still struggle to find the words and concepts. I take Ali's perceptive caution that we ought not hunt for some "indigenous Indian modernity" in this period, and I hope that I have adequately emphasized that I do not intend to situate Indian modernity in the thirteenth century. Instead, in this chapter and the next, I provide an examination of the political formation of the Yadava era in order to get at another question that Ali, too, explores when he asks, "What of everyday forms of life beyond the designs of the state's civil authority, forms of practice whose political connotations were now silent?"[12] To get to those everyday forms of life, we must pass through the elite and exclusive world constructed amid everyday life by the preeminent political force of this age and place, the Yadavas. This is the membrane of the archive, so to speak, that must be crossed. However, my aim is not an intervention into the fertile debates about what constitutes the "state" in premodern India, and I hope my reader will allow me to dodge this in favor of stepping into perhaps deeper potholes down the road.

One of these potholes involves what to call the various institutions enacted, financed, and protected by the Yadavas through their inscriptions. The inscriptions of the Yadava state, as we will see, are dominated by gifts and entitlements to individuals, families, groups, and communities for the support of some state-supported function, such as the maintenance of temples, monasteries, and institutions of learning, or the general well-being of important individuals, families, and caste groups. Among the recipients, the vast majority were Brahmin males. How to describe this social order, largely created through imperial gifts from the Yadavas that buoyed a network of entitlements and institutions, which, while not directly within the ambit of the court, were nonetheless essential to Yadava political stability as well as to the creation of vernacular literature and the nascent public sphere in Marathi?

Given my invocation of Habermas in the introduction, one term that comes to mind is *civil society,* which I understand to mean those institutions that exist and mediate between state and society, that are authorized or sanctioned by the state but not under its control, and that function to stabilize the political sphere, often in the name of the "common good."[13] As many other scholars do, I consider the economy and the private sphere of the family to be outside the purview of civil society.[14] As such, civil society is a domain administered, if not entirely populated, by the "elite" of a given social order; indeed the very status of being "elite" is often conditioned by one's proximity to the state in civil social organizations.[15] For many reasons, the term *civil society* seems to describe a cognate to that sociopolitical space in medieval India between the royal court and the institutions the court either supports or simply tolerates.

And yet the term brings with it more problems than solutions, perhaps. For one, the term is inextricable from Habermas's formulation of the public sphere, where civil society mediated relations between state and population, elevating issues of private concern to public discourse, often through institutions, associations, and groups that were granted autonomy and liberty. In Habermas's assessment, the public sphere arbitrated relations between the state and civil society, or, rather, it *is* that intermedial space in modern liberal democracies.[16] Though I do believe a nascent public sphere comes into shape in the Yadava century, a civil society, as it is so often discussed and generally conceptualized by scholars, seems impossible to unmoor from its anchoring in liberal modern democracy.[17] Furthermore, the sphere that seems to occupy the space of "civil society" in the Yadava century is entirely clientelist, dependent upon the largess and goodwill of the Yadava state—it has no autonomy. And it is a field dominated by Brahmin males, as I have already pointed out. Using the term *civil society* threatens to mask the crucial asymmetries of gender, caste, and power that are at the heart of the subject at hand. But if the term *civil society* won't do, what will?

A surfeit of support for Brahmins and Brahminic activities deeply conditioned educational establishments, religious institutions, temples, and other such organizations funded by Yadava endowments. In particular, the Yadavas directed state resources to supporting a single language: Sanskrit. The sphere of Brahminic activities that would intersect with both state and economy, and yet exist independently of both, is the sphere I refer to as the Brahminic ecumene, borrowing a term from the work of Rosalind O'Hanlon.[18] This is an ecumene that fed the systems of royal patronage that privileged Brahmins and Brahminic social capital, particularly around education, ritual, and literary production in Sanskrit. Yet as a semi-independent sphere, the Brahminic ecumene possessed its own social structure and logic. Part of this logic involved the valorization of literacy, a key feature of Sanskritic cosmopolitanism, and the high value placed on literacy is part of the impetus for the commitment of Marathi to literary forms during this period. The two figures at the core of this book—Jnandev and Chakradhar—are situated within the Brahminic ecumene of the Yadava period, but neither existed within the structures of the Yadava state or the institutions outside the court funded by the Yadavas that make up the formal locus for the Brahminic ecumene. However, both figures invested literacy with high social capital, imported, I will argue, from their positions within the Brahminic ecumene. And so, in lieu of "civil society," I submit the Brahminic ecumene as a space outside the inner domains of the Yadava court, but a space the Yadava state sought to construct and influence by finance and property regimes, several of which will appear in what follows. I will speculate on why the Yadavas, a non-Brahmin dynasty family, concerned themselves so obsessively with Brahminic literary, religious, and social production, but my primary point is to show how Jnandev and Chakradhar were emblematic of a new sociopolitical integration linking the Yadava state via the Brahminic ecumene to the public of the Yadava century through the process of vernacularization.

Figure 1.1 represents a simple conceptualization of the sociopolitical order of the Yadava century before the advent of vernacularization. The graphic shows the discursive discontinuity between the Yadava state and the Brahminic ecumene, on the one hand, and a discontinuity with quotidian society, on the other. Undoubtedly, there is great interdependence here in terms of economy, agrarian order, military conscription, and so on, but a discursive link, I propose, was not significant before literary vernacularization. The field of discursive circulation, much less production, existed in a closed system that excluded the general population of the quotidian world. Discursive power was a closed loop.

Figure 1.2 suggests the way literary vernacularization linked the Brahminic ecumene—in the figures and concerns of the Brahmins who are emblematic of the literary vernacular turn—to the public, but also linked the public to its vernacular polity, a key subject of chapter 2. In this sense, Marathi literary vernacularization completes a coil of interconnection

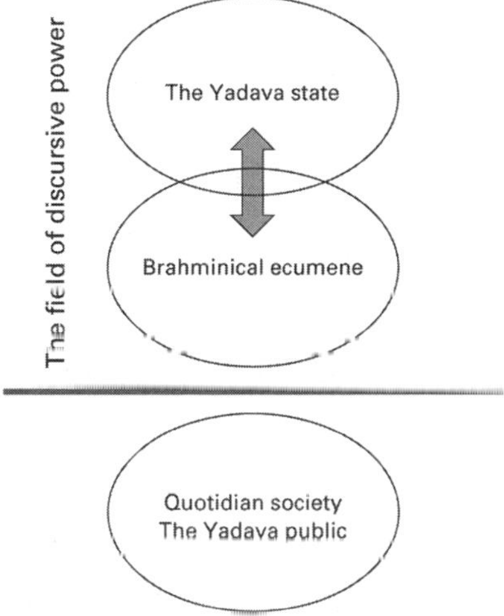

FIGURE 1.1. The field of discursive power before vernacularization. Graphic representation of the Yadava century sociopolitical order. Author original

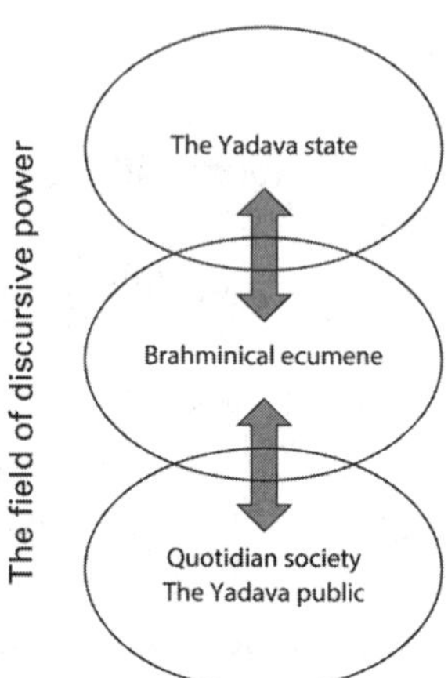

FIGURE 1.2. The field of discursive power after vernacularization. Graphic representation of the function of Marathi literary vernacularization in the Yadava century sociopolitical order. Author original

already begun in economic, agricultural, and militaristic realms; it is the discursive inheritor of the space where elite and nonelite society meet. This also implies new flows of power within the discursive field, new possibilities "from below," as it were, that might recondition the field of discursive power during and after vernacularization. This disruption occurs as the quotidian enters, in whatever small manner initially, the larger discursive field of the Yadava century.

My basic graphic here attempts to illustrate the social and political ecology of medieval public culture, the flow of discursive power, and how vernacularization links the quotidian to the sphere of power—the state, the Brahminic ecumene, and so on—in the Yadava period. This is the distinctive feature of the rudimentary public sphere that I seek to highlight in this work, the way in which this nascent public sphere articulates power from an imagined "people" or "public" to governmental, political, military, and economic elites. Certainly this "public" was connected intimately to the economy and military of the Yadava period, but not to its discursive power, contained in inscriptions, court literary production, records of state, and so on. It is this discursive world that is accessed by Marathi literary vernacularization. In particular, through the figures of Jnandev and Chakradhar (as well as the early Mahanubhavs), the Brahminic ecumene and its high regard for literacy prompted the first two works of Marathi literature that we have today. Yet these works— the *Līḷācaritra* and the *Jñāneśvarī*—are quite explicitly *not* intended for circulation and communion with the wider Sanskrit cosmopolis that the Brahminic ecumene draws upon for its social, political, and religious capital. Rather, the texts produced by these highly literate Brahmin males are directed toward an ostensibly *new* audience, not just the quotidian world in general, but a specific one, where Marathi is the medium of everyday interaction, and a world where Brahmin males were vastly outnumbered. Marathi literary vernacularization shows a synthesis between a Brahminic impetus toward literary production and a commitment to creating a new discursive field in Marathi that is, in principle, available to all people, to the world and citizen of the everyday, if only by mere attention. Vernacularization forges a literary connection between the elite spheres of the Yadava century and the quotidian world. In doing so, it opens a channel of power—discursive power perhaps, but power nonetheless—to flow from those elite worlds into the worlds of everyday life. What happens when the flow reverses, when power moves from the quotidian to the elite, is the core of other, later revolutions in the centuries that follow.

The Sevuna (Yadava) Dynasty

The Yadavas began, like many South Asian premodern polities, as a family overseeing a vassal state. From their origins in the early ninth century,[19] the Yadava line served the dynasties of the Rashtrakutas (sixth to tenth centuries) and the Western Chalukyas (tenth to twelfth centuries), forming a political order and alliance filling out the northern third of these polities, reaching toward the Narmada River. The first ruler of this dynasty to receive mention in regional inscriptions is Dridhaparahara in the early ninth century, but the dynasty acquires its name, in part, from his son, Sevunachandra I (r. c. 850–874). However, the sovereign reign of the Yadavas would not come until the time of Bhillama V (r. c. 1173–1192), who took advantage of a weakened Chalukya state, besieged on all sides by entrepreneurial militaries, and formed an independent kingdom from the northern portions of the Chalukya realm. A decade of warfare and expansion ended around 1186–1187 CE with a new political-governmental order in the region and a new capital for the dynasty in Devgiri.

The Yadavas controlled a large section of the Deccan plateau; the Hoysalas, their bitter rivals, oversaw a kingdom to the south, in the region of modern-day Karnataka; the Kakatiyas absorbed the region of modern-day

Andhra; and the Konkan coast was under the control of the Shilaharas and Kadambas until they become vassals of the Yadavas. A tenuous northern line of kingdoms stood between the Yadavas and the Ghurid Sultanate further north, a line that would thin and collapse within two centuries when the armies of the Delhi Sultanate would enter Devgiri as victors. But the Yadavas registered little concern for this brewing political force, enmeshed as they were in the typical feudalistic condition of constant war that set one sovereign polity against another and embroiled each in internal political negotiations of words, conflict, and compromise with its own vassal entities.

As Ethan Kapstein says, "war is economics by other means,"[20] and, though besieged by aggressor states on all sides, the Yadavas prospered in war and conflict. Under Singhana II (r. 1200–1247)—the grandson of Bhillama V and usually just referred to as "Singhana"—the kingdom was expanded to its farthest stable point and stretched between the Narmada River in the north and the Tungabhadra River in the south, with the Godavari River running across the middle. The map in figure 1.3 imagines the scope of the Yadava dynasty at its apex, laid over a contemporary map of India, and one can see that it occupies much of the region that will later become the modern state of Maharashtra.

Though war was a constant feature of medieval life throughout South Asia, a century of relative stability ensued in the regions of the Yadava Empire following the reign of Singhana; war was a feature of the periphery, though not usually the core. Jaitugi, the son of Singhana, was quickly replaced by the resolution of an internal battle over succession that saw Krishna, the grandson of Singhana, installed as emperor around 1245. Krishna's reign, while not more than seventeen years, was productive not only militarily but culturally as well, as we see an efflorescence of Sanskrit literary production under his rule. Krishna is also the first dynastic-political leader mentioned in the *Līḷācaritra*. Mahadev (reign c. 1261–1271) was appointed by his older brother, Krishna, to succeed Krishna and to hold the throne until Krishna's son, Ramachandra, came of age. However, Mahadev appeared to have been a rather bad general and likely lost battles with the neighboring kingdoms of the Kakatiyas, particularly when the Kakatiyas were under the rule of the queen Rudramba, around 1261; he fared little better against the Hoysalas four years later. In both cases, his enemies have recorded a hasty surrender and retreat by the Yadava ruler.[21] No doubt this poor showing in the field of politics and war

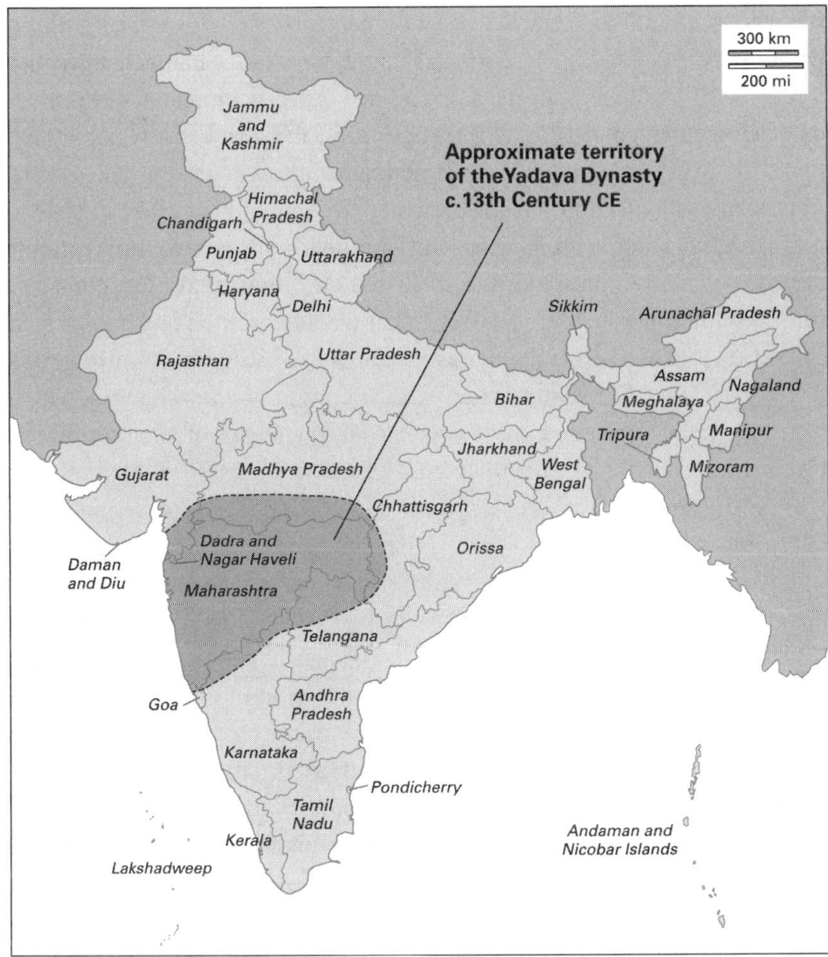

FIGURE 1.3. Contemporary political map of India with superimposed outline of the Yadava territory of the thirteenth century. Used by permission from http://d-maps.com/carte.php?&num_car=24868&lang=en

weakened any succession claims his own heir might have had over the maturing Ramachandra.

Despite this, Mahadev's son, Ammanadeva, attempted to take over the throne after his father's death, contrary to his father's agreement with Krishna. Within a year, Ramachandra had acquired the throne through a coup d'état, apparently helped by key ministers and generals who had served Mahadev, but who supported the agreement that the line of

succession would go from Mahadev to Ramachandra. In a daring plot—
which is perhaps myth but curious enough to repeat—Ramachandra and
a retinue of loyal soldiers are said to have entered Ammanadeva's court
by posing as a female dancing troupe, then mounted a surprise attack
upon the usurper. In some records, Ramachandra gouges out the eyes of
Ammanadeva as retribution for breaking the vow of his father; in others,
Ammanadeva languishes in prison until his death.[22] Upon reaching its apex
of power under Ramachandra (r. c. 1271–1311), the Yadava Empire's cultural production accelerated, a trend that would continue until the period
1303–1311, during which the dynasty crumbled and finally dissolved.[23]

Literary Marathi is not attested until the reign of Ramachandra, which
history recalls witnessed the two texts at the heart of this study, the
Līḷācaritra attributed to Mhaibhat in 1278 and the *Jñāneśvarī* attributed to
Jnandev in 1290.[24] It is therefore in the rule of Ramachandra, beginning in
1271, that the very brief "Golden Age" of the Yadava century could be said
to have begun. Lasting a mere twenty-three years,[25] this age would witness the creation of a new literary vernacular cultural politics of which the
Jñāneśvarī and *Līḷācaritra* stand as emblems. It is in the period of Krishna,
Mahadev, and Ramachandra that the literarization of Marathi is remembered to have occurred. For it is in this mere raindrop of time that the key
figures and moments of this book are all situated. This is when a nascent
Marathi public sphere was remembered to have begun, carrying an ambivalent social critique dominated by debates about caste and gender around
questions of linguistic and religious access and the very social inequities
that had established the shape of society of the time.

Landscapes of Language

Inspired by Pollock's idea of a "vernacular polity," we may now ask, what
was the relationship between the vernacular (Marathi) and the polity (the
Yadavas)? The territory of the Yadava dynasty encompassed several linguistic regions where people spoke Kannada and Marathi and, to a lesser
extent, Telugu and Gujarati, as well as early Konkani; these, anyway, are the
languages attested in sources, but there could have been, and likely were,
many more languages spoken, including Arabic and Persian.[26] This was a
polity with many vernaculars. While Sanskrit remained a central language
of state decree for almost all of the regions south of the Ghurid line across

north-central India, the language of everyday life likely was determined
by the languages of the subregion within the Yadava realm. The origin of
the Yadavas, like that of many such localized dynasties of the age, is uncertain with regard to linguistic culture, however. The Yadavas likely emerged
from within a Kannada-speaking context in the early ninth century, and
the names of the Yadava rulers—with only a few exceptions—evince a
Kannadiga affiliation. Given this fact, it is interesting to see that almost
all Maharashtrian historians claim a "Maratha" or North Indian origin for
the Yadavas.[27] The Yadavas themselves asserted a North Indian genealogy,
particularly from the regions of Mathura and Dvaravati or Dvaraka, from
where they claimed a line of descent from the mytho-historical lineage of
Yadu, one of five "tribes" described in the *Rig Veda,*and hence one name for
themselves was "those [in the lineage] of Yadu"—or "Yadava."[28]

The Yadu lineage's most famous figure is Krishna, remembered to be a
prince and (likely later) *avatara* of Vishnu and a key figure of purana and
bhakti literature, deity of the epic *Mahābhārata* and the central voice of the
Bhagavad Gītā. While Krishna's caste identity in the *Mahābhārata* is a curious
problem, most kings and others who claim descent from the line of Yadu
did so (and do so today)[29] in order to establish their high-caste Kshatriya
varna status. Not only the Yadavas in this era and area made this claim
to the line of Yadu, but so too did the Rashtrakutas, Chedis, Kalachuris,
Shilaharis, Wodiyars, and the Hoysalas; notably, however, the Kakatiyas
of the Andhra region claimed Shudra descent.[30] The act of establishing
illustrious genealogies for newly established ruling families is an age-old
practice in India, and one that continued into modernity.[31] In addition,
often Brahmin scholars would be contracted to produce fresh genealogies
tying a new king to either the hoary solar or lunar race of kings; the Yadavas
claimed the latter lineage. D. D. Kosambi writes, "as for the Deccan Yadavas,
the Brahmins who found a genealogy which connected them to the dark
god [Krishna] had no deeper aim in the forgery than to raise the chiefs
of a local clan above the surrounding population."[32] When the Yadavas,
and most of their neighboring rivals, maintained such descent, they were
authorizing a royal, high caste, Kshatriya imprimatur on their genealogical
line. However, I dissent from Kosambi's idea that they did this to elevate
themselves above the surrounding population or that this lineage represents a "forgery." As we will see, the surrounding population worshipped
Krishna in the form of Vitthal, the deity of Pandharpur, then a new though

emergent socioreligious community. As chapter 2 will show, the Yadavas took an interest in Pandharpur that may have served to connect their caste genealogy with the public worship of Vitthal/Krishna. Rather than raising themselves above their subject population, the Yadavas were actually normalizing or "naturalizing" themselves within it by a claim to the genealogy of Krishna. This claim may have been mythic, but it was certainly common practice; thus calling it a forgery misses the political convention's role. One cannot have a myth that is also a forgery. In any case, these claims may not tell us about the ancient history of the Yadava dynasty, but they do tell us about a collective emphasis on authorizing high-caste Kshatriya status within the royal field of the region and time, and in the lineage of Krishna; in other words, varna status and religiomythic status mattered to the Yadavas.

However, when referring to themselves, the Yadavas usually used the term *Sevuna* (*seūṇā, sivaṇā, seyuṇā*) and this is the dynastic name their neighbors used for them as well.[33] As we have seen, Sevuna is derived from the name of Sevunachandra, the ninth-century king credited with fully establishing the dynastic line; but Sevuna also refers to the region of the Godavari Valley, the Yadava heartland. In this sense, *Sevuna* registers the "vernacular polity" as a polity situated in time and regionality; the word *Yadava,* however, given the way the term is shared among other dynasties, even bitter rivals of the Yadavas, suggests a cosmopolitan political idiom, a claim to be more than one's vernacular/place restrictions allow, to be linked to a transregional genealogy, and hence it is a term that joins the vernacular culture of the region with a cosmopolitan mythic politics. Still, the dynasty was regularly called Yadava in South Asian Islamic historiography in the centuries just after the reign's end, especially by notables like Amir Khusrao, Ziauddin Barani, and Firishta. The convention of referring to this dynasty as Yadava, inspired by these ethnohistorical premodern sources, became adopted by colonial historiography, and remains how they usually are known today. The term, unfortunately, erases some of the specific aspects of the Yadava genealogy that I have outlined.

The expressive linguistic field of the Yadava dynasty reflects the hybrid origins of the rulers themselves. From the Yadava court, we have two kinds of expressive documents that form the core of our historical archive. These are inscriptions in stone and copper, on the one hand, and texts written in the court or under the support of state funds, on the other. Within the inscriptional record, we have some five hundred or so inscriptions throughout the Yadava lands—many more are awaiting discovery. These are primarily in Sanskrit, Kannada, and Marathi. The majority of inscriptions issued by the Yadavas are in Kannada and the second most common language of inscription is Sanskrit. Of the five hundred inscriptions, perhaps two hundred display some Marathi, usually as a translation or addition of text to a Kannada or Sanskrit inscription.[34] In other words, Kannada and Sanskrit, not Marathi, are the most common languages of Yadava written expressive culture.

Yet there is a shift in the use of different languages over time. In the early years of the Yadava reign, Sanskrit and Kannada are the primary languages for state inscription.[35] However, in the last half century of Yadava rule, Marathi came to form a central position in epigraphy, perhaps reflecting, as I will argue in the next chapter, an attentive Marathi public in the Yadava realm. This increase in Marathi inscriptions, particularly during the reign of Ramachandra, is likely an expression of the Yadava desire to distinguish themselves from the Kannada-speaking Hoysalas, as S. B. Joshi (1951, 1952) has argued, and perhaps from their own Kannada origins. This may have been part of the process of adaptation to the geocultural zone that became the Yadava heartland, where Marathi was likely the dominant language of everyday life, something the inscriptional record discussed here and in the next chapter suggests. As Pollock showed is common in South Asia, the first instances of the literization of the vernacular, in this case Marathi, are in the context of state records and royal decrees.[36] However, as mentioned, the rise of literarization, of the first literary works in Marathi, occurred outside the purview of the state. Thus, Pollock's distinction between literization and literarization is also a distinction, in the case of Marathi literary history, between the state (the harbinger of literization) and a religiously inflected public culture (the harbinger of literarization).

Marathi literization precedes the Yadava century by several hundred years. Marathi as a written language is perhaps first attested in a portion of a copperplate inscription from 739 CE found in Satara.[37] The first full use of Marathi for inscription certainly is in place by the middle to end of the eleventh century, usually appended to an inscription in Sanskrit or Kannada.[38] Several records tend to vie for a position as the first Marathi inscription.[39] One is a stone inscription from Akshi Taluka (Raigad) with a probable date corresponding to 1012 CE under the reign of the northern Konkani Shilaharas (see figure 2.1);[40] a second, also of the Shilaharas, is a copperplate inscription at Dive outlining the institution of an *agrahara,* or land endowment, in this case, as in most cases, to a Brahmin, and with a date of 1060 or 1086 CE;[41] and a third inscription of two short lines records a grant by the Mysore Hoysalas to the Mahalakshmi temple of Shravanabelgol with the date 1118 CE.[42] These inscriptions mark the moment of the language's full literization, its existence as a standard written language. The Yadavas therefore inherit a region already witnessing the public expression of written Marathi. Their own adoption of this quotidian medium is a political inheritance rather than an innovation.

Royal and donative inscriptions by the Yadavas (and others) in Marathi grow substantially after 1187 CE and throughout the Yadava century. From the presence of these written inscriptions, we might infer the existence of a Marathi public that could consume and contextualize the message of the inscriptions in Marathi as early as the tenth century. Yet at this point we still have no record of any actual literary production in Marathi, no example of the language's literarization. For this, we must wait until the latter part of the thirteenth century.

This rise of Marathi in inscriptions during the Yadava century suggests to some scholars that Marathi may have been the standard language for common notations of state records on paper as well, though no artifacts are available today. We have no physical evidence of this claim, to my knowledge; no surviving paper documents from the Yadava period. Nor does it seem logical to me that the languages of public inscription necessarily would match the languages of court, for the practical purposes underlying these two uses of language are very different. In any case, if one is to make assumptions about a private courtly language based on the frequency of an inscriptional language, then it is more likely that Kannada was the "domestic" language of the Yadavas until the reign of the dynasty's last three rulers.

In spite of this lack of physical evidence of Marathi as a courtly language in the Yadava period, we find the interesting and commonly held position that Marathi was so widely used as the regular language of state record that a new script called *modi* was said to have been developed, for the florid writing of Marathi, around the latter half of the thirteenth century.[43] This is not likely to be an historically accurate claim, however, and we find no evidence of *modi* in any inscriptions of the Yadava era, though one can imagine that the professional inscriber may not have found the shorthand script of *modi* as elegant as the longhand calligraphy of *devanagari*, often called *bālbodh* in Marathi.[44] In any case, claims, true or false, about the use of Marathi in official functions at the later Yadava court further point toward the idea of a vibrant and literate Marathi-speaking public in the region, though they do not establish the use of Marathi as a courtly language beyond its tertiary inscriptional use.[45]

As mentioned earlier, the written materials produced at the Yadava court or under its patronage are of two kinds: epigraphical materials in Sanskrit, Marathi, and Kannada of the early twelfth century onward and Sanskrit treatises composed at the Yadava court or under its elaborate system of state patronage, particularly of Brahmins, within the Brahminic ecumene. However, with the emergence of literary Marathi, a third layer of historical material is added: that is, Marathi texts composed outside the Yadava state system or the Brahminic ecumene, yet within public culture. Emblematic of such texts are the *Līḷācaritra* and the *Jñāneśvarī*.

In terms of historiography, each of these three types of material serves a purpose for the modern historian. Materials in the first category, that of epigraphy, provide the core documentation for reconstructing the political and economic history of the Yadava period in most modern histories, and these are often set alongside epigraphical data from other dynasties and kingdoms. Epigraphical records provide the usual details about the function of the state and wealthy individuals, recording land grants, battles, political succession, temple donations, gifts to Brahmins, and other such moments.

These materials are sometimes supplemented in historiography by Sanskrit compositions produced under the umbrella of the Yadava state, chief among them the *Caturvarga Cintāmaṇi* of the thirteenth century, attributed to Hemadri.[46] As we will see, although these Sanskrit documents are almost uniformly of a nonhistorical sort, comprising for the most part commentaries on Dharma Śāstra or astronomical or mathematical subjects, some "history" is preserved in them, particular of dynastic order in appendixes. The third category of material, especially the *Līḷācaritra*, supplies for historians the primary data for all social and cultural history of this period, providing details of everything from the price of vegetables to marriage practices and caste relations. My point here in highlighting how these three sets of materials are used in historiography is to note that the texts discussed in this book are not only a product of the thirteenth century, they are also the sources by which we know something historically about the period, particularly about matters of culture and society.[47] The *Līḷācaritra* and the *Jñāneśvarī* are not only taken to be the first works of Marathi literature, but they are also, in some sense, the first works of Marathi cultural history or ethnohistory.

All of these records reach a crescendo of quantity and quality in the "Golden Age" of the Yadava century around 1271 CE, but they are not records that exist as simple utterances—they are embedded in a cultural and linguistic politics of difference. For example, non-Brahmin professional scribes called Kayasthas composed almost all inscriptions by the Yadavas, and we know this because they would sign their names and give their designation as Kayastha. At the same time, male Brahmins wrote almost all the Sanskrit texts of the period.[48] Of course, Brahmins might author inscriptions, and Kayasthas might produce texts, but in general, the literary record of this period suggests a rather clear delineation of literary form and jati. Though Brahmins are by no means the sole authors of Sanskrit texts throughout Indian history, our records suggest that they dominated this field of literary production in the Yadava century, even while Kayasthas appear as a kind of rival to them in the literary sphere, as we will see in chapter 4. While no donative inscriptions, to my knowledge, record gifts to Kayasthas, we have at least one record of a prominent gift by a Kayastha guild to the Pandharpur Temple in 1273.[49]

Thus we can assume that Kayasthas were powerful, but that this power was restricted to the literary sphere of royal courts, the source of their primary employment. Brahmins, however, were equally ubiquitous at the Yadava court and in the networks of the Brahminic ecumene supported by the court and recorded in donative inscriptions from the age. The Brahminic ecumene, in this sense, linked the court with sociocultural institutions like the monastery and temple, as figures 1.1 and 1.2 illustrate. As we will see, a vast economic and social system of value was in place to fund Brahmins primarily engaged in ritual and literary activity around the production of Sanskrit texts. Importantly, even in the third category of historical source material, material produced outside royal courts—the Mahanubhav literature and the *Jñāneśvarī*, for example—the purported authors of these texts were also Brahmins. This link, as I have mentioned, is important because I argue that though the Brahminic ecumene may not have compelled these figures and their followers to compose in Sanskrit, it did compel them to compose *literature* and to write things down: the cultural capital of literacy was transposed from the field of literary Sanskrit and written inscriptions to this new field, what I am calling a nascent public sphere. Jnandev and the early Mahanubhavs (including Chakradhar)—all Brahmin males—transferred the cultural capital of literacy from the Brahminic ecumene into the field of everyday life.

Why they chose Marathi rather than Sanskrit is a motivating question for this book to consider in the chapters to come. At this point, however, we might explore the Brahminic ecumene in some depth to understand the high position Brahmins held in the Yadava century. This context helps inform an answer to the question of why two male Brahmin figures, in this period of great social security and prosperity for Brahmins, would be remembered to have produced (in Jnandev's case) or inspired (in Chakradhar's case) literary texts that undermine, each in its own way, the very Brahminic orthodoxy that enfolded the figures in the first place. This conundrum—the divisibility of the value of literacy from Sanskrit—is likely the key technical innovation of all instances of vernacularization on the subcontinent.

The Brahminic Ecumene

The existence of such a monochromatic historical archive in which Brahmins are primary agents in the Yadava century—and so focused on Brahmins and Brahminic activities—suggests their power in this period. However it also implies that the spheres of the Brahmin and of the "Brahminic" were not identical, but betrayed significant heterogeneity and emerging fault lines.[50] As we will see, not all Brahmins are the same, not under the Yadavas or at any other time. Yadava records detail a plethora of jati and *gotra* or "clan" genealogical distinctions among Brahmins, often in contention with one another.[51] In addition to Brahmins, the emergence of the Kayastha class, as well as Guravs (non-Brahmin temple caretakers and priests), engendered a set of jatis that are in almost constant contention in economic realms—symbolic and actual—and vie for elevated varna status from the eleventh century,[52] at least, and even up to the present. Indeed, the story that unfolds in this context is of direct contention between Brahminic groups as well as between Brahminic *sabhas* or "courts" and members of particular jatis who wish to acquire varna status as Brahmins authorized by such sabhas.[53] Yet alongside these individuals and communities seeking to avail of the opportunities afforded by patronage in the Brahminic ecumene, we have other Brahmins and other high-caste individuals pursuing quite different ends, many seeking some vision of egalitarianism across social strata and in relation to language. Outside Maharashtra, the figure of Basava (1134–1196) is emblematic, a Kannada Shaiva Brahmin who is remembered to have rejected temple and court in favor of a peripatetic life composing and performing *vacanas*, "utterances," throughout the Kannada public culture of his time.[54] In similar vein, the leaders and hagiographers of the early Mahanubhavs and the figure of Jnandev and the *Jñāneśvarī* stand as our exemplars in Maharashtra.

In both cases—of a Brahminic orthodoxy or a challenge to that orthodoxy undertaken by certain Brahmin figures—a precondition is set in which Brahmins dominate the state-funded institutions of the Yadava period. The ascendancy of powerful Brahmins in the political, literary, educational, and economic fields of the Yadava reign is indisputable, and almost every key historian of this dynasty—in Marathi or English—does not fail to mention the dominance of Brahmins in such institutions, though often they impute a concomitant Brahmin dominance in politics, which I do not think was necessarily the case. The Yadava rulers were not Brahmin, and their chief subject of glorification was their own dynasty, their own Yadava-Krishna Kshatriya glory. The Brahmins who served their court and benefited from Yadava largess in the institutions of the Brahminic ecumene were clients of state funds, not masters of the state. Yet the figure of the Brahmin receives vaunted stature under Yadava rule, for reasons about which I will speculate.

The sustenance of power within Brahmin circles lay in the elaborate and extensive systems in place to fund what were considered "traditional" Brahminic activities: instruction in the Vedas, the production of ritual texts and practices, the running of temples and monasteries (*matha*), theorization of Dharma Śāstra ideas, the patronization of traditional philosophical schools (in particular the sociophilosophical school of thought, Purva Mimamsa, and the astronomical and mathematical sciences), and the training of professional accountants, scribes, genealogists, and chroniclers.

These were professions that valorized and prized literacy—whether in literary production or through the means to read and maintain ritual or legal texts. The *Līḷācaritra*, for example, records a story where two monks battled for the ownership of the books of a monastery after the death of the monastery's founder.[55] The judgment of who should inherit the books, and thus the monastery, was decided by who could *read* the books—the preeminent skill of the monastic order was literacy. These literary technocratic fields, though populated at times by high-caste non-Brahmin males, nonetheless remained epitomized under the sign of the "Brahmin," that is, within the field of the literary Brahminic ecumene.

If we turn to the donative inscriptions of the Yadavas to trace the Brahminic ecumene, we can see that a majority of the inscriptions in all of the three primary languages of epigraphy within the Yadava realm communicate gifts, donations, land grants, and revenue rights to Brahmin individuals and institutions.[56] Sanskrit and Kannada inscriptions convey the largest number of such donations, though they appear in Marathi regularly as well. This benevolence toward Brahmins also seems to be the case for the inscriptional records of dynasties that preceded the Yadavas, especially the Shilaharas and Hoysalas. For example, one of the oldest Marathi inscriptions, the Shilahara Dive grant of c. 1060 CE, is just such a grant of land, revenue, and gold in trust to a particular Brahmin leader, Mavalabhatta, for the maintenance of a community of Brahmin scholars.[57] Likewise, the Shilahara Akshi inscription, possibly of 1012 CE records a donation to a Mahalakshmi temple along the Konkan coast, likely a temple under the control of Brahmins.[58]

Several Marathi inscriptions from 1144 CE onward found in Amba Jogai similarly demonstrate multiple donations for the maintenance of temples, families of Brahmins, and Brahminic monasteries—at least two of these donations made by the famous Brahmin Yadava general Kholeshwar in 1228 CE and later.[59] In 1957 Alfred Master collected fourteen representative inscriptions in Marathi on stone and copperplate from 1060–1300 CE.[60] Of these, ten record donations to Brahmin scholars or societies of scholars, Brahminic monasteries or schools, or temples run by Brahmins. Two of them record donations to temples whose proprietors are not named, but they were likely Brahmins or perhaps Guravs.[61]

We can survey those Marathi inscriptions collected by S. G. Tulpule in 1963 in the *Prācīn Marāṭhī Korīv Lekha* or "[A Collection of] Old Marathi

Inscriptions," the most thorough collection of Marathi inscriptions to date. Of the seventy-six Marathi inscriptions collected by Tulpule, thirty-four are dateable to the Yadava era.[62] Of those, twenty-six were issued by the Yadava court or its affiliate figures or vassal rulers.[63] And of those twenty-six Marathi inscriptions, fifteen clearly provide funds in the name of, or for the benefit of, Brahmins and Brahminic activities, such as temple rituals, Vedic rituals, Dharma Śāstra schools, Sanskrit education, and monasteries.[64] Another six record funds for rituals and temple maintenance, and these were likely temples at least partially under Brahmin control.[65] Thus probably twenty-one of the twenty-six Marathi inscriptions recording funds given by the Yadava state were directed, in part or in whole, to Brahmins. As many Marathi and Indian historians of this era note, whether in Marathi, Kannada, or Sanskrit, the primary subject of early Konkani, Deccani, and Yadava-era inscriptions was the gift of something to a Brahmin for some Brahminic endeavor.[66]

However, these inscriptions within the Brahminic ecumene also address the non-Brahmin, and at times the tension between the Brahmin and the non-Brahmin is apparent. This is a tension that is not external to the Brahminical ecumene, but rather contained within it. We find an example in the regular donation of funds and land for the specific maintenance of temples and temple grounds that required a negotiation of power between Brahmins and non-Brahmins. From inscriptions as early as 1080 CE in Marathi, Guravs were listed alongside Brahmins as the regular recipients of donations. As non-Brahmin temple priests and proprietors Guravs served all the vital functions that a Brahmin would serve, but often for non-Brahmin constituents. Guravs likely considered themselves on par with Brahmins or perhaps as Brahmins themselves.[67] As we will see in the next part of the book, the *Līḷācaritra* may record a contentious state of affairs between Brahmins and Guravs in the Yadava period, and this contention is registered in the careful wording of Yadava inscriptions. For example, the Tasgav copperplate inscription of approximately 1251 CE distinguishes the two groups.[68] "In the temple (*devasthala*), the Gurav is the master; in the charity distribution center (*sattrasthala*), the Brahmin is the master. [The Brahmin] should oversee the [temple's] offerings; the Gurav should oversee the care of the God." In several inscriptions we find such dual gifts and a careful demarcation of "territory" and "rights," as if to assuage any potential conflict or rivalry between Brahmins and Guravs.[69] In the main, the inscriptional record of the Yadavas displays a preponderance of state support for Brahmins and Brahminic endeavors, yet it also reveals the fault lines of social order that may have helped open up the vital connections between elite spheres of Yadava society and the quotidian world in general, the intermediate space in which vernacularization emerged.

It is interesting to note that similar tensions do not appear to exist with temples, monasteries, agrahara land grants, or *brahmanapuri* grants of village revenue to a Brahmin family or set of families. The distinction here, I think, is a public one. Only the temple was a public entity, where (most of) the general public could come and go with some regularity and freedom. Monasteries and other institutions were ostensibly "private" in this sense—they were not the locus of regular and relatively unregulated public interaction. The other examples of land and revenue rights (agrahara, brahmanapuri) were financial instruments that also implied a very localized political power, but not an unregulated public place of social interaction. I suspect the temple was the site of the most contentious struggles between Brahmins and Guravs because of its public nature. I hope to support this contention in chapters 4 and 5 with evidence from the *Līḷacaritra*.

Through donative inscriptions of this era, we get a sense of how the Yadava state, and preceding regional states, funded various sorts of Brahminic enterprises, including *mathas* or monasteries, *sattras* or charity distribution centers primarily for Brahmins (as above),[70] and *khaṇḍikās* or vocational schools teaching temple rites and other rituals, often associated with a particular Vedic branch of ritual. In the process of formalizing these systems of Brahminic patronage, the Yadavas constructed a "Brahminized" network of institutions, which, however, they conscientiously shaped and controlled. The mechanisms for funding these endeavors included direct grants and endowments made by the state, but several other forms of financial support appeared dominant, tied to land and its agricultural revenue, including such practices as the *vritti*, a small hereditary land grant given to sustain single Brahmin families. We also find that Brahmin land grants benefited from lower tax rates.[71] Thus, the temple was by no means the most lucrative nor the most direct source of revenue for a Brahmin family.

The most common financial instrument apparent in these inscriptions was the agrahara, which, as mentioned previously, was a type of land and profit grant. The word literally means "seized (*hāra*) for the prominent (*agra*) or elite" and the term denoted a system in which a village's annual tax, usually the purview of the king, was given to a group of Brahmin (and rarely Gurav) professionals for their maintenance, along with the governing rights over the village. The agrahara was a practice throughout South Asia, but especially in the western and southern regions of the peninsula; Karnataka in particular retains this word in the names of some contemporary villages and towns. Other common sources of revenue for agraharas included donations from trade guilds, the economic stronghold of the Vaishya (also *vāṇī, vāṇika,* and *vāṇija*) in the Yadava century. Brahmin recipients of an agrahara were called *mahajana*, and the adult male Brahmins formed the governing body of that agrahara village. It is important to note that not all villages were agraharas, and not all of a given village with an agrahara was governed by that agrahara. Rather, the carefully calibrated practice of agrahara linked economic and political power for many Brahmins in the Yadava period, all under the benevolence of the sovereign non-Brahmin Yadava state.

Typically, an agrahara was granted for service of a "religious" type (Vedic learning, temple maintenance, etc.), as well as scribal, educational, literary, and even Ayurvedic medical services or achievements. Less commonly, agraharas were granted to Brahmins who had distinguished themselves as military commanders and combatants, yet even in such cases the explicit reason given for the agrahara would be some literary merit. Many of the key military leaders of the Yadava period were Brahmin: for example, Hemadri, who was a highly decorated commander under Mahadev as the leader of the Yadava "elephant brigade," and the famous general Kholeshwar (fl. c. 1220 CE), who served under Singhana II as his chief military leader of expeditions into Gujarat.

The beneficence of the Yadava court toward Brahmins attracted Brahmin entrepreneurs from outside the Yadava realm, from the regions of modern-day Madhya Pradesh, Gujarat, Benares, and the region of Malwa, in the North, as well many areas of the South, such as the regions of Karnataka, Telangana, and Andhra. Indeed, Hemadri's family is said to have emigrated from the south to reach the Yadava kingdom, with the hope of entering its service; in medieval India a new polity meant new opportunities for Brahmin and other literary technocrats. Clearly, the Yadava realm was a good place to be a Brahmin male. The effect of these institutionalized economic incentives was to create a system whereby the state not only supported a caste-varna group—Brahmins primarily—in a highly systematic way but also reinforced a very particular relationship between being Brahmin and doing something designated as Brahminic—or, in Sanskrit and Marathi, *brahmanatva*, "Brahminness." The Yadava state formalized a relationship between caste and class, which carried an important association with language and with the production of Sanskrit texts. Yet this association also conveyed a deep sense of clientelism and entitlement. As we will see with the early Mahanubhavs—almost all of whom were Brahmin—they carried with them a sense of *brahmanatva* that led them to believe they were entitled to benefits—good food, clothing, shelter—given free by the general public, by virtue of their caste status. The Yadava century's institutionalized privilege of Brahmins trickled down into the quotidian world.

This expansive system of financial support for the perpetuation and preservation of Brahminic activities, particularly literary activities, did not, however, engender a plethora of literary subjects among the Brahmin technocracy or intelligentsia; indeed, the financial incentives offered by the Yadavas served to drastically narrow the themes of literary production. There was very little Sanskrit literature produced in the Yadava reign in the genres of drama and poetry, and there were few philosophical texts either, but retellings of epic and purana literature appeared to be a common entertainment at court. Though the Yadava kings, like all kings, were often referred to as "patrons of the arts," the literary art of the Yadava period in Sanskrit appeared to come primarily in one flavor: the study and reification of an ideal social order around an analysis of Dharma Śāstra, the cosmic or soteriological social science of classical and medieval Hinduism.[72] While there are a few exceptions,[73] under Yadava reign the vast majority of Sanskrit literary production took the form of commentaries and *nibandhas* or "essays" based upon Dharma Śāstra texts, though we also find a few commentaries and distillations of the *Bhagavad Gītā,* such as Bopadeva's *Harilīlā,* composed by an apparent protégé of Hemadri. Under the patronage of the Brahminic ecumene I have described, other works were produced by Brahmin luminaries of the time, including the figures of Vijnaneshwar and Aparaka.[74]

By the end of the Yadava century, Hemadri was the titular figure at the apex of this vast system of reifying the power of an orthodox social Brahminism, and he is also the figure most commonly associated with an anxiety about its erosion. If Dharma Śāstra commentary was the subject that dominated the literary sphere of Sanskrit in the Yadava period, Hemadri was the star of this sphere who epitomized the ascendency of Brahmins. The Sanskrit literary compositions of Hemadri are among the primary resources for all Yadava dynastic histories. However, about Hemadri before his rise to power as a minister of state we know very little.

While his dates are not clearly known, Hemadri appears to have been born in the southern, Kannada-speaking region of the Yadava realm into a Madhyadina Shakha Brahmin family, migrating to Devgiri to approach the center of Yadava ministerial power. He served Mahadev as a commander of the army and chief adviser and continued as prime minister when Ramachandra came to power, spanning a period from 1259 to perhaps as late as 1285 CE. This vaunted role may have been given to him for his support to Ramachandra in his coup d'état against Ammanadeva. Hemadri also stands as the chief archivist of the Yadavas, having supplied an extensive genealogy of the dynasty in his *Caturvarga Cintāmaṇi* and throughout his works, recording the affairs of the Yadava state in his time and before. He is regularly credited, dubiously, with being the figure who formalized the records of state in Marathi in *modi* script, a claim that rests on shaky ground, as mentioned earlier.[75] In fact, Hemadri appears to have composed or oversaw the composition of nothing in Marathi other than perhaps simple state records and inscriptions, for which we have no record in any case and thus no basis for speculation. The many works, around thirteen extensive treatises, for which he is well known were all composed in Sanskrit. He wrote no "literature" of any kind, no poetry or drama or commentary on poetics. Though he also wrote about astrology, astronomy, mathematics, architecture, and Ayurvedic medicine, his primary subject was *dharmic* "social science" and in particular a study of how to sustain orthodox relations among varnas.[76]

Hemadri's voluminous *Caturvarga Cintāmaṇi* is considered his greatest achievement, and we can observe this text as a snapshot of state-society concerns during the Yadava century's conclusion. This text is multifaceted and is often discussed as a kind of response to the emergent social order of the Yadava realm. Hemadri appears to direct his text to the common person, in particular when discussing "vows" or *vratas* appropriate for everyday life, ritual life, and special occasions.[77] As a text concerned with prescribing norms of society in everyday life, it stands above most others in this period, not only because of its extensive erudition but also because of the considerable political power wielded by its author, and thus the influence, though brief, the text had on Yadava court thinking about society. So influential was this text in the later Yadava century that it is often simply referred to as *Hemādrśāstra*, "Hemadri's [social] science." This Sanskrit compendium detailed the scope of orthodox rites, rituals, observances, and social mores incumbent upon each of the four varnas in the *varnashramadharma* system.

Divided into four parts, plus an appendix, the *Caturvarga Cintāmaṇi* melds political, social, and *dharmic* themes. The first part, the "Vratakhaṇḍa," examines *vrata*, the proper procedures that everyday people ought to follow for various kinds of vows, rites, rituals, and practices, particularly within the quotidian sphere. However, for Hemadri, the practice of *vrata* was deeply tied with charitable gifts, primarily to Brahmins and Brahminic endeavors.[78] The second part is devoted entirely to ways of giving or *dana*, especially for endowments for Brahminic activities. The third section explains the importance of pilgrimage and the dharmic necessity of maintaining places of pilgrimage or *tirtha*. The final portion discusses the means by which one attains *moksha* or "liberation." This section reveals that Hemadri appears to have been particularly influenced by the orthodox philosophical system known as Purva Mimamsa, which deals with a "fundamentalist" extension of the early books of the Vedic corpus and an examination of the laws of karma, cast within the orthodox typologies of varna. It is distinctive in part for its view that good karma can only yield ever better and higher births, eschewing a focus solely on moksha. It is a philosophy that asserts that people should follow the rules, as it were. This perspective serves to reinforce a strict social orthodoxy for "doing one's duty" according to varna; performing rituals and rites properly provides the only means of improving one's spiritual self. The work includes an appendix that lists certain key subjects: the *devatā* or the appropriate deities one should worship, the proper time (*kāla*) for worship, the correct actions or methods (karma) of worship, and what to do to atone when one has transgressed any of the many rules and regulations of life outlined by Hemadri, which is the act of "purification" or *prāyaścitta*.[79] Within his text Hemadri interlaces dynastic matters, including an extensive genealogy of the Yadava rulers, embedded in the "Vratakhaṇḍa," which suggests the importance of this section and its prescriptions for the ritual quotidian.[80]

Thus in the figure of Hemadri several spheres of power intersected. Another of the Sanskrit works attributed to him is a treatise on writing and literature itself, *Lekhana Kalpataru*, a testament to the intersectionality of caste, class, power, and literacy within the Brahminic ecumene.[81] His position as a chief adviser to Mahadev and as prime minister to Ramachandra provided the opportunity to further buttress this nexus of interests through patronizing Brahminic literary work around social science and also to turn the socially conservative philosophical perspectives epitomized by the *Caturvarga Cintāmaṇi* into state legal practice and norm. Several sets of evidence suggest that the Yadava period, particularly the later years under Hemadri's tenure, was a time when the state and its agents strictly enforced caste rules.[82] Already we have seen evidence of this in the elaborate systems in place for financially supporting traditional Brahminic activities. A sphere of self-replication was firmly set, producing texts and experts on social order and segregation. The state commitment to lavishly fund traditional Brahminic occupations is clear evidence of a caste-based political order of privilege. Furthermore, the fact that the chief subject of these funded endeavors was the production of texts and ritual instruments for the maintenance of traditional varna social norms further emphasizes the degree of caste enforcement dominating a particular view of society as well as a theory of state-society relations in this period.

In addition, several state inscriptions reiterate the demands of traditional social order. Ramachandra is described as the protector of the varna system and a figure who would extol the virtue of Sanskrit learning.[83] Thus it is common to find donors referred to as *vedārthāda* or "expounder of the Vedas," and *sarvajñasārasvati*, "one omniscient like the [Vedic goddess of learning] Saraswati," or *daśagranthī*, "one who knows ten books [of Vedic learning]," and so forth. Plates that record a land grant by Ramachandra to the Brahmin minister Purushottama, which Purushottama in turn donated as an agrahara to a group of Brahmins, praise Purushottama for his commitment to maintaining dharmic order and for making his subjects "conform to the rules of conduct as laid down in the varnas and *āśramas*."[84] Another inscription, from the era of Yadava ruler Krishna, cited by S. Ritti, states that the primary role of the Yadava ministers was to maintain the "four legs of dharma," which indicates the varna social system.[85] And one of Krishna's primary Brahmin ministers, Jalhana, was granted his agrahara as a reward for the relatively unusual practice of writing an anthology of

Sanskrit poetry c. 1250 CE, the *Sūktimuktāvalī*, one of the few such poetic compendiums of the period. It is important to note that, though a powerful minister of state, the grant awards him the agrahara for doing something Brahminic (composing a Sanskrit poetic text, which perhaps was enabled by his position of privilege), not for being "powerful" in the political sense—though probably his vital role in the affairs of state was the predominant reason for his agrahara.

The valorization of Brahmins even stood as a literary trope in inscriptions. For example, the inscriptional grant to Jalhana states in Sanskrit: "He who grants to a Brahmin even a cubit of land is honored in heaven for sixty thousand years." This proclamation is more than an appeal to the belief in karma, but a demonstration of class through a specific kind of philanthropy. On the other hand, to take away an agrahara or other donation from a Brahmin will earn one a future birth "as a worm in shit for sixty thousand years."[86] Here, from heaven to earth, from salvation to excrement, we see the move from the cosmopolitan to the quotidian—karma is the trope of this expression, but it functions to distinguish the people who give to Brahmins from the people who do not or, worse, who oppose or rescind such giving. The high registers of Sanskrit composition supported by court endowments, the vaunted stature of Brahmins in the Yadava century—this world of the elite gazes down on the quotidian world. Given such grants that cross a literary-political divide, we must conclude, as Pollock has suggested, that the literary and political, in the vernacular moment, are linked. The fission of this orthodoxy, the split in this dharmic atom, occurs when the exclusive link between the Brahminic ecumene and literacy is broken—when the social practice of literature shifts into the vernacular idiom and everyday life—and this is the source of energy for the quotidian revolution.

Brahminhood and the Social Capital of Literacy

We arrive at a view of the Yadava period that would seem to militate against Marathi literary vernacularization. The apparent indifference of the Yadavas to Marathi, combined with the already well-established system of patronizing another language, Sanskrit, throughout the Brahminic ecumene, all would seem to make it very unlikely that a new literature would emerge in Marathi in the thirteenth century. And yet we see the opposite.

Toward the end of this period, we have two voluminous texts in Marathi that indicate a range of literary idioms already in place in the language in this period and suggests that though these are our first text records of Marathi literature, they were composed in the context of both a history and a present of Marathi literary production. As we will discuss, the *Līḷācaritra* reveals a prose idiom that anticipates that of the *bakhar* or chronicle genre, which will arise some centuries later, yet also records within it instances of Marathi poetry (such as the *dhavaḷe* attributed to Mahadaisa/Mahadamba),[87] folk stories, and all the other forms V. L. Bhave (in his *Mahārāṣṭra Sāraswat*) suggested were in vogue in this period. And the *Jñāneśvarī* displays an advanced poetic meter and aesthetic sensibility that is highly unlikely to have grown sui generis in the context of this single text, but probably reflected a heterogonous aural literary world in Marathi. However, if any of this aural literature was ever written down, we no longer have it. What we do have are the shadows of such literature cast along, within, and between the lines of both of these key texts. It is possible, and even likely, that the Yadavas at court patronized Marathi performances, recitals, compositions, and many other forms of entertainment for their private pleasure.[88] However, in the realm of official state sponsorship of Marathi literary production, the record is not only silent, but speaks to the converse application of Marathi; that is, not as a lofty poetic language but as a language to communicate with, and at times intimidate, the general public, as chapter 2 will show.

The conditions under which Marathi literarization occurred are deeply connected to the historical context laid out in this chapter and the next one. Several strands intertwine to generate the conditions for vernacularization. One important factor is the political stability afforded by the Brahminic ecumene that the Yadavas set in place. The high regard in which Brahmins were held was a programmatic and strategic decision on the part of the non-Brahmin Yadava state. Some have viewed the "power" of Brahmins in this period—registered in donations as well as high places of state administration—as a sign that the Yadavas, as Kshatriyas, recognized the ritual and social superiority of Brahmins, as if actualizing in political economy the theoretical varna typology of ritual society. This argument assumes that a system of sustaining Brahminic orthodoxy was a feature of the subservience of Kshatriyas to Brahmins, of the former's dharma or "duty" to the latter. This is a theory that is matched by many proclamations of Dharma Śāstra literature, particularly in the *Manusmṛti*—a text Wendy Doniger describes as not only *"by* priests [Brahmins] but to a large extent *for* priests."[89] It is tempting to conclude that the Yadavas simply believed the proclamation of these orthodox texts, which were the reigning subject of the state-supported Sanskrit literature of the time—that they believed themselves inferior to Brahmins and subjected their polity to the power of the Brahminic ecumene.

However, such notions belie an actual inversion of the varna theory's hierarchy. Even Dumont, who emphasized the role of ritual purity that placed Brahmins at an apex of an imagined social order, states: "in theory, power is ultimately subordinate to priesthood, whereas in fact priesthood submits to power." By "theory" Dumont means Sanskrit texts written by Brahmins, and by "power" he means royal force.[90] The display of caste and power that seems actualized in any given moment in Indian history demonstrates the way rulers would *use*, rather than submit to, Brahminic power. Even in the rare though not irregular instances in Indian history when a Brahmin would serve as a polity's sovereign, not to mention as a general or other military figure, we still see that the "Brahminic" is subjected to the demands of state power. We can observe here a familiar downward flow of power from Kshatriya or "King" to Brahmin that many historians and historical anthropologists have noted before.[91] This is clear even in the history of the Peshwa period of the Maratha Confederacy, for example, when Brahmins served as kings in dynastic succession for a century—Brahmins dominated the Peshwa polity not because they were Brahmins but because they were kings: they held territory with force, and with force took territory from others.[92] Indeed, the fact that they were Brahmins—surrounded by "confederate" states whose kings were not Brahmins, who bore the august names of Maratha-caste families, such as Holkar, Shinde, Gaikwad, and Bhonsale—led in part to the disputes about sovereignty and caste that broke apart the Maratha Confederacy.

As Pollock writes of the political context for cosmopolitanism, there are good reasons to find a consistent tether between kingship (of any caste) and the sociopolitical value of the Brahminic ecumene: "If the preservation of language sounds (varna) that grammar achieves was linked essentially to the preservation of the social order (varna) and so to that of the polity at large, the obligation to maintain the order of language was no less than, and perhaps no different from, the obligation to maintain the political and spiritual order."[93]

Thus the function of kingship in South Asia, particularly in central and southern India, has long been served by patronizing Brahmins and Brahminic activities, if only in the context of an "honor" economy vacant of political power in many cases. In the Yadava context, even when donors were Brahmin, their stature was conditioned largely by their achievements as warriors, generals, merchants, ministers, or kings, including figures such as Hemadri, as well as Purushottoma and the famous Yadava general Kholeshwar. Such Brahmin figures earned their fame and fortune through service to the state, by fulfilling a "traditional" role more akin to the varna typology of the Kshatriyas. The donative sphere itself circumscribed the scope of the Brahminic and largely defined what it meant not only to be a Brahmin but also to live as one. What is "Brahminic" is what a Brahmin was given funds to undertake; what is not Brahminic is usually what generated these funds in the first place—war, conquest, or trade capitalism. The very fact that the Yadava state structure appears to empower Brahmins suggests that the flow of power moves from the non-Brahmin Yadava state downward to the Brahminic ecumene, not the other way around. We see this relationship replicated at the village level, where the village chief or *deshmukh* was usually non-Brahmin, whereas the *kulkarni* or village accountant, who answered to the *deshmukh*, was almost always Brahmin in this period.[94]

So why do such institutions appear to invert actual political power? Why would a non-Brahmin ruler go to such lengths to patronize the collective Brahmin community? There are many answers to this question—from the cosmic to the practical—and one will find these in many works of history, anthropology, sociology, and religious studies. My own inclination is to assume that kings benefited from the social stability that Brahmins helped to author, if not "authorize," through their creative genealogies of elaborate state-religion rituals and texts prescribing normative social order. At least in the Yadava period, it appears Brahmins were charged with creating the script of culture itself, of writing the discursive boundaries of social order, evident through the plethora of work on Dharma Śāstra and varna orthodoxy. The Brahminic ecumene formed a network that existed at the pleasure of the non-Brahmin Yadava state and served its political-strategic ends. In the case of the Yadavas, they seem to have followed a well-trod path, particularly in southern India, of creating a network of

Brahminic entitlements that were discrete but structurally the same. This network of autonomous entitlements created a stable political sphere in the Yadava realm composed of a clientelist Brahminic ecumene. A network of scholars operating temples, monasteries, and Sanskrit schools, buoyed by the generosity of royal decrees of land and revenue, served to stabilize the geopolitical realm of the Yadavas with a Brahminic ecumene that had minimal access to military or agricultural power (they acquired wealth by rent and revenue) and whose rule of property remained one of the client rather than the master. This was not a new strategy, but a well-formed one, as scholars such as Cynthia Talbot, Arjun Appadurai, Carol Breckenridge, Burton Stein, and many others have pointed out.[95] Yadava support for the Brahminic ecumene should be read not as a reflection of devotion to Dharma Śāstra injunctions of kingship, but as a practical and well-understood feature of the science of politics in the thirteenth century.

I emphasize here the effect of stability, tied to a discursive and symbolic economy, that likely reflected a stable market economy as well. The contours of the Yadava economy are beyond my ken in this book, and have been engaged by others elsewhere, though the economy is a subject adjudicated by remnants and guesses, like most subjects of the thirteenth century. However, a general scholarly consensus is that the Yadava century was stable—politically, economically, and socially—and this stability bears on my argument about the formation of a nascent public sphere. As Habermas convincingly argued, most public spheres are preceded and made possible by a regulated and rationalized market economy, and this process of rationalization stabilizes various aspects of society—governance, a civil society, the vast implementation of infrastructure, and so on. In some sense, then, the stabilization of the political and social sphere of the Yadava century is a precondition for the emergence of a rudimentary vernacular public sphere.

What this means for literary vernacularization is that a period of political stability—brief by any historical yardstick—helped create the opportunity for a public culture to thrive in the Yadava century, and this stability allowed figures like Chakradhar and the early Mahanubhavs, as well as Jnandev, to flourish in a world where they could become social, religious, and literary entrepreneurs. Importantly, this was a public culture surrounded and influenced by Brahminic values and mores that would lead both figures and their followers to the impulse to compose literature, and then also to write literature or inspire the writing of literature in Marathi.

The Brahminic ecumene had the effect of instilling a highly valued place for literacy at the junction where this ecumene met general public culture. I think the reason the agents of vernacularization—Jnandev, and Chakradhar through his Brahmin circle of followers (Bhatobas, Mahadaisa, etc.)—were mostly Brahmin was that they existed within a cultural context where literacy was not just an acquired skill but a social value and a mark of distinction. As we will see in the pages that follow, these figures explicitly retained a sense of the value of literacy and writing, though they rejected the use of Sanskrit; they remained Brahmins and Brahminic, in this sense, even while declining other aspects of this social ontology. The reason why these Brahmin agents of vernacularization rejected Sanskrit is a subject I address in later parts of the book. Here I merely want to point out that the Brahminic ecumene and its culture of Sanskrit literary production had the effect of placing a high value on literacy in those contexts where the Brahminic ecumene intersected with general public culture. At this inter-section, Chakradhar, the early Mahanubhavs, and Jnandev are our epitomes. A technology of elite power, literacy, would, in their names, become the new vehicle for Marathi literary (rather than merely literate) expression, and they would reject the idioms of Sanskrit for the idioms of everyday life in a regional language and literature.

As I close this chapter, I would like to emphasize that the argument here has meant to show the power of the Brahminic ecumene in Yadava society, but not the dominance of Brahmins in the Yadava political order. To speak of "dominance," one would need to engage the broad economic history of the period, both domestic and among competing dynasties, and such an engagement is beyond the scope of the discursive power structures I have identified here. Brahmins, it should be said, *served* the Yadavas, not the other way around. The Yadava state provided opportunities that Brahmins hoped to access. Brahmins, in turn, provided a social thesis, a normativity that could serve to stabilize and characterize a "Yadava" social world. And though Brahmins did dominate the literary sphere, as the rest of the book will show, at least two prominent Brahmin figures broke ranks with their comrades and transposed the Brahminic capital of literacy to a new mar-ket: the vernacular sphere.

Maintaining the rules of orthodox Brahminic understandings of varna was central to Yadava political and social self-imagination. And this self-imagination, if we see it reflected in the Brahminic ecumene built by the treasure and beneficence of the Yadava state, supported a system largely dedicated to producing Sanskrit texts on social orthodoxy. Given this abundance of support for Sanskrit literary production, how can we approach what the Yadavas themselves might have understood to be the role and value of Marathi? What was the social use of Marathi to the Yadava state and Brahminic ecumene in this period? It is in this sphere of the quotidian, and particularly the contours of a "public" encoded in Marathi inscriptions of the Yadava state, the subject of the next chapter, that we might yet find some evidence for how the Yadavas viewed the use of Marathi, its force in social contexts, its cultural capital in general, and the social world, the public, that it sought to affect.

CHAPTER TWO

Traces of a Medieval Public

A commonplace understanding in scholarship and popular memory about the Yadava century is that the state supported the production of Marathi literature. As we will see, this is a claim made largely through circumstantial associations: the assumption is that because Marathi literature emerged during the latter half of this period, it must have enjoyed the support of the Yadava state. On the contrary, we have reasons to believe the Yadavas were quite indifferent to Marathi, which they appeared to consider a language of the quotidian world, though that indifference may be better described as a benign ambivalence. They may have enjoyed Marathi, even literary Marathi, at court or in private, but they have left no evidence of state funds directed toward its production or patronage, and it has no place in the Brahminic ecumene discussed in chapter 1. There may be precursors here to what will become, in the modern period, "linguistic nationalism" linking Marathi and the Yadava state, and we may see here rudiments of the way in which an "imagined community" will be formed in Marathi in the centuries to come, particularly under the Marathas, the Peshwas, in the colonial period, and in the formation of the modern state of Maharashtra. Yet here, to read too much of this history into the past will be to risk missing the truly startling innovations of this period, to see this period only as a trough for the present moment. My aim in this chapter is to scrutinize how Marathi was viewed through Yadava materials—inscriptions primarily. In this process, I hope to show how and why the Yadavas evinced a benign ambivalence toward Marathi, but also to show how the writing of Marathi and the culture it accessed did serve the Yadavas and their political-social aims. In particular, we will see how what I view as a fear of the public was present in inscriptions that gave gifts of revenue and land to particular individuals. At the same time, we will note how this fear of the public could be expressed also as a valorization of it, as is particularly witnessed in inscriptions by the Yadavas around the famous Vitthal Temple in Pandharpur.

This chapter will show that, precisely because the Yadavas did not officially patronize Marathi as a literary medium, vernacularization could flourish outside royal courts and within the public cultures of the Yadava realm, leading to the ironic assertion that by not engaging in patronage of Marathi literature, the Yadavas enabled its development within the relatively stable context of their rule. Here I will pursue the question of the place of Marathi within the Yadava century, for in understanding how Marathi was viewed in the elite spheres of court and the Brahminic ecumene, we can better understand the cultural politics that surrounded using Marathi as a literary language in this period.

Inscriptions as Public Performances

Our primary archival materials are Marathi inscriptions from the eleventh to early fourteenth centuries. This is, of course, a written archive, but it is a very unique form of writing. Inscriptions, I believe, are public declarations, for the most part. By this I mean that they are social texts, expressed outwardly and propelled into time and space. In this sense inscriptions are less like manuscripts and more like genres of public performance; they are examples of a self-conscious literary public performance. Though inscriptions may be intended as communication among literate elites, they are still available for public observation. Even if they are situated in private spaces, they are composed with materials meant to endure over time and certainly transcend the lives of individuals and even the spans of kingdoms. They are "workly texts," to use Pollock's phrase, in terms of the actualization of their proclamations, but they also do work well beyond the plans of their authors or agents.[1] They may share with manuscripts a workly conveyance of information, but they are situated in space in a much different way. Inscriptions do their work because they are social texts and public performances.

What makes them "public" is the way in which they are made available for the attention of an audience that happens to be present by virtue of social forces in a given region or space. For example, an inscription may be outside a temple, directed toward the "outer" world of people that might be oriented, for any number of reasons, to a given temple at a given moment. And an inscription might be inside a temple, a space circumscribed by sect, gender, caste, and class, yet also available to the public formed by admission to the temple—those who may enter a temple or care to do so. Alexis Sanderson, in his recent study of inscriptions and what they yield about the "mundane realities" of the world of classical Shaivism refers to inscriptions as within "the public domain." In a sense, an inscription is a text without a cover.

Inscriptions, especially those placed out in the open where they are easy to observe, convey a message that has no confines other than the restrictions of the audience that pays attention to it. While we think of language difference as a high bar for the conveyance of knowledge, we also know that multilingual oral literacy has long been the norm in heterogeneous societies. An uneducated, poor child of a major urban area anywhere in the world who interacts with international tourists will likely speak her mother tongue, the various languages of her region, as well as functional versions of English and any number of European languages; she will have a linguistic breadth far in excess of the wealthy and educated tourists she encounters. The sphere of oral literacy was likely as vast and heterogeneous in the Yadava era as it is now or, perhaps, well before the dominance of global English, the variety was even greater.

Sanskrit texts are circumscribed by a tight circuit of attention, the "Sanskrit cosmopolis." This is a literary sphere spread wide by geography, but narrowly construed by sex, caste, and class. Conversely, the field of the "vernacular language" is tightly circumscribed by region, but heterogeneous by sex, caste, and class in that region. It is easy to imagine that, given the individual empowerments of these two language spheres, a thriving group of amateur Sanskritists has always existed on the subcontinent and elsewhere, ready to "vernacularize" the "cosmopolitan" on the fly and orally.[2] As Pollock notes, "listening to rather than reading literature long remained the principal mode of experiencing it,"[3] and this engenders what I think of as a kind of aural literacy. Indeed, it is possible that just such an informal culture of orally translating Sanskrit inscriptions and other texts into regional languages is part of the impulse felt by figures like Jnandev. In any case, it is my assumption that inscriptions, in whatever language they may appear, were not consumed simply by reading but by being heard and being translated, in situ, throughout the subcontinent, including within the Yadava realm. And when inscriptions are in a language largely intelligible to everyone in a given region, like Marathi in Maharashtra, then it is likely that the public performative nature of inscriptions is routine and the cultures of interpretation and conveyance that accompany them are expansive.

I do not think this fact was lost on the people who composed inscriptions in thirteenth-century Maharashtra. I believe they recognized the general public that attended to their decrees, and they used language to signal particular kinds of symbolic capital and not necessarily to exclude particular audiences. In other words, a public proclamation in any language is ultimately conveyed in content and affect to the world around it, one way or another, and often by means of aural restatement. For these reasons, I treat all inscriptions as publicly intelligible, even if they are in Sanskrit, a language unknown to most of the population of the quotidian Yadava world. I also understand these inscriptions to be *intended* for a public audience and so I read in them one layer of address: to the public around the inscriptions themselves. I am not claiming that an imagined public is the primary subject of address—in most cases it is certainly other elites. But I am asserting that those who composed or ordered these inscriptions knew that they could not control who would encounter this message and thus always wrote *also* with this general public in mind. To search for this recognition of the open nature of inscriptional discourse is one important way to write the history of publics in the premodern world and, in particular, to search for vernacular publics and even a nascent public sphere well before the printing press or the Irani café in India. It is the ever present force of an observing public that is one factor in the composition of inscriptions. And while most inscriptions do not explicitly address this public, I will examine those, in Marathi for the most part, that do, for if Yadava-era public culture was primarily a Marathi-speaking culture, then Yadava-era inscriptions in Marathi speak to that public culture explicitly. And at the earliest layer of the public address in inscriptions in Marathi, we find the curious case of the donkey curse.

The Donkey Curse and the Fear of the Public

Among the Yadavas, as I mentioned in chapter 1, Marathi was not the primary language, but rather the tertiary language of expression, trailing Kannada and Sanskrit in number of inscriptions. Yet we can glean from the use of Marathi how the language was understood by elites within the Yadava century. The use of the language clearly indicates a population that aurally understood Marathi (as well as Kannada and perhaps Sanskrit), and this strongly suggests a Marathi public culture in place, and perhaps even a Marathi literary sphere as well—these are, after all, inscriptions, even if most of the population of the Yadava realm would not have read them but rather heard them read aloud. In addition, the way in which Marathi appears in inscriptions is often to reiterate a proclamation already articulated in Kannada or Sanskrit. Thus the use of Marathi is, in inscriptions, often a replication of those parts of the inscription in Kannada or Sanskrit. However, one interesting exception to this practice is to be found in the realm of the curse. It is here that we get a glimpse of the way elites within the Yadava court and the Brahminic ecumene viewed Marathi.

The curse in general is an ancient feature of Sanskrit, and other inscriptions throughout the "Sanskrit cosmopolis," and it appears in multiple vernaculars, as it does in Marathi.[4] For example at the conclusion of an inscription from Amba Jogai from 1144 CE, granting funds for a Brahmin community of ascetics, a rather typical curse in Marathi is given—"upon him who severs or removes this agreement the lightning bolt of the Yogini will fall."[5] Another grant, at Savargav, for the upkeep of an Amba Devi Temple, likely in the care of Brahmins, in 1164 CE ends with this threat: "Remove [this decree] and you'll become a dog, a village beast."[6] At the conclusion of a grant of 1202 CE (the "Jaitra Savanta" copperplate inscription perhaps of Jaituga I's reign, 1191–1210 CE) reinforcing the taxation rights of a Brahmin agrahara, we have two curses. The first declares, "The one who takes even one cow, one coin, or one finger's worth of land will attain hell until the end of the world," and the other states, "whoever defiles this agreement, is a dog, a donkey, a Chandal [Untouchable]."[7] An inscription in Velapur of 1300 CE, which records the donation of funds for the upkeep of a Brahmin monastery, states succinctly, "the protector [of this decree] wins heaven, the one who doesn't protect [this decree] goes to hell."[8] Such curses are preeminent examples, particularly within the field of Yadava-era inscriptions in Marathi, of Pollock's idea of a "workly text" that functions as a "speech act" rather than as a simple act of documentation.[9]

The most often repeated curse in Marathi in these inscriptions is also the single most repeated phrase in Marathi in any inscriptions of the Yadavas, and so it demands some attention here. This is the perennial "ass" or "donkey" curse. The curse is not unique to Marathi or Maharashtra, and is a mainstay of Indic epigraphy and the Sanskrit cosmopolis in general, where it appears in Sanskrit and other languages. But the curse has an important and unique place in Yadava-era inscriptions. It is not only the most common curse, it is actually the single most common phrase in Marathi across the inscriptional record.

The donkey curse warns that a donkey would have forced sexual intercourse with the mother of anyone who would contravene a gift of state.[10] In the Marathi-speaking regions of the twelfth to fifteenth centuries, the donkey curse appeared regularly in inscriptions across at least four polities, from the Shilaharas and the Yadavas, to the Bahmani Sultanate, and in the Vijaynagar period under Harihara and Devaraya.[11] Often along with the curse would also appear a graphic illustration etched into the stone, called a *gadhegal*. In Marathi, *gāḍha* or *gāḍhav* means "donkey" and *gal* indicates either a "stone" (*gaḷa*)[12] or a "profanity," (*gāḷa*) related to the common term for a "swear word" in northern India, *gāli*. These *gadhegal* then are "donkey curses" etched on stone, and so they are often called "donkey curse stones" in English. They are found throughout Maharashtra and Goa (see figures 2.1 and 2.2). Importantly, as S. G. Tulpule points out, this curse was invariably in Marathi, not Sanskrit or Kannada or any other language of inscription. The fact that this curse appeared only in Marathi, and with such regularity, is a key fact in understanding the value of Marathi in the Yadava century. Sometimes the verbal curse would be absent, and only the graphic illustration would stand as implied imprecation: further evidence of the visual, aural, and material performative work of inscriptions.[13] In these contexts it would appear following a certain decree in an inscription.

Our oldest example of the donkey curse is implied rather than written. The Akshi inscription (which Tulpule, as noted, places in 1012 CE, against the opinion of some other scholars) is the oldest extant example we have of the visual depiction of the donkey curse (figure 2.1). Importantly, this also is probably the oldest example we have of Marathi, according to S. G. Tulpule, as noted earlier. This point is important to highlight, for while the Akshi stone does not record the donkey curse textually, it depicts the curse graphically along the bottom half. Because we know that the verbal curse in Marathi will become de rigueur in the subsequent century, we should note here the link between written Marathi (probably the first instance of it here in this inscription) and the curse (the first instance of its visual depiction in the region). There seems to be an important link between Marathi and the donkey curse.

A similar stone, which carries an inscription in Marathi with the image but not the language of the curse, is found on a stone in Paral (better known as Parel, in central Mumbai), attributed to the Shilahara reign of Anantadeva (figure 2.2).

The first time the written donkey curse is joined to its visual depiction is also from a Shilahara inscription in Parel, but of 1184 CE, and it is important to note that the curse here is the only section of the inscription in Marathi.[14] The inscription in Marathi reads: "Now, whomever contradicts this order, the blade of Lord Vaidyanath will fall upon his family. A donkey will have sex with his mother."[15]

An example of this link between curse, image, and Marathi in the era of the Yadava king Ramachandra can be found on a second Akshi stone, with a date of 1291 CE, and this stone bears both the image and the donkey curse as verbal formula (figure 2.3).

Indeed, Maharashtra has many such stones or *gadhegal*, especially along the Konkan coast in the former areas of the Shilahara polity, which became a vassal state to the Yadavas in the thirteenth century.[16] In most cases a curse of any sort, and especially the donkey curse, would follow a donation to a Brahmin or for a Brahminic activity, that is, a donation in support of the Brahminic ecumene, as the examples above indicate.[17] A recently discovered *gadhegal* (without the verbal curse) in the Raigad region of Maharashtra, dated to 1254 CE, bears a gift of the Shilahara king, likely of land, to two Brahmins (Ram Mandalik and Ganapati Nayak).[18] The frequency of the verbal appearance of this curse increased significantly during the reign of Ramachandra, which is the period during and after Marathi literarization. The donkey curse, then, is the most commonly repeated single phrase in Marathi inscriptions across four centuries, especially in the later phase of the Yadava century, generally invoked to protect a donation to the Brahminic ecumene. It is not by chance that the most elite and prestigious of royal gifts is protected by the most vulgar of curses.

FIGURE 2.1. (*top left*) The Akshi stone inscription with the donkey curse, c. 1012. Courtesy of Shailendra Bhandare

FIGURE 2.2. (*top right*) The Parel stone inscription with the donkey curse, of the Shilahara king Anantadeva, c. 1081. Courtesy of Shailendra Bhandare

FIGURE 2.3. (*bottom*) The second Akshi inscription with the donkey curse, c. 1291. Courtesy of Shailendra Bhandare

The donkey curse—as inscription and graphic depiction appended to donations to Brahmins (in the main)—both suggests the importance of such donations and reveals an anxiety over the stability of the social, political, and economic order those inscriptions fueled.[19] It also tells us something about how Marathi was understood in this period with relation to gender and "class" in a sense. I should note that the penalty for contravening such grants, particularly those offered by the state or its agents, was likely something other than what is portrayed in the donkey curse. We have records of the penal regimes of the Yadavas, and the donkey curse is not mentioned as actualized consequence.[20] The curse is purely formulaic, as curses are, yet also indicative of anxiety. But anxiety about what?

Several theories have been presented about the function of the donkey curse and the *gadhegal* image. Scholars who study them most commonly refer them to as "boundary markers." These scholars note that the stones exist usually at the periphery of a territory given as a gift in the inscription.[21] R. C. Dhere understood the image to serve a semiotic function within a folk-belief system, understanding the female figure to represent divine nature and the donkey to represent the Goddess of smallpox and pestilence.[22] Dalal, Kale, and Poojari, in their recent study of four newly discovered *gadhegals* suggest that the stones, while they may bear such a symbolic weight, also conveyed the threat of an actual punishment. However, as noted, there is no evidence of this kind of punishment in the Yadava period in other texts, and it seems very unlikely to be a real punishment.[23] It also seems unlikely that these stones were worshipped, while *vīragal* or "hero stones" were objects of veneration, as Dhere has so amply demonstrated. While both theories are possible, they do not provide a general theory for the imprecation (that could include those noted previously regarding yoginis, worms, etc.), nor do they account for the visual and aural power of the donkey curse.

As an alternative to these two ideas, I situate the donkey curse within the context of the larger "evil eye" prophylaxis, a feature of the global history of human culture, but one with particular relevance here to our examination of a medieval Marathi quotidian "public." The evil eye and the various prophylactic responses to it, from talismans to rituals and invocations, appear to be an almost panhuman convention from ancient times to the contemporary.[24] One essential feature of the evil eye belief complex is the idea that a public display of one's good fortune—such as a donation or other acquirement—risks attracting the envy of others. This envy then causes something bad to happen to the recipient of good fortune. The evil eye prophylaxis wards off both the initial envy as well as the resulting bad fortune. The way the prophylaxis works is by diverting the envious gaze, with a distracting phrase or charm, but often with a vision of something else, something out of place, unexpected, or even outrageous. In India today this is commonly done by dressing baby boys as girls, giving the boys temporary female names, or simply marking a spot of "lamp black" or *kājal* on their person or as an outline around their eyes—all of which are intended to divert the general, free-floating malevolency of "envy" and hence the "evil eye" from alighting on a boy child.[25] In the various recipes for evil eye prophylaxis, the oral, aural, and visual combine to ward off the threat.

I argue that the *gadhegal* depictions and verbal donkey curse inscriptions are a form of evil eye prophylaxis.[26] These are "outrageous" depictions in image and word that both seek to distract the attention of the reader (or more likely listener) from the material of the donation to the possible curse that awaits the person who envies or acts with envy. The punishment depicted in the donkey curse is shocking and peculiar, but not actualized. It is an "empty" threat, and so we should treat it as a symbolic one, as evil eye countermeasures are. Such countermeasures exist in the register of the semiotic, even if they are believed to have real-world effects as well.

The donkey curse and the *gadhegal* ward off envy, and, in so doing, these practices reveal a recognition of the threat of the public that surrounds inscriptions. All evil eye cultural forms exist in this context of the fear of the public, of public envy and desire. It is in social spaces, out in the open, that a person is susceptible to the evil eye, and this is the same social space for the inscriptions the donkey curse—text and image—accompanies. The donkey curse, as a representative example of an attempt to ward off the evil eye, indicates not only a recognition of an attentive public, but a fear of that public, in the mind of the originator of the inscription.

There is more to the donkey curse, other social effects that are also related to evil eye prophylaxis. As a device that draws away envious attention and intent, evil eye prophylaxis must also invite interest and catch a person's attention. The visual depiction of the *gadhegal* similarly invites interest, and thus the material inscribed on the stone is communicated and "advertised." Though I find nothing humorous in this image or curse, the figure of the donkey, and the idea (threat, description, etc.) of someone having sex with another person's mother are common features of South Asian humor today, as they are in Western humor, and likely over several thousand years.[27] The "humor" is of course operationalized through the violent objectification of women and a world of threat directed toward a man's female relatives, the object of his patriarchal "protection," but also possession. This aspect of the function of the curse perhaps also reveals a predominantly male audience, a gendered audience that the works associated with Chakradhar and Jnandev will seek to transcend. It is possible to read in the donkey curse, and in other curses as well, the intention of crude humor (though the image depicted is violent and not humorous, in my opinion). Taken this way, the donkey curse image and text with its shocking (or humorous, to some) message serves the dual purposes of deflecting the envious gaze by distraction, while at the same time drawing attention to the material of the main proclamation. As Melanie Dean has pointed out in her work on contemporary evil eye (*tiruṣṭi*) practices in Tamil Nadu, the evil eye prophylaxis not only protects against the natural and supernatural effects of the evil eye but also serves to display the relative benefit and gain of the person in the first place—it attracts and repels simultaneously and by the same rationale. As Dean puts it, such practices represent and resolve a "dialectical tension between the desire to display one's wealth to one's peers and the fear that the visual attention of one's peers will cause harm."[28] The visual and written donkey curses similarly resolve this dialectic as they both attract and repel attention; they mediate the attention of the public, channeling it in culturally appropriate ways. The fear of the public is challenged by the violence of this graphic curse, while the curse also serves to index the value of the gift—for why would one need a curse to ward off envy if it was not an enviable gift in the first place?

Given the "folk" nature of the evil eye belief complex, it seems likely that the historical origins of the donkey curse in South Asia are similarly within the field of the "folk," of the quotidian world. Though the first examples of the ass curse outside of Marathi are in Sanskrit and from around the turn of the Common Era, we might assume that Sanskrit absorbs into its inscriptional authority this "vernacular" tradition of warding off "evil." While Sanskrit may exist "as the language of the Gods" within an elite literary sphere above and beyond the quotidian, the inscription is the exemplary moment when Sanskrit comes down to earth, when a verbal formula is expressed to the public, etched on a stone for all to see and hear read aloud, likely drawn from the cultural idioms of a region, not the literary tropes of the Sanskrit cosmopolis. For the work of the Sanskrit inscription, like all inscriptions, is to produce a monodirectional proclamation into the quotidian sphere, into the space of a region, amid a local people, and within everyday life where the rule of law that undergirds gifts of state is always tenuously maintained. The donkey curse was perhaps a way to translate yet further, from language to idiom, to put the "sacred" or inviolable aspect of the content of the inscription into terms a local, non-Sanskritic population could better understand. The inscription speaks to many audiences, such as other class and caste elites and members of the Brahminic ecumene, as well as elite aspirants to such gifts of state. And it speaks into the future as a "legal" record of a gift meant to endure for years. But inscriptions also exist within the world of "mere attention," as Michael Warner described the sphere of publics, and they occur in social spaces that are difficult to mediate or that go almost entirely unmediated.[29] The donkey curse, preserved only in the regional language in the case of Maharashtra, and in its highly colloquial register bordering on slang, shows us that those who inscribed this curse also sought to direct this speech act to the general population going about their everyday life. The public is unmistakably one of the objects of address in the donkey curse as text or image, and it seeks to ward off a fear of the public. Bourdieu, in his analysis of state formation, makes a perceptive and relevant observation: "Force is always on the side of the governed, only opinion can sustain the governors."[30] The evil eye that the donkey curse sought to ward off is none other than the surveillance (and possible ill opinion) of the state by its subjects, the governed.

If we search for any kind of "special" use of Marathi in the Yadava period by the state or the Brahminic ecumene, we find virtually nothing in the spheres of the literary, philosophical, poetic, or aesthetic. So the fact that the donkey curse in Yadava-era inscriptions is only in Marathi, never in Sanskrit or Kannada, suggests to us that the Yadavas and the Brahminic ecumene they supported regarded Marathi as a language suitable for threatening and cajoling the general population, the masses of quotidian life.[31] We see that they patronized Marathi as an inscriptional language, a tertiary linguistic medium to convey the most pungent of their curses because it was the language of the everyday. But, aside from the inscriptional record, do we see evidence for the support of Marathi in the Brahminic ecumene, at the Yadava royal court, or in any other context that might indicate Yadava patronage?

Marathi Patronage and the Yadava State

One of the enduring assertions in modern historiography about the Yadava era—and one that provides the clearest link between that era and the contemporary period—is the idea that the Yadavas supported and encouraged Marathi literary production. Many scholars—writing in Marathi and English[32]—have made this claim, and it becomes common by the mid twentieth century when, for example, the famous scholar of Maharashtra, Irawati Karve, writes in the *Maharashtra State Gazetteer* issued by the state Government of Maharashtra in 1968 that Marathi was patronized by the Yadavas.[33] Yet the historical sources of this idea are fuzzy at best. Karve, for example, cites only the fact that Jnandev praises Ramachandra at the conclusion of his *Jñāneśvarī*, which actually tells us nothing of what Ramachandra or any other Yadava potentate may have supported or why Jnandev might have included such a tribute. In the absence of any definitive inscriptional or textual record issued from the Yadava state, scholars have tended to rely on such circumstantial evidence to substantiate the claim that the Yadavas were patrons of Marathi and Marathi literary production.

Perhaps the scholarly origin, or at least one prominent origin, of this assumption is found in the pioneering work of V. L. Bhave (1871–1926), whose *Mahārāṣṭra Sāraswat* is the first grand history of Maharashtra and Marathi literary culture and a text that is foundational in Marathi cultural historiography, a kind of source text and touchstone for all the major historians of Marathi literature who followed, both Indian and non-Indian. Bhave began publishing the work that would form *Mahārāṣṭra Sāraswat* around 1898–1899 in serialized form and this culminated in its first publication in full as a monograph in 1924.[34] To my knowledge, Bhave's text is the earliest and most powerful (and most often cited) articulation of the idea that the Yadava court supported the production of literary Marathi.

In this work Bhave recalls secondary accounts and proofs of Marathi's literary existence through texts and references to children's folktales in Marathi as well as citations of women's folk songs in Marathi in such texts as Someshwar III's Sanskrit *Mānasollāsa* (c. 1138 CE).[35] While none of the texts mentioned in such secondary sources are available to us today, I think Bhave was right to take references to such compositions as evidence that a kind of oral literary Marathi was likely in place before the actual literarization of the language, before its written form, in the late thirteenth century. He asserts that among the quotidian masses, whom he calls "Vaishyas, Shudras, and others" (a phrase that he may have drawn from *Jñāneśvarī*, as we will see), a vibrant Marathi folk-story culture existed in the century before the first historical record of Marathi literary work. Through such references, Bhave establishes that Marathi was a spoken-poetic language, likely even a literary language, that contained "texts," either oral or written, well before the advent of the *Līḷācaritra* or the *Jñāneśvarī*, which is a historical observation I believe is likely true.

After establishing the existence of some kind of Marathi literary-oral sphere by the twelfth century, Bhave connects this sphere to the royal court of the Yadavas by reference to a story in the *Līḷācaritra* that recalls a chance meeting between Chakradhar and the Yadava king Krishna at Lonar.[36] In this meeting, the king attempts to give money to Chakradhar, but Chakradhar refuses to accept the money or indulge the king, leaving the king's presence.[37] Krishna then uses the money to build a wall at the Kumareshwar Temple in Lonar. Bhave implies that Krishna's interest in such figures moved his son, Ramachandra, to patronize Marathi at his court.[38] Here, as with the reference to Jnandev's vote of thanks to Ramachandra, we have circumstantial evidence at best, and none that suggests actual patronage expressed by a Yadava ruler. Even in the case of Chakradhar, if we accept this encounter with the Yadava king Krishna as historical fact, it merely establishes a connection between a king and a particularly prominent saintly figure. The endeavors of many such saintly figures were indeed financed through royal patronage—a phenomenon we will note in greater detail when we discuss the *Līḷācaritra*. Furthermore, Chakradhar was not a figure of literary Marathi in this story: we should recall that he did not compose any Marathi literature of any kind—the *Līḷācaritra* was the work of his followers within a decade after Chakradhar's departure from Maharashtra. And so there can be no question that the story of the Yadava king Krishna's attempt to give Chakradhar money had any relationship to Marathi literary work, or at least extant work. This was an attempt to give a gift of state to a Brahmin mendicant, not a Marathi literary figure.

The only connection Bhave makes between the Yadava court and Marathi literary production during or before the time of the *Līlācaritra* and *Jñāneśvarī* is through recourse to Mukundaraja and his Marathi texts, the *Vivekasindhu* in particular. Marathi scholarship long held this text to be the first example of literary Marathi. However, by the mid-1960s a general consensus formed around a later date for this text. The argument that Mukundaraja lived in the twelfth century and that the colophon of his *Vivekasindhu* gave the date of composition as 1188 CE are highly suspect and are discounted by most scholars; the only manuscript with a colophon gives the date of transcription as 1656 CE. Indeed, there is ample evidence that Mukundaraja and his text come after Chakradhar and appear to constitute a kind of offshoot of Chakradhar's own teacher lineage (*guru paramparā*). Thus Mukundaraja's dates would be either coterminous with Chakradhar's dates or, far more likely, at least one generation later.[39] Despite the fact that most linguistic historians understand Mukundaraja's text to be from the fourteenth century at the earliest (which better matches its style of Marathi), it is still common to find this text cited as the "first" instance of Marathi literature.[40] Bhave's text thus situates Mukundaraja, whom he considers the first Marathi literary author, producing the first Marathi literary work, at the court of the Yadava general and feudatory ruler Jaitrapala (r. c. 1192–1202 CE)[41]— both this connection and this time frame have been challenged and emended by successive Marathi scholarship over the last five decades. It is highly unlikely that the *Vivekasindhu* is a text that precedes either the *Līlācaritra* or *Jñāneśvarī*.

A second claim made by some scholars involves another story from the Mahanubhavs that remembers a Brahmin poet named Narendra who, in 1291 CE, composed an early work called the *Rukminī Svayaṃvara* or "Rukmini's Choice of Groom."[42] Indeed, the story of Rukmini's elopement and marriage to Vitthal/Krishna forms a minor literary genre, not just among the Mahanubhavs, but among the Varkaris as well (and outside of Maharashtra), likely signaling a popular topic of public performance in the Yadava period.[43] The fourteenth-century Mahanubhav text *Smṛtisthaḷa* recalls that Narendra and his two brothers were poets who recited their poems for the Yadava king Ramachandra.[44] Narendra composed a poem on the subject of Krishna's wife, Rukmini, and her choice (*svayamvara*) of Krishna for a husband, and this poem, in Marathi, so pleased Ramachandra that he offered to buy the rights (essentially to buy "authorship") of the poem from Narendra. However, Narendra declined, saying that to take money from the king would tarnish the reputation of his community of poets (*kavikula*).[45] The story tells us that it is after this experience that Narendra goes to Bhatobas and becomes a Mahanubhav, bringing his poem with him.[46]

As with all hagiographical work, there is reason to be suspicious of its historical claims, particularly claims that portray relatively ordinary figures meeting kings and other temporal rulers.[47] However, as I will detail in the next chapter, the Mahanubhavs in particular sought to record the lives of their leaders—Chakradhar, Bhatobas, and Gundam Raul especially—with great historical detail, in the mode of literary realism to be sure, and the *Smṛtisthaḷa* verse that records this episode is just such a text, wedded to at least the trope of historical accuracy. If we take this as historical fact, even heuristically, it is still unclear what "courtly patronage" might entail. We have no corroboration in inscriptional or other evidence issued by the Yadava state, though one can imagine, in an informal context of courtly entertainment such moments might have happened with a high degree of frequency but with little documentation. Indeed, my argument that there is no evidence for Yadava courtly patronage of Marathi even approximating their lavish patronage of Sanskrit is not also an argument that the Yadavas did not speak Marathi or consume courtly entertainment through the medium of Marathi. On the contrary, I think there is every reason to believe the Yadavas entertained themselves in every way possible, including with performances of Marathi plays, poetry, and other pleasures, as well as perhaps the same in Kannada, Sanskrit, or even other languages.

However, this recollection in the *Smṛtisthaḷa* does not record state patronage of Marathi, but rather the impulsive offer of a highly impressed Yadava king. Furthermore, Narendra *rejects* Ramachandra's offer—the "courtly patronage" actually does *not* happen, even in the story. Obviously, scholars who invoke this passage do so to suggest that if Narendra was offered money for his poem, though he refused it, it is likely other Marathi composers were likewise offered such rewards and accepted them. Yet Narendra's response is curious, and it undercuts such an assumption for his rejection is not based on an idiosyncratic position but on a position he attributes to all his fellow poets as well. For Narendra tells the king that he must reject his reward, for to take it would denigrate all Marathi poets, it would "cast blame" upon them—that is, people would begin to speak badly about his *kavikula*, his "community of poets." Narendra is not yet a Mahanubhav either, though the text tells us he had heard Bhatobas speak. Still, his community of poets must reference other professional poets, perhaps limited to his family, but more inclusive of all poets composing Marathi poetry in oral public culture (and perhaps written literary culture) at the time.[48]

What is it exactly that Narendra refuses to sell? The text of the *Smṛtisthaḷa* tells us that it is authorship of the poem, the work itself—"the work's ascription," the entire copyright, as it were (*granthācā abhaṅgu*)—that Narendra refuses to sell to Ramachandra.[49] Therefore, if this story tells us something in general about Marathi poets and kings of the Yadava era, it is that Marathi poets *refused* to accept courtly patronage and sell their authorship of poems to kings. So if anything is corroborated by the lack of inscriptions offering support for Marathi literary production, it is this: that Marathi authors rejected courtly patronage even if (when) it was offered. This story, rather than describing courtly patronage of literary Marathi, is a story that tells us that writers of Marathi literature may have functioned outside the context of court as a matter of principle; they sought their "patronage" elsewhere. Whether or not this was the case historically, my point is that to use this particular example to establish that the Yadava court patronized literary Marathi is also to misread this very example.

My discussion here involves the literary record of Marathi, but it does not answer the question of what might constitute the first "work of Marathi literature" in some absolute sense. The first work of Marathi literature *that we have* is the *Līḷācaritra*, but that text, alongside the *Jñāneśvarī*, suggests to me, in any case, that Marathi has long had a literature, well before these two texts were composed. And this literature may have been oral primarily—perhaps even a fixed oral form in various cases, an aural literary form—or it may have been written, but we no longer have that written record. Yet it is hard for me to imagine the *Līḷācaritra* or the *Jñāneśvarī* emerged sui generis, and I am very suspicious of such declarations of "firsts" in history in any case. However, it is beyond my ability to prove the existence of any text before these two or to establish a field of oral Marathi literature before the late thirteenth century. Despite this, it is my own conviction that such literature—likely not only orally preserved but also written—did exist. Yet I am restricted by my sources here, and so I treat the *Līḷācaritra* and the

Jñāneśvarī as the first two works of Marathi literature, as a statement of current historical contingency.

Early Vitthal Devotion in Pandharpur and a Bhakti Public

Another common claim that the Yadavas supported literary Marathi points to the inscriptional evidence of gifts for the maintenance of the Vitthal Temple in Pandharpur made by various rulers of this dynasty. These inscriptional gifts are preserved in a set of three inscriptions from: a) 1189–1190 CE; b) 1273–1277 CE; and c) 1311 CE.[50] None of these inscriptions denotes funds to support Marathi literary production, it should be stated.[51] However, they do reveal the cultivation of the veneration of the deity Vitthal at his temple in Pandharpur by the Yadava state and establish the recognition by the state of a large group of devotees who gathered there, and thus the state's sense of the power of Vitthal devotionalism among the general population of the region. Yadava interest in the Vitthal temple may have been a strategy to unsettle the claims of their rivals, the Hoysalas, over the same temple and community. We can see that the Hoysala king Someshwar in 1237 CE and at other times supported the Vitthal temple with gifts of state, making it clear that Vitthal devotion was not the sole purview of the Yadavas (or of the Marathi-speaking world). As R. C. Dhere has noted, the broad swath of polities taking on the mantle of "Yadava" in this period and region all appear to worship the deity of Pandharpur—another commonality with, in particular, the political rivals of the Yadava dynasty.[52]

In order to explore with care the relationship between the Yadavas, Vitthal worship, bhakti, and literature, we must parse from the materials we have the role of literature, particularly the bhakti literature that will come to form a core of Marathi literature in the centuries to come, through the figures of Jnandev, Namdev, Eknath, and Tukaram, among many others. While the Yadavas made gifts to the Vitthal Temple, there is no mention of patronage for literary works, nor support of Jnandev and Namdev, the two earliest literary figures claimed by the Varkari faith. What do we find in these inscriptions, I will argue, is the recognition of what I have called a "bhakti public," a social sense of a general devotion shared by many people in the region yet not confined to any given sect, religious order, or explicit community. Though later the religious community we now call the Varkaris will form, at this period—in these inscriptions and also in the *Līḷācaritra* and the *Jñāneśvarī*—there is no mention of such a community. Still, a public culture of worship clearly surrounded the Vitthal temple, and this is what we glean from the inscriptions of gifts in Pandharpur. Observing these gifts to Vitthal's temple provides a rubric for understanding the devotional public culture at large, the general sphere from which our key texts will emerge.

Scholars will often connect the support of Pandharpur, Vitthal's temple, and Vitthal's devotees by the Yadava court to the devotional literature that marks the Varkari religion in the centuries that follow. This is a flawed assumption for several reasons. The only work attributed to Varkari figures that can be even conjecturally applied to this period or to Pandharpur would be the work attributed to Jnandev and Namdev. Namdev makes no mention of the Yadavas, and the Yadavas make no mention of Namdev, and so it is far too tenuous to draw a link between these two, quite aside from the significant problems with locating Namdev in history.[53] What is more, as I've pointed out in other work, Namdev disavows literacy, the conceits of literature, and the very idea that writing is useful.[54] In addition, the dates suggested for Namdev's life—1270–1350—overlap with the outer limit of the historical period covered here. For these reasons, and for others, it does not seem that Yadava patronage of the Vitthal Temple can be connected to what will later become the literary song-poem corpus associated with Namdev and his companions, even if we accept his traditional dates of life as historical fact.

The case of Jnandev, likewise, carries significant difficulties. Jnandev makes no mention of Vitthal or Pandharpur in the *Jñāneśvarī*, and we hear of Vitthal only in later *abhang*s associated with him, which many scholars consider significantly later than the *Jñāneśvarī*, perhaps by a century or more.[55] In other words, the Jnandev of the *Jñāneśvarī* does not present himself to be a Varkari, much less a devotee of Vitthal.[56] I am not stating that Jnandev was not a Varkari—he is presented since at least the sixteenth century as a Varkari and devotee of Vitthal, Varkaris revere his texts and memory, and hence Jnandev is undoubtedly a Varkari. Instead, I am simply stating that he did not explicitly present himself as such in the *Jñāneśvarī*. Varkaris and Jnandev's own followers acknowledge that between the time of the *Jñāneśvarī* and the later abhangs of Jnandev, a time when he comes to encounter key figures, like Namdev, and other low-caste and female *bhakta*s, Jnandev undergoes a change of heart and a conversion to the worship of Vitthal. The story of this "conversion" is attributed to Namdev, in a set of biographical and autobiographical songs called Tīrthāvaḷī or "the journey."[57] In part, this story and its effect on Jnandev's public memory will be noted in the conclusion. I should also state here that Jnandev also never mentions Namdev in any text attributed to him, to my knowledge.[58]

My point is neither to challenge the strong Varkari belief that Jnandev was a Varkari (which he was, without a doubt) nor the idea that Jnandev and Namdev were companions (they certainly were), but instead to show that it is anachronistic to read direct Yadava support for the Vitthal Temple in Pandharpur throughout the thirteenth century as support for literary production in Marathi in the idiom of Vitthal bhakti that will flourish in the fourteenth century under these names. It is quite possible, even probable, that the support shown for the Vitthal Temple by several states and polities in the thirteenth century, especially by the Yadavas, spurred the creation of Marathi literature in subsequent centuries. Indeed, the root of this support is important to note here, for it registers a keen awareness by the Yadava state (and others, such as the Hoysalas) of the vitality of an emerging quotidian Marathi public, one major focal point of which was the bhakti world that surrounded Vitthal and Pandharpur. And so while support for the Vitthal Temple and the worship of Vitthal by the Yadavas from 1189 to 1311 CE cannot indicate support for the Marathi bhakti literature that would later be associated with Pandharpur, Vitthal, and the Varkaris, it does tell us what made it possible, in part, for the Varkari tradition to flourish in social and literary worlds, and for Jnandev to be enfolded into the Varkari religion.

The three sets of inscriptions that we have from the Yadava era recording gifts to Pandharpur all indicate an interesting sociopolitical story, one that connects the Yadava state with public culture, bhakti, and religion, drawing the Vitthal Temple and Pandharpur into a dynastic vision of society in a way quite unique in this period. The historical beginning and end of the Yadava dynasty are literally marked by state donations in Marathi to the Vitthal Temple in Pandharpur, and so it seems inevitable to read these Marathi inscriptions as gifts to a temple for the sake of "religion" as also statements about statecraft, soft power, and the recognition of a public culture both active and powerful within the Yadava century.

The first donation recorded was given in 1189 CE, attributed to the Yadava king Bhillama—often considered the founder of the sovereign Yadava dynasty, as mentioned earlier.[59] Here is a translation of the readable portions of the inscription:

> In the year Shake 1111 (1190 CE), Friday, know that the Chakravartin
> [Bhillama Yadava] and the Mahajans [Brahmins], for the whole of the family
> of God [lit. *devaparivar*], with the seal of Vitthal Deva Nayak, they all [give]
> to this small temple (*lān maḍu*) some maintenance from the [royal] granary.
> And as long as the moon and tide exist, no one should consider this [grant]
> to come to an end. To those who don't know, [tell them that] it is the seven
> chiefs [who give to this temple].
>
> And whoever challenges [this decree], they would be going against
> Vitthal.
>
> If anyone destroys this work, that person maligns the Creator/Father.
> [He will acquire bad . . .] karma.[60]

The donors in addition to Bhillama are listed as the *mahajans* or Brahmin
elite of the region. The donors, including the king Bhillama and Brahmin
elites, claim this gift to the Vitthal Temple is for the *devaparivār*, the "family of the God" as a whole, which would include themselves, as donors, but
also implies the general public of devotion.[61] The inscription refers to the
Vitthal Temple in Pandharpur as a "small temple" (*lān maḍu*), and the grant
is given to enlarge the temple, support the devotees of Vitthal, and expand
the worship of Vitthal.[62] This inscription, like many others, extolled the
virtue of giving to the temple, where one's karma would increase by such
a gift or decrease in the absence of giving. Many scholars have referred to
this inscription in order to demonstrate that the worship of Vitthal and
the temple in Pandharpur grew from a small, pastoral deity site to a major
temple complex under the care of the Yadavas (but also the Hoysalas).

Why invest in this "small temple"? The reasons are several. Politically,
Pandharpur exists in a region of contention, especially between the Yadavas
and the Hoysalas, and the town has suffered the wrath of warring polities because of its location through the centuries. Bhillama's support for
the temple and for Pandharpur is also a political signal to the Hoysalas
and others, a way to claim territory that is both geographic and cultural.
Indeed, another inscription some decades later in 1237 CE describes the temple as lying within the realm of the Hoysalas, suggesting that Pandharpur
was at the center of land under dispute and unrest throughout the thirteenth century, as it was in the century after.[63] Yet it is also a reflection of
its popularity in the everyday world of the emergent Yadava realm that
this modest temple had a sufficiently grand number of devotees to attract

such an investment of state funds. The bhakti sphere that surrounded the Vitthal Temple, marked by this inscription, is one piece in the larger growth of a devotional, Marathi-based field of public religious practice, a field in which Jnandev and Chakradhar, though neither expressed devotion to Vitthal in the texts of this study, are yet to be situated. And though the word bhakti does not appear in a Marathi inscription anywhere at this point in time, to my knowledge, we can still see that the *devaparivar* circumscribes a devotional social sphere of elites and non-elites alike who shared devotion to Vitthal.

As I have argued elsewhere, bhakti fundamentally produces publics, contexts of social "sharing" (a root meaning of the word), and interaction.[64] As Jack Hawley has argued, bhakti also produces "networks" that link people, places, and politics.[65] The social work of bhakti is apparent here as a fulcrum around which social cohesion adheres, and thus it is an opportunity to invest both cultural and economic capital in the growth of a potent symbol. But we should also note that the Yadavas supported many other temples with far more lavish funds. And, as we will see, this was not a one-time investment, but a first installment in a relationship of financial and cultural capital that would endure until the end of Yadava rule.

Beginning in 1273 and lasting through a long series of inscriptions of gifts, the last dated to 1277, we have our second major donation in Pandharpur. This is a Yadava-era donation, from the reign of Ramachandra, but unlike the inscription of 1189 CE, issued by the Yadava king Bhillama, this one has a vast assembly of donors, with each name and date of donation listed serially. This is important to note. Often, when scholars invoke this set of inscriptions, it is referred to as a Yadava gift, or the donation of Ramachandra or his minister Hemadri. Yet the names of these two august figures are rather muted in the litany of donors. The donation is actually recorded in a substantial set of inscriptions—seven in total—with long lists of donors offering funds for the growth and maintenance of the Pandharpur Temple to Vitthal.[66] The name of Ramachandra is but one of the many names given here, preceded by the name of Hemadri. Hemadri is donor number twenty-three in the list, and Ramachandra number twenty-four.[67]

The inaugural statement of the inscription that precedes the long list of names is not clearly legible, but it appears to contain names and specifics about donations. However, the second portion in Sanskrit is clearer and it reads: "I pay joyful homage to Vitthal, who is endlessly praised by sages and Gods, known in the Vedas as supreme, the lotus-eyed beloved of Shri about whom celestials happily sing pleasing songs, who is celebrated by the fervent populace of devotees (*bhaktajana*) with bristling hairs and eyes filled with happy tears as they honor the son of Nanda, who looks after the joy of his devoted attendants (*bhaktānugam*)."[68] The Marathi inscription follows immediately after this and it reads: "In the auspicious holy year of 1195 [1273], called Shrimukh, details are given here of various [amounts of] money [donated] by the leaders of devotion (*bhaktimāliāṃ*) to Lord Vitthal of Pandhapur for flower garlands [to be given] three times a day for as long as the sun and moon [exist]."[69] As the first inscription of 1189 CE suggested, giving to the temple and to the devotees who come to Pandharpur—here in 1273 called *bhaktajana* in Sanskrit—was a way to accrue merit and, to be sure, having one's name inscribed in stone ensured both a public and a personal register of that merit.

After a long line of names and gifts, we arrive at Ramachandra's gift, which reads: "King Ramachandra, who is the chief of Vitthal's congregation in Pandharpur (*pāṇḍarīphaḍamuṣya*), who is the bearer of tradition, of the powerful majestic auspicious Yadava Narayana dynasty, who is the universal monarch (*cakravārttiṃ*), he will bestow a well for the All Powerful, Victorious, King, who is the Chief Deity of the Holy Temple, Shrimangala Mahashri Lord Shri Vitthal."[70] Even Ramachandra's terms of self-aggrandizement, the very bread and butter of the *prashasti* or royal panegyric form, are still balanced by an equally august set of titles for Vitthal. And included in Ramachandra's lofty description, first and foremost, is not the idea that he is a king among men but that he is a chief among devotees. What is interesting about this inscription is the way the presence of primary figures of the Yadava state—Hemadri and Ramachandra—is relatively downplayed, nestled as their gifts are within a long list of others. These two key figures of Yadava rule are enumerated among many other elites and enfolded within the general world of the bhaktajana, the people of devotion to Vitthal. It seems the prime reference for donation in these inscriptions is devotion or bhakti itself.

To my knowledge, these are some of the first instances, in 1273, of the words *bhakti* and *bhakta* appearing in inscriptions in the region, in Marathi or Sanskrit.[71] These instances conjoin *bhakti* and *bhakta* in compounds that express companionship and sociality, as in *mali* or "leader," in the Marathi inscription, and *anuga* or "attendant" and *jana* or "people" in the Sanskrit one.

Thus the very first explicit appearances of the idea of bhakti in inscriptions in the Yadava era invoke social organization.

The donors are identified in the Marathi inscription as *bhaktimali*, the leaders of devotion. The phrase is odd—the text may read *bhaktamali* instead—but the point is essentially the same: the donors who have given to the Vitthal Temple are the luminaries and benefactors not only of the temple but rather of bhakti itself, of public devotion. The individuality and singular attention usually given to a donor in inscriptions is not a convention we find in the donations inscribed to the Pandharpur temple around 1273 CE, and this is unique. One gets the impression that patronage of the devotionalism, the bhakti, associated with Vitthal, is the driving force conveyed in the inscriptions. This suggests a conscientious effort to valorize a general public, the bhaktajana, or the people who make up the field of bhakti, the devotees of Vitthal, in whose name, in some fundamental sense, these inscriptions exist.

The growth of the Vitthal Temple between 1189 and 1273 reflects not only an increase in the popularity of Vitthal bhakti in the Yadava realms and throughout the region but also the rise of the political usefulness of Pandharpur and its large quotidian populace of devotees.[72] These inscriptions align the political state with public devotionalism, and while this alignment does not indicate support for literary Marathi production, it does reveal support for the quotidian world of bhakti, the field in which the Marathi public sphere will first emerge. Though offered to a private temple, this gift identifies a kind of "public good," a benefit to which all are entitled. I say this not to assert that the Pandharpur temple was public in a modern sense. It is not. Access was restricted in all the usual ways, and the funds given would have been in the control of the temple's Brahmin proprietors.[73] But there is something unique here. Most gifts to temples in the Yadava period carefully name and enumerate the people and jatis that received funds and rights to ceremonies. The invocation of a general bhaktajana in this massive inscription is both anomalous and suggestive.

A final inscription of a donation to the temple in Pandharpur is made in 1311 CE, several years after the Delhi Sultanate had captured Devgiri (1294) and the year that Malik Kafur finally made subject the Yadava dynasty, the same year in which Ramachandra died and his successor, Singhana III, mounted an ill-fated rebellion against the Sultanate army in the region.[74] It is unclear who has given this last donation of the Yadava reign to

Pandharpur, however.[75] The inscription records a gift to Pandharpur and especially, again, to aid in the service of the bhagatajana, the "people of devotion."[76] Here is a translation of the relevant portions of the inscription:

In the prosperous year 1311, named Virodhakrita, on the seventh day in the bright half of the month of Margashirsha, on a Thursday, in the holy Dvaraka of the South, where the Lord of Pandharpur resides, [he who gave] Pundalik a boon, [he who] supported the Pandavas, who supports the bhagatajana, who gives constant happiness and support to all people . . . [lines 1–3].

. . . one gold coin is given [for the maintenance of Vitthal] by a *bhakti kinkar* [a servant of bhakti][77] to build a sanctuary (*caitrā*); the family of God (*devaparivār*) offer the five elements[78] once a day to Pundalik's lord . . . [line 7]

Those who do not uphold the dharma or cut off [the gift], they are sinners (*maḷaka*). But those who defend the dharma forever, [they are] the Marathe devotees (*parivaṇḍe marāṭhe*), the servants of Vitthal, the lord of this land (*khetrapati*), and they [will be] fortunate [lines 10–12].[79]

This inscription does a lot of work. We have some continuity from our first two inscriptions in that a devotional public is again invoked. We hear of the bhagatajana or bhaktajana, "the people of devotion," that surrounds Vitthal and Pandharpur, and a "family of God," a *devaparivar*, is cited again as well, likely indicating the community of devotees. We also have the peculiar description of the first donor as a *bhaktikinkar*, that is to say, a servant of devotion or bhakti itself, though this may be an orthographic mistake. Yet it would reinforce the reading in the inscription of 1273 of a *bhaktimali*, which may also contain a reference to bhakti itself. Bhakti, here, appears as a fully formed concept linking theology and sociology, a belief attached to a population making of it a social unit. The gift also invokes the memory of Pundalik, who is a hoary figure of Pandharpur credited with convincing Vitthal into staying in Pandharpur by displaying his deep and unending devotion (bhakti) to his parents.[80] Pundalik is the quintessential figure of the common man in bhakti spheres, a son whose filial devotion demands he ignore even the deity Krishna standing at his threshold, whom he tells to wait until his interminable piety to his own parents is done. Finally, the inscription also notes that it devotes its funds to the "constant happiness

[and] support of all people" (*sadāprasanna samujjīvailoka*), a direct invocation, to my mind, of the public at large.

The last lines of the inscription are particularly curious to note in relation to the outline of a concept of a public culture in these edicts. The inscription invokes the term *Maratha*. We have the word *Maharashtra* attested several decades earlier, in the *Līḷācaritra* and elsewhere, as a designation of place, the Marathi-speaking region, as we will see again in subsequent centuries. But here we have something more: a designation of place that is also a designation of social distinction. Here Maratha means more than just Maharashtrian, but instead also implies Marathi-speaking, and, by extension, devotee of Vitthal. It does not yet indicate a caste or jati, as it will in later centuries and as it does in the present. The final line equates the Maratha *parivanda*, or the Maratha devotee, with the Vitthal *sevak*, the servant of Vitthal. We find a direct correlation between being Maratha and serving Vitthal. To my knowledge, this is the first instance of a term—*Maratha*—that designates the people of Maharashtra as a social collective, a group beyond simply a language or geographic unit, but as a distinctive social group, made coherent by their shared worship, the shared bhakti, of Vitthal.[81] It reminds me of a line from Irawati Karve's well-known essay about traveling with the Vitthal pilgrims in 1950. She wrote, "I found a new definition of Maharashtra: the land whose people go to Pandharpur for pilgrimage."[82] We now have a state-issued inscription that articulates a region, a polity, a language, and bhakti itself all intertwined around the idea of being Maratha, being Maharashtrian.

We can read into these three inscriptions three key points in the history of the Yadava polity. The first inscription of 1190 CE is one of the earliest inscriptions in Marathi we have for the Yadava dynasty. Historically, it marks the beginning of an era, of Bhillama's reign, and it announces the power of a new political order. And yet the donation is a small one and to a small temple. It is an investment of economic, social, and religious capital. The second inscription beginning in 1273, at the height of the Yadava period, was composed within a few years of the time when the *Līḷācaritra* and the *Jñāneśvarī* purportedly were completed. Whether or not these materials are so close in time to one another, they appear to suggest a period of relative stability and prosperity—the inscription took at least four years to complete—the kind of massive undertaking that implies resources of both material and human sorts were plentiful and appropriately applied. The massive inscription of 1273 is a list of names of donors, a public display of benevolence addressed to a quotidian world and the historians of the future. It is important to note that at the apex of Yadava power, and attached to a religious site of contention with the Hoysalas, the Yadavas chose to "stake their claim." This demonstrates the stable and powerful polity the Yadavas had become, but it also suggests the way in which they conceived of the Pandharpur Temple, Vitthal worship, and bhakti in general in relation to that power: the bhakti public in the region was also a political force, and "public opinion" had to be cultivated.

The final inscription of 1311 is perhaps the swan song of the Yadavas—we have no Marathi inscriptions attributed to them extant after this period. Its last lines appear as a final plea to be remembered, to bind the reader or listener to the "defense" of the dharma that appears to link Marathi, the region of Maharashtra, and the worship of Vitthal (the Lord of the Land) to the temple in Pandharpur that can memorialize the eventful era drawing to a close in 1311. This is a declaration to a public, both present in 1311 and into the future—a poignant request to not be forgotten. The fact that this statement comes so thoroughly entwined with bhakti as a social and religious concept seems clear: as the political might of a great dynasty was evaporating, a tenuous hope remained that the power of devotion would obtain. But who were the people described in these inscriptions—donors and others who would benefit from these gifts—and the general people described as bhaktajana, the "people of devotion"?

A Medieval Marathi Public

The reader might be wondering at this point: what has happened to our donkeys? None of these three inscriptions of gifts to the temple in Pandharpur threaten a person with a curse of any kind. They all simply state a fact. If you countermand a gift to Vitthal, it is bad karma, our first inscription tells us. Our second says nothing about countermanding the hundreds of gifts enumerated, perhaps because the hubris and hegemony of the ascendant Yadava century and its elites, donors to the temple, blinded them to the many forces threatening their stability. Our third inscription merely states a fact: that only a foul sinner, a *malaka*, would do such a thing as countermand a gift to Vitthal's temple. The register for these gifts to the Pandharpur temple appears to be well outside the purview of the evil eye, of the acquisition and display of benefit in public that might engender envy. The donkey is not needed here, for the evil eye cannot attach to a general public. This is because the gifts are not given only to Vitthal and his temple, but to the bhakti public that surrounds him. The evil eye is negated by the fact that these gifts are ostensibly for everyone.

My argument is that these are gifts that identify a general public of devotion, not necessarily confined to Vitthal and Pandharpur, and the donors associate themselves, and make honorifics of, their association with devotion, with bhakti, itself. The gifts indicate the public cultural realms that will be the primary subject of the next chapters. These inscriptions of gifts to Pandharpur point toward the power of an evolving public, situated within the ordinary world of devotees, and how elites sought to register their explicit support for this public, circulating around the temple in Pandharpur. In other words, these inscriptions further suggest the public power of bhakti in general and the existence of a recognizable public culture in Marathi. Even while they cannot be considered evidence for state support of Marathi literature, and the first layer of literature to emerge is not "Varkari" literature per se, they are evidence for the support of the cultural sphere out of which literary Marathi will grow.

These inscriptions help us understand the preconditions for Marathi literary vernacularization. They display the importance of bhakti, one important sphere of "religion," at the intersection of public culture and political power. We can see at this juncture the beginning of the bhakti network that will form. These inscriptions also show the power of an evolving public, situated within the ordinary world of devotees. With the donkey curse, we saw the state's fear of the public, a fear of the effects that property and entitlement—configured around caste and gender—might have on the excluded citizens of the everyday world. On the other hand, the Pandharpur inscriptions register how elites seek to make explicit their support for the Vitthal Temple and, through that support, appeal to the same society of the everyday addressed by the donkey curse. Only now they valorize this public rather than restrain its impulses.

This world of gifts to Pandharpur, in which a bhaktajana, a people of devotion, is consistently invoked, may seem to be in contrast to the world threatened by the donkey curse imprecation and image. But the two are the same world, I think. They both are addressed to the public at large, to the sphere that not only surrounds (and potentially threatens) the Yadava polity, but that also supplies the labor, market, and humanity that make up the Yadava century. If, in one register, this public is kept at bay with the donkey curse, in another register, that same public is beckoned, and even beseeched, in the three Pandharpur inscriptions. Marathi links these two approaches to a single world, the sphere of everyday life. We are left with a view of Marathi in the Yadava century that shows, at best, indifference by the state toward the official production of Marathi literature. Yet, perhaps in an ironic sense, the Yadavas did in the end "patronize" Marathi literature by neglecting it entirely. For in the absence of any state control over Marathi literary production, a new literary public in Marathi could emerge in the Yadava century under the benign ambivalence of the royal court.

Perhaps this is the mark of a great civilization that it may create the opportunity for its own social sphere to challenge some of society's most entrenched values, making way for new and surprising social forms to arise. Throughout the long thirteenth century, the Yadavas maintained a relative equilibrium in state and society such that a new cultural politics around vernacular language, caste, and gender could emerge, crafting the contours of a new Marathi public sphere where subjects of the "common good" would be discussed. Though the Yadavas were not the agents of the emergent Marathi literature of the thirteenth century, they were nonetheless patrons of the arts, as so many similar rulers liked to be called, for they created the social world in which public culture could be reflected in a new literary idiom in a new literary language, and central questions about social equality could be raised and exemplified. The Yadavas created the world in which Jnandev and Chakradhar, and the legacies that surround them, could come into being.

CHAPTER THREE

The Biography of Literary Vernacularization

I have waited until now to introduce Jnandev and Chakradhar as "historical" figures, that is, as figures with a biography in time, in part because I seek to avoid the "great man" theory of history, of appearing to argue that two individuals were the sole instigators of literary Marathi's origins. As I argued in an earlier book (2008b), the device of biography is a historiographic device—a history of an age that is contained in the retelling of a life story. It is beyond my ability to determine the truth or falsehood of any particular claim to the biographies of the two figures at the center of this book; what is possible is to see how, through the device of biography, a history is told or, if you prefer, a historical memory is preserved. This is not a history of an individual, but of a collective, of a public, changing through time and often disagreeing with those who had gone before. Here individuals serve as memorial devices and the memories of their lives are metonymic biographies, representations of the larger story of Marathi literary vernacularization itself.

In this book I read into and through the vernacular literary moment in which the lives of these two figures are vital. I want to uncover something like the idea of a "social imaginary," as sociologists use this term, to outline a vision of the world that reflected back upon itself a view of a social, moral, and political order. To do so, however, is also to invest in the remembered lives of figures such as Jnandev and Chakradhar. I would not argue that Jnandev and Chakradhar are simply agents of change, but rather they are bright stars in a constellation of historical currents. Yet historical memory often conforms around individuals, and we use them to anthropomorphize history, in a sense, which is also what we do with celestial constellations, finding in them shapes that reflect our present cultures, metonyms for our timely concerns.

This chapter seeks to provide the essential biographical data imputed to Jnandev and Chakradhar, drawn from sources said to be coterminous with their lives. My intention here is emphatically not to reduce the moment of literary vernacularization to the genius of these two men. We remember Jnandev and Chakradhar, or any figure of history for that matter, because of the ways a collection of memorial materials have been assembled around them. And, to understand this assemblage, we need to get a sense of figures at the core, if only through the translucent lens of "biography." In order to understand how this assemblage works, and why, I will propose we see such figures in relation to the kinds of moral, spiritual, scriptural, political, and financial economies that I outlined in the first two chapters. The goal of this chapter, then, is to draw to a point the received biographies of Jnandev and Chakradhar in relation to the literary vernacular moment, but also to provide one way to understand these figures as reflections of the social imaginary of their age.

The two previous chapters have laid out the social fields in which Chakradhar and Jnandev are positioned. Along the way, I have noted how this Brahminic ecumene forms its own kind of economy of literary and religious merit linked to financial and political rewards as well as how this economy is nestled within the feudalistic world of the Yadava period. This chapter provides a final layer, delving into the remembered biographies of these two figures and their social contexts, arguing that we must see them within the fields of these various overlapping social ecologies or even "economies" of the Yadava era.

I will argue here that Jnandev and Chakradhar serve a role something like what Foucault called the "author-function," that these figures as "authors" of literary vernacularization represent "the principle of thrift in the proliferation of meaning."[1] To press this further, I will attempt to show how, as a new field of Marathi literature emerged in the thirteenth century, the biographical assertions around Jnandev and Chakradhar—and the texts associated with them—register a new kind of symbolic economy, the symbolic economy of the emergent literary vernacular. I do not examine Jnandev and Chakradhar as historical entities, but as principles of social and religious organization in time, and I adopt the organizing concepts of symbolic capital and spiritual economy to do so. Around these figures a new spiritual economy takes shape, borrowing old patterns and subjects—new in that it is in Marathi yet old in that it returns to the figure of the common person. Kumkum Sangari, in a powerful essay that engages the "spiritual economy" deployed in the compositions of Mirabai and Kabir, suggests that "the liberalizing and dissenting forms of *bhakti* emerge as a powerful force which selectively uses the metaphysics of high Hinduism . . . in an attempt to create a . . . transcendent value grounded in the dailiness of material life."[2] In a similar way, I use the idea of a spiritual economy to suggest that vernacularization, in the Marathi case, the "dailiness" or quotidian quotient, provides the very means by which the spiritual economy can be reconfigured around the topos of the everyday and, in particular, its public composed of "women, low castes, and others." As we will see in the chapters that follow, such "dailiness" is a constant feature of the reconfiguration of the high metaphysics of Hinduism here—especially the very idea of dharma, which will be brought down to daily life in the *Līḷācaritra* and will form the core ethics of salvation of the *Jñāneśvarī*.

As I have suggested in the previous chapters, vernacularization as a discourse around the topos of everyday life is well established in much earlier sources, such as the epics, the purana literature, and, of course, in the *Bhagavad Gītā* itself. Yet these were Sanskrit texts, even if their stories were unrestricted to any single language and circulated in the oral/aural sphere of myth, folk tale, and legend. With the shift into Marathi in the thirteenth century, the figures of Jnandev and Chakradhar provide nodes of orientation; they present a human, rather than textual, accommodation to the quotidian. We might adapt Foucault's term, "the author function," here and see the process whereby individuals are inscribed within broad social change in this particular case as the "the sant function." It is in part this position within a new spiritual, social, and literary economy that I think makes Chakradhar and Jnandev unique and important and allows them to function as principles of thrift within the various meanings that Marathi literary vernacularization bears through time.[3]

In this chapter I flesh out the received biographies of these two figures, with reference to the resources available, and then move on to a discussion of how to understand the public memory of both of them within the symbolic economy of the era. Each biographical description, however, comes with certain challenges. With Chakradhar, we have only biography, a stark literary realism conveyed in the *Līḷācaritra* and other texts, composed with the primary intention of relaying everything that Chakradhar said and did in exact detail. On the other hand, we have no biography of Jnandev until *after* he is said to have composed the *Jñāneśvarī*. As the ample later hagiography is a vernacularization of Jnandev himself, I feel it is anachronistic—even diegetically so—to import that later hagiography into the earlier context of the *Jñāneśvarī* and apply it to the remembered author of that text. So I restrict the outline of his received life story to what can be gleaned from his eponymous text; as a result, there is relatively less biographical information for Jnandev to engage here, but those limited details are nonetheless vital. Since the next four chapters deeply draw on the life of Chakradhar in the *Līḷācaritra* and on the sense we have of the social ethics of the figure of Jnandev in the *Jñāneśvarī*, here I engage only those salient issues that locate these two biographically constructed individuals in relation to the prevailing norms of the Yadava century, but also set them against those norms in ways that reveal the nature of the unique innovations ascribed to them and which they represent.

Speaking of the lives of saints is a risky business. Hagiographical materials are hardly "historical" materials in the sense in which they present a positivist historiographical archive—they are of a different sort than land revenue records, state inscriptions, bureaucratic red tape, statistics of populations, ethnological data, and the like. Yet they are indisputably records about the past and about human life. All lives—in history, biography, or hagiography—are imagined into being, whatever the proximity to that written account and the actual events of the life depicted. But, at the onset, let me recognize that my use of the materials that convey the contours of biography here—the *Līḷācaritra*, other texts of the Mahanubhavs, and the *Jñāneśvarī*—provide the only archive we have for reimagining the lives of these figures. I allow the reader to decide whether the lives I outline here and throughout the remainder of this book are real or fictional or somewhere in between. For me, these biographical materials are evidence of a public discourse in Marathi that links questions of social inequality with the possibilities of spiritual salvation, and so I treat these lives as "real" and "factual" within this discourse. I do not make claims that either Chakradhar or Jnandev or others did or did not live, did or did not do this or that—I have no doubt that they did live. But my analysis here is premised on tracing the facts of their public memory; the truth claims behind this public memory are not for me to judge. My interest is in how these figures—their lives, their companions, their contexts, and the texts associated with them—form primary documents in the evolution of a nascent public sphere, a conversation in the vernacular about what society ought to be.

The Memory of Two Lives

Chakradhar (c. 1194)[4]

The life of Chakradhar and the emergence of literary vernacularization in Maharashtra are in some fundamental way the same subject, for our primary text for Chakradhar's life—the *Līḷācaritra* (completed c. 1278 CE)—is also the oldest surviving work of Marathi literature.[5] Yet the first life story given in the text is not that of Chakradhar but of another figure, Changadev Raul. The *Līḷācaritra* opens with an explanation, as given by Chakradhar, of the origins of the Mahanubhav spiritual genealogy that he typifies.[6] The Mahanubhavs worship five "Krishnas" or *pañcakrsṇa*, and hence they comprise a Vaishnava Krishnaite religion in a formal sense. The five Krishnas are the Hindu deities Krishna and Dattatreya,[7] and three human incarnations of those two deities, Changadev Raul, Gundam Raul, and Chakradhar, all purported to have lived within the thirteenth century.[8] Despite these five forms of Krishna, Mahanubhavs consider themselves monotheists—each of the five Krishnas is a manifestation of the "Great Lord" or Parameshwar.[9]

The *Līḷācaritra*'s first several episodes or *lilas* (literally "plays")[10] tell us that Changadev Raul, born into a Karharde Brahmin family in Phaltan, in Maharashtra, received *śakti* or "divine power" from the deity Dattatreya while living in Dvaraka in Gujarat.[11] Changadev, in turn, passed the sacred lineage to another human figure, Gundam Raul, or Govinda Prabhu of Riddhapur, in Maharashtra, and Gundam Raul's story is the subject of the *Rddhapurlīḷā*.[12] Gundam Raul was born in Riddhapur, Maharashtra, into a Kanava Brahmin family.[13] The *Līḷācaritra*'s emphasis on specificity and fact is apparent in the careful way it records the sociocultural backgrounds of its key characters, and caste is a preeminent subject to recall. The *Līḷācaritra* then tells of how Changadev Raul was beset upon by a powerful female yogi, or *yoginī*, named Kamaksha or Kamakhya,[14] who insisted upon sexual intercourse with Changadev, even though he had sworn to Gundam Raul to remain celibate, a *brahmacārī*.[15] Rather than submit to Kamaksha, Changadev Raul "left his body," that is, died of his own volition, freeing his soul to migrate elsewhere. At this point the *Līḷācaritra* shifts perspective to "Gujarat," and here starts the biography of Chakradhar.

Changadev's soul entered the body of the son of a royal minister, a *pradhan* to King Malladeva (r. c. 1154 CE) in Bharavasa or Broach (now Bharuch) in Gujarat in 1193 CE.[16] The son was named Haripal, and his birth corresponds to the period of a series of incursions into this region by Jaitunga's Yadava armies, a fact registered in the *Līḷācaritra*.[17] Haripal's father's name was Vishaldeva and his mother's name was Malhandevi. In his youth Haripal was married to a woman named Kamalaisa. The *Līḷācaritra* tells us that Haripal was a particularly ill-behaved young man and appeared to be addicted to gambling.[18] At some point, Haripal fell ill and died. It was at this juncture, as he was being carried to the funeral pyre, that the soul of Changadev, escaping the yogic lust of Kamaksha, entered the body of Haripal, and the minister's son revived.[19] Thus Haripal, who later takes the name Chakradhar, is both the son of a Gujarati royal minister and a kind of reincarnation of Changadev, a Karhade Brahmin from Phaltan; also, he is considered as one with Gundam Raul, as well as the incarnation of both Krishna and Dattatreya.

At this point, we might ask: what was Chakradhar's caste? Can one even speak of the caste of a figure with such a complex cosmic-genetic nature? This is an important question to ask because caste designation is an essential part of the life-descriptions of most figures of the *Līḷācaritra* and also of Jnandev in the *Jñāneśvarī*. Yet it is also a curious feature of the *Līḷācaritra* that Chakradhar's caste remains somewhat vague. Even while the caste—jati and varna—of almost every other major figure of the text is made explicit, as with Changadev and Gundam Raul, there is no such clarity regarding Chakradhar, the very subject of the *Līḷācaritra*.[20] Not only is there no scholarly consensus on this question,[21] Mahanubhavs themselves seem not to be in agreement regarding Chakradhar's caste.[22] Furthermore, from a theological point of view, the question is moot for Chakradhar, like Gundam Raul and Changadev, declares, as God, to be beyond all caste distinction.[23] It may be that this caste indeterminacy, so unusual in the *Līḷācaritra*, is part of a way such a maverick figure defies conventional matrices of social order, a feature of his own "heresy" in the cultural field that surrounds him. And yet the text leaves us with clues, and the question of how the *Līḷācaritra* and other texts may have conceived of Chakradhar's social status seems an important issue to investigate.

In an early lila Haripal and his family are described as *raje*, a word that draws its meaning from a root that means "king" and might therefore imply Kshatriya varna status.[24] However, as we have seen, kings can be of any caste (jati or varna), and the varna term is a theoretical one, a term that exists in ritualistic fields of symbolic capital. In any case, the term *raje* in Old Marathi is not the plural of *raja* or "king" but rather a derivative of *rajya* or "royal."[25] Feldhaus and Tulpule in their *Dictionary of Old Marathi* gloss *raje* as "rule; administration," a word attested to, for example, in an old copperplate inscription from Khategram issued within a century of this period.[26] In other words, the designation *raje* likely means here a person or thing associated with the royal court; it is not an ascription of caste, jati, or varna.

The first time a suggestion of Chakradhar's caste is made is during a curious episode early in the *Līḷācaritra* when Chakradhar gets married, for a second time, while at Warangal in the Andhra country.[27] During negotiations for the wedding, the father of the bride-to-be asks Chakradhar about his caste. Chakradhar says he has no caste, but, when pressed, says his caste is "Lāḍ Sāmak,"[28] a jati title that appears to indicate a Brahmin caste group who recite the Sāma Veda and who are from the Lad or Lat region of Gujarat, the region in which present-day Bharuch is located.[29] This ascription of caste to Chakradhar is repeated again when a group of Mahanubhavs is discussing the variety of wedding rituals practiced in the region. One of Chakradhar's followers responds to Chakradhar's description of his own wedding by saying, "No sir! That is not our way. That is your way among the Lāḍs."[30] Similarly, there are many other points in the *Līḷācaritra* that appear to reinforce a claim that Chakradhar is a Lad Brahmin of the Sama Vedi branch from Gujarat.[31] Still an ambiguity over Chakradhar's caste is a feature of the narrative of the *Līḷācaritra* at many points, as we will see in the chapters that follow.[32]

Haripal, the *Līḷācaritra* tells us, continues to live a wayward life, even after the spirit of Changadev comes to inhabit his body. He has a wife and son, but neglects his family in favor of gambling, at which he loses disastrously. One day, when he demands money from his wife, Kamalaisa, to pay his gambling debts, she shames and ridicules him. Feeling dejected at his own addiction and the low point to which he has sunk, he asks his mother and father to allow him to go on a pilgrimage to Ramtek in the region of Maharashtra. Though his parents resist, they eventually allow him to go. He makes his way to Riddhapur in the district of Amravati in modern-day Maharashtra, which is some four hundred miles from Bharuch.[33] In Riddhapur, he is said to meet Gundam Raul, who, as we have seen, received "sacred knowledge" or *jñānaśakti* from Changadev himself, now incarnate in young Haripal. Upon meeting, Gundam Raul gives *prasad* to Haripal in the form of a half-eaten sweet, which Haripal takes and is thus initiated by Gundam Raul and given the name Chakradhar, "the one who holds the discus," a reference to the Hindu deity Krishna.[34]

After this initiation, the hagiography of Chakradhar generally divides his life into three parts.[35] The first part, sometimes called the "solo" part or *ekāṃka*, describes his time living alone in the mountains for twelve years, undertaking a vow of silence. After those twelve years he decides to return to society, much like Nietzsche's Zarathustra, and begins to associate with other ascetics.[36] He initiates a period of wandering through the political-linguistic region of the Yadava dynasty and into areas along its southern borders, particularly to the regions of Karnataka and Andhra, where he is apparently known as a Natha yogi adept.[37] His facility with yoga is apparent in several contemporary depictions of him, such as the one in figure 3.1. During this period Chakradhar appears to match the more or less conventional attributes of the wandering yogi. He has some followers, some students, but is generally peripatetic.

The second phase of Chakradhar's hagiography, usually called the "Pūrvārdha" or "Initial Half," begins when he takes up residence in Paithan. This geographic stasis allows a group of followers to grow around him there. They take vows, enact daily routines, enter initiation, and see to Chakradhar's veneration as their ritual core. Significantly, this phase is inaugurated when Chakradhar accepts the first of his devotees who will form the core of the Mahanubhav socioreligious community,[38] in particular a woman named Nagubai, a Deshastha Brahmin of apparently lofty pedigree whom Chakradhar comes to call Baisa.[39] In Paithan his circle of disciples grows along with his fame, and it is at this point, as the next two chapters will show, that the following of Chakradhar flourishes. He innovates a new social order, tied to the use of colloquial Marathi among his followers,

FIGURE 3.1. Contemporary poster art depiction of Chakradhar. Author's collection

though his own first language would have been Gujarati.[40] Despite the fact that we find many examples, some to be detailed, of Chakradhar's expertise in Sanskrit, he does not use Sanskrit with his followers. Many of his followers, Brahmin males, were conversant and even experts in Sanskrit, yet Marathi becomes the lingua franca of their community. The ethical rationale for the use of Marathi within the Mahanubhav order is the subject of chapter 5.

Given this rejection of Sanskrit, the location of the original community of the Mahanubhavs in Paithan is significant. The town was well known then, as it still is today, as a center for Brahminic learning and Sanskrit literary production; it was the intellectual capital of the Brahminic ecumene in the Yadava century. A Brahmin male of high learning, royal pedigree, and superior Sanskrit like Chakradhar would have been a regular sight in Paithan, though we have no evidence from the *Līḷācaritra* that Chakradhar chose Paithan for this reason. Yet we can imagine that a spiritual innovator with an eye toward reordering social relations within a given cultural field would find Paithan to be the ideal ground for recruiting like-minded elites. Chakradhar does not belong to the dominant Brahmin jati of the town, the Deshastha Brahmin community, and in many other ways, as we will see, he stands in stark relief to Brahminic culture in Paithan, in part as an outsider and in part because of his retinue of followers, which appears constituted by a majority of women. Yet he does belong there in other ways, and his many Brahmin followers circulate within this region, brought here, directly or indirectly, by the gravity of the Brahminic ecumene itself. It is in and around the Brahminic ecumene that many of the significant events of Chakradhar's life will take place.

The last phase of Chakradhar's hagiography, usually called the "Uttarārdha," or "Latter Half," is marked at the point when Chakradhar meets and inducts Nagadev, later to be called Bhatobas, a Brahmin devotee who has apparently given up a life as a highly successful mercenary to follow Chakradhar and who succeeds him as head of the Mahanubhav order when Chakradhar departs Maharashtra.[41] This phase of the *Līḷācaritra* describes short visits to areas around the Godavari River, but focuses primarily on Chakradhar's efforts to establish the contours of his order and transmit his teachings. He appoints Bhatobas as his successor and dictates restrictions on his followers' actions and movements. Bhatobas's life is the primary subject of the *Smṛtisthaḷa* (c. 1312).

It is worth observing that a certain kind of affinity is displayed between Chakradhar and Bhatobas: both are Brahmins, yet trained in the arts of state and war—we see Chakradhar's own skills with a sword on at least one occasion.[42] They are both "warrior" Brahmins—Brahmins who have been schooled in the craft of politics or *raje*. As such, Bhatobas and Chakradhar are intermediary figures, ideal types of the nexus of state and Brahminic ecumene that characterizes the Yadava period.[43] Indeed, the *Līḷācaritra* will detail several stories that convey the interest of successive Yadava rulers—Krishna, Mahadeva, and Ramachandra—about Chakradhar and the Mahanubhavs, an attentiveness that turns from curiosity to admiration to hostility.

At the end some versions of the *Līḷācaritra* we find a set of stories describing Chakradhar arrested by Yadava soldiers and persecuted by the state on the orders of Hemadri.[44] As mentioned in the "Note on Translation," many Mahanubhavs do not believe these stories to be historically true, and I do not endorse them as true in this book, but rather engage them as remnants of the larger story of vernacularization. In some versions of the *Līḷācaritra*, soldiers bring Chakradhar to a temple and a tribunal accuses him of impropriety in teaching women, a charge with multiple implications. The tribunal of Brahmins and others, including Hemadri, purportedly puts Chakradhar through a public trial, an event that we will examine in detail in chapter 5.[45] Chakradhar is portrayed as indifferent to the tribunal's affairs and encourages the august gathering to do as they see fit. They order him brought to another temple where allegedly his nose is cut off as a punishment, what some versions of the *Līḷācaritra* describes as Chakradhar's "sacrifice" or *pūjā*.[46] Later, responding to the anguish of his followers, Chakradhar allows his severed body part(s) to be regenerated.[47]

At the end of the *Līḷācaritra*, Chakradhar begins to make arrangements to leave the region of the Yadavas.[48] He appoints Bhatobas to succeed him as the group's leader following his departure.[49] The Yadava state, however, continues to persecute Chakradhar, according to some versions of the *Līḷācaritra*. Indeed, though this *lila* is likely a later addition, in one episode Chakradhar apparently predicts the ruination of the Yadava state at the hands of *mlechha* or "Muslims," a reference to the Delhi Sultanate's advance into the region in 1294 CE. This prophecy of dynastic doom suggests a theme of animosity between Chakradhar and the Mahanubhavs, on the one hand, and the Yadava state, on the other.[50] In Belapur Chakradhar is apprehended by Yadava soldiers again and brought to a mountainous area, where he is purportedly beheaded.[51] However, after the soldiers leave Chakradhar's body, the lila tells us that his head and body rejoin, a feat witnessed by a group of Natha yogis. It is important to reiterate here that some Mahanubhavs do not accept the veracity of these stories, even while they are present in the scriptural record of the *Līḷācaritra*.

Revived, Chakradhar begins his final journey north, toward Ujjain, but not before encountering his former follower, the Brahmin teacher and now minister of the Yadava state Sarang Pandit, who, in Judas fashion, had betrayed his friend and mentor at the tribunal mentioned earlier. Filled with shame, Sarang Pandit tries to hide his face from Chakradhar but is noticed.[52] This, and another chance meeting, are related to Bhatobas and Chakradhar's followers as eyewitness testimony reassuring them that their master is still alive and is journeying northward.[53] Indeed, though some Mahanubhavs accept the stories of Chakradhar's mutilation and decapitation, and some do not, most Mahanubhavs believe that Chakradhar lives still in the Himalaya. The *Līḷācaritra* ends as Chakradhar leaves the region of Maharashtra toward Ujjain.[54] The general date for the end of the historical memory of Chakradhar in Maharashtra is 1273 CE. Many of his followers retreated to Riddhapur, to remain under the tutelage of Gundam Raul and collectively recall the life of their departed leader. This recollection is said to have taken the form of the *Līḷācaritra* in 1278 CE, compiled and written out by the Brahmin follower Mhaibhat or Mhaimbhat.

Jnandev (c. 1271)

As mentioned, a significant asymmetry of biographical data from the period of this study exists between Chakradhar, portrayed in the *Līḷācaritra*, and Jnandev, portrayed in the *Jñāneśvarī*. Though the life story of Jnandev is perhaps one of the best-known biographies in the Marathi-speaking world, the texts that tell us of his life come some decades, perhaps even centuries, after the purported time period when the *Jñāneśvarī* is composed. These are the biographies of Jnandev that emerge when the subject of his life is taken up by a person considered to be of a Shudra or "low" caste, a tailor or Shimpi named Namdev (1270–1350 CE).[55] These biographies are divided into three parts (an organizational theme in many hagiographies, as we see above with the *Līḷācaritra*). The three parts of Jnandev's biography attributed to Namdev are thematically arranged in this way: the story of Jnandev's parents and his childhood (called the "Ādi" or "Beginning"); Jnandev's meeting with Namdev and other low caste and female sants, as well as a journey with Namdev to pilgrimage places in northern India (called the "Tīrthāvaḷī" or "The Journey"); and Jnandev's voluntary entombment

in the place of his birth, Alandi (called the "Samādhi" or "Entombment").
In terms of philological historiography, the "Ādi" and "Tīrthāvaḷī" are represented in texts as early as the seventeenth century; the "Samādhi" is
represented later, but, for various reasons, I suspect that it was composed
around the same time as the other two texts.[56] In terms of public memory,
all three texts are said to have been composed by Namdev *after* Jnandev
completed the *Jñāneśvarī* (which is a moment that closes the story of the
"Ādi"); the "Tīrthāvaḷī" and the "Samādhi" would, according to diegetic
logic, have been composed after those events as well. This means that even
if we take Namdev's hagiography of Jnandev at historical "face value," the
latter two parts would have been composed after 1296 CE, and the first
part at or after this time. For these reasons—the philological and diegetic
position of this biography *after* the composition of the *Jñāneśvarī*—I do not
draw on these biographical details in my analysis given here of the Jnandev
portrayed in the context of the composition of the *Jñāneśvarī* and hence
the biographical outline of its purported author. Instead, I draw from the
Jñāneśvarī itself whatever biographical details we can glean and I restrict
myself to this sphere, though I do return to the biography attributed to
Namdev in the conclusion.

Nonetheless, the biography of Jnandev attributed to Namdev and composed after the *Jñāneśvarī* was completed has fascinating implications for
how we read the content of the *Jñāneśvarī* over time. The biographical
details attributed to Namdev that come some years or centuries after the
composition of the *Jñāneśvarī* serve to vernacularize Jnandev himself, to
bring Jnandev's life story into line with the social politics that the Varkari
religion—epitomized by Namdev—will impute to Jnandev over the centuries. Some of the key features of that biography include stories of how
Jnandev and his siblings—his brothers, Nivritti and Sopan, and his sister,
Muktabai—are designated as "outcaste" because of their father's choice
to renounce the world while still a "householder." To reclaim their caste
status, the children must appear before a Brahmin tribunal in Paithan. It is
before this tribunal that we get one of the most famous stories of Jnandev's
life, the moment when he compelled a buffalo (also named Jnana) to recite
the Vedas as a way to demonstrate that a "soul" resides in men and animals
alike, a way to challenge the "social distinctions" of caste that formed the
subject of the tribunal. Stories such as this one—along with stories about
Jnandev's deep fellowship among low-caste and "Untouchable" men and

women recorded by Namdev (but not present in the *Jñāneśvarī*)—would all appear after the composition of the *Jñāneśvarī* as a means of using biography to explain the prevailing social ethics later ascribed to Jnandev. Indeed, Namdev's biography of Jnandev conveys the image of a figure who undergoes a transformation of his social politics in Namdev's company and in the company of Vitthal's bhaktajana, his public of devotion. Yet, as we will see in this book, Jnandev's social ethics displayed in the *Jñāneśvarī* reveal carefully wrought fault lines for the emergence of a literary sphere in Marathi. Since there is no biographical material that is contemporary with the creation of the *Jñāneśvarī*, to engage the biography of Jnandev beyond the barest of details gleaned from the *Jñāneśvarī* itself is, in a sense, to impose a diegetic anachronism, or at least an unwarranted historical reconstruction. The conclusion, however, will provide us with a chance to return to the more spacious details of Jnandev's later biography and see how those details emend the ethics we will draw from our close reading of the *Jñāneśvarī* in chapters 6 and 7. For now, we have only a basic biographical sketch of Jnandev—quite in contrast to Chakradhar—but our reading of the *Jñāneśvarī*, if we are to link text and the image of its author intimately, will tell us a great deal about the fascinating figure of the sant.

The biographical details we can glean from the *Jñāneśvarī* begin with a name, Jnandev. This is the self-designation of the person composing the text; we do not see the name Jnaneshwar, the root of the eponymous popular title of the work, anywhere in the text. The *Jñāneśvarī* suggests that its author lived around 1290 CE when the text's colophon tells us it was composed,[57] and he lived in the region of Nevase in Maharashtra, a town sixty kilometers south of Devgiri and about that far to the west of Paithan; in other words, a town within the nexus of major urban areas of the Yadava century and along the key circuits of the Brahminic ecumene. Jnandev does not tell us his caste in this text, though it is implied in several ways, as we will see in later chapters, that he is a Brahmin. As noted, his later hagiography will position Jnandev within an ambivalent social ontology—an "outcaste" Brahmin who both attempts to return to caste status (along with his siblings), but one who becomes deeply critical of caste distinction (as the *Jñāneśvarī* will show and as his later hagiography will emphasize). The *Jñāneśvarī* assumes that Jnandev is a Brahmin and displays this indirectly in many ways.

One reason to assume Jnandev is a Brahmin is that he is clearly a scholar of Sanskrit, for his primary text is the Sanskrit *Bhagavad Gītā*, which he quotes throughout the text; he is also not a "scribe" (thus unlikely a Kayastha), for the *Jñāneśvarī* is an oral performance transcribed by a figure who calls himself "Satchidananda Baba" in the text's colophon. Jnandev delivers the *Jñāneśvarī* as an oral performance to an audience who, at least theoretically, attended a discourse composed of over nine thousand verses in Marathi in the town of Nevase at the end of the thirteenth century. This indicates that Jnandev had a following within the region; which is also suggested by the fact that this text exists at all. He may not have had "devotees," but he had an audience who viewed him as an authority. He describes this audience, in ideal terms, as including "women, low castes, and others" (*strishudradika*).[58] My point here is that Jnandev's diegetic audience implies a circle of attentive listeners (if not so much a following) and a community that is at least socially capacious in terms of caste, gender, and class.

The content of the *Jñāneśvarī* reveals that Jnandev is aware of a broad range of Sanskrit material in philosophy, Dharma Śāstra, mythology or purana, aesthetics, poetry, and even apparently *haṭha* yoga, among many other things.[59] Jnandev, therefore, is a Sanskrit expert, though he does not take on epithets of such distinction, such as *paṇḍit* or *ācārya*. Instead, he makes several self-deprecating statements, even while displaying his mastery of the field of Sanskrit knowledge. Jnandev tells us that his guru is Nivritti, who may also be his brother—this is a claim of later hagiography and not made explicit in the text, but there is clearly a jocular intimacy between Jnandev and Nivritti that seems to extend beyond the social mores of a teacher-student relationship alone; that is, Jnandev tends to act like a "little brother" might. But whatever this familial relationship, Jnandev clearly declares Nivritti to be his guru, and, through Nivritti, Jnandev traces a lineage for himself within the Natha yogi genealogy.[60] The popular depiction of Jnandev in figure 3.2, seated in the lotus position, upon a small platform, raised above a diegetical audience, conveys some of the features described here.

Though Jnandev is a Sanskritist, it is perhaps most obviously a feature of his biography that he is a speaker of, and literary artist in, Marathi. Whereas Chakradhar and the early Mahanubhavs—all very much like Jnandev in their positions as Brahmin male Sanskrit experts (particularly Mhaibhat, the overall "editor" and compiler of the *Līlācaritra*)—use Marathi

FIGURE 3.2. Popular representation of Jnandev. Author's collection

conscientiously as an ethical and practical means, Jnandev explicitly seeks to create a high aesthetic value for Marathi and engender a new Marathi literature. He not only has an ethics around salvation and access to the *Bhagavad Gītā* for all, but he also has an artistic agenda with Marathi—to make the language a medium for literature. In this sense, Jnandev is an innovator in literature itself. He is a "new wave" author crafting a new idiom of art.

The diegetic setting of the *Jñāneśvarī* has but two explicit characters—Jnandev and Nivritti—and a general audience that Jnandev sometimes addresses, but that is not described. We hear no biographical details of Jnandev's parents or other siblings and nothing about other companions. In terms of his "community"—religious, social, and so on—we have no further information. This is important to note. Though Jnandev would later become a key figure in the Varkari religion,[61] focused on the worship of the deity Vitthal/Pandurang in the town of Pandharpur, we hear nothing of Vitthal, Pandurang, or Pandharpur in the *Jñāneśvarī*. In other words, the *Jñāneśvarī* does not indicate reverence for Pandharpur or Vitthal, nor does it suggest that Jnandev is a "Varkari," though this does not of course mean that he did not revere Vitthal or that he was not a Varkari. In later hagiography and in the abhangs or "songs" attributed to Jnandev, he is indeed a Varkari and Vitthal devotee. He may have been a Varkari before and during the composition of the *Jñāneśvarī*; however, this text simply does not address these issues and does not mention Vitthal, Pandharpur, or other sants of the Varkari tradition.

It is perhaps related to this latter point that we also see a clear critique in Jnandev's text—and even in the existence of his text—of the elitism surrounding the exclusive use and transmission of Sanskrit among upper-caste males. As we will see, Jnandev utterly rejects the idea that the salvational materials of Sanskrit should be inaccessible to a majority of humanity, especially women, low castes, and those deemed "Untouchable." In some sense, his later biographies will seek to explain why this is the case, how it is that this erudite male Brahmin Sanskrit scholar chose to write a commentary on a Sanskrit text in everyday Marathi and present within it explicit rejections and condemnations of elitism around caste and gender difference in relation to the literary and religious treasures of Sanskrit. In the *Jñāneśvarī* we have an intellectual, philosophical, and theological engagement with many things, including an evolving social ethics around language and salvation; but we have almost no biographical narrative, no romantic journey of our hero as he reaches the height of his literary powers.

What this tells us in terms of a biographical sketch of Jnandev is that he was a self-conscious innovator, aware of the dynamics of the cultural fields that surrounded him, particularly of the intersection between the literary field and the Brahminic ecumene. Jnandev, in distinction to Chakradhar, is in this sense an "author," an agent and a producer, who contends with the relational nature of the cultural field, seeking to press out the boundaries of some aspects of that field while retaining other boundaries, as we will see. While both Chakradhar and Jnandev are spiritual and cultural innovators, it is Jnandev who leaves us with a text that has an agenda, what I've called a "vernacular manifesto," that conveys a cultural politics beyond the confines of a particular religious group. If Chakradhar and the *Līḷācaritra* speak to the circle of initiates within the frame of the Mahanubhav religion, Jnandev will speak to a field very similar to the one identified in chapter 2 in the last inscription of the Yadava era in Marathi, the gift to the Pandharpur Temple of 1311. In that inscription, *marāṭha*, meaning a region, a language, and a field of devotion, is an idea quite similar to what Jnandev will propose—that Marathi is not merely a language but a medium for social unity and soteriology. The two do not map onto one another (Jnandev does not invoke Pandharpur or Vitthal as the 1311 inscription does), but they are both expressions of a distinctive public crafted from the materials of everyday life. In the *Līḷācaritra* Chakradhar will circumscribe a boundary for his followers—the sphere of "Maharashtra"—but this is a physical sphere of limitation, a territory. For Jnandev, however, Marathi (though not "Maharashtra") is a way to cross over borders and boundaries, reaching "women, low castes, and others" to whom he is compelled to offer the salvational benefits of the *Bhagavad Gītā*. Jnandev's innovative spiritualism is a blueprint for a future yet to be constructed, but one that will be built in part from Marathi.

The "Sant Function" in a Changing Spiritual Economy

I want to expand here on a heuristic adaptation of Foucault's "author function" with the idea of the "sant function." It is not only a feature of South Asian history, but of the history of the world, that figures emerge from time to time to form new spiritual and social paradigms, and in the bhakti milieu of western and northern India the term often used for these figures is *sant* or "good person." Though the term is often rendered in English as "saint," one hopes that the Christian connotations are erased or at least sublimated. The biographies of innovation ascribed to these sants are crafted in part from the materials of the old regimes recombined with new ideas, models, and semiotic systems. These figures may be called prophets, visionaries, gurus, etc., and they may also be called heretics, revolutionaries, traitors, and madmen or madwomen.[62] Such figures venture in new directions within a given semiotic system and form new spiritual paradigms. I juxtapose these figures with those spiritual leaders who continue within a given spiritual or religious lineage, even as innovators yet wedded to a preservation of that lineage's orthodoxies.[63] My interest here is in understanding Chakradhar and Jnandev as emblematic of a radical restructuring of the symbolic capital of a given field, in this case the field of literature or rather of public literary expression. These are perhaps figures with an inordinate share of what Weber called "charisma" and "charismatic authority" and, similarly, their success is predicated on the process of "routinization" of their new ideas in their wake, a process that often requires the institution of a "sacred biography" of the person.[64] My interest here, however, is not in this routinization but rather in the moment of innovation. I want to illuminate the moment of a new route being formed through the cultural and political power of an age. In this way the "sant function" is a device of history. The social relations involved in this moment of innovation are tracked by the way these figures and their followers are seen to interrupt and disrupt flows of power in society. The figure may or may not be a historical figure, but he or she certainly is an index for historical change.

In thinking through what it is that makes Jnandev, Chakradhar, and the early Mahanubhavs part of a "quotidian revolution," I am inspired in part by Pierre Bourdieu's idea of a "cultural field" as a field of forces in competition to moderate value, the material of symbolic capital. Though a now well-worn set of concepts, Bourdieu's ideas still inspire useful ways of thinking about social change. Bourdieu uses the idea of a "field" to express a social sphere of people in relation to one another by virtue of a shared set of values and defined by that relationship—what he calls "relationality," a constant negotiation that, in part, creates a given field.[65] A field is constructed by "agents" in relation to others who share a stake in the subject of that field, such as art, culture, politics, sports, academia, and so on. The people who produce and consume culture, for example, constitute "a space of positions and position takings" in an "objective relation" to one another.[66] I take this to mean that human relationships construct the fields of value (or "distinction") that give things like art, literature, sports, or politics their social value. This idea expresses the core of what makes an economy something people "believe in," having "faith in the value of the dollar," for example. Each field is conditioned by a "circle of belief," even a force of "faith," in the value of that field's products, and each field has specific "rules of the game." Each field involves the trade of symbolic capital, what is valued in that field by agents and others. Within such fields, a normative system of "belief" in value is enacted that sustains the field. Though Bourdieu had little to say about religion, one can easily see here in his terminology a deep Weberian dependence on the cosubstantiation of religion and economy as means of symbolic interpretation.

One can imagine the Brahminic ecumene as the dominant agentive force of the literary field of the Yadava century. Until the advent of "Marathi literature" the literary field was also contained *entirely within the Brahminic ecumene.* The Brahminic ecumene does not ignore the nonelite, quotidian world, but it does not gather its symbolic capital by virtue of general public attention and consent. Within this context, I suggest that it is the effect of the "sant function" to reorder the symbolic capital of the literary field and reformulate the set of relations that constitute it. Around the public memory of Jnandev and Charkardhar a new literary economy is engendered and remembered. This new literary economy is also a new spiritual economy, for the impetus behind the texts considered the first works of Marathi literature is a spiritual and, at times, social, salvational promise.

The transformation of a given field, the literary or spiritual field, for example, is possible because fields are not necessarily stable. Bourdieu in particular was interested in change, in how fields mutate with new agents and intersections with other fields. He describes the literary field, for example, as "a field of forces, but also a field of struggles tending to transform or conserve this field of forces."[67] A field's stabilization of symbolic capital, what Bourdieu calls its "orthodoxy," is often disrupted by "heresy," where the heretics, the new "prophets," emerge to reorder symbolic capital and social relations. Sometimes such figures are quelled and disposed of by the prevailing orthodox agents of the field, but sometimes the heretics prevail and a new set of "rules," a new symbolic capital and habitus, is engendered.[68] Again, though Bourdieu is analyzing the fields of literary production, his language resonates with the categories of Western and Christian religious institutionalism.

I position the public memory of Chakradhar and Jnandev as innovators within the dominant literary field of the Yadava Century, yet "heretical" (in Bourdieu's sense) to it in important ways, many of them running contrary to prevailing social norms. As argued in the previous chapters, the Yadavas did not patronize literary Marathi—they preferred to patronize socially orthodox Dharma Śāstra literary production. Yet their patronage of writing as a technical and aesthetic skill—their support for the professional skill of writing and reading and its various aesthetics—conditioned the social capital of literacy as a value in and of itself. Jnandev and the early Mahanubhavs who composed the *Līḷacaritra* transposed the social capital of literacy from the dominant literary field (in which Sanskrit was the preeminent and perhaps the only language of literature) to a new language, Marathi. Indeed, we will observe that literacy itself, for the Mahanubhav male Brahmin leaders, was a kind of habitus, an ingrained, semiconscious disposition of action. Their orthodoxy was to maintain the symbolic capital of literacy, but their "heresy" was to transfer this symbolic capital to Marathi. As noted already, an appeal to speak for the quotidian world has a long history in Sanskrit; shifting that appeal into the very language of the quotidian world is the character of the vernacular turn as we know it.

The sant function highlights the notion of a collective undertaking, in which an individual may be central but an endeavor that is on the whole a fundamentally asocial, nonindividualistic one. Such an individual may be remembered as an agent in a given field, yet we know of the person, and history marks his or her existence, only because of the endurance of the field, of the social sphere around the agent, not because of the "charisma" of the agent him- or herself. I follow Bourdieu when he argues of the literary field in particular that it "requires . . . a radical break with the substantialist mode of thought . . . which tends to foreground the individual . . . at the expense of the structural relations."[69] Again—this is not a great man theory of history. A spiritual innovator may be an individual, but he or she is a principle of organization for a social order within a new field. My interest is, therefore, not in arguing the historicity of an innovative spiritualist, but rather the history of the cultural field that is said to have been inaugurated by that figure. Chakradhar and Jnandev can be seen as vehicles for the restructuring of a field's symbolic capital: not the bearers of old orthodoxies, but the prophets of new ones. Around their public memories we see a reconfiguration, and sometimes an entirely new economy of belief and practice arises. My argument here and in the remainder of the book is that Jnandev and Chakradhar are conceived of as agents who inaugurate the religioliterary field of Marathi by combining a predisposition for literacy with a desire to offer salvation to the quotidian world. And thus Marathi becomes their natural medium. They are conceived as such in the texts we will study in the next four chapters, and this conceptualization is both explicit and juxtaposed to prevailing norms. Whether or not they exist as historical individuals, they certainly exist to organize a particular history, the history of Marathi literary vernacularization.

What this means, in terms of this chapter's aim, is that we can only peer back through the prism of the newly engendered literary field of Marathi to its first substantive texts to unearth biographical data. This is because the only materials available to us to portray an image of the lives of Jnandev and Chakradhar are themselves the inaugural texts of Marathi. We are like the proverbial dog that chases its own tail: we have to return to the tail, but this is not the same thing as a beginning. My aim has been to extract from this circular discourse some sense of the biographical components of this study and of the two figures at its core and to provide a set of ideas to orient our sense of the biographical in the story of Marathi vernacularization. Spiritual innovators within the "sant function" context convey the ontology of the metonym—they are merely the human or "humanistic" part of what is also an economy, a market, an aesthetics, a social allegory, and (importantly for these subjects) a new and more equal opportunity for spiritual salvation. Jnandev and Chakradhar are not only remembered as spiritual innovators but also as indexes of innovation itself.

A new spiritual innovator exists as an organizing principle among many kinds of "economies": spiritual, religious, social, cultural, literary, financial, political, and so on. The intersection of markets, economies, and fields—mediated by the field of power—is a key idea for Bourdieu, and I think we see it here too.[70] The highest reaches of the Brahminic ecumene, of the literary field of Sanskrit, intersected with the fields of political power (in terms of state ministerial positions, for example) and the field of the economy (in terms of rewards through instruments like the agrahara). High cultural capital in all these fields meant a socioeconomic mobility that is a hallmark of the Yadava century; "markets" of all sorts—economic, religious, social, artistic—are linked and trade in capital.[71] Both Chakradhar and Jnandev demonstrate high symbolic capital within the symbolic economy of the Brahminic ecumene. With Chakradhar in particular, we will see other fields—of politics and economics—intersect with the religious field in which he operates. Jnandev, I will note, reflects several other fields in the *Jñāneśvarī*, though his interactions are less "heretical" in these contexts and more in line with social norms. And yet both appear to have rejected all access to the financial economy of their age (award through state entitlements, for example) in order to fully invest in the spiritual economy of their age, which, if it is set counter to the prevailing norms of the Yadava century, would also mean a rejection of the financial field of benefit. Bourdieu described the field of art as an inversion of the economic field and, as such, related to it in symbolic form. Similarly, the new field occupied by and expanded by figures like Jnandev and Chakradhar, carved in the process of Marathi literary vernacularization, reveal an inversion of the field of social, political, and economic power in the Yadava century. The idea of poverty and abnegation of worldly accumulation is a long-held value in the ethical and aesthetic systems we associate with "religion."

Jnandev and Chakradhar were mavericks within the Brahminic ecumene, and as such they are figures of some risk. Just as Bourdieu saw the field of literary production as an inversion of the economic field in modern Europe, so we might see the reconfiguration of the spiritual field, and its association with the social fields of the Yadava age, as also an inversion of the economic field. Through the figure of Chakradhar in particular, we will see someone who actively rejected state and financial benefit—literally running away from kings and powerful ministers bearing gifts—in order to fully invest himself in a reconfiguration of spiritual and social value. We will see this sense of risk clearly in the latter part of *Līḷācaritra* that documents the end of Chakradhar's life in Maharashtra, a period that concludes when he is persecuted by the Brahmin elites of his time in the name of the Yadava king Ramachandra. And we may sense some of the mitigation of risk as well in the *Jñāneśvarī* toward its conclusion when Jnandev explicitly thanks King Ramachandra for his benevolence. As we will see, being a spiritual innovator, restructuring the sociospiritual capital of an era, is remembered to be a very risky endeavor.

My use of the ideas presented here—the "sant function" or the "spiritual innovator"—are meant to serve as heuristic tools. While the contours of the lives I invoke remain essential to understanding how the texts and contexts associated with them present the social and religious critiques of the literary vernacular moment, I hope the reader will find that the concepts of this chapter help illuminate particular aspects of the received memories of Jnandev and Chakradhar. For example, the idiomatic pattern of the spiritual innovator is apparent in the brief outline of Chakradhar's life given in this chapter. Initially, as a yogi and public preacher, his power was drawn from the symbolic capital of his many intersecting social ontologies: male, Natha yogi, Brahmin, someone with deep expertise in Sanskrit and Sanskritic literature, a man familiar with politics and statecraft. Any or all of these qualities would have provided several opportunities for livelihood in the Brahminic ecumene or perhaps the ministerial functions of the Yadava state. Yet the "venture" of Chakradhar's innovations in social, religious, and, later, literary contexts involved other, apparently "radical," decisions: to disavow Sanskrit and adopt Marathi, a second language to Chakradhar; to found his new order with a preponderance of female devotees; to insist on the almost complete rejection of caste distinctions within the ambit of his initiates; and to reject apparent overtures of royal beneficence or support from within the Brahminic ecumene or the royal court. In the figure of Chakradhar, the conveyance of some of the symbolic capital of the Brahminic ecumene—a good deal of its esoteric philosophy and the value of literacy—are matched by a rejection of many of that ecumene's core socioreligious values. Heresy and innovation are seamlessly intertwined.

Jnandev's spiritual and social innovation is a feature of the apparent contradictions between his received biography—elite Brahmin male Sanskrit scholar—and the ethics of his text—a critique of elite Brahmin male exclusive access to a Sanskrit text about human salvation. As a figure who would have had access to high symbolic capital in the literary field within the Brahminic ecumene, Jnandev most explicitly transfers that capital to a new Marathi literary idiom. This is a powerful and creative reconfiguration of the literary field in the Yadava century. While the Mahanubhavs composed their text in Marathi, they did not evince self-consciousness about literary form. Jnandev, on the other hand, appears aware of his many "heretical" interventions, such as his perspective about providing access to salvational materials for non-Brahmins and women, but also the creation of a new literary world in a regional language that he champions. I consider Jnandev and Chakradhar epitomes of the sant function because their public memory recalls them as having innovated from the old a new social economy of religious, literary, and cultural value, and so they stand as human emblems of that much broader social change.

Chakradhar and Jnandev represent figures that recondition the symbolic capital of a given field. Bourdieu refers to fields as defined by relationality, by humans negotiating value and belief relevant to the conditions and products of a given field. In the quasi-Marxist (and Weberian) synthesis of Bourdieu's thought, this involves understanding how agents in relation to other agents distribute and authorize symbolic capital. Spiritual innovators like Chakradhar and Jnandev enter a given field, perhaps by virtue of the possession of a modicum of relevant symbolic capital, but they operate within this field in opposition to the prevailing norms and relations of the field. In other words, they enter a given field to realign symbolic capital by renegotiating relationships among people within that field or, rather, to stand as indexes of that renegotiation. For Chakradhar, this involves entirely dissolving caste and gender hierarchy within his circle of initiates, but largely tolerating such hierarchy outside that circle. Jnandev's venture comprises founding a new literary field entirely, "Marathi literature," that can convey the salvational power of the *Bhagavad Gītā* to a common audience. This discursive soteriology is tempered and circumscribed by the social mores of the age, mores that are part and parcel of the idioms of Marathi Jnandev uses, the cultural distinctions that give the language its autochthonous and quotidian meanings.[72] And yet, subverting an apparent acceptance of these social mores, we will also see the seeds of social equality planted within the *Jñāneśvarī*.

Chakradhar and Jnandev are not remembered simply as novel gurus or new guides. They stand in for a social force that reconfigures the spiritual economy itself and, in so doing, alters the social worlds around by inaugurating a critical public debate. Jnandev and Chakradhar may not have had the benefit of a civil society in their age, but they made claims about civility in society in the medium of the vernacular. Their innovation is not merely a new technology of the self, a new brand of worship, a public discourse on social equality, or a redirection of social value, but a combination of them all: they are human supernovas in the course of the history of spirit, streaming their stardust into the present.

PART TWO

The Vernacular Moment

We have observed in the preceding chapters how, through the Yadava rulers' benign ambivalence toward Marathi, an environment was created for a flourishing Marathi public culture to engender a new literary medium. Two Brahmin spiritual innovators emerged from this context, and each became associated with a text that enunciated that figure's cultural politics while reflecting the conditions of the times. These texts and their purported authors transmit two different features of the emergent moment of Marathi literature.

This chapter and the next one will take a fine-grained approach to exploring the cultural politics of vernacularization at this crucial period in Maharashtrian, and Indian, history by using the *Līḷācaritra* as an archive for this historical instant, the vernacular moment. This chapter will examine the ways that the *Līḷācaritra* registered and responded to social inequity. I argue that the *Līḷācaritra* represents the cultural politics active during the process of vernacularization, a process that likely preceded the creation of the *Jñāneśvarī* by several decades, as the periods depicted in the *Līḷācaritra* appear to cover the first three-quarters of the thirteenth century. For this reason, we will study the content of the *Līḷācaritra* first, before we examine the nature of the text, its ethics and the logic of its creation as the first work of Marathi literature. This may seem to the reader a backward sort of way to do things, but my rationale is derived from my impression that the *Līḷācaritra* is a text that responds to its time, rather than a work that consciously precedes and envisions a new world, which is an attribute of the *Jñāneśvarī*. The social conditions the *Līḷācaritra* records fundamentally constitute the rationale for the creation of the text itself—those conditions are part of the sacred and social landscapes through which Chakradhar traveled. We begin by exploring the social ethics of Chakradhar and the early Mahanubhavs, a subject amply recorded by the *Līḷācaritra*.

Brahminic Anti-Brahminism?

One of the salient features of the narrative of the *Līḷācaritra* is the ubiquitous presence of Brahmins, an indication that this text emerged from the social sphere attached to the Brahminic ecumene of the Yadava century. This is a text situated within, and reflecting, a Brahminic point of view, but a view that stridently critiques Brahminism itself, and, along with it, caste and gender inequity, as well as the social divisions created by language. Aside from Chakradhar, who was probably a Brahmin, as I argued in the last chapter, the other two human incarnations of Krishna worshipped by the Mahanubhavs, Changadev Raul and Gundam Raul, are explicitly remembered to have been Brahmins. My rather rough estimate of times when Brahmin characters are introduced in the *Līḷācaritra* suggests that around 60 percent of all the lilas given in the *Līḷācaritra* feature a Brahmin character other than Chakradhar or one of his followers. Another rough estimate can be made with reference to the list of people who came into contact with Chakradhar during his life, which is contained in a prologue to the *Smṛtisthaḷa*, a record of the early years of the Mahanubhavs after Chakradhar had left their community.[1] In that list of 110 names, at least 50 indicate their caste identity to be Brahmin.[2] If we add to this all the important Brahmin figures within the *Līḷācaritra*,[3] and almost every other key follower of Chakradhar, as well as several of his Brahmin adversaries who reappear, we can see that perhaps 90 percent of the lilas feature a Brahmin figure. Of course, if one accepts that Chakradhar himself was a Brahmin, then *every story* in the text features a Brahmin. It is perhaps an irony of history that primarily people who are not Brahmin today populate this religious tradition; most Mahanubhavs today are Marathas by caste. One cannot read the *Līḷācaritra* and not come away with the sense that Brahmins are not only central to understanding the text's cultural politics and context, but that a statement about caste and society lurks amid this overdetermined host of characters—there is here a Brahminic critique of Brahminism, an example of what I have elsewhere called the Brahmin double.[4]

Throughout the *Līḷācaritra* we hear details about Brahminic privilege and elitism. For example, we learn of lavish practices of feeding Brahmins and other high-caste figures and we find stories of diehard Brahminic puritanism in which various Brahmin jatis are positioned against one another within their larger varna grouping.[5] In a rather comical lila, we hear that Chakradhar's male follower, the Brahmin Daimba, is mistaken for a particular woman's husband. Though Daimba is not this woman's husband, he brings the woman back to meet Chakradhar. Chakradhar settles the dispute by asking the woman's jati (or rather her father's jati), which is Madhyajan Brahmin, rather than Daimba's jati, which is Karhade Brahmin.[6] If they are not of the same Brahmin jati, the social logic follows, then it is very unlikely they were married. This story is noteworthy because it highlights the deep practices of endogamy, rife within and between jati and varna groups, registered in this text, in which it would not only be against social norms to marry outside one's varna, but even to marry outside one's jati *within* the same varna. For Brahmin jatis alone, we hear of many: Madhyajan, Karhade, Dixit, Laad Samavedi, Deshastha, and so on. The text appears keenly aware of the minutiae of the Brahminic social world. In addition, there is great awareness of those jatis that intersect with, and often compete with, Brahmin jatis, such as those of Kayasthas and Guravs. And the multiple divisions of caste enumerated within the text are significant. We hear of an assortment of Brahmins, as mentioned, as well as Kayasthas and Guravs, who appear as direct challengers to Brahminic power. But we also hear of multiple "Untouchable" jatis, such as Mahars, Chamars/Chambhars, Matangs, Mangs, and Dhoras, among others, as well as Mhalas and Kalals. We also hear of Shudras and Shudra jatis, such as those of the Shimpi, Teli, Mali and Kunbi, Koli, as well as many middle castes, such as Gondhols and many, many others.[7] In its depth of detail about the social conditions and conventions of its time, the *Līḷācaritra* forms its own veritable ethnology of caste and caste practices. This is in part a result of Chakradhar's ascribed personal interest in the ethnological subject. At one point he imitates the way Shudras worship at Shiva temples—recreating their vocalizations and actions—something that he can do because of his own careful observations of Shudras' rituals of action and language.[8] We will return to this story a little later on.

The text also registers the anxiety of Brahmins around questions of pollution. Early in the *Līḷācaritra*, Chakradhar meets a key character, Dados, who is also a guru, and who will become an ambivalent associate of Chakradhar, but later a Mahanubhav himself. We learn that thieves had killed Dados's father and that he and his household were in mourning, thus their home was "polluted" by their father's death. Expecting that Chakradhar would hold to the same conventions of pollution, Dados asks that he be allowed to take food to Chakradhar so that Chakradhar will not have to visit Dados's polluted home to dine. However, Chakradhar dismisses this highly conventional notion of pollution, saying, "that means nothing to me."[9] In another incident, his Brahmin follower Lukhadeoba returns from Devgiri, where he had drunk "the polluted water touched by a Dhora" and a "Chambhar"—two jatis considered "Untouchable."[10] As a way to purify himself, he shaved his head. Chakradhar, noticing Lukhadeoba's shaven head and, hearing what had inspired it, teases his Brahmin follower for this display of adherence to the conventions of Brahminic ritual purity, mockingly calls him "Punya Mahatma" or "The Mahatma of Merit."

In some fundamental way, the *Līḷācaritra* is a "Brahminic text" and also a text about proper social behavior, thus it is in line with the dominant subject of the age within the Sanskrit Brahminic ecumene of the Yadava century. It is not a text about the conventions of Dharma Śāstra in the way, for example, Hemadri's *Caturvarga Cintāmani* is. But it is a text about dharma, as is the *Jñāneśvarī*. As I argued in part 1, the dominant literary and philosophical subject of the Yadava century was dharma in some form or another. And while the *Līḷācaritra* rejects Sanskrit, it absorbs this primary subject of Sanskrit texts of its age. However, the *Līḷācaritra*'s engagement with normative social dharma is one of critique, not support. The stories recounted suggest that though this is a Brahminic text, it is not particularly positive about Brahmins or the conventional interpretation of dharma associated with Brahmins and with Dharma Śāstra. Indeed, the text registers a consistent critique of Brahmins and Brahminism, referred to as *brahmanya* and *brahmanatva* at various points in the text, as we will see. In this way, I view the *Līḷācaritra* as a text that links the Brahminic ecumene with the quotidian world via a critique of Brahminism itself, and thereby sets up the context in which this small group of Brahmins who had gathered around the figure of Chakradhar would forego—or at least try to forego—their caste prejudices while observing such prejudices in their own community and in the world around them.

This point is made immediately in the *Līḷācaritra,* for the text spares no time in critiquing Brahmins. While still discussing the life of Changadev Raul,[11] we learn about a Brahmin who is robbed by thieves on his way to Dvaraka in Gujarat to offer meals to one thousand Brahmins.[12] His wife cleverly holds her gold earrings in her mouth during the robbery, and they use these secreted earrings to purchase their offering. Changadev, who was among the thousand Brahmins, is served first and quickly consumes the equivalent of five hundred meals before any of the other Brahmins can even begin eating. The Brahmin's wife complains about this behavior, and Changadev stops eating and leaves the meal. The Brahmin, enraged, says to his wife, "Die, die, you sinful woman! Why did you do that? Giving him [alone] the meals of one thousand Brahmins would have been the same as feeding one thousand different Brahmins!" This story's primary emphasis is perhaps to make clear the holy nature of Changadev, but both the Brahmin characters' actions implicitly carry a critique of Brahminic behavior as mechanical, unreflective, concerned with quantity, and always in the service of some gain.[13] It is perhaps unfortunate that a female Brahmin must stand as the object of this critique, however, given the great number of Brahmin female followers of Chakradhar and their vital role in the Mahanubhav order and its preservation. And this is of course a parody of Brahmins, not an accurate portrayal. In any case, while we may see the Brahmin's wife as someone who mistakes quantity for quality, the reaction of her husband is extreme, and he emphasizes, again, a simple arithmetic of merit and a crude understanding of the divinity and message of the object of his devotion, Changadev. The lesson is clearly not to go on feeding a holy figure like Changadev, but rather to give up the very practice of feeding Brahmins for merit and find one's virtue in other forms.

At another point, shortly after this episode, Changadev finds a dead dog in the street and carries the carcass on his head, disposing of the body outside the village square.[14] The responsibility for removing such carcasses would normally fall to the village "Untouchables" and hence the Brahmin Changadev appears to disrupt normal caste expectations. Furthermore, his mode of carrying the dog's body is particularly startling—to bear such impurity on the purest part of the body, the head. These very opening sections of the *Līḷācaritra* focused upon Changadev presage the critique of caste that runs throughout the stories that follow the life of Chakradhar.

After the narration of Chakradhar's early years, we learn that he travels southward to Andhra where he has several encounters that express his lack of adherence to caste distinction, especially while seeking alms, a lesson he will later struggle to teach his own followers. First Chakradhar dines at the home of a member of the Teli or oil-presser caste, considered a Shudra in Maharashtra and Andhra in that period,[15] and later he observes Gundam Raul accepting food from Matangs,[16] an "Untouchable" jati.[17] While in the Vindhya Mountains bordering northern Maharashtra, Chakradhar again breaks caste taboos by dining at the home of Gonds, who are classified as a Scheduled Tribe in contemporary India and bear the prejudices attached to "tribals" in the period of the *Līḷācaritra* as well.[18] These episodes all clearly register the fact that for divine beings, such as Changadev, Gundam Raul, and Chakradhar, caste distinction is utterly meaningless; yet, diegetically, the stories are told in the context of the shock these actions provoke within the quotidian world around them precisely because of the caste distinctions of the time in which their human incarnations existed.

Perhaps the most poignant early example of caste prejudice and its sometimes violent effects occurs after Chakradhar returns to the region of Maharashtra, to what is now the district of Beed. Here we encounter a curious story about Chakradhar's association with a Chambhar, a member of an "Untouchable" jati that, in Andhra Pradesh and Maharashtra, was associated with shoemaking and leatherwork.[19] The Chambhar and his wife happen upon Chakradhar. The Chambhar man is hypnotized by Chakradhar's radiance, praising him as "without equal"—this, we will see, is a regular reaction to the public's encounter with Chakradhar. The Chambhar's wife demands that he leaves Chakradhar's presence so that they can continue on their way, but the man refuses. Curiously, the woman then threatens that she will divorce him if he doesn't move along, and he flatly responds, "Divorce me." She apparently does so and, as promised, goes her way.[20]

The man is then initiated by Chakradhar and begins to sit in the town square and preach. The villagers object that he is only "playing at" being a holy man—for how can a Chambhar have the authority of a Brahmin? They call a Brahmin legal expert in Dharma Śāstra who declares that the Chambhar man is polluting the village with his presence.[21] When the Chambhar man refuses to leave, the Brahmin declares his judgment: the man will be buried in a water-limestone pit, a particularly horrible form of capital punishment in which the limestone "burns" away the person's flesh very slowly. While the sentence is being carried out, a bystander declares that he has just seen that same man in the market, garlanded and strolling carefree. When the people rush to the market and find the Chambhar man there, as described, they repent, falling at his feet and declaring, "we are all like sinful Chandals ["Untouchables"] [because] we harassed you."[22] Given how few stories there are in the *Līḷācaritra* about "Untouchables," it is significant that two long lilas at the beginning of this text tell the story of this Chambhar man, who is also one of the earliest initiated devotees of Chakradhar.

These passages suggest a harsh reaction to caste transgression in the Yadava era and the violent means required to reinforce caste-based social codes. The villagers, we should assume, were not mostly Brahmin, though they call a Brahmin expert in Dharma Śāstra to adjudicate the situation. We might also note the irony that the villagers, in repentance, declare themselves "Chandals," a general term for "Untouchables," even while they have punished a man for being an "Untouchable" displaying "uppity" behavior befitting a social station above that ascribed to him.[23] The text indicates this social situation by quoting the villagers' language, in which they describe the Chambhar as "playing at" being a holy man.[24] It is ironic that, in apologizing to an "Untouchable," these villagers would refer to themselves as "Untouchables." The irony is perhaps present in this text: the villagers at once apologize for their actions because they realize he is a "God man," but they do not apologize for almost brutally killing a Chambhar who dared to sit in the town square; in other words, notwithstanding this miracle, they seem to believe their horrific actions would have been justified in normal instances, but that this was an exceptional instance. The use of "Chandal" as a self-directed insult reinforces the caste prejudice the story conveys, albeit as a secondary social commentary: the primary meaning of the story is the greatness of Chakradhar's ability to transfer sacred power to others.[25] Yet, in the context of the previous stories, this tale of an "uppity" Chambhar is also a story of social inequity and injustice wrapped up in the language of caste prejudice of the thirteenth century, all carefully recalled by the composers of the *Līḷācaritra*. This lila and many others show that the authors of the *Līḷācaritra* were keen to represent caste inequity prevalent in their age, which may seem an odd thing for a group of presumably privileged Brahmins to do.[26]

At several points the text gives us evidence of the physical separation of castes within villages of the Yadava realm. We learn, for example, that graveyards and cremation grounds are places where Mahars live and work,[27] and they are entitled to the items used to adorn or accompany dead bodies. In an early lila, Chakradhar is at a burning ground in the area of Patur, in the district of Akola, and takes some cloth that had been on a dead body.[28] Chakradhar is at first accosted by a Mahar man who claims that such rags are his right alone to take, but when the Mahar realizes Chakradhar's nature he gladly gives the rags to him. The long-held association between the management of dead bodies and "Untouchability" is reinforced here, as are the kinds of "rights" associated with castes who are obliged to undertake this work. In two other lilas we come to understand that Mahars in particular were not allowed to live within the village proper, but confined to *mahārvāḍas* or Mahar areas outside villages. In one story, rife with ironic humor, thieves, who had originally planned to rob Chakradhar, instead offer to guide him home safely. They helpfully inform Chakradhar that they ought to escort him through the "Mahar neighborhood" because, as the thieves point out (with no apparent irony), it is an area full of thieves.[29] In another episode, Akaisa, a Brahmin female devotee, leaves old bread "at the edge of the village" where it is touched by a group of Mahar boys and becomes "polluted," and so she allows the boys to have the bread, which, we can guess, was always her intention; the "pollution" is just a rationale within the divisive logic of social norms.[30]

The emphasis in the *Līḷācaritra* on authentically representing Chakradhar's speech, and hence the argots of the region and time, reveal a linguistic world differentiated by caste. This is apparent when Chakradhar imitates the vocalizations of worship by Shudras, for example, as mentioned earlier. But it is also apparent in the kinds of jokes and even playful insults Chakradhar offers. There are at least three points in the *Līḷācaritra* when Chakradhar gently derides his Brahmin female follower, Ausa, by calling her a "Dhora," which is the jati name for a caste of "cowherders," which is both an "Untouchable" jati name as well as an insult for someone who is perceived as only useful in pulling around cattle.[31] It is not clear why Ausa, in particular, receives this epithet so regularly, but one can speculate that the reason is because she has a particular attachment to her Brahminic status and anxiety over that status, which is displayed several times in the text.[32] As we will see with Jnandev in the *Jñāneśvarī*, this is an example of the use of a Marathi colloquialism that is likely not meant to insult Dhoras but is a way to chide Ausa, a Brahmin. However, the use of the term to tease a Brahmin woman conveys the implicit understanding that to be a Dhora is a bad thing. It also suggests a colloquial culture where calling someone an "Untouchable" of some kind is an insult. The nature of such colloquialisms will also be an important subject when we examine the *Jñāneśvarī*.

In addition to these hierarchical views of caste difference, we get a few stories that display caste prejudice and rivalry outside Brahminic contexts. For example, to explain a folk origin story of how three *lingas*, aniconic forms of Shiva, come to be arrayed outside a temple by a drainage ditch,[33] Chakradhar tells a story about a Koli and a Gauli—a low-caste fisherman and a cowherd according to their jati associations. The two were close friends and hunting companions, an association that did not contravene the norms of caste. One day, however, the Gauli told the Koli that he wished to dine at the Koli's house. The Koli refused, saying, "How can you come to my home to eat? I am a Koli and you are a Gauli." They ultimately dined together at the Gauli's home. Though this story appears to be an analogy for the meeting of Shiva and the soul,[34] generated perhaps from Chakradhar's Natha Shaiva yogic pedigree, the social description that underlies it is the separation, not simply between high castes and low castes, but among all castes, even very close ones in normative rules of purity, along lines of endogamy and commensality. This passage also reinforces the fact that Shudras were not allowed inside temples in the Yadava realms, in suggesting that the Shaiva symbols were placed at the drainage ditch by the low-caste Koli and Gauli because they could not enter the temple.[35] But the story also expresses the fact that Shiva is intimately associated with these two low-caste figures, and thus the divine realm can transcend the social one.

The denial of temple entry, sometimes to Shudras, and almost always to "Untouchables," is a common feature of South Asian Hindu temple culture, and this was one of the several key reform subjects of the colonial and postcolonial periods.[36] Temple restrictions did not just apply to people of a low caste, but also to any woman who was menstruating; this "taboo" extended to many other kinds of ritual ceremonies and contexts as well, and such gendered rules of purity tend to be greatest in number for higher-caste women than for those of lower castes. For example, at one point in the *Līḷācaritra*, Umaisa, a Brahmin follower, is menstruating, and so hesitates to touch Chakradhar's feet, her usual mode of greeting him.[37] Chakradhar rejects the idea that Umaisa is in an "impure" state and touches her himself, to Umaisa's great shock. He further declares, in a mix of philosophical logic and good humor, that if the flow of human effluvia were to force devotees to avoid Chakradhar, then every devotee who defecated each morning would be required to avoid Chakradhar for that day, and so he'd have no followers at all.

Chakradhar's rejection of gender distinction is equally strident. Arguably his first and most central follower was a woman, Baisa; the majority of his followers thereafter were women; and several of them were widows as well, carrying with them the stigma of "impurity," which clearly Chakradhar rejected. In one very direct and poignant episode, Chakradhar's occasional follower Sarang Pandit (who would later betray him before the tribunal), arrived to find many women had gathered around Chakradhar to listen to his teaching. Sarang Pandit was annoyed that he would have to wait for their lesson to conclude, and he complained to himself that this group of "plumpies" (*guluguliyā*) would delay his own worship of Chakradhar, and felt that they should "all be sent to Telangana to pound rice" (i.e., thresh rice).[38] Realizing the odiousness of his thoughts, Sarang Pandit went to bathe in the river and purify his mind. When he returned, Chakradhar (who must have heard Sarang Pandit mutter to himself) chastised his devotee, saying, "Why should women not come for instruction to fulfill their desire for dharma? Why do you act like such an oaf (*toṃga*)? You have a soul (*jiva*); do they not also have souls? Does one God protect you and another God protect them?" The force of this passage is clear, and while it expresses Chakradhar's condemnation of his devotee's sexism it simultaneously reveals the sexist assumptions of the age, which Chakradhar seeks to countermand. It is interesting here to see Sarang Pandit's own struggle with this issue, for he voluntarily admits the fault of his thoughts. Much of the *Līḷācaritra* will express these sorts of struggles, as an innovative social movement presses against the mores of its age.

Despite what seems a radical rejection of such social orthodoxies, we do see Chakradhar and the Mahanubhavs holding to other conventions of social interaction. Chakradhar seems aware that his community of devotees might run afoul of social convention to their endangerment, so another theme woven through many stories in the *Līḷācaritra* concerns proper behavior in society. Chakradhar teaches his followers to be polite, which has a more direct relationship to the seeking of alms, especially by Brahmins, amid the wider population. He scolds Bhatobas, whom the *Līḷācaritra* portrays as particularly arrogant and bombastic, for speaking rudely to people, as when he yells at a group of scholars who have followed Chakradhar to a monastery and insist on singing songs to him. When Bhatobas speaks to them impolitely, Chakradhar scolds him, saying, "A Mahatma must speak sweetly. If not, then who will give things to us? And if no one gives things to us, then from where will we receive what we need?"[39] Similarly, Bhatobas enters a village to beg but finds there are no Brahmins. He then approaches a group of Kunbis seated in the town square and rudely asks them for uncooked grains. Bhatobas wants the grains uncooked so that he might avoid the pollution that he, a Brahmin, would risk by taking cooked food from a lower-caste Kunbi.[40] Chakradhar does not comment on this clear casteism, but rather berates Bhatobas for his rude speech.[41] At another point, Bhatobas is discourteous to a group of Guravs, using informal language to address them.[42] Chakradhar demonstrates for Bhatobas how to speak nicely to other castes, consistently calling the Guravs "Lords" or *rana* and making solicitous inquiries about their families—a fascinating example of thirteenth-century "small talk."[43] This leads to better results in begging, the lila tells us, as the Guravs give food, perhaps because they are a generally prosperous and high-caste community, and they also direct Bhatobas to the homes of generous Brahmins, their close associates in the temple economy of the Yadava century.

One senses that this rather utilitarian logic—be nice to people so they will give you alms—is Chakradhar's attempt to teach the highly practical Bhatobas a lesson. Not all stories of social decency are so instrumental, and Chakradhar's egalitarianism is apparent throughout the *Līḷācaritra*, even if this point is made directly only episodically in the text. This is perhaps a reflection of the Brahminic point of view that dominates this text—a point of view that does not valorize Brahmins but is nonetheless told from the vantage of Brahmins. For example, we hear of relatively few core followers of Chakradhar who were not Brahmin, and hence none that might carry forward a memory and subsequent narrative of a different sort than that which the early Mahanubhav Brahmin followers have provided in the *Līḷācaritra*. We are left to imagine what stories exist in the shadows of this dominant Brahminic recollection of the life of Chakradhar.

One exception to this general rule comes in the story of Dako, described as a "Chambhar Gond," thus an "Untouchable" and a blacksmith, as well as a regular, long-standing worshipper of Chakradhar, that is, a Mahanubhav. On a particular day when Chakradhar was in Bhingar, Dako arrived with a five-color blanket he had made for Chakradhar as a gift. He stood outside the building in which Chakradhar was being honored by the Brahmins of the nearby village. Dako would not approach the building, but called out to Baisa to tell Chakradhar that he had come. When the worship was over, Chakradhar came out and asked Dako why he had waited outside, implying that he should have entered the building—an odd question that must have been rhetorical, as it is hard to imagine Chakradhar did not know the answer. Dako gave no response but the listener to the story would know that the Brahmins would not have allowed him inside the building. After the gift of the blanket to Chakradhar, Dako and Chakradhar dined together outside the building. The lila then describes that this blanket is the very one that Chakradhar used thereafter, three times a day, throughout his life. When he departed, the blanket was taken to Gundam Raul, who used it until his death. This small detail, about a beloved blanket, hints at what we cannot see behind the narrative of the *Līḷācaritra*. Did Chakradhar keep this blanket because of its five colors or its exceptional comfort? Or did he keep it to remind his followers of all the others who revered him, who simply existed outside the confines of their small community? The story also implies that Chakradhar, through his life, in action and word, articulated a critique of caste and gender, and this is one of the most important messages conveyed by the *Līḷācaritra*.

The Social Critique of the Early Mahanubhavs

Almost every story about caste, gender, and purity norms in the *Līḷācaritra* involves the discipline of the inner circle of Chakradhar's mostly Brahmin followers, when they are with Chakradhar and when they are without him, in the presence of Gundam Raul after Chakradhar's departure. If there is a "critique" of social inequity within the *Līḷācaritra*, one that travels with the momentum of the Marathi literary vernacular turn, then it is in stories that relate such moments. In other words, the external observations of the early Mahanubhavs reflected caste and gender inequity in the world around them, but it is in their small, intimate circle of initiated devotees that they sought real social change and a radically new egalitarianism.

While the basis of the "system" that governs caste hierarchy may be, at the most essential level, a question of endogamy and all that goes with it—property possession, maintenance of bloodline, consolidation of social power, repression of women and their sexuality, and so on—the way in which caste difference is often expressed is in terms of "purity." As I have shown, the transgressions of caste and gender difference we see in the *Līḷācaritra* are primarily along these lines of purity rather than a contravening of endogamy—most of Chakradhar's followers were elderly, widowed, or had already renounced their family ties. I know of only one tale of exogamy in the *Līḷācaritra*, and it is largely a kind of "fable," which I will relate in this chapter.[44] However, there are ample incidents regarding "purity" in the text, and almost all involve commensality of one kind or another, either between devotees of different castes within the ranks of the Mahanubhavs or between Brahmin Mahanubhavs and low-caste members of society. The reason commensality, far more than endogamy, is the feature of the "caste system" highlighted for critique in this text is because the Mahanubhavs, and Chakradhar, are wandering mendicants who rely on requesting food from strangers as they travel the countryside, and they are celibate.

There is yet a deeper significance here attached to food and sociality. As Brahmins, they are already entitled to being fed by strangers as a means for the person offering food to them to accrue merit. This is an old stereotype—the Brahmin grown fat on the many feasts offered to him by a caste-bound ritual culture—and we see a hint of that with the story of the Brahmin who intended to feed a thousand Brahmins himself to gain merit.[45] Changadev's miraculous ability to consume a thousand meals is both a humorous play on this stereotype and a subversion of it. However, this type of ritualistic reception of offerings of food is significantly different than the kind of begging and mendicancy Chakradhar prescribes for his followers. He tells his followers that they must beg as ascetics, as people who have renounced caste and all else in the social world. In other words, they are not begging *as Brahmins* but as renunciates; they must abandon the pleasure of food and the pleasure of caste status that was related to the pleasure of food. Chakradhar tells them that they must take whatever food is offered, mix it all up, avoid any pleasing foods, and never return to the same place twice to ensure that their caste status as Brahmins remained hidden and that no bond formed that might lead to special treatment.[46] Chakradhar advises his followers in many lilas about how to properly beg, instructing in one: "You should beg from all four castes as the Dharma Śāstra instructs. Do not be selective among the houses you visit, and do not the visit the home of someone you know."[47] It is in the context of this kind of begging—not as Brahmins but as ascetics—that issues of caste and caste relations with the outside world are highlighted through discussions of what it is to "act like a Brahmin," that is, to display brahmanatva, "Brahminness." It seems that this fine distinction—between being fed lavishly as a Brahmin and being fed scraps as an ascetic—is a difficult matter for the early Brahmin Mahanubhavs to grasp.

As the circle of Chakradhar's followers grew, and his fame expanded within the Yadava realm, the urgency of dictating proper ways to interact with the general social order, as Mahanubhav ascetics, became more acute, and food occupied a central role in such interactions. And so we see that the latter portion of the *Līḷācaritra* (Uttarārdha) contains several explicit engagements with the nature of "being Brahminic," of practicing brahmanatva, where this issue arises in the context of seeking food alms. For example, Chakradhar's followers, like Chakradhar himself, show a proclivity for asking for alms at the homes of Brahmins (hence the admonition about going to the homes of all four castes [varna]), even while Chakradhar will also accept food from anyone of any caste. Nathoba is scolded for donning his "sacred thread," the mark of his Brahminhood, when he begs so that he is given better food.[48] In another story, when Sadhe returns from seeking alms at the homes of Brahmins,[49] Chakradhar teases her, telling her that the home she believed belonged to Brahmins actually belonged to a "grocer" or *vāṇī*, a Vaishya varna. When Chakradhar asks what she will do, having eaten the food of a lower caste, she says that she'll drink the water of Chakradhar's footbath to purify her stomach. Chakradhar then assures her that it was indeed a Brahmin's house to which she went, but tells her, "You should understand the deeper meaning of my sarcasm." This deeper meaning, we can guess, is a critique of her casteism and her attachment to Brahminic privilege and social norms.

At two points in the *Līḷācaritra* Chakradhar tests his followers, particularly those attached to their caste status and the special treatment they receive as Brahmins. While in Barshi, Chakradhar quizzes Sadhe: "Oh Sadhe, with whom should one go out asking for alms, with Ausa . . . or with Bhatobas?"[50] Sadhe replies, "I will not go with Ausa [because] she is a yogini [thus pays no attention to social distinction] and she begs from all four castes. I will go asking for alms with Bhatobas." Bhatobas, as we noted, has a tendency to seek out only Brahmins when he enters a new village or to seek alms that are uncooked in order to avoid pollution; he does not, apparently, go to the homes of low-caste people. When they return from seeking alms, Bhatobas complains that Sadhe asked for buttermilk from the homes to which they went—buttermilk is a common "digestive" that people, especially Brahmins in Maharashtra, consume after a meal. Chakradhar responds to Bhatobas, saying, "Should a great soul give up their religious discipline (dharma) for a trifling thing like a little buttermilk?" In this statement, Chakradhar appears to soften his position, hoping not to strain the devotion of his followers because of rules about begging, perhaps. Chakradhar tells Sadhe that she can have at least one of four things she craves when she begs—a vegetable, spices, buttermilk, or salt—and that she shouldn't be too worried about which she gets. As he says, "Don't trouble yourself [with certain foods]. The tranquil soul will become troubled [if it worries about what it will get when begging] and will go seek out sense pleasures. [A troubled soul] will go to the ends of the land; [a troubled soul] will accept all kinds of immorality (sarvādharmatva) and Brahminness (brahmanatva). . . . If a small sin means a greater evil can be avoided, then let it be avoided."[51] Chakradhar, here, explains that the focus of their practice is not a particular kind of begging or a superficial austerity, but a general diminishment of the attachment to the social self. He feels his Brahmin followers especially are attached to this sense of self around their high-caste status, their brahmanatva. Chakradhar would rather see his followers fail in small ways than big ways, even while their caste conceits, and entitlements, present a profound problem in the context of Mahanubhav mendicancy.

Chakradhar describes this desire to engage with sense pleasures, and the tendency to go "to the ends of the earth" to be satisfied, as "immoral" or "irreligious," using the negative of the word *dharma*, that is *adharma*.[52] He also identifies this desire to seek sensual pleasure, particularly around caste pride, as "Brahminic" or *brahmanatva*. Given the extensive discourse around dharma in this period, and the association between Brahmin caste and producing normative dharma prescriptions, this is an important and powerful description, to equate "immoral" and "nondharmic" with "Brahminness," with what Brahmins do as *Brahmins*. It is a highly counterintuitive claim for the zeitgeist of the age. Chakradhar appears to hope that if his followers' caste pride is assuaged in some small way—a bit of buttermilk here, some salt there—then they will remain on their ascetic paths, which will mean the reduction or elimination of casteism in other aspects of life. But Chakradhar does seem to fear that too much asceticism is itself a threat to his own teachings, for it will revive the "Brahminic" latencies of his followers. Chakradhar preaches asceticism, but he also preaches equilibrium and measure. He is a careful manager of his spiritual flock; he knows their limits as well as their potential. Chakradhar balances the eradication of caste and gender difference with the fact that these differences are deeply ingrained in society and human habitus in this period and place.

At a later point in another lila, Bhatobas quotes Chakradhar's phrase about "immorality" and "Brahminness" and asks for clarification: can someone return from this state of "Brahminness" (and "immorality") to the right path?[53] Chakradhar tells Bhatobas a story of a soldier—a tale apt for Bhatobas who, as we know, was a soldier by profession before he encountered Chakradhar. The story recalls a soldier who runs away from battle, but when he finds there is nowhere without war, changes his mind, and returns to fight and die as a soldier.[54] Similarly, a person troubled by the desire to be "Brahminic" and "immoral" can return from indulging those vices, when they realize that they cannot escape their fate, that is, the rule of karma that governs their "salvation."

Mirroring the story of Sadhe, we have a similar story occur later in the *Līḷācaritra*, only this time Ausa is the subject of Chakradhar's lesson.[55] Chakradhar asks her, "Who is purer, Ano or Markand?" Ausa replies, "Ano is *not* the purer one [because] he goes begging to all the four castes. Markand is purer." Chakradhar replies, as he often does with Ausa, rather harshly: "Tend cows [that's all you're good for]![56] Ano is polluted because he gave up all of his Brahminic (*brahmanya*) ways, his sacred thread and tuft? This makes Markand, someone who always lies,[57] better [than Ano]?" Ausa replies, "Swami Jaganatha, I'm ignorant of all this." She has considered Chakradhar's question as one about normative ideas of purity and hence believes Ano is not "pure" in this sense. Neither is she, if the earlier lila is to be understood here, for we know Ausa herself is a "renunciate" who begs from all four castes. Chakradhar's instruction here enacts an inversion of socioreligious norms of purity, finding that the notion of "impurity" is a feature of "Brahminic" ways, again a reference to the desire to be treated in a special way as a Brahmin or high-caste person. It also is interesting to see that Chakradhar insults Ausa again by calling her a Dhora, a cow-tender, an "Untouchable" caste in the region—yet another way that quotidian language encodes prejudice and insult by reference to caste. And this strikes a fascinating contrast between explicit and implicit meanings: explicitly Chakradhar has scolded Ausa for choosing the normative world of ritual purity over her ascetic ideals in her answer, and yet his choice of insult—to deride Ausa as a Dhora—would implicitly reinforce the very social distinction he had explicitly rejected. While Chakradhar means this not as an insult to Dhoras but as a good-natured chiding of Ausa, the phrase cannot have its effect without reference to the very social structure of caste inequity. This double bind, inherent in the use of colloquial Marathi to articulate a rejection of colloquial culture, will be a feature of the *Jñāneśvarī*, explored in chapter 7. The passage is also puzzling because Ausa *is* impure in the eyes of Brahminic society because she begs at all four castes, and so in this way she is like a Dhora. Chakradhar's argument is a complicated one.

The larger point, however, seems to be that Ano, because he has entirely rejected his Brahminic ways, is the "purer" of the two, even though he contravenes conventional ideas of purity. This inversion of caste and purity, based not on birth but on action, is a common theme in South Asia over the millennia. The Buddha famously is said to have stated that birth does not determine whether one is a "Brahmin" or a "low caste" but rather action decides one's merit.[58]

One larger significance of these stories about Chakradhar's exhortation of his Brahmin followers to mitigate their "Brahminism" as they beg for alms is to reiterate the relations of power these stories reveal, which mirrors the relations of power demonstrated in the system of donations to Brahmins reinforced by the non-Brahmin Yadava state. Here, too, while Brahmins receive special privileges, they receive them at the goodwill of the general population. The Brahminic ecumene and its clientelist relationship to the Yadava court is mirrored in the similar relationship that Brahmins who seek alms have with the general public that supplies those alms as a perceived act of merit. Chakradhar's insistence that Bhatobas speak politely to all people is directly tied to the way in which they rely on the generosity of others, which is to say, on the public. It is, I would argue, Chakradhar's acquiescence to the social norms that prevail, but this is an acquiescence not for the sake of Brahmins (he does not seem to care if Brahmins are well fed in society), but rather a polite way to defer to the closely held beliefs of the general public. There is here, of course, the obverse view: that Chakradhar is afraid of how the public might turn upon his followers if they are too neglectful of social mores. Chakradhar's purported persecution will be premised on contravening social mores—around caste and gender as well (I will argue) as language. The "fear of the public" that I outlined in chapter 2 bears some force here, as Chakradhar guides his followers between the paths of social normativity and a radical reconfiguration of social norms within his community of believers. As a spiritual innovator, he must take risks and mitigate risks simultaneously as he crafts a new path for himself and his followers in the Yadava century.

This idea recurs throughout devotional literature in South Asia, and Chakradhar echoes this sentiment in another lila where Mahadaisa insists on going to Varanasi with Dados.[59] Chakradhar tries to convince her not to go, for her reasons are entirely related to her Brahminic pride and social normativity: a pilgrimage to Varanasi is the height of Brahminic accomplishment, and it will raise her stature among her caste fellows. To dissuade her, Chakradhar uses two stories of caste exogamy. In one he relates the story of a Brahmin girl who falls in love with a low-caste Koli boy and must give up everything for her love of him. Chakradhar asks Mahadaisa, "For her desire of sensuous pleasure, she gave up caste, family, and daily attachments. For a life of the love of God can't you sacrifice a bit?" But this does not convince Mahadaisa (and, indeed, the story is ambivalent),[60] so Chakradhar tries another story, this one about a Brahmin man who falls in love with a Mahar woman.[61] The Brahmins of the village ostracize him—not allowing him to access the village well, not inviting him to feasts, making him eat on broken plates (a common treatment of "Untouchable" castes by upper castes in general in this period). Chakradhar says, "Like this, the people who are supposedly knowledgeable [i.e., Brahmins] are like idiots, and thus they achieved nothing [by their actions]." He explains these stories by saying, "Ignorance is better than [such] 'knowledge'; the person who is a Chandal by caste is better than the person who is a Chandal by actions." This passage might remind us of the famous saying of the Buddha cited previously, only in the Buddhist context we have a positive connotation: a Brahmin is a "good" person by actions not by birth, and this of course implies that being Brahmin is good. Here, however, we have the opposite: being a Chandal is a bad thing, and even a high-caste person can be like a Chandal if he or she isn't a good person. These are two stories of counternormativity that work against the other social interests of the stories' protagonists—being excised from one's family, being rejected by one's community. The force of public hegemony is ever present, and there is a cultural politics that Chakradhar attempts to impart to his followers.

We may also notice that by "knowledge" Chakradhar apparently means things like learning, social mores, and various "norms" for society, particularly associated with Brahminic learning—we may infer that he has in mind the Dharma Śāstra–inflected worldview that dominated the Brahminic ecumene of the region and age. Given the emphasis on Varanasi and doing something "Brahminic" in traveling there, we can guess that Chakradhar is indicting Brahminic social orthodoxy, not to mention the way this story invokes a regular network of literary exchange, an extended network of the Brahminic ecumene, between Paithan and Varanasi. Chakradhar then is critiquing the entire edifice of Brahminic "knowledge" that compels both Mahadaisa's behavior and the harsh treatment meted out to the characters in his two allegories, and yet he uses a metaphor that reinforces the fact that being a Chandal or an "Untouchable" is a negative thing. My point here is that Chakradhar is not declaring to his followers: if you follow me, if you reject caste the way I do, then you will have a happy life. Instead, he is telling them the opposite, that they will not be happy, that they will be "out-caste," but they will be liberated through their devotion to Chakradhar. Mahadaisa, in this story, is not yet fully ready for this path.

Toward the end of the *Līḷācaritra,* as the Mahanubhav order is consolidating its practices for a future without Chakradhar in Maharashtra, we see these themes recur in an exchange between Pathak (a Brahmin devotee), Bhatobas, and Chakradhar about the correct way to beg.[62]

One day Pathak said: "Sir, sir, I will go now. Then while going I will beg."

Chakradhar nodded in consent.

Then Bhatobas said, "Sir, sir! How should we go about begging?"

Chakradhar said, "Whatever I have avoided, you should avoid. Whatever it is I've told you to do, do it that way. For example, one avoids wells and tanks; one avoids village water sources; Shiva temples or the homes of Vishnu you must avoid. There's trouble there [because you'll get good food]. When a peaceful soul is troubled that person will go to the end of the land and take on all types of immorality (*adharmatva*) and Brahminic behavior (*brahmanatva*). If by a small sin a great evil can be avoided, then let it be avoided."

Upon this, Mahadaisa said, "Sir, sir! Of what good is it to accept just a little discomfort? Whatever obstacles there will be, we will tolerate them."

Chakradhar said, "My children! You will be subjected to many trials. How will you endure [all] the obstacles of suffering?"

"Yes, if we cannot bear them, then we won't [overly] trouble ourselves."

Chakradhar thought about this.

Then Mahadaisa said, "Sir, sir! Let us dine on food until we're satisfied. Should we not be capable of eating just once [a day] or even just twice [a day], then may we eat three times a day?"

Chakradhar said, "That is okay, woman. If you cannot do it, then what else is there to do but beg three times a day?"

This passage returns us to Chakradhar's effort to accommodate some leniency in his prescription of abject asceticism—the phrase he uses regarding immorality and Brahminism, and allowing a "small evil" to replace a "greater evil," is a direct replication of what he had said earlier. This passage mediates the temptations of the public world, but also allows some personal discretion, some degree of accommodation. For, as human beings, his followers will remain within the social world in one way or another.

We can see that the question of suffering, especially of requesting alms and eating the food of strangers, is a source of high anxiety for Chakradhar's followers, and this is a direct result of their attachment to caste norms that privilege them as Brahmins. The one privilege in particular they seem to cling to is having good food given to them. This is not, of course, the sole root of the idea of Brahminism used here—we see that Chakradhar must constantly correct Bhatobas's superiority when he addresses those he thinks of as beneath him in a social hierarchy for example. But seeking alms is the most consistent example in the *Līḷācaritra* for the problems that this sect of renunciate Brahmins will face in public life. This is a dual challenge: from within, as they try to maintain the standards of the casteless but private social world their founder has prescribed for them; and from outside, as they try to sublimate the entitlements of their social standing within society.

Immediately following the lila in which these issues of caste and the desires of Chakradhar's Brahmin followers are discussed, we have a lila that appears to extend, by metaphor, Chakradhar's insistence that his followers try, with all their might, to minimize their caste prejudice. Yet it is a lila that appears to rely on caste stereotypes itself to convey its message. Chakradhar describes the simplicity of a Shudra who knows happiness because he does not have "knowledge."[63]

> One day Chakradhar said, "There was once a Shudra. He washed his hands and feet at the river. He viewed Shiva's *linga* and then went home. He would sit near [his] bed and bend down, taking out a wooden stool [from underneath the bed]. Then [his wife] would cook warm millet. He'd take the warm millet on his plate. She would make seasoning in oil in a ladle and put it on his millet. He'd have lentils on his plate. Then he'd mix them and press many holes in them. Then have a ladle full of eggplant in a sauce. And he'd eat. Afterward he'd drink buttermilk from an earthen pot. He'd wash his mouth, then wash his hands and on a well-shaped mattress he'd lie down. He'd chew a dried, blackened betel leaf as small as a tiny berry. This was his after-dinner digestive. His two runny-nosed daughters would roll around on his stomach and he'd say, 'I'm very happy.'"
>
> Chakradhar said, "Thus is one person's happiness; he knew nothing else."

This story is ambivalent, and perhaps this is intended. Coming, as it does, after a conversation about how much his followers suffer when they don't eat a lot, it is perhaps not by accident that Chakradhar's story is a review of a delicious meal set within the social form of the family, all conventions and normativities happily in place, all domestic delights the Mahanubhavs have rejected. He seems to be telling his followers that, if all they want is a good meal and two "runny-nosed children," they are no different than the Shudra character of his story. Yet I sense he does not judge either his followers or his Shudra character here. He merely juxtaposes the simple life of a householder with the life of a renunciate, the one chosen by his followers. Whatever they thought was "knowledge" within the Brahminic ecumene, "learning" they could trade for good food or other benefit, was nothing of actual importance. Just as the Shudra is content, so they could be content. The "knowledge" of social normativity is equally illusory for the Shudra as it is for the Brahmin: both think they know what happiness is, but neither really does know, it seems. Or rather, they both have a happiness that is relative and fleeting rather than the happiness of liberation. In whatever way one reads this parable, it is clear that its core referent is the quotidian, normal world—what average people are like or what kinds of ordinary challenges to austerity might be tolerated. And this is certainly the pedagogical meaning of the use of the Shudra character: he is emblematic of everyday life. He is neither poor nor rich; he is just "ordinary."

Though Chakradhar allows his followers to gradually, or even incrementally, renounce their Brahminhood, and though he evinces a proclivity to accept the beneficence of Brahmins himself in the *Līḷācaritra*, the text still marks several moments when he provides a direct challenge to his followers' sense of caste superiority. As we have seen, Chakradhar eats, on a few occasions, the food offered by and in the homes of low castes and "Untouchables," yet he does not seem to insist on this kind of behavior from his followers. While Chakradhar clearly sees himself as a model for his followers' actions, he rarely forces them to radically transgress caste norms outside their small circle.

However, one prominent exception can be cited. Halting at the Yogeshwar Shaiva Temple near Paithan, three Matangs (again "Untouchables") come as close as they can to see the temple's spire, which is the nearest they can come to the image of God resting inside directly below the pinnacle.[64] Two continue on their way, satisfied with this distant, prescribed vantage, but the third Matang says he will not leave until he has "seen (*darshan*) God": he knows he cannot see the one inside the temple, but he would like to see the living one come outside the temple, that is, Chakradhar. The Matang approaches Ausa (who, we may recall, has rejected all caste distinctions) and asks her to tell Chakradhar that a "soldier" (*pāīka*) has come to see him; he does not call himself a "Matang."[65] The fact that this character calls himself a soldier is important, for it displays a self-declaration of identity as something other than derivative of caste, even while the text of the *Līḷācaritra* calls him a Matang and not a soldier. It also suggests that, as in the early colonial period, "Untouchables" were often soldiers. Ausa follows the man's instructions and tells Chakradhar that a soldier awaits him outside the temple. Chakradhar hands Ausa a sweet (prasad) that he has brought from inside the temple to give to the Matang. She gives him the sweet, but he still refuses to leave. Chakradhar then comes out, and the Matang bows to him and returns the sweet, before leaving. Chakradhar takes the sweet, now touched, and likely partially eaten, by the "Untouchable" and distributes it to his Brahmin followers as prasad, as a gift from God, from Chakradhar. His followers appear to balk at the thought of touching the sweet, much less consume it, but Chakradhar scolds them, "Which of you would not reach out for rice and clarified butter? Who wouldn't reach out for fine garments among you? You'd take filthy water from me and call it 'a great offering (*mahāprasād*).' *This is prasad.* Why would you not take it?" He has produced a paradox for his followers that strikes directly at their sense of the limits of commensality and caste. Of course his followers take and consume the prasad.

Chakradhar upbraids his followers not only for their casteism but also for their general desire for only the very best in alms: rice and clarified butter or fine garments, a subject raised throughout the *Līḷācaritra,* as noted earlier. Yet this parable conveys not direct contact with a Matang or other low caste but contact mediated through the purifying force of Chakradhar himself—a story reminiscent of the opening story of the Chambhar. While Chakradhar traps his followers in a paradox—they don't want to touch the food touched by an "Untouchable," but they won't refuse food offered by God/Chakradhar—he also releases them from the constraints of the paradox: the food is blessed by Chakradhar, thus purified, for purity is a quality above the mundane.[66] Caste prejudice is defied here, but caste norms are maintained in a sense. Chakradhar manages to do both things at once: challenge social orthodoxy and also acquiesce to it in some small measure. In the end, however, the lesson cannot be lost on his followers or on us: caste distinction is unjust in the context of salvation.

We see that Chakradhar asks his followers to challenge as well as maintain caste norms in ways that seek to minimize offense toward the general public in many stories. For example, in one story Chakradhar is invited to the home of a Brahmin, Tikavanayak, a relation of Mahadaisa, for a feast to mark the end of a period of mourning following a death in the family.[67] When it is time to serve Chakradhar and his followers, Tikavanayak says he will serve the Brahmins first, and does not give a plate to Chakradhar because he is uncertain of Chakradhar's caste.[68] Mahadaisa, outraged, gives Chakradhar her plate of food. When Chakradhar has finished, she brings it into the kitchen, but Tikavanayak protests, saying that it should go outside. He says, "This is not the right way to do things . . . should we not find out what Chakradhar's caste is?" Mahadaisa tells him angrily, "Why do you need to know Chakradhar's caste? Chakradhar is God. What else could he be?" But Tikavanayak persists: "Yes, sure, sure. Chakradhar is God. But what is his caste?" The next morning, Tikavanayak tells Chakradhar what had transpired the night before. Chakradhar addresses Mahadaisa then and says, "Oh Woman! What Tikavanayak says is the way it is. Is a person a Brahmin, or a Kshatriya, or a Vaishya, or a Shudra, or whatever, how does one know?"

This story displays an accommodation to "polite" society, and it also recalls Chakradhar's ambiguous caste status, discussed in chapter 3. Chakradhar is socially "unknown," which is likely a result of his origins outside the region, for, as many scholars have argued, caste, like other social distinctions, is highly contextualized with localized power structures—of family, village, town, city, and state.[69] Chakradhar is out of his element, so to speak, and so his markers of quotidian social ontology cannot be determined. Indeed, Chakradhar's social indeterminacy is an undercurrent throughout the *Līḷācaritra*. Rather than simply declare his caste, which he might have done given that the *Līḷācaritra* tells us the caste of every other major character in that text, Chakradhar instead responds by reinforcing social norms and reaffirming the social interactions of everyday life. In the quotidian world—outside the unique environment of the small circle of Mahanubhavs—such moments of social interaction are not to be violated. Just as it was deemed rude by Chakradhar for Bhatobas to speak down to Guravs, so it is rude here for Mahadaisa not to accept and respect the caste discrimination inherent in Tikavanayak's actions. Chakradhar's reformation of society is highly restricted—limited to his narrow band of followers. His radical reconfiguration of social norms has a natural limit within the sphere of his initiates. Yet this accommodation contains an immanent critique as well, for Chakradhar's question is rhetorical: how does anyone really define such a socially dependent designation as varna or jati? Chakradhar's statement at once reinforces social normativity and yet calls into question the very fact of social subjectivity.

The "caste question" in these contexts is almost always a question of the place, role, and particular problems of the "Brahmin" and of Brahminism as the text construes it. Though the *Līḷācaritra* also registers the vicissitudes of caste society and its many injustices, the focus of these stories is on the way to mediate the ills that accompany being a Brahmin—for being a Brahmin is a social affliction for the early Mahanubhav renunciates. The liberation of the soul of each of Chakradhar's followers is thus linked to their ability to transform themselves from people harboring significant caste prejudice to people who have, by and large, overcome such prejudice. This is important to note: the salvation Chakradhar offers his followers involves an engagement with the nefarious conditions of caste and gender inequality in society. Salvation may be attained without these social considerations actualized, but, given how important such moments of observing and challenging social inequity figure in the *Līḷācaritra*, it seems that Chakradhar taught an ethical sociology along with his theology. Yet Chakradhar, conversely, does not call on his followers to change that society in total. Instead, his revolution and radicalism is limited and restrained but set along an unmistakable trajectory.[70]

Given this relatively nonradical approach to equality in quotidian society, it may be hard to see what, exactly, was the social challenge posed by the Mahanubhavs within the Yadava realm or the Brahminic ecumene in general. It is clear that the Brahminic ecumene is the context from which the *Līḷācaritra* is composed, and upon which the text reflects, but it also is clear from the text that Chakradhar took exceptional care to maintain social convention, to not offend needlessly, and to respect social custom in many cases. Gundam Raul, for example, evinces far more transgression of social norms and at times displays outrageous antisocial behavior, such that he is described as "mad" at several points in his biography;[71] he utterly disregards the "caste system" or any rules of ritual purity or commensality and as such would seem to pose a much greater threat to the Brahminic status quo than Chakradhar, who carefully calibrates his actions in conventional social situations. Yet Gundam Raul, to my knowledge, is never described as persecuted by forces of the Yadava state or the Brahminic ecumene, unlike Chakradhar. It would seem that a "madman" poses no threat, but Chakradhar, with his highly refined sense of social decorum, does present a serious hazard to those invested in the Brahminic ecumene. It is perhaps in the contours of very specific caste animosities that we can see the terrain in which the early Mahanubhavs posed this particular challenge.

Temple, Scripture, and Cultural Capital in the Brahminic Ecumene

We can assume that caste politics was endemic in the social world of the thirteenth century, as it is today.[72] Certainly caste politics in premodern India could not take the form of caste-based voting blocks and democratic activism, but it would be hard to imagine a more central feature of social life in India than caste/gender norms, and undoubtedly the caste question motivated alignments of power in the thirteenth century. I have already pointed out the tensions and also rationales involved in the support of a Brahminic ecumene by a non-Brahmin ruling family. As with many other things, the perspective on such caste cultural politics presented in the *Līḷācaritra* emphasizes not a general view of society but the specific rivalries involving Brahmins with other Brahmins and between Brahmins and others. Given the high status of Brahmins in the Yadava century, this is a good place to look in order to find some of the cultural fissures that may have been endemic to literary vernacularization in Marathi. In this case, we can identify two rivalries between Brahmins and other caste groups that received state sponsorship by the Yadavas. These other patronized groups are Kayasthas and Guravs, and a contention between Brahmins and these groups appears particularly marked in the *Līḷācaritra* and other early Mahanubhav writing. The reason for this, and the relative nature of these rivalries, implies a great deal about the cultural politics preceding and surrounding the literary vernacular turn in Marathi and the spiritual "economies" that innovators like Chakradhar and his followers appeared to threaten. These are the economies that linked temples, monasteries, and literary endeavors, all subjects of royal patronage.

Caste politics in India takes many forms, and often Brahmins are described as archetypical perpetrators of caste injustice, as they are allotted the lion's share of responsibility for the construction of a socioreligious orthodoxy in classical and medieval India through such texts as the *Manu Smriti* and other Dharma Śāstra materials.[73] However, the sociology and ethnology of caste, particularly since the colonial era and into the present, shows that most incidences of caste rivalry and violence are between caste groups, that is, jatis, that are close to one another in terms of either theoretical designations along the spectrum of varna, or socioeconomic designations along the lines of class, or are in close proximity in the context of village economies or other locales governed by the rules of labor-exchange such as the *jajmani* and *baluta* systems.[74] In other words, most caste violence is not between the "highest" and the "lowest" of some given typology, say Brahmins and "Untouchables," in a defined region (village, territory, linguistic region, etc.), but rather fault lines are most strained between those who border one another in such a typology and hence tread upon one another's social and economic "territories" more frequently, particularly those of property and economic obligation.[75] The story of the Koli and Gauli expresses this idea, for example, where two low-caste, non-Brahmin men of different jatis preserve the rules of commensality even while they freely interact socially in other ways. My point here is that the cultural politics of caste in most cases is systemic, not "top-down," and Brahmins alone do not buoy these caste politics, as much as they might participate in them. At the same time, to call the contexts of these multiple caste fissures a feature of "Brahminic society" is not to attribute agency to Brahmins, but to metonymically name a social order emblematic of a concern with hierarchy, purity, endogamy, commensality, ritual status, and honor in ways that are crafted through the texts and practices associated with Brahmin producers.

The fact that most caste politics occurs between jati groups in close proximity to one another along various vectors ("purity," property, economy, etc.) is one reason that the *Līḷācaritra* hardly deals with encounters between its Brahmin principal characters and either Shudras or "Untouchables." We can imagine that between the latter there are many unrecorded social and economic struggles. But our records for this period—as chapter 1 expressed—are all remnants of the Brahminic ecumene in one form or another. That said, the *Līḷācaritra* appears to focus narrowly on rivalries between Brahmins and two other non-Brahmin but high-caste groups who were regularly in contact with them within the economies of the Brahminic ecumene: the Kayasthas, non-Brahmin literary professionals, and Guravs, non-Brahmin temple priests, caretakers, and ritual specialists. Brahmins, as we know, are well represented, if not dominant, in the "literary economy" of the Yadava century around Sanskrit, and also in the "temple economy," where they have long been in control of temples throughout India, especially in Maharashtra. Guravs, then, as non-Brahmin temple priests, represent a particular competition within the sphere of the temple economy, and Kayasthas, as a non-Brahmin literary group, represent competition within the sphere of the literary economy. This is not to say that these rivalries might not also lead to cooperation or that other modes of contest were not present. Yet the *Līḷācaritra* appears to highlight rivalries between Brahmins and these two groups. Furthermore, we have already seen the management of distinct roles in temples for Brahmins and Guravs in the Yadava inscriptional record, and so we must assume that such rivalries are not simply the idiosyncrasy of the *Līḷācaritra*. This all suggests that something about the cultural politics of these caste groups had an impact on the formation of literary vernacularization.

Kayasthas and Brahmins

Designating a class of literary professionals under the title of Kayastha is common throughout central, western, and northern India from at least the sixth century CE, if not earlier.[76] In Maharashtra, by the fifteenth century onward, debates about their social rank and function, particularly within the Brahminic ecumene, were the site of significant disagreement.[77] From the eleventh century, and throughout the Yadava period, the title Kayastha was commonly used to denote the scribes of inscriptions in particular.[78] It was unclear even at that point, however, and remained unclear for centuries to come, where exactly Kayasthas fit into the various typologies of caste, even while it seems that, in the period of the *Līḷācaritra*, Kayasthas formed a jati or caste group distinct from either of the groups from which they are said to have been drawn, that is, Brahmins or Kshatriyas, in the varna typology. A Brahminic theory of the origin of Kayasthas suggests that they are the offspring of exogamy, of a Brahmin man and Shudra woman.[79] However, the likely origin of the Kayasthas is of a class of people drawn from high castes who were distinguished by their literary service, as scribes and inscribers. The typology of the Dharma Śāstra is highly idealistic in terms of the replication of an endogamous group; Kayasthas represent a kind of intermediary position, tied not to varna but to their central role in the production of literary materials, both in physical terms—as scribes—and in intellectual terms—as authors. Given this status as producers of literary and inscriptional materials, it is no surprise that the *Līḷācaritra* and other early Mahanubhav texts that are presented from the point of view of Brahmins in the Yadava century would register an endemic social conflict between Brahmins and Kayasthas.

It appears that, in the thirteenth century, Kayasthas may have been considered either as equal to Brahmins or simply within the Brahminic ecumene, this despite the fact that modern-day Kayasthas in Maharashtra understand themselves to have arisen from the Kshatriya varna and are thus an intermediary caste between Brahmins and Kshatriyas.[80] In the Yadava era Kayasthas are regularly mentioned in inscriptions as the *lekhaka* or *kāraṇika*, or "writer," though they are not regularly in receipt of donations, as are Brahmins and Guravs. However, in some cases, individuals and associations of Kayasthas have made donations, as they are recorded to have done in Pandharpur around 1277, which suggests their deep involvement in the merit economy of Yadava reign.[81] We can assume that during the Yadava century, Kayasthas—as individual literary professionals and as either a guild or a caste block—were more prominent within the state structure than within the Brahminic ecumene, that is, they were closer to the core of power at the royal court, yet further from the stabilizing structures of temple, monastery, and educational institution. In this sense, the social vicissitudes of the Kayastha are more deeply entwined with a given royal court and so less likely to flourish over successive political upheavals. This may account for the close connection we find between Kayasthas and Kshatriya varna status across South Asia as well as the way in which Kayasthas filled an intermediary space within the varna echelon between Brahmin and Kshatriya. As professionals tasked with discursive mediation, it only makes sense that we would find them "in the middle," as it were.

Kayasthas appeared to consider themselves on par with Brahmins and Brahminic practice in the Yadava period. For example, we can observe the figure of Haridev Pandit, a Kayastha introduced early in the *Līḷācaritra*, who is an admirer of Chakradhar, though not quite a true follower.[82] He engages in a debate with Chakradhar about the *Bhagavad Gītā* and ancient lore literature (purana), thus emphasizing his Sanskrit learning. Like other Kayasthas encountered in Mahanubhav literature, Haridev also takes the title *Pandit*, referencing his expertise on the Puranas (a *pauraṇikā*), which is usually associated with Brahmins, further indicating the link between these two caste groups with the literary sphere of the Brahminic ecumene. This proximity of Brahmins and Kayasthas appears to have resulted not in harmonious coexistence but in significant caste prejudice. For example, in the *Smṛtisthaḷa* a story is recorded of an encounter between Umaisa and a follower named Kothaloba, a Kayastha.[83] When Kothaloba takes a sip of water from Umaisa's cup, she gets angry at the pollution she perceives and calls him a Shudra, which is intended as an insult. The fact that two figures *within* the Mahanubhav sect express animosity suggests that such enmity may have been even greater in more general public contexts.

Although the early Mahanubhav literature suggests this rivalry between Kayasthas and Brahmins, it is not an overdetermined subject for these early texts. This may be because the early Mahanubhavs, though they were mostly Brahmin, were not, by and large, members of the "scribal" profession, with the possible exception of Mhaibhat and Kesobas.[84] In other words, the spheres of culture inhabited by the early Brahmin Maha-nubhavs did not significantly intersect with the spheres of the Kayasthas; when they do intersect, though, we can detect a rivalry under the surface.

This conflict between Brahmins and Kayasthas perhaps reveals a struggle over the "economy of literacy," which is not quite the literary field as it is also a field dominated by technocratic literacy rather than "creative" work, such as poetic composition. This was a highly significant locus of power within the Yadava century and the Brahminic ecumene in that period, as we have seen in part 1. But its relatively minor representation in the early Mahanubhav literature implies not only the general lack of significant contact or conflict between the Brahmin Mahanubhavs and Kayasthas over literary issues, that is, the professional literary world of the Yadava court and the Brahminic ecumene it financed, but it also suggests that the Mahanubhavs did not occupy anything like a "literary" sphere. The literary economy, at the center of which Kayasthas existed, did not intersect with the world of Chakradhar to a great degree. This is important to note, if, as I have argued, the *Līḷācaritra* portrays the historical conditions that *precede* the literarization of Marathi rather than those that accompany this moment. This would suggest that the Mahanubhavs did not register as a threat or a presence within the literary sphere at all. This appears to happen later in Mahanubhav history, a subject the conclusion to this book will touch upon briefly, but the early Mahanubhav works, in any case, do not position the Mahanubhav community in contact with, or conflict with, agents and actors within the literary sphere attached to the Yadava court over issues pertaining to literature or writing.

Chakradhar's own position on literacy and writing is difficult to discern. In one interesting episode from his life we see the nexus of literacy, the

Brahminic ecumene, and social value. The story concerns the succession of power in a monastery after the death of the monastery's leader, a story mentioned in chapter 1.[85] In this lila we learn that the monastery's chief had two servants. One servant tended to the leader's personal needs (much as the early Mahanubhavs tended to the needs of Chakradhar) and the other servant tended to the monastery's collection of books. This meant that the former servant could not read or at least not as well as the latter could. On the death of the chief, the servant who has tended to the books inherits the monastery based on a simple argument: the monastery belonged to the person who could read the monastery's books. Chakradhar encounters the servant who looked after the monastery's chief and who therefore did not have the level of literacy of his rival. Chakradhar directs the dejected man to challenge the other former servant to a public debate in which they will read the monastery's books. It is unclear whether or not Chakradhar coaches him, but Chakradhar assures the man that in the debate he will be able to read. A sabha is formed (usually this would mean a tribunal of Brahmins and other high-caste elites) to adjudicate the debate. The sabha members and the monastery's other adherents observe that this servant who was considered illiterate can now read. They then grant the rights to the monastery to him.

This lila expresses the social value of literacy—in the form both of the treasure of books but also the ability to read them and explain them. However, what is curious here is the way Chakradhar appears to privilege a different kind of service, the practice of selfless service to one's master over the practice of service to books and the field of literacy. Though Chakradhar intervenes in such a way as to preserve the high value of literacy, he also subverts that value by presumably helping the formerly unlettered servant, who was devoted to his master rather than to his master's books, and therefore implicitly undermining the rule that the monk with the greater literary facility ought to inherit the monastery. Yet the fact that it registers a process of succession that we might assume was normative at the time, and that clearly privileges the literary work of the monastery, is a signal of the great value of literacy in the age. Despite this, through Chakradhar, we have a relative devaluation of literacy and a greater emphasis on service. I think the parable here functions to downplay the value of literacy, not only for Chakradhar's followers, but with the culture of the era as well, to note that literacy excludes among social groups. Or to put it another way, this story puts literacy in the service of social justice. This issue will arise again when Chakradhar undergoes his trial, and we will extend our discussion of the social value of literacy among the early Mahanubhavs in the next chapter. But, to find the greatest social fault lines apparent in the *Līḷācaritra*, we have to look to another rivalry demonstrated in this text.

Guravs and Brahmins

The *Līḷācaritra* reveals a more contentious caste opposition between Brahmins and Guravs, non-Brahmin temple priests and proprietors, than it does about issues of literacy. In contemporary Maharashtra, the caste status of Guravs is uncertain. They have sought to be recognized as Brahmins in some cases, while generally being considered non-Brahmin, both by other castes and sometimes by members of their own caste.[86] Some Guravs wear the sacred thread usually associated with Brahmins, and they perform many, if not all, of the same rituals Brahmins perform, especially within Shaiva temples. As opposed to the varna status of Kayasthas, it is even harder to determine the varna status of Guravs in and around the period of the Yadava century. Throughout the *Līḷācaritra* and in inscriptional evidence from the Yadava state, we can see that Guravs were distinguished from Brahmins, but they shared responsibilities at temples and gifts of state to temples, especially Shaiva temples, but also, in particular, Goddess and Hanuman temples.[87] Guravs have often also appeared as spiritual teachers—indeed, Guravs themselves trace the etymology of their jati title to the Sanskrit word *guru*, while the more likely, though not entirely unrelated, genealogy for Guravs can be derived from the Kannada word *gorava* or "Shaiva mendicant." [88] In Chakradhar's time, Guravs considered themselves high-caste and hardly secondary to any other caste; indeed they may have thought of themselves not just as equal to Brahmins but *as* Brahmins. In any case, it is clear that a rivalry existed in the temple economy of the Yadava century between Guravs and Brahmins, which the *Līḷācaritra* records.

If Kayasthas represented a threat to the dominance of Brahmins within the literary field, then Guravs represent a threat to the dominance of Brahmins in the temple economy of the Yadava century. More importantly, perhaps, given that temples are loci for other things as well—social groups, economic activity, points of information exchange—the friction between Brahmins and Guravs also indicates a rivalry over space that approximates a "public" common context.[89] We have seen temple inscriptions that dedicate funds and land to Guravs for the maintenance of temples; indeed, next to Brahmins, Guravs are the chief recipients of state and other grants recorded in the Yadava inscriptions.[90] The *Līḷācaritra* suggests that Guravs may also have been the beneficiaries of agrahara donations and enriched by many of the same conventions of alms-giving that Brahmins enjoyed,[91] evidence that they were considered high-caste in the Yadava century.[92]

Instances of enmity between Guravs and Brahmins are found in the *Līḷācaritra*. As noted, Bhatobas is often rude to Guravs, speaking down to them in most contexts. Chakradhar, on the other hand, insists on calling them "lords" or rana. This may be more than an attempt to compensate for his followers' rudeness; rather, it may have been a regular convention of colloquial Marathi at the time to refer to Guravs as rana. Another early follower of Chakradhar, Dakhala (who is apparently a Brahmin), rudely disrupts the worship of a Gurav at a temple situated at the origin of the Godavari River by pouring out all the water collected by the Gurav responsible for the temple.[93] The Gurav demands compensation from Chakradhar for his follower's behavior, and Chakradhar obliges. Dakhala, in the midst of this reparation by Chakradhar, carries on insulting the Gurav man by saying, "What is so special about your water? You're a Gurav. You're not of the lineage of the Rishi Gautama. You're nothing to me." The reference to one of the seven mythological holy men, or *saptarṣi*, invokes a common Brahminic lineage in India, and also refers to one myth of the origin of the Godavari tied to Rishi Gautama.[94] Dakhala appears to be upbraiding the temple's Gurav for daring to speak to a Brahmin man, that is Dakhala himself, in such a manner. Yet clearly Chakradhar recognizes the sovereignty that the Gurav holds over his temple grounds. This territoriality is apparent in another lila when Baisa inquires of Chakradhar whether Lord Krishna is the deity of Guravs, as the Guravs claim him to be, or a deity of the Brahmins (*vedavākta*, the "ones who speak the Vedas"), as she has understood.[95] Chakradhar resolves the problem by pointing out that *he* is Krishna and the God of all, so Baisa's question about social distinction is immaterial. The question, however, reveals the cultural politics of caste and temple economies that engenders it, rooted in a rivalry between Brahmins and Guravs in this period.

The hostility between Guravs and Brahmins is further played out in a long lila that surrounds the theft of a coconut.[96] Chakradhar and his followers are guests in the cave-home of a Gurav when the Gurav accuses them of stealing from his cave a coconut that contained some money.[97] Chakradhar asks Bhatobas to take the matter to the local judicial council, but not before Sadhe abuses the Gurav, calling him "greedy," to which Chakradhar gives the command he had given to Bhatobas: to be polite to Guravs is the way of the Mahanubhavs (suggesting that few Mahanubhavs *were* Guravs). The council, composed of Brahmins, decrees that the Gurav is wrong in accusing Chakradhar and his followers of such a crime, and they demand that the Gurav, as a penance for false accusation, cover his body with mud and cow dung and grovel at Chakradhar's feet, which he does. Later, Chakradhar informs the Gurav that his friend (also a Gurav) took his coconut. These insults to the Gurav—verbally from Sadhe, physically from the Brahmin council, and narratively, as he is the fool of this story, betrayed by his own friend—further illustrate the tension between Guravs and Brahmins.

An image of the rivalry expressed between Brahmins and Guravs may be captured through the figure of Dados, one of the most consistent characters to appear in the *Līḷācaritra*. Dados is central to the narratives of the *Līḷācaritra,* even while he is not, at least entirely, a Mahanubhav; he remains a very close figure to Chakradhar, but also a figure of rivalry and bitterness. Dados is introduced as a temple caretaker early in the *Līḷācaritra,* and I suspect that this description implies his Gurav status.[98] He quickly becomes fascinated by Chakradhar and shadows him throughout the text, caring for him on occasion. The term used to describe Dados as "having become the caretaker of the Vateshwar Temple" is the word *kaṭhīyā,* which means not only "temple caretaker" but also is often used to describe non-Brahmin temple priests, especially Guravs.[99] While the jati designation of Gurav is never explicitly given to Dados, it does seem that other devotees of Chakradhar did not consider him a Brahmin, as we will see. In my opinion, it is highly probable that Dados was a Gurav.[100]

In the course of the text, Dados's own fame as a spiritual figure appears to grow, in part through what he has learned from Chakradhar. Dados inadvertently brings several of his own followers to Chakradhar, including, importantly, Mahadaisa and Bhatobas, as well as Abaisa, Umaisa, Alhaisa, Indrabhat, Baisa, Padmanabhi, and others.[101] These devotees of Dados are all Brahmin, and they all eventually leave Dados to follow Chakradhar.[102] However, it is interesting to note that caste seemed no bar to these Brahmin devotees when they were followers of Dados. Yet one senses in the various episodes involving Dados that he is angry not only that his followers have left him for Chakradhar, but that they have left him for a Brahmin guru. Toward the end of the *Līḷācaritra*, Dados appears openly hostile and jealous of Chakradhar and is perhaps a party to Chakradhar's persecution, even while he is not invited to join the jury (probably because he is not a Brahmin), as was Chakradhar's other close associate, the Brahmin Sarang Pandit.[103] However, by the time of the *Smṛtisthaḷa*, after Chakradhar's departure from Maharashtra, Dados will have become a Mahanubhav and will die a member of their fold and in their company.[104]

If Dados is a Gurav, this helps us understand a number of conflicts that surround him in the *Līḷācaritra*. In one episode, Lakhubaisa, a Brahmin devotee, is sweeping, and dust from her actions falls on Dados.[105] Bhatobas, still at this time a follower of Dados, complains to Lakhubaisa about the dust. Lakhubaisa responds, "First, think of who you are, then of who your Dados is." This statement makes Bhatobas furious, and he says, "What am I?! What is my Dados?! I'd give my head to save a hair on his!" Lukhubaisa coolly responds, "Give up your head then." Chakradhar then intervenes and says, metaphorically, that just as one must like the son of a king, even if the son is born from a queen who is not liked, so Lakhubaisa must like Dados.

The episode is somewhat enigmatic, but one possible reading is that Lakhubaisa is reminding Bhatobas of his caste superiority over Dados. She does not like to see a Brahmin like Bhatobas complaining to her, another Brahmin, about an affront to a lower-caste person like Dados. It seems that Bhatobas understands this, and thus his retort with all its self-righteousness. Chakradhar's interjection is likewise enigmatic, but seems to imply that though one may be born into the world in an inferior status, the same deity (i.e., in this case, Chakradhar) reigns over all creatures. Here, again, we see Chakradhar's ability to accommodate social difference and disagreement yet also to reject it. If we understand Dados to be a Gurav, then Lakhubaisa's comments make more sense. And given the fact that Bhatobas will one day become a devotee of Chakradhar, and will evince a strong dislike of Guravs, it may be that we see here a reason for this prejudice—it is a remnant of his spiritual "divorce" from Dados.

Dados is not only a victim of such antagonism, but he also perpetrates his own. At a temple near Ramnath, Mahadaisa, who has earlier renounced

Dados as her guru and accepted initiation from Chakradhar,[106] takes some water from the temple and washes the dust from Chakradhar's feet, a daily ritual shared among the Mahanubhavs.[107] Later, as is customary, she drinks the water as a blessing (prasad). Dados then accosts his former disciple, suggesting to her that, given her proclivity for purity, she should take a bath in order to purify herself, for the water from the temple was the water of a Gurav. She responds that this is the water purified by the dust from Chakradhar's feet, so there is no need for a bath, and besides, if it had been water touched by a Gurav then Chakradhar would have protested as well (another indication that Chakradhar is understood to be a Brahmin, though perhaps a low estimation of his clear egalitarianism). Dados may be responding as a Gurav and thus metaphorically recalling his own association with Mahadaisa—the Gurav's water, purified by Chakradhar's dust, is a metaphor for Mahadaisa's own spiritual progression toward Chakradhar and regression away from Dados. Dados is clearly hurt and offended, perhaps not merely for losing a beloved devotee, either. This passage seems to imply that he believed, or at least suspected, that Mahadaisa left his company because she would constantly have carried with her the fear of "pollution" from him as a "lesser" person in some way.

Whether or not Dados was a Gurav, the rivalry between Guravs and Brahmins appears more prominently in the *Līḷācaritra* than the contest between Brahmins and Kayasthas. I think this fact highlights the particular sphere of circulation of the Mahanubhavs. Though they come to occupy the center stage of Marathi literary vernacularization, the particular rivalry with Guravs here suggests that a kind of "temple economy" linked to a "guru economy" of wandering spiritual teachers was the sphere that the Mahanubhavs threatened, more so than the Sanskritic literary economy of the time. As we have seen, the three major gifts to the Pandharpur Temple that "bookended" Yadava sovereign reign (in 1189, again around 1273, and finally in 1311) are,[108] to my mind, the only inscriptions that record a gift of state to anything like a "bhakti public," in this case, to the devotees of Vitthal and by the devotees of Vitthal, the bhaktajana, rather than for specific individuals or a collection of individuals associated with a temple, monastery, school, or other institutions. The Pandharpur Temple, like many other temples (especially in South India), was a site that linked multiple spheres of society and political economy. During the Yadava century, this temple represented a connection between the state and the public, as it was a node for social organization within the sphere of "religion" sponsored by state gifts as well as private donations.[109] I believe that the relative severity of conflict between Guravs and Brahmins, registered, in part, in inscriptions, and clearly in the *Līḷacaritra*, suggests that temples were the places where new spiritualists recruited followers and that new religious cultures circulated within the geocultural spaces linking major temple areas in the Deccan. Thus state and nonstate evidence suggests that the temple was a key location in the evolution of a new public culture in the thirteenth century. That Marathi literature would be so conditioned by the cultural sphere of Pandharpur, and devotees of Vitthal, in centuries to come, is therefore no surprise. Marathi literature, conveying new modes of salvation for a Marathi public, was not in conflict with rarefied realms of literary production—in Sanskrit or otherwise—but rather it emerged in relation to, and perhaps as an alternative to, the social locus of worship in the temple. In other words, the *Līḷacaritra*, like the Matang who refused to leave before he saw "God," represents a way to "see God" outside of a temple, accessible to everyone of any caste or either sex.

It may be that one of the key innovations of Chakradhar and the early Mahanubhavs was to decenter the prominence of the temple, much as Basava did in the century before in Karnataka.[110] Therefore, the social order that the Mahanubhavs challenged was not primarily a literary one; the "vernacularization" they represented was not about literature but about *place*, the temple and networks that surround temples, and about the economy that formed around the entrepreneurial spiritual teachers of the age. They were radical egalitarians in their community yet sought good relations with the outside world. And a new literature grew not from a new literary intervention but from an intervention that displaced the centrality of the temple—under the control of a Brahmin or a Gurav—by emphasizing the importance of the localized holy figure, like Chakradhar or even Dados, who taught out in the open in public.

Vernacularization is displayed here as the conversion of the center of power from the temple to the center of power in quotidian public culture of the thirteenth century, in the public discourse of Marathi, which becomes the sphere of the new spiritualist. Chakradhar did not make literary interventions in the world but public, social ones. This further reinforces the idea that it was not the production of literature that was the key feature of vernacularization, but a new political order centered on conventions of everyday life, and it is this shift that set the conditions for a new literature to emerge, fleshed out with a conversation about social inequity. We will see a full shift of focus from "temple" to "text" with the *Jñāneśvarī*, as the effect of a previous decentralization in public culture, which is recorded here in the Mahanubhav works.

The scriptural economy is highly restricted—in relation to the state especially. The Yadava court evinced no interest in supporting the production of Marathi "literature," even while it used Marathi as a language of state on occasion and often as a language of address to the denizens of everyday society. The temple economy, on the other hand, is the locus for something approximating public interaction, and so it is here in "religion" that we can locate the emergence of the vernacular public accessed by a new Marathi literary world. This is perhaps why the court is not the epicenter for vernacularization; instead, it is the general public, in which the temple is being decentered, ironically, by spiritual innovators, who will engender the production of a new literature, typified by the *Jñāneśvarī*. The royal court, rules of literary aesthetics, or economies of literature, are not the interest of Chakradhar or the early Mahanubhavs. Instead, they grapple with social inequity, within their community, and outside, in the quotidian world around them.

We can see that Chakradhar was at the center of a changing tide in the public culture of his age. The rivalry between Guravs and Brahmins and, secondarily, between Kayasthas and Brahmins, and also the challenge Chakradhar appears to have given to the standard-bearers of the Brahminic ecumene of his age—these are all signs of this social transition. In this context it appears that the primary anxiety of this ecumene was not about a threat that Chakradhar, or others like him, posed to the literary, scriptural world of Sanskrit, but more about a threat he may have posed to an allied world of religious power, that of religion in public culture, circulating not just around the temple and its control, but within the burgeoning market of new spiritualisms.

As Cynthia Talbot has pointed out, in Andhra of around the same time, the Hindu temple was a node that connected several cultural worlds, public and religious, economic and political, among others. Thus the culture of "temple Hinduism" is much more than the temple itself. I would extend this argument to see that the rivalry between Brahmins and Guravs reveals a consistent struggle over some key aspects of public culture in thirteenth-century Maharashtra. If this was the nature of the rivalry noticed here, we can see, in the next chapter, another rivalry play out, one that may have been more detrimental to Chakradhar and the early Mahanubhavs, which sets up an opposition between them and the larger sphere of control within the Brahminic ecumene.

Chakradhar challenged Brahminic authority within his sect, but he did not necessarily encourage such a challenge outside his group of followers. An outright rebellion against social norms, as one finds among the "radical" ascetics of India (Kalamukhas, etc.),[111] or in the figure of Basava, would hardly have had the same effect as a more conservative, restricted, one might say "strategic" calibration of social critique, set more by example than by imposition. Thus, inside the world of the Mahanubhavs, caste and gender were subject to a radical new ethics, but, outside it, Chakradhar urged his followers to accommodate prevailing social practices. The creation of a literature was a natural extension of the Brahminic value of literacy at its core. However, the effects of that literarization would be to allow the restricted critique of caste and gender, inherent in much of the history of vernacularization in South Asia, to enter into literature in Marathi as a dominant theme. This combination of forces, a restricted critique of social inequality that accommodated everyday life and a challenge to the physical epicenter of the oral Marathi public sphere—the temple as emblematic—is the heart of the vernacularization that the *Jñāneśvarī* inherits.

However, we might now ask: why did the Mahanubhavs compose in Marathi? What purpose did this serve? How did the particular social ethics of the Mahanubhavs, within the field of the Yadava social world, induce the early Mahanubhavs to create the first work of Marathi literature, especially as their founder, Chakradhar, seemed rather uninterested in the literary world? In answering this question, we get a clearer image of the nature of the challenge and threat the Mahanubhavs posed to prevailing social norms in their age. We will see that the challenge was contained not so much in questions about a new literary medium as in the underlying social change such a shift in the field of the literary sphere would cause, creating lines of intersection between elite spheres of society and the quotidian masses that would threaten the heart of Brahminic orthodoxy in the Yadava century.

CHAPTER FIVE

The Mahanubhav Ethic

The greatest site of conflict in the Yadava century was within the realm of public religiosity, in which innovative spiritualists competed for followers and prestige. Conversely, little contest was apparent within the sphere of professional literary production. The seedbed of vernacularization was laid primarily in the field of public religious life, not in preexisting fields of professional literary production, but vernacularization would come to take a concrete form in the field of literacy. How did this social and religious movement come to represent itself in Marathi literature and thereby create our first extant record of Marathi literarization? What ethics underwrite this first work of Marathi literature?

The followers of Chakradhar are purported to have inaugurated Marathi literary vernacularization (or literarization) by producing the *Līḷācaritra* in 1278 as the written legacy of their founder's life. I have argued that this occurred because the Brahminic ecumene supported by the Yadavas instilled an impetus especially among Brahmins to set things down in writing, a literary habitus that motivated their actions. The relative indifference of the Yadava state and the Brahminic ecumene to Marathi literary production created an open space for Marathi literarization to occur, not in royal courts or institutions of state patronage, but rather in the field of public religious life in the world of the everyday. Into this field, Brahmin figures at the core of the Mahanubhav religion imported the social value of literacy inherited from the Brahminic ecumene into the new field of literary Marathi. This transfer of symbolic capital from a Sanskritic world to a

Marathi world is an essential feature of literarization in Marathi. Whether or not the *Līḷācaritra* was actually the first work of Marathi literature, my argument is that the literary field of the Brahminic ecumene motivated a new literary world in Marathi. The question for this chapter is: can we detect an ethical impulse residing within this literary innovation?

This chapter takes up the issue of literarization by exploring how and why the early Mahanubhavs elected to commit to literary form the words and deeds of Chakradhar in Marathi rather than in Sanskrit or another literary language. In addition, it discusses what Marathi meant in this period, particularly in contrast to Sanskrit, a question pertinent to the early Mahanubhavs because their founder was likely a Brahmin with high literacy in Sanskrit materials. In addition, as pointed out, almost all the key devotees of Chakradhar were Brahmins as well; many of the males among them were likely experts in Sanskrit literary materials, and this is especially true of Mhaibhat, the purported editor of the *Līḷācaritra*. The early Mahanubhavs, as well as Chakradhar, Changadev, and Gundam Raul, were all situated in relation to the Brahminic ecumene where Sanskrit was valorized along with literacy. Exploring why Marathi rather than Sanskrit was chosen as their primary literary medium helps us understand the cultural politics at work in the creation of the first vernacular literary text of the region. This allows us to tie social ethics and action with a new composition in an emergent literary language. This ethics will further reveal the "conversation" in public for which the *Līḷācaritra* serves as our antenna, allowing us to make out the lineaments of a discourse about social equality carried out in Marathi among elites and nonelites alike.

The *Līḷācaritra*

Immediately after the departure of Chakradhar from Maharashtra around 1273, his followers gathered under Bhatobas's leadership to record and transcribe their memories of Chakradhar in the *Līḷācaritra*. The text is said to have been written down and edited in 1278 by Mhaibhat, a highly learned Brahmin of Maharashtra. The election of Mhaibhat for this role is interesting, as we will see, for he is clearly a recruit from the upper echelons of the Brahminic ecumene in the Yadava century. Though he joins the Mahanubhav order rather late in its formation, he is also most clearly in possession of the highest literary capital and experience of the group.

The *Līlācaritra* inaugurates centuries of literary production by the Mahanubhavs; indeed, next to the Varkaris, there is no single social entity that sustains such a rich or prolific body of literature over the centuries and right up to the present.[1] Though we think of the Mahanubhavs (like the Varkaris) as a religious community, they are also a *literary community*, resembling the Varkaris in this as well. How this literary community began, and why they chose a particular language as the primary literary medium of their community, is the story of this chapter.

Chakradhar did not compose the *Līlācaritra*, but rather his followers after his departure did so; yet the content of the *Līlācaritra* is Chakradhar's life, words, and actions. In some fundamental sense, he is its object and subject, its "prime agent," I would say, though he is not the text's literary composer. While we often refer to Mhaibhat as the author of the *Līlācaritra*, he was in fact its editor and compiler, according to historical memory, a person who took down the details of the remembrances of others; Mhaibhat was a scribe and editor in the main, and as a late addition to the Mahanubhavs (perhaps joining them six to twelve months before Chakradhar's departure), he depended on long-standing members of the community to convey the data he required, the remembrances that are called lilas or "plays" in this text. Where the *Jñāneśvarī* has a purported author—Jnandev[2]—the *Līlācaritra* is a text with many authors, but a single subject—Chakradhar. The figure of Chakradhar is the prevailing logic of the text in every way including language. In this study, therefore, I consider the *Līlācaritra* to be a text whose agent is Chakradhar, and, as such, the text serves to transmit his voice and actions—whatever the historical reality of that content.

The *Līlācaritra* is as unadorned a reflection of Chakradhar as possible, keeping in mind the ways in which human memory operates when recalling the past. I say this knowing that the text, as with all texts perhaps, may be "unreliable" in a positivist historical sense; as a product of many centuries of human preservation the text, like all texts, has changed over the years. And so I take it that the *Līlācaritra*, in the form in which it is conveyed in historical memory in general in Maharashtra, encodes the life, words, and deeds of Chakradhar as collectively chronicled by his followers. For this reason, text and agent are inseparable—Chakradhar and the *Līlācaritra* join to form the first work of Marathi literature that we have.

The *Līlācaritra* is interesting in another way. While the *Jñāneśvarī* is clearly a work of theology, philosophy, and (secondarily) social critique, it is all couched within the sphere of dharma, the quasi-religious, quasi-social concept of the proper functioning of society and cosmic reality, and so the text is primarily a theological and philosophical treatise. As such, the *Jñāneśvarī* is fundamentally a didactic text. The *Līḷācaritra*, though it also engages dharma, theology, and philosophy, in addition to politics, history, culture, economics, and many other subjects, is still fundamentally a text meant to accurately record of the life of Chakradhar above all. Because of this deep commitment to "the facts" of Chakradhar's life, the prose of the *Līḷācaritra* conforms to a kind of historical literary realism.[3] Chakradhar commands his followers to "remember me as you have seen me," and the implication of veracity in this command is faithfully carried out by his followers in the *Līḷācaritra*.[4] Certainly the text is devotional, as the source of Chakradhar's teachings, as well as hagiographical, as it records the life of the founder and deity of the Mahanubhav community. Yet the aesthetic and intended effect of the text is far more similar to the Marathi chronicle genre that will emerge a few centuries later, called *bakhar*, than it is to either the *Jñāneśvarī* or to the devotional songs of the sants of the region (abhang), or to the hagiographies that will emerge after Namdev (1270–1350).[5] Thus the first text of Marathi literature is a text that one can describe heuristically as a work of historical literary realism.

If the *Līḷācaritra* is a historical chronicle, and the primary subject of its history is Chakradhar, which also makes it a biography, I hesitate to call it a hagiography for reasons I will discuss further on in this chapter. I use the term *historical* here not to assign this text a place in Indian literary typology—the lack of the existence of such a form has been at the center of a long and ongoing debate in South Asia studies.[6] This is not a subject that must be belabored: those who do not think that India has "history" before modernity are grappling with a problem germane to modern historiography, not to India's record of its past. I refer to the text as "literary realism" to touch upon the way it sought to preserve a record of the past in exact detail, with particular attention to everyday life, as an unadorned record of actual events in chronological and geographical order—to historicize as exactly as possible and with great attention to location was inherently a feature of the religion and devotional orthodoxy of the Mahanubhavs. It is essential to the theological purpose of the text to give the richest possible details to their remembrance of Chakradhar so that nothing would be forgotten. This means the *Līḷācaritra* contains vivid, even tedious, details of everyday life. Political events and the names and lives of political leaders, kings, and ministers are amply recorded. We have notes about all sorts of features of daily life: food and food prices; weather conditions; descriptions of towns, villages, and cities; common rituals of all sorts; various trades and occupations; the curiosities of specific Marathi argots and euphemisms, and so on.[7] Almost every lila records a dialogue, and often this dialogue is inflected with efforts to record argot, accent, and so on; on more than one occasion an observer notes that Chakradhar speaks Marathi well for a Gujarati; in several cases Chakradhar imitates the speech of others, and this is captured in peculiar Marathi phonetics. Another sign of this realism, and the historical impetus behind it, is the fact that we get a picture of Chakradhar that is "warts and all." He is displayed as quick tempered sometimes, as somewhat harsh at other times; he appears to gamble, and this is carried forward into stories in which it appears Chakradhar does not like to lose games, even to children, who cry when they are defeated by Chakradhar.[8] These are of course the features of lila, and Mahanubhavs interpret these episodes as the unique configuration of the Chakradhar's divine status, of the fact that Chakradhar does things that are beyond human fathoming. One final effect of the literary realism of the *Līḷācaritra* is the relative lack of "miracles" for a story about a divine person. This is highly unusual in South Asia or elsewhere—such as in Catholicism where every saint must evince a miracle in order to qualify for sainthood. There are almost no miracles associated with Chakradhar, save those that surround his purported disfiguration and decapitation. Instead, we see Chakradhar as a highly skilled human being with a tremendous charisma, yet perhaps more than any "normal" person. For example, at one point in the *Līḷācaritra*, as we will see, Chakradhar is poisoned. He does not cure the poison through a miracle, but rather through assiduously drinking milk, and his treatment takes a great toll on his health, as the text records. For this reason I find the term *hagiography* too loaded with assumptions about divine intervention and miraculous effect to adequately describe this unique text. There is no doubt that the Mahanubhavs worship Chakradhar (as well as Gundam Raul and Changadev) as deities (manifestations of the one deity, Parameshwar), and it is part of their theology of his divinity that each of his actions and words should be preserved exactly as they happened. In the *Līḷācaritra* historical literary realism is technically a theological position.

In describing the *Līḷācaritra* as historical literary realism, I find a particular parallel with Sanskrit texts of roughly the same period, such as the *Rājataraṅgiṇī* (c. twelfth century) and *Prabandha Cintāmaṇi* (early fourteenth century). Daud Ali states that both texts "seemed to be characterized by great 'realism'" because they "portrayed everyday life," giving them a "tantalizingly 'historical' character."[9] Ali wisely distances himself from Orientalist-era claims that the *Rājataraṅgiṇī*, for example, was premodern India's one and only work of something like historical writing. But Ali's point is that these texts, though shot through with "the magical and supernatural," did not represent "'failed' historical consciousness, but a conceptualization of the past that was the product of significant shifts at the turn of the millennium in Western India."[10] These historically inflected narratives Ali calls "useable pasts."[11] I would argue that the *Līḷācaritra* is a preeminent example of just such a useable past, a text that sought to preserve an accurate record of the past, but in a context at a far remove from modern historical writing or modern literary realism.

The *Līḷācaritra* has very little to say explicitly about the use of Marathi rather than another language current within the Yadava century, such as Gujarati or Kannada, and especially Sanskrit. The *Līḷācaritra*'s primary statement about the use of Marathi is the text itself, that is, the record of Chakradhar's voice. The early Mahanubhavs used Marathi because this was historically accurate: it was the language Chakradhar spoke, even though it was not his first language. Yet nowhere in the text is there an explanation of why Chakradhar chose to speak in Marathi. Practical concerns would have guided him away from his native Gujarati, which would have been uncommon (but familiar) in the Deccan towns and villages where he circulated. He is also said to have traveled through the South, especially the regions of Kannada and Telugu, and lived there for many years—presumably he would have spoken the languages of these regions as well. But it is less clear why Sanskrit lost out. As the lingua franca of South Asia at the time, Sanskrit was well-known to Chakradhar, the *Līḷācaritra* tells us, and to at least his male Brahmin followers if not also, perhaps, to a fair number of his female Brahmin followers.

The remainder of this chapter will use the *Līḷācaritra* to infer a likely rationale and ethics for the use of Marathi, especially in lieu of Sanskrit. To foreground this discussion, though, we should observe two things. First, we must understand the associations not just of region but also of class, caste, and particularly gender that accompanied the use of Marathi in this period in general. We have explored this subject to some degree in part 1, confined to the uses of the Yadava state and the Brahminic ecumene, and we return to it here, placed within the larger Brahminic ecumene, the taxomonies of Sanskrit, and the possible position of a regional language like Marathi within that Brahminic Sanskrit world. Second, we can observe that Chakradhar's followers, faced with the task of preserving Chakradhar's legacy, viewed the use of Marathi rather than Sanskrit as essential to conveying their teacher's legacy in the future. We can then see more clearly the contours of a rationale for the use of Marathi by Chakradhar and the early Mahanubhavs, hence a motivation for literary vernacularization itself. We will conclude by engaging the story of Chakradhar's trial to see how the various strands of this chapter and the previous one may be read in the judgment of the tribunal, a moment that not only registers a transgression of normative everyday life but also signals the swirl of discourse in public culture around issues of caste, gender, and language, the first formations of a nascent public sphere.

Marathi and the Taxonomies of Sanskrit

How might the Brahminic ecumene described in the *Līḷācaritra*, preoccupied as it was with Sanskrit literary glory, have viewed Marathi? If, as I have argued, the language of the general literary and intellectual public sphere during the Yadava century was Sanskrit—enforced by a social and economic order of entitlements and gifts largely composed of Brahmins and deeply concerned with the production of Sanskrit texts— then it is important to understand the view this Brahminic ecumene may have taken of Marathi within the matrix of the Indo-Aryan linguistic continuum in which it is situated.

The Sanskrit linguistic world presents a view of itself and other languages ordered in a hierarchical taxonomy governed by religion, class, caste, and gender, primarily; in other words, Sanskrit, from its earliest Vedic forms to the present, has been described by its scholars and practitioners as a language suited for a very narrow and elite subset of people: high-caste males.[12] In a very general sense, then, the linguistic world is divided between Sanskrit and everything else. Sanskrit was a language used by Gods, Brahmin and other high-caste men, and at times certain women, particularly ascetics, queens, and other exceptional females who represented "power" in the male-dominated fields of Sanskrit usage. Everyone else is attributed some version of a Prakrit language, a "natural" or "ordinary" language, or of various "corrupted" or *apabhramsha* languages, primarily of northern India.[13] Marathi, like all North-Indian Indo-Aryan languages other than Sanskrit, is considered a form of this "ordinary" and "corrupted" genealogy, even though it is not likely that Marathi is "derived" from any language, whether Sanskrit or even any considered Prakrits. In other words, I do not think Marathi is *derived* from anything, but is likely a language with a unique origin on the subcontinent in the region of Maharashtra that long predates its uses in inscription or its references in other Sanskrit texts, even if that ur-language has been modified by many languages along the way. For Marathi, these would be Sanskrit, of course, but also importantly Persian, as well as Konkani, Kannada, etc. Despite this, in the taxonomies of Sanskrit historical philology, Marathi is an example of a Prakrit, a language of "nature," gendered in the feminine, and associated with the autochthonous field. In an intellectual world dominated by Brahminic Sanskritic learning such as the Yadava century, it is useful to see how this field of knowledge might have understood the literary value of Marathi.

In Sanskrit dramas, women and low-caste men would speak some version of Prakrit, such as Maharashtri, a language associated with the region of Maharashtra and in particular the Satavahana Empire (c. third century BCE to third century CE). Maharashtri is sometimes described as the origin of Marathi, though I think this is very unlikely. Instead, I find it more likely that Maharashtri is the attempt to represent the language of the region of Maharashtra within the phonological world of Sanskrit. It is, in this sense, a representation of an actual spoken language, but not an origin for that language. Marathi becomes connected to Maharashtri through its status as an apabhramsha language within the Sanskrit typological system.[14] Thus Marathi, from the point of view of Sanskrit linguistic or grammatical typology, is a language inferior in status to Sanskrit, twice-removed and "corrupted" in a sense through Maharashtri and regional apabhramsha dialects, and this inferiority is registered by the fact that it is considered a language suitable primarily for women and low-caste men—here we see age old associations with the land and nature, on the one hand, and women or the "demotic," on the other.

This taxonomy became canonical well before the Common Era. For example, Jains first used the Prakrit language Ardhamaghadi and Buddhists composed in the Prakrit language Pali in part to excise themselves from the fields of Brahminic superiority represented by Sanskrit: these new religions of the sixth and fifth centuries BCE—Jainism and Buddhism—rejected the social orthodoxy of varna and admitted women into their monastic communities, in contradistinction to what we might call Vedic Brahminic Hinduism of the age. The early rejection of Sanskrit was, in a sense, an acceptance of its taxonomic world—Jains and Buddhists excluded Sanskrit as a means to position themselves in opposition to the social and religious ideas represented by the language. Curiously, however, Buddhists in particular would return to Sanskrit for practical purposes—to make their debates with Hindus and others standardized to a single language, a reflection of a shared discursive economy among Jains, Buddhists, and the rest ("Hindus," for lack of a better word), which is to say, the Sanskrit cosmopolis.[15] Within the Sanskritic cosmopolitan sphere we also see this taxonomy in force. As noted, this is amply displayed in Sanskrit drama and epic literature, where women and low-caste men use languages other than Sanskrit, imperfect languages of place as well as social location. Yet this hierarchy did not always imply inferiority. As Madhav Deshpande notes, a key theoretician of poetic aesthetics, Rajashekhar, in his *Kāvyamīmāṃsā* of around 900, describes Prakrit as a language that is "feminine and delicate" as opposed to the "masculine and terse" nature of Sanskrit; hence for Rajashekhar, a Prakrit language like Marathi is the more appropriate medium for poetry and emotion.[16] We can draw from this not only the clear sense in which Sanskrit is a masculine high-caste language reserved for particular purposes and people, but also that the mastery of the entire linguistic spectrum—Sanskrit, Prakrit, and other "corrupted, natural" forms—was still within the domain of a certain learned Sanskritic sphere. Thus while Jains and Buddhists, at early stages of their literary production, did not use Sanskrit, they used the nomenclature and philosophical worlds inaugurated and sustained by Sanskrit, and in rejecting the use of Sanskrit they yet participated in a self-conscious positioning within the Sanskrit cosmopolis. After all, the Prakrit speech of women in classical plays and epic texts was created for the most part by high-caste men as a feature of the Sanskrit public and literary sphere, as a marker of social distinction. Whether or not this actually reflected a real-world or quotidian reality of language use is a much harder question to answer—and beyond my ken in any case. But I point this out for, as we know, the surviving materials we have that display the inauguration of Marathi as a literary language both emerge from the genius of members of the Brahminic ecumene of the thirteenth century, even if at its periphery and only to critique its origins. Like the Buddhist and Jain literary production before it, the advent of the Marathi literary field in the thirteenth century is a critique from *within* a Sanskritic Brahminic ecumene, a shared epistemology that exhibits radical and divergent interpretations, and this inner nature of the criticism of social restrictions placed on Sanskrit will naturally display a degree of ambivalence, as the last chapter on Jnandev and the *Jñāneśvarī* will make plain.[17]

The sense from within the Brahminic ecumene in which the "ordinary" and "natural" languages of India in this period are "feminine" is borne out in highly self-conscious ways in both the *Līḷācaritra* and in the *Jñāneśvarī*. As we will see in the next chapter, Marathi is referred to as a "maiden" on several occasions in the *Jñāneśvarī*; the poetic meter of the text is the *ovi*, a form associated in popular memory with women's working songs.[18] And we might also note that one of the most popular names for Jnandev in Marathi is *māulī* or "mother," a term that describes him as "mother" to his devotees, but perhaps also progenitor of Marathi literature.[19]

Similarly, the *Līḷācaritra* implies this connection between the use of Marathi and gender. Although we have no clear statement attributed to Chakradhar about why he used Marathi rather than Sanskrit as his medium of communication, we can notice that his initial followers are women, both in his "solo" period, when he first befriends a fellow yogi, the female ascetic Muktabai,[20] and when he acquires his first disciple, Baisa, in the period that marks the end of his solo time. The prominent presence of women (many of whom were widows), within the ascetical nonsexual community of Mahanubhav renunciates is one of the primary social features of Chakradhar's circle of followers, and it will also become one of the chief complaints the tribunal raises against him. In any case, a group dominated by women in the thirteenth-century Maharashtra, even Brahmin women, would be a group in which Marathi was the dominant language. Aside from a mythic morphology of the language, Marathi also has a sociocultural location relevant to gender and caste.

Though the idea that Marathi was derived in a second-order way from Sanskrit may be fanciful, the associations with gender and caste do not appear to be. As a medium to communicate among women especially, Marathi was clearly essential to Chakradhar, and Marathi was also essential for leaving an intelligible, accessible legacy for the generations of Mahanubhavs that would form and flourish after Chakradhar's departure from Maharashtra. A story in the transmission of the *Līḷācaritra* makes clear why and how women were so essential to Mahanubhav religion. The story recalls that during invasions of the Deccan by Sultanate armies in the last decade of the thirteenth century, all extant written copies of the *Līḷācaritra* were destroyed by accident during the chaos of war. The text survived because the female devotee Hiraisa had committed it to memory.[21] We can see this emphasis on gender, access, and language in the wake of Chakradhar's departure, where a push to convey Chakradhar's message to all his followers across caste and gender lines becomes a key subject. The record of this period is the *Smṛtisthaḷa*.

Shortly after Bhatobas's death in the early fourteenth century, his biography was compiled by various followers and likely completed by the latter half of the fourteenth century, in a text called the *Smṛtisthaḷa* or "A Collection of Memories."[22] This text, as Feldhaus and Tulpule describe it, shows the followers of Chakradhar and Bhatobas as they "remember, interpret, and try to apply the teachings" of their absent leaders.[23] In this text we see the early Mahanubhavs, bereft of their original leadership, struggling over what Weber might have identified as "routinization": what should the essential teachings of the order be? How should they conduct themselves? What modes of succession should then be put in place? And, vitally, what language(s) should they use to preserve their faith?

Of over three hundred works attributed to the Mahanubhavs from the thirteenth century to the beginning of the nineteenth century that Ian Raeside records, we find twenty-two texts written in Sanskrit.[24] Most of those Sanskrit works appear in the early, formative years of the religion in the fourteenth century, when a good number of devotees were Brahmin.[25] Most of them are commentaries on the *Līḷācaritra*, *Sūtrapāṭha*, and other aspects of Chakradhar's teachings, and they all appear to be composed (or attributed to) male Brahmin devotees (especially Mhaibhat and Kesobas), which is the norm for all early Mahanubhav literature in Sanskrit or Marathi. The remaining texts, and importantly the *Līḷācaritra*, as well as the *Smṛtisthaḷa*, *Sūtrapāṭha*, and *Sthānapothī*, among other texts, were all in Marathi. The choice of Marathi was therefore not a foregone conclusion but a conscientious decision.

The *Smṛtisthaḷa* records a debate among the early Mahanubhavs about the appropriate language to use in producing a literary archive and commentarial tradition for their sect. That this was an issue at all is a further reflection of the deeply ingrained value of literary writing already vibrant within the small Brahmin-dominated community of the Mahanubhavs. Many of these followers would have been skilled in Sanskrit and may have viewed it as the appropriate medium for so lofty a goal as recording and remembering the lives and teachings of the founders of the Mahanubhav faith. Yet, as Feldhaus and Tulpule note, even though the Mahanubhavs who produced the *Smṛtisthaḷa,* for example, were almost all Brahmins, "the world to which the group portrayed in the *Smṛtisthaḷa* sees itself opposed is primarily that of Brahminical Hinduism."[26] And part of this opposition was the practical, ethical, and historical decision to use Marathi rather than Sanskrit. At several points in the *Smṛtisthaḷa*, Brahminism, as a thing distinct from Brahmins themselves, is highlighted and ridiculed.[27] Brahmin male Mahanubhavs generally were required to cut their Brahminic "top knot" and were forbidden from wearing their Brahminic thread.[28] Thus the early Mahanubhavs evinced an irony: a group of Brahmins who opposed Brahminism, as we saw in the *Līḷācaritra* in the last chapter. And part of this struggle with Brahminism, at least as displayed in these early texts, was a struggle with the use of Sanskrit or Marathi.

While it bears repeating that Sanskrit was not the private domain of Brahmins in the history of South Asia, or in the region of Maharashtra, the association between Brahmins and Sanskrit is indelible in the Mahanubhav materials, as it is in the *Jñāneśvarī* and indeed, as I have argued in part 1, throughout the Yadava realm and well beyond the thirteenth century. The *Smṛtisthaḷa* displays the use of Sanskrit among several key figures—Bhatobas, Mhaibhat, and Kesobas primarily[29]—and these uses highlight the contentions around language among the early Mahanubhavs. For example, at one point Bhatobas differentiates between two devotees, Kesobas and Pandit. Although both can compose in Sanskrit, only Pandit can compose in Marathi too, a testament to Pandit's superiority over Kesobas in this case.[30]

Mahanubhavs in contemporary India regularly recalled to me two other incidents from the *Smṛtisthaḷa* when I would ask them about the privileging of Marathi as the medium of their literary materials over Sanskrit. In the first incident, recorded early in the *Smṛtisthaḷa*, Kesobas composed in Sanskrit a text, the *Ratnamāla* or "Garland of Gems," a commentary on a selection of passages from the *Līḷācaritra*. He presented this text to Bhatobas, who praised it.[31] However, when Kesobas proposed to compose a portion of what would become a chapter of the *Sūtrapāṭha*, the sayings of Chakradhar, Bhatobas instructed him not to use Sanskrit, for, if he did, this would "deprive" his *mhātāriyā*, his "elderly women."[32] The word used by Bhatobas for "deprive," *nāgavane*, literally means "to undress," to strip naked, and implies theft, shame, and ruination—a description particularly potent when applied to the female followers among the Mahanubhavs. The implication is that all women (but also non-high caste men) would have no access to Chakradhar's teachings if they were preserved in Sanskrit. This injunction, delivered with some vehemence, quells Kesobas's desire to represent the direct teachings of Chakradhar in any language other than Marathi, though commentaries, translations, and other texts in Sanskrit were permissible and do exist, as noted. This incident is drawn from a rather simple reality of the quotidian world: women, by and large, did not know Sanskrit, nor did the general public of the Yadava century. The rationale is hardly theological and just barely registers a social ethic. It is really much more a matter of "common sense," but its effects will be profound.

The second incident often cited by contemporary Mahanubhav devotees to me as a rationale for the use of Marathi implies a theological and didactic rationale for Marathi, and a historical one, based on the life of the religion's founder. This was also the incident they most often recounted about why the early Mahanubhavs used Marathi rather than Sanskrit, perhaps because it carries some of the humor so often present in early Mahanubhav literature. Again, Kesobas raises the issue of Sanskrit: "One day Pandit and Kesobas were conversing [with Bhatobas]. Kesobas asked a question in the Sanskrit language. In response, Bhatobas said, 'Pandit, Keshavadeva, I do not understand your "hences" (*asmāt*) and "whences" (*kasmāt*). Chakradhar taught me in Marathi. Ask [questions] in that [language].' Then they agreed [to do so]."[33] Bhatobas chides his two followers by using the Sanskrit words *asmāt* and *kasmāt*, words that appear in verbal formulae within high rhetorical argumentation, as Feldhaus and Tulpule note, a kind of parody of obscure philosophical debate in Sanskrit.[34] At other points, as well, the *Smṛtisthaḷa* displays the use of Sanskrit within quotidian life in ways that both emphasize how special Sanskrit is, how it marks a particular kind of social distinction, but also how this social distinction can be a subject of humor. In one episode Mhaibhat and

Lakshmidharba are mistaken for thieves. As they are about to be beaten, Mhaibhat says to his companion in Sanskrit, with a kind of verbal shrug, "Either a fever or a weapon," referring to two ways to die, as in "everyone has to die of something."[35] This invocation of Sanskrit is enough to persuade the gathered crowd that Mhaibhat and his companion are not thieves—for how would a common thief speak Sanskrit?

Such moments may appear to contradict the praise Bhatobas gave to Kesobas for his Sanskrit commentary on sections of the *Līḷācaritra*, the *Ratnamāla*. The passage in which Kesobas and Pandit questioned Bhatobas in Sanskrit, however, portrays a pedagogical, living environment, and it appears as if Bhatobas, in addition to citing historical precedent, is protesting the gender and caste exclusion that such group discussions would imply if they took place in Sanskrit. For this reason, perhaps, he invokes Chakradhar to remind Kesobas and Pandit, and others, that the primary medium of instruction while Chakradhar was among them, particularly oral instruction, was Marathi. This injunction to speak in Marathi would become a kind of linguistic orthodoxy among the Mahanubhavs where Marathi would become the standard language for oral instruction and the de facto language for textual preservation for similar reasons in Maharashtra.

Put another way, Marathi was the language of the quotidian—of the "elderly women" as a rather sexist (and ageist) metonym for the everyday sphere of interaction—the language Chakradhar used every day, when a theological lesson might emerge during a stroll, a meal, a wrestling match, or the waning of a long day. Commentary and other kinds of materials could be composed in Sanskrit, and appreciated, but the essential transmission of the Mahanubhav teachings, formed during the routines of everyday life in Chakradhar's presence, would require Marathi, not because of a particular regional or cultural pride associated with the language, but because this was the language of Chakradhar, a language he used so that he could communicate with all his followers, women and non-Brahmins especially.

Vernacularizing Chakradhar Through Marathi in the *Līḷācaritra*

Among all the subjects the *Līḷācaritra* enfolds, one is a statement about the cultural politics of Marathi vernacularization, even while its chief character is not "Maharashtrian" but "Gujarati" and not a native speaker of

Marathi but of Gujarati; indeed, as Haripal (Chakradhar's father) points out, Chakradhar goes to reside in enemy territory and a foreign land when he leaves Gujarat for Maharashtra. Chakradhar is an émigré. This represents a cultural politics that is deeply tied with the concept of place as well as an investment in the culture of place. As we saw in the last chapter, Chakradhar observes his surroundings with ethnographic precision, imitating language, actions, and the habits of the people that draw his attention. If part of vernacularization is the transformation of a place into a literary medium and affect, the *Līḷācaritra* is emblematic of this process, a text deeply invested in its location, both geographic and cultural, as well as political, as we will see.

One of the ways in which the *Līḷācaritra* is both eminently historical and vernacular is the way in which it pays very careful attention to the exact places Chakradhar visited while he was in the region of Maharashtra. When one reads the *Līḷācaritra*, one notices that nearly every lila begins by situating its narrative in a place, and almost all places enumerated in the text are restricted to the region that the Mahanubhavs themselves call Maharashtra in the *Līḷācaritra*. In other words, the general form of any given lila is to locate itself first in a place, and often in time as well (usually time of day), which is to "vernacularize," in a sense. Yet the *Līḷācaritra* begins with Chakradhar outside Maharashtra, in Gujarat (where Changadev also chose to reside, after leaving Phaltan, in Maharashtra, to travel to Dvaraka). And the *Līḷācaritra* ends with Chakradhar leaving Maharashtra, moving toward Ujjain, while he commands his followers to remain behind. The text therefore constructs notional geopolitical borders, or, as Anne Feldhaus perceptively argues, at least oppositions, distinctions between regions; it is a Maharashtrian text in language and geography.[36] In this sense the *Līḷācaritra* is a text that not only uses the language of place, but one that uses place itself to root the text in what I consider a careful outlined geography that will later become a sacred geography to the Mahanubhavs. The Mahanubhav religion is initiated and sustained in this region, and the *Līḷācaritra*, providing the primary material for the *Sthānapothī* or "Book of Places" that recalls where Chakradhar traveled, knits together a sacred geography for the Mahanubhavs that is coterminous with the region they call Maharashtra. The vernacularizing effect of the *Līḷācaritra* is not merely in its choice of the language of the region as its medium but also in the full embrace of geopositionality, of making "place" a key logic to the text as well.

As Chakradhar's time in Maharashtra comes to an end, we see him consolidating his theology and ethics with his core group of followers. In this context he makes several demands of them, which become the canonical statements of the *Līlācaritra* and the *Sūtrapāṭha*.[37] Here is Anne Feldhaus's translation of those statements preserved in the *Sūtrapāṭha:*[38]

Stay in places where you know no one and no one knows you. || XII.22 ||

Do not go to the Kannada country or the Telugu country. Those regions
　　are full of sense pleasure. There ascetics are honorable. || XII.23 ||

Stay in Maharashtra. || XII.24 ||

Do not go to Matapura or Kolhapura. Those proud places create obstacles
　　for those practicing religion. || XII.25 ||

Throw away your life at the foot of a tree at the end of the land. || XII.26 ||

These sutras or statements of instruction given by Chakradhar are primarily meant to convey to the early Mahanubhavs that they should not seek out places of comfort where ascetics will be treated well, such as the Kannada or Telugu regions (also places of Chakradhar's early life) or Matapur or Kolhapur. They should stay in Maharashtra "at the foot of a tree at the end of the land." But why? Anne Feldhaus has presented several compelling answers to this question. She notes that Chakradhar demands that his followers speak and compose in Marathi, and so restricting the movements of his followers to Maharashtra confines them to this linguistic area but also reveals their loyalty to Marathi.[39] While Kannada, more often than Marathi or Sanskrit, is the language of inscription among the Yadavas, particularly in the time of Chakradhar's floruit, the areas around Devgiri, the areas traversed by Chakradhar for the most part, are within the Marathi-speaking heartland.[40] Chakradhar's commitment to Marathi, a language foreign to him,[41] is not for the love of the language itself—whereas for Jnandev his love of Marathi *as a literary language* will be apparent. Chakradhar likely chose Marathi because this is the dominant language of everyday life in the regions around Devgiri, where most of his life and teaching took place. Marathi was the language of the quotidian world in which Chakradhar flourished.

Feldhaus also points out that the injunction in the *Līḷācaritra* and the *Sūtrapāṭha* to "stay in Maharashtra" appears to indicate that Chakradhar does not want his followers seeking easier lands in which to live.[42] Maharashtra is a difficult place to be for the wandering mendicant, or so it seems, and suffering is a key component of the religious practice of the Mahanubhavs—hence Chakradhar commands that they stay in a land not amenable to them, the land of Maharashtra.[43] This may strike the reader as odd given that it seems Chakradhar and the Mahanubhav order flourished in the Yadava century, that is until Chakradhar ran afoul of Hemadri and other powerful Brahmin figures. This statement to stay in Maharashtra, located toward the conclusion of the *Līḷācaritra*, comes as Chakradhar's fortunes have turned in the region.[44] It is a curious injunction—that his followers remain in a land of jeopardy. Feldhaus points out the irony here, noting that in later commentaries Maharashtra is praised as a land of "physical and psychological benefits . . . [and] moral superiority."[45] I get the sense that Chakradhar implores his followers to stay in Maharashtra because the land has been marked by his presence—its geography is also his own history.

As Weber pointed out, in religion, as in states and other formations of society, the personal charisma of a figure gives way, after his or her death, to a routinization of that charisma.[46] Literally, the routes of Chakradhar, trailing through an inhospitable land for his followers, become the sacred geography for the movement he founded and thus their "home," however rough it may be.[47] Hence Feldhaus's observation about later commentaries referring to the region as a "great land" that is "blissful and beneficial."[48] The passages seem to indicate two things at once: stay out of places where you will find too many comforts and stay in Maharashtra, where you know the language and you know your way around, where you will find the places Chakradhar has been. It appears to argue that one's own "vernacular" (place, language, culture), even if it be hard and inhospitable, is better than another's vernacular, however enticing it may be.

The function of this routinization is to domesticate and make "local" the foreign figure of Chakradhar, to make him "Marathi" in some fundamental sense. Chakradhar, literally and literarily, is vernacularized by the *Līḷācaritra*, and by extension, the *Sthānapothī*, *Sūtrapāṭha*, and other texts. He is written into the language of the place—Marathi—and into the place itself, through the network of *sthāns* or locations where he halted during his life and the many sutras in Marathi that record his teachings. The *Līḷācaritra* is not a literary endeavor in terms of its primary aim, but it is an endeavor to vernacularize a figure whose life and sayings, preserved in a language of place, will become the core of a new religion. The literary realism of the text is instrumental in configuring a vision of vernacularization that collapses time, place, language, and idiom. In a reverse sort of way, Chakradhar has vernacularized Maharashtra. Just as we saw in chapter 2 with the inscriptions from Pandharpur in 1311 that described Maharashtra as a land of Vitthal devotees, for the Mahanubhavs Maharashtra becomes the land of Chakradhar's life's legacy, a map drawn by the places he has been—in both cases land and faith become one and the same.

The goal of the *Līḷācaritra*, in this sense, was not to inaugurate a new literary genre in a regional language, but to articulate a foreign religious leader, Chakradhar, with the geocultural zone of Maharashtra and its everyday life (time, place, language). The process of vernacularization was not literary but contextual, a process of situating Chakradhar in the quotidian contexts of Maharashtra. And this geocultural zone is not merely "Maharashtra" but encompasses its particular public culture, its "hostility" perhaps but also its "blissful and beneficial" qualities. Marathi, not Sanskrit, circumscribes the boundaries—linguistic and geographic—of the early Mahanubhavs and their texts, and this linguistic medium expands a different set of boundaries, those of caste and gender in particular, in the formation not just of a vernacular literature, but a vernacular space. Chakradhar speaks the language of heterogeneity rooted in place.

It is clear, I think, why the Mahanubhavs chose Marathi to convey Chakradhar's teachings into the future, but it is less clear why Chakradhar himself used Marathi when he could have preserved his teachings in Sanskrit, which would have allowed them to spread over a much wider, and far more elite, field of literature.

Chakradhar, Language, and Cultural Politics

Chakradhar was clearly a polyglot. The *Līḷācaritra* records him speaking Marathi, primarily, but also Gujarati and Sanskrit, as we will see. Given that Kannada was one of the routine regional languages of the Yadava century, we may speculate that he knew Kannada as well; and since he also lived in the Andhra region, his followers might have remembered him to be a Telugu speaker too. Indeed, Chakradhar's comfort with language is a common subject in the *Līḷācaritra*. At several points in the text people comment upon how well Chakradhar speaks Marathi despite his foreign origins. Naturally, we must assume he spoke Marathi to communicate with his followers in Maharashtra, but can we detect other reasons for the use of Marathi attributed to Chakradhar?

One consistent feature of Chakradhar's personality repeated in the *Līḷācaritra* is his ability to mimic aspects of culture, especially conventions of caste and language. We can observe a fascinating example, given toward the end of the *Līḷācaritra*, in which Chakradhar confounds his followers by his seemingly strange behavior outside a temple, a passage foretold earlier in the book, that tells us of how Chakradhar understood Shudras to speak and worship:

After the morning worship was over, Chakradhar wandered off to a temple. Baisa was understood to be the leader among the devotees who accompanied Chakradhar. In the temple's assembly hall, Chakradhar removed his shirt and hung it up; he wrapped his turban around his waist. He applied ash to his forehead like the Shudras do. Then he went by the drainage line [outside the temple] and stood there. He joined his hands together.

Then he said, "Sorathi Somnath! Aundha Naganath! Paraliya Vaijanath! One hundred Lingas! One thousand Lingas! One hundred thousand Lingas! [I do] prostration [to them]! [I do] one prostration [to them]! Bless Saya! Bless Maya! Bless Kaya! Bless Saubai! Bless Maubai! Bless Kaubai!"[49]

And then Chakradhar folded his hands and came towards the devotees [and said], "O Elders, this is pure! O Elders, this is pure."

Then Baisa said, "What is this, sir?"

Chakradhar said, "Woman, this is how the Shudras encounter God."

This story appears to depict Chakradhar replicating the way in which Shudras were required to worship at Hindu temples, in particular, at a Shaiva temple, and doing so by repeating physical actions and especially verbal formulae in an argot of Marathi that we are to understand is particular to Shudras. That Shudras were forced to remain outside of the temple, standing near the drainage line that would have carried the leavings of offerings from within the temple to the outside, is clear from this passage. This was perhaps the opportunity afforded to Shudras for acquiring prasad or materials offered to the deity in the temple, blessed, and then returned to devotees in part. Standing at the drainage line, Chakradhar intones a specific verbal formula in which he calls out names of other famous Shaiva temples and provides a verbal "prostration" to them all. He then asks for the blessings of three boys and three girls by name, and the alliteration of their names implies naming practices, or at least stereotypes about these. He concludes by addressing his own followers as if he were a Shudra, "in character," in a sense, calling them elders and declaring that his act is pure, that he has not transgressed any rules of purity; this too we might conclude was a verbal formula required of Shudras. Chakradhar's followers are sufficiently unaware of Shudra practice that they must ask for clarification, and so we might also assume that none of Chakradhar's followers are Shudras in this moment.

Chakradhar seems to be linking language and caste, situated in a quotidian moment of daily worship, to demonstrate to his followers the narrow confines of their own experience. As a foreigner, an ethnographic "other" in a sense, Chakradhar participates and observes in order to teach his followers a socialcultural lesson about inequity, to show them "how the other half lives," as the saying goes. The link between colloquial language, on the one hand, and caste and gender, on the other, is not severable in South Asia. Though nowhere, to my knowledge, does Chakradhar say that he uses Marathi to unravel and reveal caste distinction, moments such as these seem to present a clear cultural politics around language and caste. Chakradhar knows the ways Shudras worship; he worships *as a Shudra*, though he is not a Shudra. The vernacular here—in terms of ritual and language specific to a caste group in a given region—drills down deep. Chakradhar is not only a subject of vernacularization, for him vernacularization is a social science—he is an ethnographer of his times, a kind of anthropologist of social difference.

Conversely, we can notice those few moments in the text when Chakradhar speaks Sanskrit, a language associated with high-caste males exclusively, when he takes on the social affect of a Brahmin male of high learning rather than the affect of a Shudra. In one story a character named Prajnasagar, a figure who appears throughout the *Līḷācaritra* and was likely a learned Brahmin of the Brahminic town of Paithan or Pratishthan, approaches Chakradhar.[50] Prajnasagar figures significantly in the last days of Chakradhar's time in Maharashtra, as we will see. We first encounter him querying Chakradhar on esoteric theological matters. When Chakradhar insists that salvation or moksha is attained by service to God and not by mere knowledge of the self, he appears to us listeners to be criticizing Prajnasagar's own haughty and prideful sense of self.[51] Shortly after this interaction, Prajnasagar again approaches Chakradhar to ask about his caste this time, by generally asking "Who are you?"[52] To this, Chakradhar replies not in Marathi (though Prajnasagar puts the question in Marathi), but in Sanskrit. Here is Anne Feldhaus's translation of Chakradhar's answer in Sanskrit:

> I am not a man, nor a god or Yaksha
>
> Nor a Brahmana, a Kshatriya, a Vaisya or a Shudra.
>
> I am not a celibate; I am not a householder or a forest hermit.
>
> Neither am I a mendicant, I who am innate knowledge.[53]

This Sanskrit passage is repeated in the *Sūtrapāṭha* and is also attributed to Gundam Raul in his biography, thus it forms a kind of verbal formula bearing some weight of irony.[54] No explanation is given here for why Chakradhar would speak in Sanskrit to Prajnasagar when questioned in Marathi, but, given what we know of Chakradhar, we can be sure it was not unintentional. When the same phrase is used in the biography of Gundam Raul, there is some rationale. In that context a "Dravidian" Brahmin comes to Riddhapur to meet Gundam Raul, having heard of his divine nature. The Dravidian asks Gundam Raul essentially the same question, and Gundam Raul gives the same response, verbatim. However, in this latter story, we learn that since "no one could understand" the language of the Dravidian, Gundam Raul speaks to him in Sanskrit, the cosmopolitan language of Brahmins. This lack of mutual comprehensibility in any language other than Sanskrit would explain, perhaps,[55] Gundam Raul's choice of Sanskrit. But what might have been the rationale for Chakradhar to use this language when Marathi would have done just as well?

To help answer this question we must look ahead to see how and why Prajnasagar appears in subsequent lilas. He appears twice more, once during the trial of Chakradhar, as one of the judges adjudicating Chakradhar's alleged crimes. Immediately after this lila, which results in Chakradhar's nose purportedly being cut off, Prajnasagar and fellow adjudicator Mayata Hari are apparently so disturbed by the outcome of the trial that they leave

"Maharashtra" entirely, as we will see.[56] Prajnasagar is thus, like Sarang Pandit, a figure who appears at once to be fascinated by Chakradhar, but also threatened by him, ultimately participating in his trial even while he protests its proceedings. Prajnasagar is a key member of the Brahminic ecumene, as his place at the trial makes clear, and he is a man with a stake in preserving the moral integrity of the Brahminic ecumene, as he sees it.

The reason Chakradhar responds to Prajnasagar in Sanskrit, that is, the logic proposed within the omniscient narrative structure of the *Līḷācaritra*, is to highlight the challenge to the social capital of Sanskrit linguistic and literary prowess that Chakradhar embodies; Chakradhar is speaking to Prajnasagar who serves as a metonym for the Brahminic ecumene itself. A Brahmin, in Marathi, asks Chakradhar about himself, and Chakradhar answers in Sanskrit. His answer conveys information about him, about his species (he is divine), as well as his "station" in life, but importantly also about his caste in relation to the usual social conventions of Brahminic orthodoxy. Chakradhar, in his response, links Sanskrit and caste in such a way as to present an answer embedded in an irony. For in answering in Sanskrit, Chakradhar is revealing his high caste-status, if not his Brahminic status, even while he claims to recognize no such status at all. He thus gives Prajnasagar two answers: I am a high-caste divine male person who is beyond all such distinctions—which is, in some sense, the declaration of Krishna in the *Bhagavad Gītā* as well.[57] It is indeed the sole privilege of the elite to reject elitism. Chakradhar is using the language, and the habitus, of the elite as a technique of criticism.

The juxtaposition of Sanskrit and Marathi, situated within a cultural politics, is made more explicit when toward the end of the *Līḷācaritra* we first encounter Mhaibhat, a Brahmin described as a kind of rising star in the Brahminic ecumene and a skilled Sanskrit scholar, undefeated in debate, who hears of Chakradhar and seeks to challenge him in rhetorical contest.[58] Mhaibhat is also associated with the Yadava state in some capacity, as he is described as undertaking "political activities" (*rājakāya*).[59]

In preparation for the debate, Mhaibhat asks his teacher, Ganapati Appaye, "Is he [Chakradhar] a philosopher?" Appaye says, "No, he is a Mahatma." Mhaibhat appears unimpressed by this august honorific and asks "Well, does he know the Sanskrit texts?" Appaye answers, "I do not know what he knows or doesn't know. But he does speak Marathi fluently." Mhaibhat replies with what appears to be sarcasm: "So he's a Mahatma and he speaks Marathi, but how will he speak with [someone like] me? He may speak Marathi, but I will debate in Sanskrit!"[60] Chakradhar and Mhaibhat meet, but Mhaibhat is too overwhelmed by Chakradhar's presence to begin the debate. Chakradhar initiates their discussion, in Marathi. When their interchange gets going, and Mhaibhat realizes Chakradhar is getting the better of him in the vernacular, Mhaibhat switches to Sanskrit, only to find that Chakradhar can also debate in flawless Sanskrit. This lila that describes the meeting of Chakradhar and Mhaibhat is one of the longest in the entire *Līḷācaritra* and ends when Mhaibhat admits defeat. A series of lilas follow that convey core philosophical teachings of Chakradhar, couched within the scope of a narrative debate and subsequent discussion with Mhaibhat. However, it would still be some time before Mhaibhat would become a follower of Chakradhar.[61]

Chakradhar's first encounter with Mhaibhat is instructive in many ways. First, it is clear that Mhaibhat will become a repository for Chakradhar's philosophy and theology, and Chakradhar prognosticates about Mhaibhat's evolving role in their order.[62] Though Mhaibhat and Chakradhar's encounter begins as a confrontation, for Chakradhar it appears to be something more like a job interview: Chakradhar is sizing up Mhaibhat, for he appears to seek a highly skilled, sensitive, and literate person who can help codify in writing his new religious teachings. In this sense, Mhaibhat's skills as an "agent" within the Brahminic ecumene are vital for the transference of his symbolic capital into the nascent Mahanubhav order. It is only Mhaibhat's arrogance that initially blocks his entry into the Mahanubhav faith, and over the course of many long lilas, in which Chakradhar imparts key teachings through debate with Mhaibhat, and wears down his ego and attachment to glory, we see the Brahmin scholar's arrogance dissolve into devotion.

Chakradhar both rejects the Sanskrit philosophical sphere in confrontation with Mhaibhat as well as shows his mastery of that sphere. Furthermore, these debates with Mhaibhat provide primary articulations of Chakradhar's philosophy, as if to say that the best person to understand such lofty ideas is another Brahmin with scholarly acumen. Indeed, alongside Bhatobas, Mhaibhat appears to fulfill the job of reflecting some aspect of Chakradhar's Brahminic past: Bhatobas, though a Brahmin as well, mirrors Chakradhar's legacy as the son of a state minister in Gujarat, trained in martial arts and political theory; Mhaibhat mirrors Chakradhar's high

Brahminic learning and facility with Sanskrit. While Chakradhar defeats them both "at their own game" (he outwrestles Bhatobas, challenges him at races, etc., to show his physical and martial dominance),[63] they both exhibit some aspect of Chakradhar's charisma after his departure.

The sphere of the Brahminic ecumene appears to surround Chakradhar, and this is revealed in several ways. The many encounters Chakradhar has with Brahmin spiritual teachers suggest an environment where spiritualists and philosophers sought out new disciples, grew their fame, and pursued access to the benefits given by the Yadava state and other benefactors for such ventures. These were not all Brahmin figures,[64] but it appears that the Brahmin figures vying for or seeking to preserve their place within the Brahminic ecumene posed the greatest threat to Chakradhar, perhaps because they perceived that Chakradhar posed a threat to them. Chief among these figures were Mahadashram, Sarang Pandit, and Hemadri, all figures associated with the Brahminic ecumene of the Yadava century, and they would all play their role in Chakradhar's trial. Hemadri, in particular, represents the height of achievement within this context as the prime minister of the Yadava state under Ramachandra. Given that Chakradhar's trial will take place at the intersection of the Yadava state and the Brahminic ecumene, it is necessary to understand how the Yadava state, and political matters in general, are registered within the *Līḷācaritra* and in relation to Chakradhar.

Chakradhar and the Yadava State

Pollock's argument that literary vernacularization deeply involved the engagement of the royal court may have some parallel in the case of Maharashtra through the portrayal in the *Līḷācaritra* of the relationship between Chakradhar and the early Mahanubhavs, on the one hand, and the Yadava state and the Brahminic ecumene, on the other. While it is not the case that Marathi literary materials emerge at the Yadava court or through courtly patronage, it is clear that the benign ambivalence about Marathi evinced by the Yadava court is a vital aspect of the history of Marathi vernacularization, as chapters 1 and 2 suggested. At the same time, the *Līḷācaritra* amply records that the Yadava kings,[65] as well as key figures of the Brahminic ecumene, took great interest in Chakradhar and the early Mahanubhavs. The *Līḷācaritra* also makes fascinating comments about the machinations of the state politics in its age. This interest in governmental-political affairs, the "political field," to use Bourdieu's term, hints at the vitality of the range of subjects within the nascent Marathi public sphere. Whether or not such interactions record historical fact, the emphasis on them in the *Līḷācaritra* suggests that vernacularization occurred at the intersection of state and public culture, which is the location of the public sphere in general.[66]

Chakradhar first attracts the interest of the Yadava state early in the *Līḷācaritra* when the king Krishna hears from a temple Gurav of the wondrous beauty and luster of Chakradhar, a story already discussed in this book.[67] Krishna sends messengers with gifts of gold coins to Chakradhar, who refuses them. When Chakradhar does not touch a bag of gold coins that the king and his younger brother Mahadev attempt to give him,[68] the king then donates the funds to a temple for the repair of a wall, which is perhaps represented in an unreadable Sanskrit inscription at the temple of Lonar.[69]

Following this encounter, another political figure named Ramdrana, a regional governor in Amravati, near the town of Achalpur, hears of Chakradhar's majesty. Ramdrana entices Chakradhar to stay for ten months in his palace.[70] During this time, it appears as if Chakradhar takes on the position of the guru of Ramdrana, and even accepting, as the lila says, a temporary role as a political adviser or minister (*rājyadharma svīkarile*). It is curious that though Chakradhar refuses the funds of the Yadava king, he responds to the invitation of Ramdrana, serving as his political guru and surrogate ruler. The lila implies that the instruction Ramdrana received from Chakradhar was in governance, not solely religious matters. These two unusual interactions with political power, it should be noted, come quite early in Chakradhar's life in Maharashtra.

Shortly after this encounter, we meet one of the key figures of the *Līḷācaritra*, Sarang Pandit, who, though he appears throughout the text and is vital to the narrative of Chakradhar's life, is not a follower; indeed, Sarang Pandit struggles to assert his peer status with Chakradhar.[71] Sarang Pandit will follow Chakradhar throughout the *Līḷācaritra*, appearing at times to be his admirer and worshipper, at others as a skeptic and potential enemy. Dados is a kind of new spiritualist, as mentioned earlier, and Sarang Pandit is a similar figure, though he chooses to enter and rise in Yadava state service and the Brahminic ecumene rather than gather an informal following drawn from general public culture. Sarang Pandit is one of the key judges in the trial that ends the *Līḷācaritra*, as mentioned, and he is also one of the last people to see Chakradhar before he departs for the North.

We learn early on that Sarang Pandit was a reciter of lore, a *pauraṇika*, and thus a scholar of Sanskrit, who served a figure named Gadonayak, probably a minister at the court of Mahadev. Enamored of Chakradhar, Sarang Pandit first begins to worship him, and they appear to strike up a relationship somewhere between friendship and devotion. One lila tells an interesting story. The queen of Mahadev, Vaijarani, commissioned a temple to be built near Paithan and gifts were made to Brahmins in perpetuity. Sarang Pandit appears to have felt dejected that he has not risen in the ranks of his caste fellows within Yadava social orders to attract the benevolence of the king and queen through such a donation. Chakradhar assures him that if he goes to Paithan to visit the queen, who is in temporary residence there, he will see his name among the honored Brahmins, which of course is the case, as Sarang Pandit discovers.[72] As if this assistance were not enough, Chakradhar cures Sarang Pandit of a fever shortly thereafter. This intervention in the life of Sarang Pandit marks the ascent of his career within the political realms of the Brahminic ecumene, which brings Sarang Pandit and Chakradhar into conflict as the *Līḷācaritra*'s narrative progresses and Chakradhar gathers the ire of various Brahmin figures of power and is taken to trial. What is interesting here is to see reflected in the *Līḷācaritra* the cogs in motion within the Brahminic ecumene buttressed by the non-Brahmin Yadava state. Sarang Pandit, as a charismatic professional expounder of Sanskrit mythology, is a good candidate for state sponsorship in the Yadava century.

When Chakradhar went to stay for a while at Verul, twenty kilometers from the Yadava capital in Devgiri, the *Līḷācaritra* tells us, his fame had spread throughout the northern reaches of the Yadava territory and into the coastal areas of the Konkan.[73] Eminent figures visited Chakradhar during this period, bringing offerings and listening to his discourses. However, two prominent Brahmin administrators in the court of King Mahadev, Mahadashram and Brahmasan, grew jealous and plotted against him. Learning that Charkadhar never refused offerings of food, they poisoned him with such offerings on two occasions. The text narrates how Chakradhar showed the physical signs of poisoning but went into seclusion for three days, drinking only milk, and recovered from these attempts on his life. In a dialogue that hints, again, at the humanistic humor within the *Līḷācaritra*, Baisa asks why, if he knew the offerings were poisoned, Chakradhar accepted them. Chakradhar replies that he did not want to disappoint Mahadashram and Brahmasan after all the trouble they took to poison him. The text makes clear that the threat Chakradhar posed to the Brahminic ecumene was the way in which the attention of the Yadava kings as well as their subjects had turned toward Chakradhar. Sarang Pandit represents the middle ground between, on the one hand, the political rulers and the Brahminic ecumene and, on the other, through his association with Chakradhar, public and religious culture in general.

One day Sarang Pandit decides to visit Chakradhar along with a fellow court narrator of the Sanskrit epics, a Pandit named Gopal.[74] Meeting with Chakradhar, Gopal displays his erudition. Chakradhar is not impressed and critiques Gopal's narrative techniques. Gopal accepts Chakradhar's advice, and he returns to the court of Mahadev having significantly improved upon his skills as a result. As Chakradhar's fame spreads further and he gathers a larger audience, the *sabhāmaṇḍap*, or hall of council, at the court of Mahadev becomes empty.[75] The king is furious over this matter until he hears Chakradhar's name, at which point perhaps he recalls having met Chakradhar in the company of his father, Krishna.[76] When Mahadev's messenger tells Chakradhar of the king's curiosity about him, Chakradhar half-heartedly consents to a meeting.

What follows is both comical and curious. Twice Mahadev attempts to leave Devgiri to visit Chakradhar, and each time an ill omen and a natural act prevent his departure: the spontaneous death of an elephant and the sudden onset of torrential rains. The third day, Mahadev departs, while simultaneously Chakradhar orders his followers to pack up their belongings and leave Verul. By the time the king arrives at Verul, Chakradhar has moved to Mudkhed. This pattern repeats itself four more times, each time Chakradhar and his followers moving just before the Yadava king reaches their town or encampment. At one point Baisa asks Chakradhar, "Why won't you just meet the man?"[77] To this, Chakradhar replies that he is worried the king will visit him, become a devotee, renounce his kingship,[78] hand over his kingdom to Chakradhar, and then dominate all his other followers. In other words, the king's "political capital" will transfer to this other social realm, and this transference of symbolic capital will amount to a "takeover" of the social order. It will also change Chakradhar's own social position, forcing him to return, perhaps, to a political life he has already renounced. In addition, Chakradhar notes that the king comes to give treasures and ornaments—the implication is that he bestows benefaction, we may presume, upon Brahmins such as Chakradhar. This, we understand, would have had a negative effect on Chakradhar's followers and run contrary to his general rejection of gifts of state, as we saw with the story of the Yadava king Krishna (this antipathy to state patronage is also seen in the later story of the court poet Narendra narrated in chapter 2). Importantly, though, Chakradhar is asserting that the nature of the movement he has inaugurated must take place independently of the Yadava court as well as of the Brahminic ecumene, for these two locations of power bear the orthodoxy that Chakradhar seeks to undermine within his small community of followers.

Chakradhar's revolution is a quotidian one, not financed by state or secular power, but buoyed by the slow accretions of everyday life and an investment in that life. Here we see this clearly—the interventions of state are not welcome in Chakradhar's sphere. Even in the case of Ramdrana, Chakradhar serves the governor for some time, then departs, and he accepts no intervention within his own spiritual social world. So we see Chakradhar avoiding royal patronage and, by extension, rejecting state support. While Mahadev's interest does not suggest that the Yadava state might have pursued support of Marathi vernacularization—for Chakradhar, as we know, was not an "author" or a "writer," nor did he compose anything in Marathi—it does suggest, as Bhave and Tulpule implied, that the Yadava court took a nonstate interest in Marathi public cultural forms of instruction and entertainment, and a new spiritualist of local renown would have supplied both. The story of Mahadev finding his court empty while Chakradhar's "court" was full is clearly a story of the inversion of some social capital, a purposeful juxtaposition of royal power and a new power center out in the world beyond the court.

The series of episodes regarding Mahadev ends when a key minister of King Mahadev, Palha Dangia, approaches the encampment of Mahanubhavs at Sinnar in a final attempt to contact Chakradhar.[79] Although Palha Dangia has visited Chakradhar many times, he does not recognize him because Chakradhar has "disguised" himself with a Gujarati-style headdress and speaks in Gujarati rather than Marathi. Although Palha Dangia understands Gujarati, he does not manage to see through Chakradhar's subterfuge.[80] So Chakradhar is a master of many things, apparently also of disguise, and

Palha Dangia returns to Mahadev to tell him that Chakradhar has left Sinnar and his whereabouts are not known. We might note here the irony of this "disguise," for Chakradhar is actually a Gujarati, and so speaking and dressing as one is perhaps to return to another "vernacular" in this moment, to "go home" in idiom and affect.

This is the last we hear of Mahadev and his efforts to meet Chakradhar. This "Initial Half" ("Pūrvārdha") of the *Līḷācaritra* concludes just as two key figures of the Mahanubhav order enter the narrative: Mahadaisa and Bhatobas (as devotees of Dados). If the episodes with Mahadev and Chakradhar's encounter with secular power reveals an anxiety about social structure and leadership within Chakradhar's community, the section that follows these remembrances, the "Latter Half" ("Uttarārdha") begins to track the process whereby a stable communal leadership was established among the Mahanubhavs, centered on the figure of Bhatobas, a kind of pre-routinization period. This will also mark the period in which the persecution of Chakradhar intensifies.

Chakradhar may distance himself from the state; shunning courtly patronage, though, is not the same as remaining ignorant of politics and state power. Indeed, Chakradhar believes his devotees are obliged to observe these aspects, too, of the quotidian world. While the beginning of the "Uttarārdha" of the *Līḷācaritra* is usually marked by the acceptance of Bhatobas to the inner circle of Chakradhar's followers, this half of the narrative also revolves around a change in Yadava courtly power. We can recall from Yadava history that Mahadev had agreed to rule until his nephew Ramachandra, the son of Krishna, came of age. However, upon Mahadev's death, his son Ammanadeva attempted to usurp power from the heir apparent, Ramachandra. The *Līḷācaritra* records this political conflict as well, but with an entirely different valence: Chakradhar tells his follower Indrabhat that Ramachandra has attacked Ammanadeva and has "plucked out his eyes."[81] We get none of the bravado of the Yadava record, but rather a bare account of brutal succession. It is unclear from the text how Chakradhar knows this, but the text implies that he gathered the information from passersby. As Indrabhat was on an errand to a nearby village, Chakradhar scolds him for not gaining this knowledge himself, for not inquiring about world affairs while circulating in public. He tells Indrabhat, "You're a Mahatma, no? A Mahatma must investigate conflict and strife occurring as part of state politics (*rājyavārtā*) and the affairs of the land (*deśavārtā*).

He should live in those places that are stable."[82] The Mahanubhavs are situated within the general public culture of the Yadava era, and they remain keenly aware of the machinations of politics and state around them. This threat to stability is perhaps a further example of the prevailing stability of the age—for this bloody internal conflict, though short-lived, is perceived as aberrant for the age.

This awareness of politics compels reflections in the *Līḷācaritra* on the major political events of the age. And while some of these may be later interpolations, in part or in whole, it is curious to note that the text's authors or later editors felt such observations were essential to the work. For example, at several points in the text Chakradhar comments upon the forces of the Delhi Sultanate pressing at the northern line of Yadava sovereign territory, which presents Chakradhar as a political prognosticator, musing on the future of the Yadava realms. In an episode following the political succession, Chakradhar is at a *madrassa*, an Islamic school, in the village of Domegram (Kamalpur), 80 kilometers from Devgiri, with his female follower Sadhe.[83] They observe a man leading away a tethered cow and ox, presumably to be slaughtered. Chakradhar comments that he observed this in the North among Muslims or "Turks" and that the Turks would come to the region and would enslave people this way. A second prognostication occurs after Chakradhar's trial, but before he moves north, in which he predicts the destruction of the Yadava "nation" or rashtra by "Muslims."[84] Here we find the term *mleccha* for "Muslim," and the term *Yadava* (*jādhava*) for the dynastic rule that will be overturned—both terms will appear in the *Jñāneśvarī* as well, a testament to the routine place of Islam in the culture of the Yadava century, contradicting the idea that the "advent" of Islam in western India is under the power of the invasions of the Delhi Sultanate in the last decade of the thirteenth century. Chakradhar relates a rather unpleasant future of killing, imprisonment, mayhem, mass exodus, and an influx of new and "foreign" people to the region. A similar statement is found in the *Smṛtisthaḷa* when Bhatobas, upon hearing of the capture of Ramachandra by the forces of Alauddin Khilji in 1307, predicts that the king will be released, but implies that he will yet meet his fate.[85] This fate, Bhatobas says, is because of the way Ramachandra had allowed sants and *mahants*, holy people, to be poorly treated, perhaps a reference to Chakradhar's trial and persecution—the idea that it is the Yadava ruler and not the conquering Islamic polity that bears the guilt of persecuting Hindu holy men is interesting to highlight here. Though the "ruination" of the kingdom will come, according to Chakradhar and Bhatobas, it appears not to have yet happened at the time of the composition of either the *Līḷācaritra* or *Smṛtisthaḷa*; thus both are situated in a period earlier than 1318, we might presume, and a time of relative stability. In any case, the *Līḷācaritra* demonstrates a clear preoccupation with political upheaval and state machination, and it seeks to display a high level of intelligence regarding the politics of "place." In particular, Chakradhar's purported predictions about the rise of political Islam in the region both underscore the political awareness of the text but also remind us that such works, though they may seek to convey "history," are continuously being edited and emended.

The lila in which the coup d'état and Ramachandra's victory over Ammanadeva are mentioned marks the end of a particular political frame, one in which Yadava leaders appear to want to praise, fund, and otherwise glorify Chakradhar. However, with the ascendance of Ramachandra, and in particular that of his prime minister Hemadri, Chakradhar's relationship with state power will take a turn for the worse. He ceases to be seen by the Yadava state and the Brahminic ecumene as a curious, charismatic spiritualist from a foreign land and instead becomes a local, recognizable threat.

One can mark this point, in part, by observing how Sarang Pandit's role in the *Līḷācaritra* begins to turn from that of an ardent supporter and lay devotee of Chakradhar to one of his persecutors, albeit a reluctant one. Midway within the narrative of the *Līḷācaritra*'s "Last Half," the relationship between Sarang Pandit and Chakradhar's followers begins to sour just as Sarang Pandit's fortunes rise as an official at the Yadava court, a position Chakradhar helped him acquire, as we saw. At one point Sarang Pandit invites Chakradhar and his followers to his now lavish home to be fed. Sarang Pandit makes a point of giving Bhatobas excessive amounts of clarified butter, a sign both of his wealth (that he can afford such delicacies) and a common trope in the representation of Brahminic gastronomic excess—Brahmins are sometimes stereotypically portrayed as fattening themselves with such things as butter from meals offered by others.[86] Bhatobas understands this act to be an insult because he is an ascetic, a follower of Chakradhar, and he also perceives the caste prejudice it contains. Yet the incident delves deeper, suggesting that Sarang Pandit, while he is indebted to Chakradhar for his high station at the Yadava court, rejects Chakradhar's asceticism and, in particular, his band of followers. Chakradhar compels the final split by issuing an ultimatum to Sarang Pandit to join his ascetic order.[87] Sarang Pandit demurs, saying that although he knows all the success he has accrued in his life, such as his position of service to the royal court, is because of Chakradhar, still he prefers a world of pleasure (*bhoga*) to a life of asceticism.[88] With this rejection, it appears as if Chakradhar loses his key support among the Brahmin intelligentsia of the Yadava court.

Marathi, Quotidian Life, and the Story of Chakradhar's Trial

Before discussing the lilas that describes Chakradhar's trial, I should note here again that some Mahanubhavs do not believe this trial happened, nor subsequent events, such as Chakradhar's purported disfigurement or beheading. The lila that records the story of the trial is present in some versions of the *Līḷācaritra* but certainly not in all of them. S. G. Tulpule, in his edited version of the *Līḷācaritra*, provides the lila describing Chakradhar's trial in an appendix with a carefully worded paragraph of introduction.[89] I follow Tulpule's words here by reiterating that by engaging these controversial lilas *I am not endorsing their historical veracity*. Though these stories may not be historically true, they are represented in the manuscript archive maintained by some Mahanubhavs over many centuries. Though I engage them here as part of this literary archive, *I do not claim they describe true events, but rather relevant stories though of dubious historical truth.* I do include these lilas here for they reveal, among other things, the commitment to social equality, and particular gender equality, within the Mahanubhav order represented by Chakradhar.

The sequence of events that will lead to the stories of Chakradhar's trial and persecution in some versions of the *Līḷācaritra* begins when he again meets Mahadashram, the Yadava minister who had colluded in trying to poison him twice before. The two encounter one another as Chakradhar is walking toward the monastery of Ganapati Appaye (Mhaibhat's former teacher), where Chakradhar has begun to deliver lectures in Marathi on theological subjects.[90] Chakradhar greets Mahadashram by asking him if he has achieved *vṛdhāpya*, which is a highly Sanskritic word that means to achieve prosperity, but in Marathi can also mean to "grow old." This question resonates with a double entendre, for we know that Mahadashram represents the "old guard," that stratum of the Brahminic ecumene wedded to Sanskrit literary production via state patronage, and he is not clever enough to have succeeded in his plan to kill Chakradhar. He is a Sanskrit master who runs an endowed matha or monastery where he teaches Dharma Śāstra texts on social orthodoxy. Chakradhar's use of the Sanskrit word *vṛdhāpya* here might be taken by his followers as a comment directed toward the established Brahminic ecumene itself: that it has "grown old" and thus new spiritualists like Chakradhar and Jnandev have arisen in the region.

Chakradhar continues to Appaye's school, where he holds forth in Marathi, though the school is a *śāstramaṭha* or "social science monastery" and thus devoted to the study of Sanskrit Dharma Śāstra literature. Around him gather students not only from Appaye's school but also from the nearby school of Mahadashram. Furious at the truancy of his students, Mahadashram seeks them out, only to discover them seated before Chakradhar, who is lecturing in Marathi, and receiving his "blessings" or prasad. As with the story of King Mahadev, who finds his royal court empty because all his courtiers are elsewhere listening to Chakradhar's teachings, here too we see one court emptied—the "old" court—and a new one filled. The lila closes with Mahadashram's ominous observation: "Now Chakradhar is destroying our way of life."

Mahadashram then attempts to kill Chakradhar a second time by luring him to public worship at a nearby temple where he has constructed a booby-trapped "throne" or *yantrāsana*, which Chakradhar somehow disarms with his thumb.[91] As noted earlier, it is interesting to see that the *Līḷācaritra* does not imply that Chakradhar avoids this hazard by means of superhuman powers. Though the poison that Mahadashram uses in his first attempt to kill Chakradhar makes him ill, Chakradhar has a knowledge of poison and so also a knowledge of its cure; this is not the work of magic or miracle, but rather medicine. In Mahadashram's next attempt to kill Chakradhar, again it is the latter's knowledge that saves him. He understands the engineering of booby traps, and his knowledge of human behavior allows him to detect Mahadashram's incongruous affection and thus suspect foul play. Chakradhar is not working miracles here, but rather draws on what we presume to be his training as the son of a Brahmin courtier and possibly a military commander in Gujarat.

Toward the end of the *Līlācaritra* a series of plots against Chakradhar's life and confrontations with key Brahmin figures at the nexus of the Yadava royal court and the Brahminic ecumene compel him to consider leaving the region of Maharashtra to move "north" alone.[92] Chakradhar does not give a rationale for this decision—indeed, as we have seen, he demands that his followers stay in Maharashtra.[93] Toward the conclusion of the *Līlācaritra,* we see him and his followers consolidating Mahanubhav practice and theology through a series of lilas.[94] It is in this context—after two attempts on Chakradhar's life by jealous Brahmin ministers of the Yadava state and after his decision to move north—that we find the first of two important encounters with Hemadri, the most famous and influential of the Brahmin ministers who served Ramachandra and who stands at the apex of the Yadava state and the Brahminic ecumene.

Here we encounter a peculiar story that involves Hemadri, his wife Demati, and Chakradhar.[95]

Demati was the wife of the Pandit Hemadri. She came to the Dhoreshwar [temple]. She took *pān* from the mouth [of Chakradhar] and sandalwood from his holy feet. At first, [Chakradhar] had avoided her. But then he put sandalwood on her forehead.

Then [Hemadri] came to her place [i.e., bedroom].

She said [to Hemadri] that he may go [if he wishes], but he said no.

[Hemadri] asked, "What is this? I have never stayed here before [i.e., spent the night with you], but now I don't feel like leaving. Why is this?"

She said, "[It is because] I had gone to see (darshan) Chakradhar. I brought the sandalwood from there. Thus this has happened."

Chakradhar said, "She is a woman so she spoke frankly. He will be upset that she came to see me."

Sandalwood is regarded as an aphrodisiac in Ayurvedic practice, and this is clearly indicated here: Hemadri desires to have sex with his wife, Demati, and the reason for Hemadri's inclination, according to Demati, is the sandalwood she acquired from Chakradhar. The implications regarding Hemadri may appear less than flattering, and we might guess that listeners and readers of this text would find some humor in this passage. For our purposes, it may convey a transparent critique of Hemadri. Chakradhar may be implying a certain "impotence" to the social complex in which

Hemadri is a titular figure, which is the Brahminic ecumene as it meets and intermeshes with the Yadava state. Chakradhar's closing commentary on this lila is suggestive, first, because of the "frank" way in which he feels women speak as a matter of course. In addition, Chakradhar highlights only one aspect of this story, indicating which of the several strands of meaning here seems most important to the narrative of the *Līḷācaritra*—that is, the fact that Hemadri will not be happy with Chakradhar's involvement in his personal life. We see here a rather surprising way in which a quintessential concern of the quotidian—one's sex life—appears to enter our narrative in the context of the life of one of the most famous political and literary figures of the age. The juxtaposition—of the ordinary and the exalted—is perhaps an indication of the nature of the charges that Chakradhar will face. And, as Chakradhar predicts, Hemadri is apparently not happy.

Chakradhar's trial arrives in some versions of the *Līḷācaritra* shortly after this encounter with Hemadri's wife, and this proximity of stories implies that there is a relationship between these two events in the literary archive. Recall that Chakradhar tried to avoid Demati, perhaps because he understood that contact with her would lead to no good. For reasons we are not given, soldiers arrive from Paithan, under the orders of Hemadri, and they attempt to take Chakradhar into custody.[96] Bhatobas singlehandedly disarms the leader of the soldiers and drives all the others away. Chakradhar demands that Bhatobas relinquish the sword he has taken from the chief of the soldiers and return it to him. It is at this point that Bhatobas, unhappy to comply, returns the sword to the soldier, quipping that if he can take the man's sword he can take the man's wife as well. One gets the sense this is a common jibe among soldiers.

Chakradhar then surrenders himself to the soldiers. He is taken to a temple in Paithan, one of the key centers of the Brahminic ecumene, rather than to Devgiri, the capital of the non-Brahmin Yadava state. The trial takes place in or at a temple, in public, rather than within a private royal environment. The jurisdiction, in a sense, in which Chakradhar will be accused of his alleged crimes is situated within that nexus of worlds that Brahmins uniquely inhabited, where we find mingled temple, court, Brahminic ecumene, religious life, and the quotidian world. Here is the lila (rejected as historically true by some Mahanubhavs) that records Chakradhar's purported trial:

Then Chakradhar, having crossed the Godavari River,[97] went to Paithan, where a tribunal (sabha) gathered at the Aditi temple of Mudha. Hemad Pandit,[98] Sarang Pandit, Mayata Hari, Prajnasagar; the major leaders of the village, the Brahmin elites [mahajan], scholars, historians, holymen, celibates, Jain ascetics, members of the Natha sect—they all assembled. Chakradhar was brought into the Mudha Aditi temple. Chakradhar took a seat in the middle of the assembly hall.

They said to him, "Who are you?"

Chakradhar said, "I am an ascetic, a Mahatma."[99]

[They said,] "There is nothing more you'd like to say?"

[Chakradhar said,] "All of you gathered here are eminent people. Scholars, students, renunciates, milk fasters,[100] legal scholars, historians."

And then his gaze fell upon Sarang Pandit, and Sarang Pandit looked aside.

[Chakradhar continued,] "You who have assembled are the leaders of all eighteen families [of Paithan],[101] Jain ascetics, Natha yogis. You would not drink unknown water.[102] Then you ask yourself what it is that I am."

[They said,] "The women are attracted to you, no? Isn't this the way it is? And you are similarly attracted to the women, isn't that the case?"

Those gathered said, "Yes!"

Someone among the tribunal clapped, and they all began to quietly conspire (i.e., "whisper") with one another.

Then two people, Mayata Hari and Prajnasagar, stood up [and addressed the tribunal]: "That you conspire [against Chakradhar] is wrong."

The conspiring talk ended.

Mayata Hari and Prajnasagar said, "You [tribunal members] are bring ruin upon this country (*rashtra*) and you are acting like Chandals."[103] Then Mayata Hari and Prajnasagar left.

Chakradhar said [to the tribunal], "You each are religious experts (*agāmika*). Each of you holds a position of political importance (*pradhan*). Please consider what it is you'd like to do."

"No need, we've decided already," they said.

"Is it so? Then whatever it is you've decided, then just do it," [Chakradhar said.]

Then they took [Chakradhar] to the temple courtyard. There he voluntarily offered his nose.[104]

This is a detailed and dramatic story, a thirteenth-century courtroom drama where much unfolds. Though some Mahanubhavs reject the historical accuracy of this story, the presence of it in the literary archive of the Mahanubhavs is suggestive even as literary fiction. We find gathered together powerful Brahmin figures, ministers in the Yadava government, who have appeared throughout Chakradhar's life up to this point—Hemadri, Prajnasagar, Mayata Hari, and his erstwhile friend Sarang Pandit are principal among them.[105] The tribunal accuses Chakradhar of what appears to be impropriety among his female followers, or perhaps they object to him having female followers at all. It is unclear why Chakradhar's nose is cut off. Cutting off the nose—of people or of statues—is a form of disfigurement meant to imply degradation, emasculation, and shame, as the nose is an almost universal symbol of pride. It may also refer to a Dharma Śāstra injunction.[106] Given the conspiratorial nature of the purported trial—at least according to Prajnasagar and Mayata Hari—we can assume that whatever the crime of which Chakradhar was accused in this disputed lila, it was not the actual motivation for the alleged trial. Still, we might recall the encounter between Demati, Hemadri's wife, and Chakradhar—this is the only direct connection the *Līḷācaritra* provides that links Hemadri and Chakradhar and involves the "attraction" of a female devotee (Demati) to Chakradhar, even though the *Līḷācaritra* has many examples of women and men finding Chakradhar's charisma to be overwhelming, as we have seen. The encounter with Hemadri's wife may indeed be the fodder of an accusation of "intimate contact," misrepresented and misconstrued by the court—and hence the accusation of mendacious proceedings, that is, this is a false accusation.

If we take the charge that Chakradhar "attracted" female followers—perhaps as an extension of his apparent empowerment of Demati, Hemadri's wife, in a sexual and domestic context—then we can see that this passage appears to condemn the teaching of women in general. The verb used here for "attracted," *vedhaṇe*, primarily implies pious or spiritual devotion rather than sexual attraction; the word suggests a person deeply affected by the presence of another person. Demati, for example, was attracted to Chakradhar in just this way, and there is no hint in the text that there was a sexual attraction. Thus this does not seem to be an accusation of sexual impropriety, but rather an accusation that he attracts women to his order, and indeed many of his key and closest followers are women.[107]

This apparently contravenes the social orthodoxy preserved by Hemadri and the tribunal—in other words, Chakradhar should not teach and initiate women. As we noted, Hemadri in particular is remembered as a scholar of orthodox social order and for authoring a text that detailed the quotidian vows that men, and especially women, might undertake. We can imagine that it is on the grounds of a perceived disruption of the normal social relations of everyday life that Chakradhar is supposedly tried in this court. We have the sense here that Chakradhar, as a Brahmin, and a male, has contravened accepted social practice by teaching women as well as non-Brahmins and low-caste people. The crime with which he is charged is the attraction and instruction of women and, by extension, others outside the sphere of the Brahminic ecumene. The use of Marathi epitomizes these purported crimes, for, as we have seen, the language is intimately tied to communicating with female (and by extension, non-Brahmin) followers. In using Marathi to express the ideas of his new religious order, it is clear to the tribunal that Chakradhar's goal is to spread these ideas widely, without honoring the conventions of social distinction around knowledge and power that the Brahmin male members of the tribunal seek to uphold. A discourse in Marathi is out of the control of the Brahminic ecumene, just as an inscription in Marathi is beyond their control.

Yet there is another "trial" nestled within this one, and Chakradhar is the vehicle by which this other trial is exposed. What is it that Prajnasagar and Mayata Hari oppose? What causes them to exit the *sabha*, thus denying the tribunal, as Sontheimer notes, the possibility of a unanimous and thus unequivocal decision?[108]

Quite aside from Chakradhar's actions, it is Prajnasagar and Mayata Hari who level an accusation against the tribunal. This appears to be a challenge to something like a "speedy and public trial" by one's peers.[109] The challenge arises when Prajnasagar and Mayata Hari realize that the trial is "rigged" and an outcome has already been fixed, which is indicated by the whispering to which they object. As men of integrity, they protest, and their words of admonition are strong, deploying casteist prejudice for rhetorical force. They accuse the tribunal—which includes the state's most powerful minister, Hemadri—of having wrought "evil" or "filth" (*okhata*) throughout the "country" (*rashtra*). This invocation of the "country" may also suggest the domain that the tribunal sees as their charge to protect, an idea that bears some premonition of a legal public.[110]

As we have seen, there appears a consistent connection between "Maharashtra" and the language of Marathi, even while Maharashtra was not a monolingual region in the Yadava era, nor is it now. The *rashtra* is not defined by its political borders exclusively, nor by its languages, but there is a clear sense here that the injustice being done to Chakradhar is also an affront to a particular place, not simply a particular person or the contravening of a given law. The trial turns in this moment from a supposed crime committed by Chakradhar to a crime committed *against* him: Chakradhar is the victim of an aberration of justice, an unfair trial. We can only connect the idea that this aberration of justice despoils an entire "nation," a *rashtra*, if we understand some idea that links a public within a given cultural region with a sense of social justice or "due process." And we can only assume that such a sense of region and justice intertwined exists because it is a subject of public debate at some level.

Caste also resonates in this condemnation of the tribunal by Prajnasagar and Mayata Hari. They call their fellow Brahmins and tribunal members Chandals or "Untouchables," which is often simply a term of insult, but here may bear particular resonance, especially when directed by two Brahmins toward other Brahmins. We can see a fissure within the Brahminic ecumene open up in this moment. On the one hand, we have Hemadri and Mahadashram—the latter, we will recall, fearing that Chakradhar is "destroying our way of life." On the other hand, we have Prajnasagar and Mayata Hari, two men wedded more closely to moral principle than political preservation. For the latter two, then, the Brahminic ecumene is an edifice independent of political influence, a place of social value that they believe the figure of the "Brahmin" epitomizes—and hence the perceived opposite of the Brahmin, the Chandal, and the use of that term as a mode of rhetorical critique. When Prajnasagar and Mayata Hari see their principles so brazenly compromised, they see not a single miscarriage of justice but the downfall of an entire social order. Of course, this is also a public trial, taking place out in the open, and before a gathered audience.

An emphasis is clearly placed on Prajnasagar and Mayata Hari in the telling of this story and so also on the injustice the trial epitomizes, for the lila that follows the story of the trial is about the two of them, not about Chakradhar. In this lila we learn that Prajnasagar and Mayata Hari hastened home, packed up their things, and, with their wives, set out to flee Maharashtra. Members of the tribunal, however, attempted to waylay

Mayata Hari in particular and called out from their homes above the street, "Grab him! Grab his wife! He has deprived us of our unanimous decision (*samaya*)! Throw him out, throw him out of our Maharashtra!" Mayata Hari responded, "Take your own wife! And your father's wife too! I am leaving your Maharashtra of the Mahars!"

Terms of insult of both caste and gender return to our narrative in this passage. As Mayata Hari leaves, his detractors hurl invectives at him and his wife, in particular, and he retorts with an insult directed at the wives and mothers of his abusers. Mayata Hari again refers to his Brahmin peers as "Untouchables," only this time he uses an actual jati title, Mahar, to do so.[111] Mayata Hari's point is not to insult Mahars, however, but to insult his Brahmin peers, and particularly those who claim some sanction on the sovereignty of the political region named "Maharashtra" here and elsewhere in the text. The effect of this passage is to reinscribe several features of social order: that the Brahminic ecumene represents "Maharashtra" is one. But another is, perhaps, that Chakradhar represents a challenge because he too accesses a "Maharashtra," which *is also* a land of Mahars, and of women, Shudras, and many others who are not part of the Brahminic ecumene. As we have seen, Chakradhar has imagined his own "Maharashtra," and here we have another articulation of "Maharashtra." Both share the idea that region, culture, language, and social ethic interlace to form this concept of place. Furthermore, through the story, however apocryphal, of the trial we can see a space cleaved between the political motivations ascribed to Hemadri and the traditional justice system defended by Prajnasagar and Mayata Hari. It is through this newly opened space that figures like Chakradhar and Jnandev will proceed into the future.

Following the lilas that engage the trial, Chakradhar responds to the agony of his followers at seeing his disfigurement, and their pleas to preserve their "pride," by causing his nose to regenerate.[112] Several key stories follow in which Mhaibhat becomes a follower of Chakradhar, Bhatobas is anointed the new leader of the group, funds and other arrangements are made for the maintenance of the group, and Chakradhar delivers a series of lectures in which the vital tenets of this new religion are laid out, including the injunction to stay in "Maharashtra."[113] This is also the section in which Chakradhar predicts the downfall of Yadava rule by *mleccha* or "Muslim" rule.[114] Indeed, before departing Chakradhar proclaims, "Now I will go North and live among Muslims."[115] In a curious statement, when his female follower Ausa asks him why he'd want to do such a thing—to live among Muslims—he says, in a declaration reminiscent of Baisa's question about whether Krishna belongs to Guravs or Brahmins,[116] that all people, Muslim or otherwise, may also benefit from his teaching. This idea restates the deep humane sense of compassion the religion expounds. The statement also carries an echo of the kinds of mystic-yogic "syncretism" that will later be found in South Asia, from the Sufi saints of the medieval period to spiritual masters like Sai Baba of Shirdi in the modern period. One can imagine that figures such as Chakradhar—a person of great charisma, adept in yoga, deeply knowledgeable about religious matters, and also willing to transgress social boundaries—likely lie at the heart of the diverse meeting places of Sufis, Hindus, and Sikhs.[117]

Some versions of the *Līḷācaritra* conclude as soldiers again arrive to apprehend Chakradhar and attempt to kill him.[118] As above, these lilas are rejected by some Mahanubhavs. Yet all versions of the *Līḷācaritra*, to my knowledge, end as Chakradhar leaves for Ujjain in the region of modern-day Madhya Pradesh. On his way, he meets several people who are witness to Chakradhar's survival—most importantly Sarang Pandit, his erstwhile friend, recent persecutor, and someone who has appeared alongside Chakradhar throughout the *Līḷācaritra*. Sarang Pandit tries to hide his face in shame, but Chakradhar engages Sarang Pandit. Then Sarang Pandit invites Chakradhar to his home; however, Chakradhar appears to slip away after bathing in a nearby river, and this is the last time he is seen in Maharashtra. One cannot help but feel that on Sarang Pandit's shoulders rests the guilt of the Brahminic ecumene over the purported persecution of one of their brightest stars.

Thus we have the story of Chakradhar—immigrant to Maharashtra and émigré from Maharashtra—bookended by a linguistic-ethnic region, a region he leaves, but in which he commands his followers to stay, a region amply marked by the legacy of his remembered life. We have a non-native speaker of Marathi who engenders the first example of Marathi literature so that his teachings may be widely accessible to all levels of society in the Marathi-speaking region—a revolutionary new vision of a discursive sphere of common learning hemmed by the rough boundaries of linguistic geography. Long after the Yadavas dissipate, it will be this linguistic geography, transformed into a literary geography, that will endure as "Maharashtra" into the present.

PART THREE

A Vernacular Manifesto

As we have seen in the previous chapters, the use of Marathi by the early Mahanubhavs—and by Chakradhar in his own life as recorded faithfully in the *Līḷācaritra*—was not predicated on a valorization of a new literary idiom. Marathi here was not a language of emancipation or redemption, but the logical, simple, and "ordinary" response to a fundamental problem of social communication: how best to preserve Chakradhar's teachings or, by extension, how Chakradhar in his life and religious practice sought to reach the widest array of listeners, citing in particular access for women and low castes. Literary vernacularization, if its epicenter can be placed in the production of the first Marathi literary text, the *Līḷācaritra*, was motivated by an ethics of social inclusion, a response to a cultural politics around language that divided the population along lines of gender and caste. Marathi was not presented as the epicenter of a "revolution" in language, politics, or culture, but the use of Marathi, nonetheless, became a definitive feature of the early Mahanubhav religion, particularly through the creation of the first extant work of Marathi literature, the *Līḷācaritra*.

Though literary production was not the aim of the early Mahanubhavs—they produced the first literature of Marathi for practical reasons, and perhaps as an extension of the training many of them had in literary arts, particularly in Sanskrit—this is not to deny that the *Līḷācaritra* is a literary work of exceptional merit. Indeed, the early Mahanubhavs produced what I consider one of the most stunning works of literature I have ever read in any language. But nowhere in the text do I get the sense that the creation of a literary work is the aim of the text's agents. This fact is in sharp contrast to what we will find with the *Jñāneśvarī*, where the production of a new literature in Marathi often appears to be one of the foundational reasons for Jnandev to compose his text. In contradistinction to the *Līḷācaritra*, then, the first self-consciously literary work of Marathi is remembered to be the product of Jnandev, his *Jñāneśvarī*.

This brings us to part 3 of the book, where we will draw on the same foundational social and political milieu as in part 2 as we move to a discussion of Jnandev and the *Jñāneśvarī*. Far more well known, and bearing the full weight of being Marathi's first explicitly *literary* text, the *Jñāneśvarī* is considered to be the foundation of Marathi literature up to the present.[1] This is a fact often stated by scholars, politicians, cultural critics, and common people in Maharashtra. As such, a study of the *Jñāneśvarī* is in some sense a study of the first text to declare itself a work of Marathi literature *as* literature. In the figure of Jnandev and in the *Jñāneśvarī*, we will find the full expression of a new literary idiom in Marathi, a clear vision of the politics of this new literature, and yet a complex discourse around social equality that reveals the indeterminacy of the long, measured quotidian revolution.

In order to advance the argument of the book, I have mirrored (which is to say, "reversed") the order of analysis of part 2 that I import into part 3, which I do in order to create a dialectic between these two sections of the book. In part 2 we first examined the observation and critique of social inequity that is apparent in the *Līḷācaritra* (chapter 4) and then discussed how this critique compelled the use of "Marathi" and the conditions that surrounded this choice of language (chapter 5). The two chapters of part 3 mirror this format: we will first discuss the valorization of Marathi as a literary language in the *Jñāneśvarī* (this chapter) and then move to the observation and critique of social inequity contained in the text (chapter 7). From social ethics to the logic of Marathi composition in part 2, we move from the logic of Marathi composition back to social ethics in part 3.

The rationale for this approach reflects the explicit intentions of the *Jñāneśvarī* as opposed to the *Līḷācaritra*. The *Jñāneśvarī* is a text that presents itself as a new literary form in Marathi, as we will see, and so I think of it as a kind of literary vernacular manifesto, a declaration of a new vernacular literary idiom. This is an unequivocal aspect of the text's self-understanding, unlike the *Līḷācaritra*, which bears no self-consciousness about being a *literary* text, even though the early Mahanubhavs make explicit their choice of Marathi and adhere to the form I refer to as historical literary realism. On the other hand, the *Līḷācaritra* openly engages and challenges caste norms in restricted social contexts, even while limiting that challenge in the quotidian world. The *Jñāneśvarī*, however, has a somewhat more ambivalent reflection of caste, gender, and inequity in society at large. This is because the *Jñāneśvarī* privileges a medium—Marathi—over cultural critique. Yet both texts are generated from the same source: everyday life. The impetus behind the *Jñāneśvarī* is not to change the social world entirely, but to open to all society the possibilities of salvation inherent in *hearing* the *Bhagavad Gītā*. The social ethics that surrounds transferring the salvational message of the *Bhagavad Gītā* into Marathi is clear in the *Jñāneśvarī*, as we will see in this chapter. However, the transformational implications of this act for society in general is a subject that reveals some ambivalence in the text, as an explicit rejection of social difference in the context of cosmic reality appears tempered by the implicit use of colloquial Marathi and its attendant idioms of social difference. As we saw in the *Līḷācaritra*, here too vernacularization is as much about creating a discursive field that widens toward a public in everyday life as it is about managing the social implications and effects of this expansion. In this careful balance between satisfying social norms and transcending them, the *Jñāneśvarī* takes its cue from the text it serves to elucidate through commentary, that is, the Sanskrit *Bhagavad Gītā*.

The *Bhagavad Gītā* and Cultural Politics

A warrior, Arjuna, faces an opposing army. He sees across the battlefield his cousins, uncles, teachers, and friends. They are ready to fight and to kill him. But is he ready to do the same?

This moral quandary provides the context for what is perhaps Hinduism's most well-traveled text, both in South Asia and outside.[2] The *Bhagavad Gītā* or "Song of God" is a metered poem in simple Sanskrit of seven hundred verses divided into eighteen chapters that was composed, in its final form, sometime around 100 BCE to 100 CE.[3] The context of the Song of God is a dialogue between the divine charioteer Krishna and Arjuna, the warrior and prince who stands before his family and friends as their mortal opponent. It takes place in the context of civil war and fratricide, in which

Krishna counsels, berates, humiliates, teases, cajoles, placates, instructs, and enlightens Arjuna. The *Bhagavad Gītā* or simply the *Gītā,* as it has been known for a millennium or more, is a text about how to act when all your options appear bad.[4] It is a political text, couched as it is in the context of political upheaval, as well as situated within the central problematic of politics: making a choice that resolves one problem only to catalyze another. As a political text, it was used by figures in the modern period as diverse as the staunch nationalist B. G. Tilak, to justify violent resistance against the British, and M. K. Gandhi, who used the text to advocate non-violent resistance to British rule. In all such cases the *Bhagavad Gītā* mixes the politics of state and the politics of culture, joining them together in the context of deciding upon action.

The *Bhagavad Gītā* is at the center of what is often called the largest and longest poem ever composed and recorded, the *Mahābhārata,* a story that is perhaps twenty-five hundred years old—at least five hundred years older than the *Bhagavad Gītā* itself. The text is around ten times the length of the *Iliad* and *Odyssey* combined, though many versions of the text exist and all vary in size, alternating between poetry and prose. Yet the overall emphasis of the story is direct. The *Mahābhārata* narrates the end of an era or *yuga* of greater certitude in social action and religious belief. It marks the end of a time when people inherently knew what to do and why. The story it tells is of a civil war within a single family, moved by dark motives, where just characters meet tragic ends and heroes act at times with apparent deceit, all taking place within a larger decline marked by a descending series of eras. What begins with the era of Truth or the *satya yuga,* slowly counts down like a time bomb, through a Third Era (*treta yuga*), then a Second Era (*dvāpar yuga*), and finally the Era of Strife or *kali yuga.*[5] The *Mahābhārata* is situated on the precipice of the Second Era as it shifts toward our age, an era of discord and contention.

The *Mahābhārata* does not tell a happy story, but it is an inspirational story in its own way, one that takes seriously the complications of political and ordinary life—jealousy, desire, addiction, deceit, power, and corruption. In this last Age of Misfortune that is ushered in by the tumultuous events of the *Mahābhārata,* all values of propriety and moral obligation are set in question and humanity forgets its natural sense of right and wrong (dharma). The only solution to this decline is to relearn the ancient truths about the cosmos as well as social life. This is how the *Bhagavad Gītā* emerges, as a text with a solution to the crisis of moral decay that is at the core of the *Mahābhārata.*

The term that is used to describe the ancient truths about the proper functioning of the cosmos and of social life that the *Bhagavad Gītā* seeks to revitalize is the word *dharma.* This term literally means "to hold together," and in the *Bhagavad Gītā* as well as in the *Jñāneśvarī* the term *dharma* tends to be understood as displaying two key facets.[6] The first facet of dharma is the immutable force that holds the cosmos together. It describes the fundamental laws of reality, which cannot be transcended. This is the dharma that teaches about and encompasses familiar Hindu concepts, such as *karma* as an incontrovertible law of action and reaction; *samsara* or the cycle of karmic return and rebirth; *brahman,* the eternal and universal "everything"; and *atman,* the undying core of each living being. This concept of dharma, and variations on it, form the heart of the classical Indic religious world, not only of "Hinduism" but also of Jainism and Buddhism as well (with significant revisions of meaning in each), and the terms are drawn into other religious discursive worlds, such as Islam (especially in Sufism), Sikhism, and Christianity. The term *dharma* has even traveled as far as the American Beatniks of the 1950s and 1960s, and contemporary U.S. popular television shows like *Lost.* In these contexts it seems that this cosmic idea is what travels, the idea that a transcendent order is invested in everything, but perceiving that order is an acquired skill.

The second facet of dharma is social and contextual. This is the dharma that dictates the specific expectations of each individual, based on sex, age, or "station" in life, caste, and essential nature or *guna.* This concept of dharma is mutable and can be transgressed. Indeed, one marker of the Age of Misfortune is the very need for people to be reminded of this kind of dharma, of the fact there are right and wrong choices, and humans must make those choices. People have forgotten how to act in the Age of Misfortune and, moreover, have forgotten how all their actions are intermeshed with the cosmic forces in which they exist. This crisis over properly determining "what is right" is the impetus behind the production of various kinds of Dharma Śāstra over the last two thousand years. The very need for such a social science of action and choice is the proof of an age of discord in such understanding in society on the whole. The Dharma Śāstra attributed to Manu is the most famous of such texts, though the *Bhagavad Gītā* is also often considered a text within the social science of dharma.

This second aspect of dharma, as a social and mutable set of ethics situated within everyday life, is an important subject to flag here. In this context, of the social and variable, dharma exists within a field of debate. It is debated because it is mutable, and therefore it requires a process of adjudication and ethics, it requires *rationale* within a discursive field. In this social sense of dharma the field of debate revolves around right, rule, truth, justice, and legitimacy. Rulers throughout South Asian history have used this term to describe themselves, as in *dharmarāja*, "The Righteous Ruler" and *dharmacakravartin*, "The One Who Turns the Wheel of Dharma." Such titles indicate legitimacy by presenting rulers as the political solution to the rectification of cosmic and social dharma. The distance between these two aspects of dharma is the space of debate and the sphere of a dialogue in constant resolution. What this means is that dharma has long been a subject of social debate, and so it is a natural subject for public debate as well. Touching, as it does, upon the spaces where the cosmic and mundane meet, where sovereigns and subjects are joined, dharma represents a sphere of discursive engagement among people and social groups. The reason dharma is so centrally a concern for varna typologies is because it mediates social relationships. And the reason Dharma Śāstra is a "social" science, as opposed to a cosmic one, is because the social is the primary experience of dharma in the world and in everyday life.

While some texts may raise the discourse of dharma to levels of high philosophical abstraction, the *Bhagavad Gītā* is a text of the social science of dharma because it situates dharma within the complexity and uncertainty of human life. For this reason, the *Bhagavad Gītā* has a long history within the field of public and political life in South Asia. Though the *Bhagavad Gītā* is in Sanskrit, it signals a public debate. Even its narrative frame—a conversation between two people, in the midst of two armies, overheard by others—is a public discussion. And, like the *Mahābhārata,* the *Bhagavad Gītā* presents itself as a discourse for common people, even if its medium—Sanskrit—puts it outside their reach. And while the *Bhagavad Gītā,* as many have noted, often appears to be a highly conservative text, defending a very particular Brahmin-centered ethics, and likely doing so against the anti-Brahminic influences of Buddhism, it is still a text that presents itself as a solution to the problem of unequal access to salvation for all people. The public appeal of the *Bhagavad Gītā,* and the public framing of it, are key aspects that determined both the form and content of Jnandev's commentary in Marathi on the text.

The discipline involved in negotiating potential conflicts between these two kinds of dharma is referred to in the *Bhagavad Gītā* as *yoga.* The idea of yoga here sometimes sounds like the yoga better known in the genealogy that precedes modern forms of yoga, but here the term generally does not refer to physical activities but rather to a discipline of decision-making and through right action, salvation. The *Bhagavad Gītā* is often described as presenting three distinct yogas or ways to control the self in the face of a need to act so that the karmic debt that the self or soul (atman) normally accrues through a life of action is mitigated and minimized. These three are usually enumerated as *karmayoga,* or the discipline of "action" and renunciation of the fruits of action; *jñānayoga,* the discipline of "knowledge," of understanding the subtle machinations of the cosmos that render all decisions ephemeral; and *bhaktiyoga,* the discipline of devotion to God. These three disciplines are interconnected in this text, held in tension, and a long tradition of commentary on the *Bhagavad Gītā* draws out this strain, often arguing for the importance of one of these three yogas over another, or the presence of options beyond these three yogas or techniques. In many ways, however, the yogas of knowledge and renunciation of the fruits of action represent a highly specialized approach to the problem of action and decision, and in turn these yogas tend to appear as appropriate for the learned and highly skilled. As we will see, in these contexts social difference is erased through a philosophy and theology of transcendence. However, it is in the third yoga of bhakti that social difference becomes a more enduring problem, perhaps because it is this form of yoga that is most suited for everyday life, most accessible to the largest number of people. In the *Jñāneśvarī,* when we encounter issues related to caste and gender, and how these social factors impede the salvation of the soul, we will see an emphasis on bhakti as a way to solve this particular problem. For this reason, it seems that bhakti, everyday life, and the process of vernacularization are intertwined.

For over two thousand years, the *Bhagavad Gītā* has been a key text within the multiple expressions of Hinduism in South Asia and beyond. Its highly compressed form, poetic nature, and capacious embrace of multiple philosophical and religious trends make it an ideal text upon which one can work interpretive magic. The commentarial tradition around the *Bhagavad Gītā* began auspiciously around the eighth century CE with the figure of Shankaracharya, who was perhaps India's most famous scholar, its "Socrates" in a sense. From that point onward, writing a commentary on the *Bhagavad Gītā* became a natural course of action for the philosopher, spiritual teacher, and scholar. Indeed, though the Mahanubhavs are not well known for providing commentaries on the *Bhagavad Gītā*, at least fourteen different *Bhagavad Gītā* commentaries in Sanskrit and Marathi are attributed to Mahanubhav composers since the fourteenth century.[7]

The variegated and public discursive nature of the *Bhagavad Gītā* has always made it a text that appears to bridge the common and the cosmic, the world of the everyday and rarefied reaches of philosophy and high learning. It is this midpoint between earth and the heavens that the *Jñāneśvarī* and its author occupy. And just as the *Bhagavad Gītā* sought a détente among various philosophical, religious, and ethical streams of thought in India two thousand years ago, all couched in the context of a conversation, so too Jnandev and his eponymous text appear to mediate, on the one hand, an orthodox social consciousness, typified by Hemadri and the Brahminic ecumene in the late thirteenth century, and, on the other, an iconoclastic rejection of such orthodoxy, exemplified by Chakradhar and the early Mahanubhavs.

Though the *Jñāneśvarī* mentions neither Hemadri nor Chakradhar,[8] and largely eschews its own historical context—quite in contrast to the *Līḷācaritra*—still this text walks between the two poles of social orthodoxy and social critique (as does the *Bhagavad Gītā*), at times signaling allegiance to one, then to the other. On the subject of social equality, the *Jñāneśvarī* clearly spells out a politics of inclusion around language and the salvational possibilities that access to the *Bhagavad Gītā* affords. As we will see, by accessing the language of the very quotidian world to which he seeks to offer access to the *Bhagavad Gītā*, Jnandev must also draw in and passively reinforce some of the restrictions of that world. However, I argue that it is the effect of the *Jñāneśvarī* to plant the seeds of the potential disintegration of the social inequities of that quotidian world as well. Jnandev sees that the social critique mounted from the cosmic realm is the fulfillment of the cultural politics of the *Bhagavad Gītā* itself. Whatever the equivocations about social difference in the *Jñāneśvarī* that will be discussed in the next chapter, we will see here that the text is unequivocal about its presence at the epicenter of a new, valorized, glorified Marathi literature that makes the egalitarian salvation of the *Bhagavad Gītā* available to all.

The *Jñāneśvarī*, Its Structure, History, and Aesthetics

There is a story now canonical in Marathi popular memory that the Marathi sant Eknath (1533–1599 CE) had a dream in which he saw the figure of Jnandev seated in *sanjīvansamādhi*, a state of deep meditation, in Alandi, in a tomb underground where the roots of a tree had entangled him.[9] When Eknath awoke, he set out on a mission to refurbish the site of Jnandev's *samadhi*, the memorial or "tomb" that Jnandev is said to have entered. He also took this dream as a metaphor for the state of Jnandev's eponymous text, the *Jñāneśvarī*. In Eknath's time in the late sixteenth century, many different and diverging manuscripts and recollections of the *Jñāneśvarī* were apparently circulating in what must have been a vibrant Marathi literary sphere, as the story goes, and so the text had become corrupt, itself entangled in multiple recensions. Eknath is said to have collected together these versions of the text and edited them, producing a new edition of the *Jñāneśvarī*. Subsequently, all previous manuscripts were considered superfluous and the Eknathi *Jñāneśvarī* became the new standard.

Over the five centuries since Eknath's time, the text again multiplied, and there is no clear sense of which of the many versions of the *Jñāneśvarī* is Eknath's *Jñāneśvarī* (if indeed there is such a thing). In general, the most popular version of the *Jñāneśvarī* is the one edited by Sakhare in 1955 and reprinted regularly since then, which is said to conform to the Eknathi version. Indeed, Sakhare's editions of the works of many of the Varkari sants are the standard texts for Varkari worship as well as for the vast secondary field of commentary on the *Jñāneśvarī*. Chief among these commentarial texts is S. V. Dandekar's edition of the *Jñāneśvarī*, with his commentary and rendition of the text in modern Marathi, which follows Sakhare's text.[10] In 1909 the famous Marathi historian and philologist V. K. Rajwade claimed to have found a manuscript of the *Jñāneśvarī* that predated Eknath's time, a text he published.[11] From that time until now, perhaps fifty or more versions of the *Jñāneśvarī* have been brought out by publishing houses small and large; in addition, perhaps triple this number of various kinds of commentary on the *Jñāneśvarī*, which reprint the entire text, have also been published. And around this text exists a thriving world of public religious exposition, from small *pravacana* or "lecture" sessions all around Maharashtra, India, and the world, to social clubs and semiformal reading groups that recite and discuss the text. It is of course also a text at the very center of the Varkari religion in Maharashtra, even though it does not mention Varkaris, Vitthal, the pilgrimage to Pandharpur, or any other specific subject related to the Varkari faith. Thus the proliferation of textual representation that Eknath heroically tried to tame in the late sixteenth century appears to have only quickened its pace toward the modern era.[12]

The *Jñāneśvarī* is a long poem composed in the same language as the *Līḷācaritra*, what we generally call Old Marathi, and which also shows elements of Kannada, Sanskrit, and Persian influences, as well as a more ornate, poetic aesthetic. The *Jñāneśvarī* uses a loose oral meter referred to as an *ovi* that requires that three lines rhyme and be of more or less equal length (often eight syllables), while the final line need not rhyme and can be half the length of any one of the first three. There is some speculation that the ovi verse form was a "woman's work song" or a "song of the grinding mill."[13] While this may be an apocryphal idea, it nonetheless suggests the gendered nature of the text and its language. The reader might recall the discussion in chapter 5 of the ways a Sanskrit typology of language encodes Marathi within the field of Prakrit languages and hence a language with a "gender" as "feminine." The fact that the first poetic meter of Marathi is associated with gendered labor is highly suggestive even if not historically true. By the time Jnandev employed the ovi it was likely a well-established oral poetic medium, particularly among male performers (*kīrtankārs*) circulating in and between urban areas, and it is not considered a "women's work song" in the *Jñāneśvarī*, as far as I can tell. However, it is seen as a simple, popular, and easily understood metric form embedded within the public culture of the time.

The content of the *Jñāneśvarī* is a commentary on the *Bhagavad Gītā*, verse by verse, that usually contains the Sanskrit verse of the *Gītā*, then a paraphrase of the Sanskrit verse in some aspect of the explication of that verse. One can speak of the *Jñāneśvarī* as a "translation" only in the loosest sense of this term. The word *transfer* would be more appropriate than *translation* to convey the purported intentions of the author, for Jnandev seems to want to transfer not only the contents from Sanskrit to Marathi but also the divine aura of the text, its very nature as a thing that conveys merit and salvation. In other words, the literary symbolic capital of the Sanskrit verse, of the fact that the *Bhagavad Gītā* is originally in Sanskrit, is still a feature of this Marathi text. The reason for this is historical in a sense: Krishna and Arjuna, Jnandev implies, spoke in Sanskrit, and it is indeed the language of the Gods, as Jnandev will explicitly state. Thus, while the *Jñāneśvarī* functions in some sense as a "translation," it is not a formal translation of the *Bhagavad Gītā*, but a transfer of its words, meaning, and, most importantly, its salvational potential. The *Bhagavad Gītā* is only in Sanskrit, but the meaning of the *Bhagavad Gītā*, and the soteriological value of understanding that meaning, is a subject that should transcend Sanskrit, according to Jnandev's *Jñāneśvarī*.

The literary aesthetic of this text is complicated. It takes on the Sanskrit form of the commentary, but does not replicate the Sanskrit *śloka* form in that commentary, rather using the ovi instead. This is at least a hybrid example of what Pollock calls a "superposed cosmopolitan code" common in new regional literatures.[14] The hybridity here is contained in the mixing of the formal cosmopolitan genre of the commentary in Sanskrit with a genre not attested in the cosmopolitan Sanskrit sphere, the ovi. This blends the superimposed commentarial form upon a highly regional and quotidian Marathi poetic form. Vernacularization surpasses the use of a new language to recreate cosmopolitan Sanskritic literary idioms and presents a new aesthetic as well. In other words, vernacularization, and literary vernacularization in particular, is never merely derivative but is always novel. Here we can see the high cosmopolitan genre of commentary become domesticated, placed in a gendered form and a localized idiom. The literary structure of the *Jñāneśvarī* is a purposeful, even critical, embrace of the cosmopolitan by the quotidian, almost as though Jnandev were pulling the high Sanskrit commentarial tradition down to earth, drawing the world of Gods into the language of "men," or rather, of men as well as "women, low castes, and others."[15]

The "voice" of the commentary in the *Jñāneśvarī* is by default the voice of Jnandev; he narrates and presents the text. However, Jnandev often adopts Krishna's voice, ventriloquizing Krishna's meanings in Marathi. A rarely heard third voice is that of Nivritti, a figure described as Jnandev's guru. Though these are the only three voices of the text, there are times when Jnandev is mentioned as a third person in the text, and thus we may assume a kind of "omniscient narrator" as well. Or we may hear in such cases the narrative voice of the scribe who signs the colophon of the text, a figure named Satchidananda Baba. Despite these various voices and registers, the text, on the whole, is considered the articulation of Jnandev alone—Jnandev is its purported author and agent. This is apparent in that almost every chapter of the *Jñāneśvarī* ends with the conventional *bhanita* or "signature line" usually found in the poetry of bhakti. One finds some version of "Jnandev says" or *jñāndev mhāṇe* throughout the text and in the concluding lines of most chapters. As noted in chapter 3, the name "Jnaneshwar," from which the text receives its popular title, is not attested in the text; we have only the name Jnandev.

This somewhat complicated layering of authorial voice must be understood in the context of the oral presentation style that was almost surely the source for the *Jñāneśvarī*'s original composition, which is in the form of an oral public performance. This is the format to which Jnandev constantly returns our attention. He asks his audience to "listen," not read, even though he sometimes calls his text a "book" or *granth*.[16] Indeed, at the end of the composition he terms the *Jñāneśvarī* both a "book" and a *kirtan* or oral, didactic, and musical performance.[17] The *Jñāneśvarī* is like many bhakti and other South Asian texts in that it reveals a variety of authorial nodes and narrative voices, and these various narrative perspectives are in part a function of the medium. Though the oral and written are thoroughly intertwined here, both forms—grantha and kirtan[18]— suggest a single composition rather than a collection of discrete pieces. In other words, the *Jñāneśvarī* is not a set of distinct compositions combined into a single "text" at some later point, which is the case for most of the vast corpus of abhangs or song-poems attributed to the Varkari sants and others. Instead, the *Jñāneśvarī* was likely always a single, continuous text, even if recensions differed over its exact contents. As I detailed in *Religion and Public Memory*, the oral and literate exist along a continuum in the context of the performance and preservation of bhakti texts like the *Jñāneśvarī*, though this text, as a single discrete composition, structured around the famous *Bhagavad Gītā* finds a much more routinized material preservation in the manuscriptival record than do small, disconnected songs or abhangs that make up the great majority of Varkari devotional materials.[19]

In sum, though we can identify Jnandev as a self-described author of the text, the authority of the work involves several levels.[20] At perhaps the most basic level, the text has a scribe, Satchidananda, who is named in the last line of the *Jñāneśvarī*, in its colophon.[21] The overarching presence of the scribe is apparent when we observe that Jnandev appears as a figure in the text itself, along with Nivritti, the only other figure who speaks in the *Jñāneśvarī*. In other words, the overall narrative perspective of the text is in the third person, a perspective supplied (at least diegetically if not historically) by Satchidananda. I would argue that when we find the text referred to as a granth or "book," this "book" is technically the product of the scribe, not of Jnandev, who is the "author" of an oral discourse observed and recorded by Satchidananda. It is its nature as a book, as a written text, that allows the narrative to encompass Jnandev as a character, just as in the *Bhagavad Gītā,* where both Arjuna and Krishna are characters whose words are relayed to us by a third party observer. Jnandev even associates himself with Vyasa, who *tells* the story of the *Mahābhārata* and *Bhagavad Gītā* to Ganesh, the latter being the text's actual scribe.[22] We can think of this level of authorship as inhering in the "scribal author" of this text, who is described as Satchidananda, whereas the primary author, the "genius" behind the text, remains Jnandev. The degree to which Jnandev is the undisputed author—very much in the Western sense of this word—is amply revealed in the eponymous name of the text itself, the *Jñāneśvarī.* Yet the text carefully modulates a claim to Jnandev as its author, for this is a text *about* a text, after all, and a simple mono-nodal idea of authorship cannot describe the plural narrative phenomenon we encounter here, a fact about which the *Jñāneśvarī* appears to register self-conscious awareness.

Just as the *Bhagavad Gītā* is described as a dialogue between Arjuna and Krishna, this dialectic between Arjuna and Krishna is given a diegetic parallel within the *Jñāneśvarī,* as we are invited to imagine Jnandev offering his commentary, in public, likely in or near a temple, before Nivritti, who also appears as a "character" within the text. Jnandev's interactions with Nivritti at the beginning and the ending of chapters mimic the framing context of the *Bhagavad Gītā,* which often begins with some verbal interaction between Krishna and Arjuna (as in "Arjuna said" or "The Holy Lord said," etc.), though the bulk of each chapter of the *Bhagavad Gītā* displays Krishna delivering his teaching. This dialogic aesthetic also places the reader or listener in the position of an observing public; the text prescribes a public context of oral performance. Just as we overhear Krishna's conversation with Arjuna, we also overhear Jnandev's public presentation or pravacana to Nivritti. In a way that echoes the public trial of Chakradhar in a temple, Jnandev similarly expresses his text in the public realm—the conditions are entirely different, but the location is the same in that both figures speak into the public culture of their age, literally and through metaphorical diegetic setting.

And so the cohesive, booklike nature of this text should not also contravene its oral, performative nature. The orality of the *Jñāneśvarī* is preserved faithfully—as we will see, Jnandev invokes his audience, converses with Nivritti, and provides all the flourishes and techniques of the oral performer. I emphasize here the performative nature of the text in order to trace this important link from the *Bhagavad Gītā* to the *Jñāneśvarī* to the idea of an emergent public sphere in which this text exists amid texts of all sorts, including inscriptions, as a I argued in chapter 2. Furthermore, the *Bhagavad Gītā* is a conversation; and so too is the *Jñāneśvarī*. These are conversations overheard by others. Given this nature, they imply an interaction with the receptive publics in which they exist. If the vast proliferation of other *Jñāneśvarī* versions and the modern commentarial tradition on the *Jñāneśvarī* is any indication, then the modern public sphere in Marathi conveys this text into the present as a subject that not only registers an important debate but perpetuates that debate in public conveyed from the past.

One key feature of the orality and performativity of the *Jñāneśvarī* is the dominant use of simile (*upamā*), found here in almost every commentarial Marathi ovi on every *shloka* and usually collected into a set of similes stretching over many verses. This is a common characteristic of the *Jñāneśvarī*—the sheer volume of simile is like nothing else in Marathi literature. Indeed, the author of the text also seems self-conscious about the extensive use of simile. At the end of chapter 13, Jnandev says, "every word will be analyzed; every Sanskrit verse will be stuffed with similes."[23] In contemporary pravacana, as well as kirtan, the use of simile is a standard feature of oral performance. It is a mark of the brilliance of a performer that he or she can spontaneously construct an interconnected series of similes to explain a point. The compact nature of these similes is also indicative of the modularity of oral performance, the way in which—to borrow a phrase from contemporary film theory—each performance is also a set of "assemblages" that can be recalled in other contexts and related to new objects, inserted into new contexts. Similes abound in the *Jñāneśvarī* because it is preserved as an oral public performance.

It is important here to mark the cultural trove from which Jnandev mines his similes. One of the hallmarks of his work is his ability to transfer the high philosophical content of the Sanskrit *Bhagavad Gītā* into quotidian Marathi of the thirteenth century. In this way the everyday world that surrounds Jnandev provides him with a major source for his many commentarial metaphors. The language across the text is consciously pitched toward the "ordinary" person, the "women, low castes, and others" that Jnandev will identify. As in the *Līḷācaritra*, we find ample documentation of "everyday life" in the *Jñāneśvarī*. While far less self-consciously "historical" the text still conveys historical material from its context into the present. In the next chapter we will see that, by preserving the social assumptions implied in the use of certain colloquialisms and similes in the Marathi of his day, Jnandev reveals some limits inherent within the social ethics of creating access to the text for "ordinary" people, which is his goal.

One feature of this engagement of the "everyday" is the pleasure and play of language in the *Jñāneśvarī*. As in the *Līḷācaritra*, there is humor in the *Jñāneśvarī*. For example, throughout the text we find Nivritti chiding his disciple for his verbosity, which is perhaps deserved given that Jnandev expands upon a Sanskrit poem of a mere seven hundred verses by creating nine thousand verses of his own. In the course of the introduction to the *Jñāneśvarī*, Jnandev both praises the *Bhagavad Gītā* and deprecates himself, calling himself and by extension his text a mere "firefly" (*khadyotā*) in comparison to the sun, which is the *Bhagavad Gītā*.[24] He calls himself stupid (*neṇatu*), an idiot (*murkha*), slow-witted (*matimaṃda*), and without taste (*avivek*). This process of praising the *Bhagavad Gītā* and insulting himself is brought to a conclusion when his guru, Nivritti, interrupts him:

"Stop!" The Guru then said. "There's no need to go on like this!
Now just get to the point of your book here, and fast!" || Jn. 1.83 ||

This is good advice for any author. Jnandev appears to want to bring humor to his composition, and, though the subject is highly philosophical and in this sense "serious," he seems to be an author at play with language. Indeed, in my experience of attending lectures and performances (*pravacana* and *kirtan*) that expound the *Jñāneśvarī*, humor is an ever present aspect. This is perhaps part of the way the character of the text recalls the character of the author, who is said to have composed this text at the age of fifteen. At one point in the text Jnandev even refers to his own language as "child's talk," and in another passage he describes himself as an infant who has been separated from his "dear mother" the *Bhagavad Gītā*.[25]

Simplicity, humility, and innocence are endemic to the character of the narrator, the "Jnandev" that emerges within the *Jñāneśvarī*. Jnandev seemed to enjoy employing the rhetorical device of exasperated interjections offered by his guru, Nivritti, who is always ready with a playful chastisement to his childish but brilliant little brother. In a long digression at the start of chapter 9, Jnandev begs his audience to treat him with charity, and here, again, child metaphors are abundant.[26] At the end of a long digression, Jnandev's guru says:

"Hey, what's going on?! We get the gist already.
Now just tell us the story of Narayana (Krishna)." || Jn. 9.32 ||

And at the start of chapter 12, similarly, Jnandev causes Nivritti to say, "Stop all this talking and get on with your exposition of the *Bhagavad Gītā* already!" This happens again at the start of chapter 14. At the beginning of the final chapter, 18, Jnandev has Nivritti insist, "Knock off this babbling!"[27] And so with some regularity we are reminded of the character of Jnandev, his loquacious tendencies, his unabashed exuberance for his work, and the dialogic, public performative setting of his lecture on the *Bhagavad Gītā* that all serve to ground the text in a diegetically ordinary context, that make of the "scene" of the *Jñāneśvarī* a quintessentially vernacular moment of everyday encounter. I see this as the aesthetic of the quotidian, which is an innovation of the vernacular idiom in Marathi in this text. The *Jñāneśvarī* vernacularizes the narrative diegesis of the *Bhagavad Gītā* itself by creating symmetry between the narrative context for the dialogue of Arjuna and Krishna and that for the dialogue of Jnandev and Nivritti. The humor apparent in their exchanges, however, serves also to distinguish this text from the *Bhagavad Gītā*, to reduce both social and literary formality in a sense, to make the text intimate and autochthonous. This is a further reification of an aesthetic of the quotidian, the language of common offhanded and playful banter between brothers. The vernacular here is not just presented in the literary use of Marathi, but vernacularization is explicitly staged for us in an intimate Marathi conversation outside a temple in the heart of the Yadava lands.

Thus the *Jñāneśvarī* is many things: philosophy, theology, poetry, translation, commentary, and entertainment. Yet its message remains consistent. It is a text about "righteousness" or dharma in cosmic and common contexts. The text self-consciously articulates two otherwise discrete worlds, one of the *Bhagavad Gītā* and elite spheres of Sanskrit literacy and the other the common language of Marathi, pitched in a register that aims to reach a wide audience. This conjunction of languages—shifting the meaning of a central Sanskrit text on religion and dharma to Marathi—suggests a concomitant commitment to a certain kind of cultural or social politics. Yet the origin of whatever politics or ethics we may find in the text is predicated on the act of making available a Sanskrit text that is otherwise inaccessible to women, low castes, and others. In a search for the cultural politics of this text, we must seek to understand its sentiment around composing a commentary in Marathi on a famous Sanskrit text in the first place.

The Call for a Vernacular Literary Public

The *Jñāneśvarī* forthrightly declares the importance of its medium—Marathi—and its function as a literary device that seeks to address and even create an egalitarian, pluralistic audience in public culture. The text appears to engage the Sanskrit literary sphere of its era by making the *Bhagavad Gītā* the centerpiece of his commentary, but also self-consciously seeks to involve a Marathi public where such a commentary would have purchase.

Let me cite and discuss two passages that demonstrate the self-conscious literary venture that Jnandev undertakes. The first passage is from chapter 12 when Jnandev requests of Nivritti, whom he calls his "mother" here, that through his efforts:

> Let a gold mine of literature (*sāhitya*) be excavated from the soil of
> Marathi (*deśī*).
> Let vines of aesthetic discernment grow everywhere. || Jn. 12.12 ||

Four verses later, Jnandev declares:

> Let the knowledge of Brahman (*brahmavidyā*) abound in the city of
> Marathi (*marhāṭiyecām nagarīm*) . . . || Jn. 12.16 ||

These passages from the *Jñāneśvarī* offer a mixed set of metaphors, yet they all bear importantly upon language, social location, everyday life, and public culture. Jnandev's first metaphor is of a natural material that is transferred into capital in human civilization, and here he implies a careful refinement of Marathi, drawing a raw material into a substance and economy of value. The second metaphor invokes the expansion of nature, perhaps related to the idea of Marathi as a "natural" or Prakrit language, growing, he hopes, freely in the region. The final metaphor, of a "City of Marathi" seems to bring these two together—joining nature and human aesthetic value—in a figure of quotidian civilization, the city. The fact that his metaphor here is oddly mixed—from mining to agriculture to urbanity, so to speak—is perhaps more purposeful than is first apparent, for it signals three key features of the Yadava, or any, economy: the cultivation of capital and land mediated by urban politics.

These metaphors resonate in several other ways. They show us that Jnandev is self-conscious about the field of literature or *sāhitya* into which his text will be inserted, which is likely a reference to Sanskrit literature, a field of composition Jnandev seeks to parallel with a literary world in Marathi.[28] This passage may also imply the existence, in his time, of many other Marathi compositions of high literary merit for which we have no remaining physical evidence.[29] Jnandev is operating in a Marathi literary sphere already in existence, it would seem. The *Jñāneśvarī* does not position itself as the *first* literary work in Marathi or even, in a sense, one among few; instead, the *Jñāneśvarī* seems to address the lack of attention to an already existing literary sphere in Marathi, a "gold mine" he wishes to uncover, a thing already in place yet uncirculated in human interaction. The process that Pollock has describe as "literarization" is here well underway, or so the text seems to imply. If the *Līḷācaritra* appeared to reference already existing oral literary forms, the *Jñāneśvarī* appears to represent already existing written literary forms. The *Jñāneśvarī* is part of the movement toward Marathi literary abundance, certainly, but the text does not appear to consider itself to be singular in this world. We also have a resonance here with the Bourdieuan idea of social capital—the idea of "literature" as "gold," as capital in its own market of value. Pollock argues that a literature is present when a system or logic of aesthetics exists through which writing is analyzed and valued—that is, a system of social and artistic distinction exists.[30] These and other declarations from within the *Jñāneśvarī* are aimed at raising the "cultural capital" of this and all other such literary endeavors in Marathi of the age. I think the materialist metaphors of land cultivation and capital serve a symbolic function here of expressing the hope for a new economy of Marathi literature to emerge.

The reference to the "City of Marathi" is also important for it helps us locate Jnandev and his metaphors. In Marathi and Sanskrit in this period (as well as for centuries before and after), the word *nagara* refers to a "city" or major town.[31] Scholars have recognized the link between vernacularization and an increase in urbanization, particularly around 1000 CE in South Asia, and the connection within the cosmopolitan Sanskrit sphere among urban centers is well known.[32] Though only one of many factors that contribute to vernacularization, the connection between urbanization and language that the image of a "City of Marathi" conjures does suggest a corollary of the Habermasian café to the medieval town square or urban gathering place where ideas and cultural politics, as well as expressive idioms, could be honed and shared quickly. A city of Marathi is after all a social organization built on language or, more specifically, literature; it is, as Benedict Anderson famously said, an "imagined community," a community of literary interconnection. As we will see, Jnandev will locate his own text at the "crossroads" or chauhata of villages and cities, likely a key site of the medieval Indian public; indeed, the term chauhata itself indicates "out in the open" or "in public."[33] The *Jñāneśvarī* appears aware of the way in which urbanism and a burgeoning Marathi literature are linked. The *Jñāneśvarī* is directed toward the public square, toward the urban world and the nexus of smaller towns and villages that connected the major centers of Devgiri, Paithan, and other areas, and specifically to the places of public aggregation in these urban areas.[34] This was, and still is, the site where multiple forces meet in Indian social contexts. Leela Prasad, in her study of contemporary Sringeri, a South Indian pilgrimage town, notices how the "labyrinthine relationships between canons that prescribe conduct," such as Dharma Śāstra and other such idealized texts, meet "the complex exigencies of everyday life."[35] As in Prasad's exploration of the moral tale in public culture in Sringeri, Jnandev appears to provide a meditation on social ethics through oral performance situated at the heart of the urban world, a world not just of stone and wood but also of literary words.

Jnandev is tireless in his acclaim for Marathi as a literary language in the *Jñāneśvarī*. He regularly references Marathi,[36] which he praises throughout the text:

> I will compose my Marathi with such affectionate words and artistic
> expressions that [Marathi] would defeat even divine nectar in a contest
> over which is the sweeter. ‖ Jn. 6.14 ‖

He calls his language "direct" or "proper" (*nīta*), and claims it will charm one's senses and thus allow one to grasp the meaning of the *Bhagavad Gītā* holistically, rather than simply intellectually.[37] He declares:

> By the beauty (*nāgarapaṇe*) of Marathi, the aesthetic of peace (*śānta*) will
> outlive the aesthetic of passion (*śṛṅgāra*).
> Then these verses (*oviya*) will have become the jewels of rhetoric
> (*sāhitya*). ‖ Jn. 10.41 ‖

The term for "beauty" here is *nāgarapaṇa*, which means "the quality of being urban" and refers to the beauty of a sophisticated person of the city. The reference may be to the Sanskrit term *nagārika*, the city slicker, in a sense, who is also the subject of the famous *Kāmasūtra*. Jnandev may have the *Kāmasūtra* in mind, for he tells us that his nagārika language will have the aesthetic or *rasa* of peace, *śānta*, not the aesthetic of "beauty" and "attraction" or *śṛṅgāra*, which are among the key themes of the *Kāmasūtra*. Yet this differentiation likely runs deeper: *śṛṅgāra* is a premier subject of courtly Sanskrit poetry.[38] Jnandev is likely rejecting the Sanskrit lyricisms of the courtly aesthetic world here and asserting a purposeful break between court and everyday life. He is appropriating the cultural capital of Sanskrit through his commentary on a Sanskrit text in order to fashion a new field of literature in Marathi with its own presumptions of social ethics and literary distinction.

Yet despite what seems like bravado here, Jnandev appears self-aware of the lesser status of Marathi when compared to Sanskrit or perhaps even other vernaculars. He apologizes many times for the inadequacies of his text, as we have seen. Yet his metaphors, while they downplay his own talents and the value of his text, also manage to laud them at the same time. For example, at one point Jnandev says that the truths of his

Jñāneśvarī, though not as greatly expressed as those of the *Bhagavad Gītā*, are still the same truths, just as the vast sky, whether reflected on the surface of the wide ocean or a small pond, is still the same sky—quite a curious description of literary vernacularization from the point of view of the Sanskrit cosmopolis. This limitation seems in part related to an awareness of Marathi's status in the time of the text's composition. Jnandev, for example, calls Marathi "beautiful" (*lāvaṇyā*), but also "young" (*tārūṇyā*), describing Marathi as a maiden.[39] However, the *Bhagavad Gītā,* as well, becomes a maiden in Jnandev's similes, as he compares Sanskrit with Marathi:

> While reading the primary Sanskrit text alongside this beguiling Marathi
>> [commentary] and having understood the meaning [of the *Bhagavad Gītā*]
> You will not be able to tell which is the original. ||Jn. 10.42||

> Just like the way a beautiful [female] body is adorned with lovely
>> ornaments, so that one cannot say which is adorning which [the body
>> or the ornaments] || Jn. 10.43||

> In this way Marathi and Sanskrit occupy the same position of excellence.
> Just listen to the beauty and purity of Marathi! || Jn. 10.44||

Such reveling in the glory of Marathi, while expressing an anxiety about its inadequacies compared to Sanskrit, occurs in several places in the *Jñāneśvarī*. The link, for Jnandev, that saves his endeavor is the *Bhagavad Gītā:* by recomposing the *Bhagavad Gītā* in Marathi and offering commentary, the luster of the *Bhagavad Gītā*, which is yet more than the luster of Sanskrit, is transposed to Marathi. In this way the cultural capital of the cosmopolitan *Bhagavad Gītā* is "superimposed" (to use Pollock's term) onto the *Jñāneśvarī*, but not because the text is in Sanskrit; rather, because the text is "the song of God." But we should also notice the gendering of the medium, and hence of the message. The entire *Jñāneśvarī* is the maiden adorned with ornaments, for the text contains both the *Bhagavad Gīta* and the adornments of Jnandev's commentary.[40]

Jnandev appears precocious and even brave in the face of a daunting task and seems to see himself this way too: he tells us that he feels inadequate to bring the meaning of the *Bhagavad Gīta* into Marathi, that he fears failure, yet he will be daring (*dhiṭīmvā*) in his plan. Jnandev thus seems to sense the gravity of his work, bearing the weight of literary vernacularization on his shoulders. He compares himself to Vyasa, as noted: just as Vyasa had distilled the discourse of Krishna and Arjuna in Sanskrit, so does Jnandev in Marathi. At the very end of the *Jñāneśvarī*, he tells us that he has decorated the *Bhagavad Gītā* with the adornments of Marathi.[41] These boasts of beautifying the *Bhagavad Gītā* with Marathi are also confessions of anxiety, for Marathi, as Jnandev consistently says, simply adorns or ornaments the *Bhagavad Gītā,* but never replaces the original Sanskrit text. This sense of a hierarchy of languages, however much Jnandev challenges it, remains preserved in such metaphors. Yet the hierarchy of texts is something Jnandev is willing to challenge; he reserves particularly strident critique for the Sanskrit *Vedas* and even for Sanskrit itself.

Jnandev's concerns are literary, this is clear, but they also extend well beyond the merely literary or aesthetic. Jnandev articulates a moral compulsion to attend to his paraphrase and commentary on the *Bhagavad Gītā* that reveals a social ethics of equality around language access in society. He is explicit about the need to open the text to many listeners. He compares the Sanskrit *Bhagavad Gītā* (and its various elements) to a confluence of three famous rivers (Ganga, Yamuna, and Saraswati), which meet in Prayag/Allahabad, the site of the Maha Kumbha Mela. Two of the three rivers are visible waterways—the Ganga and Yamuna; the third, the Saraswati, is an invisible, "spiritual" river, which is nonetheless real to its devotees. Jnandev tells us that:

> The River Saraswati is a hidden river and this is the [essence of the]
>> *Bhagavad Gītā;* and the two other visible rivers of emotion flow into it.[42]

> Thus a sacred confluence of three is truly made, O Elders! || Jn. 11.7||

> By listening to [the *Jñāneśvarī*], anyone can easily enter this sacred
>> confluence.
> Jnandev says, "My benefactor has done this through me. || Jn. 11.8 ||

> From these Marathi words I have built steps to cross over the impassable
>> banks of Sanskrit.
> Because of Lord Nivritti, this treasure of *dharma* [the *Jñāneśvarī*] has been
>> composed. || Jn. 11.9 ||

Therefore, now anyone at all (*bhalata*) may bathe in these sacred waters
  as if they were at Prayag viewing Krishna's form as the Universal Lord.
And upon achieving all this, a person might just give up the world!"
  || Jn. 11.10||

The ethical message of this passage is multivalent. The *Bhagavad Gītā* is a sacred river that is inaccessible because of its medium, Sanskrit. It is specifically inaccessible to women, low castes, and others. He uses in his metaphor the location of Prayag or modern-day Allahabad, where the Maha (and Purna) Kumbha Melas occur. Though the pilgrimage was not nearly as large in earlier centuries,[43] the idea of this site as both a holy place and a place that (almost) anyone can visit makes this metaphor particularly important. Unlike a temple, the public nature of the river implies socially egalitarian access to something considered sacred and also purifying, a place where the concerns of the everyday (fetching water for drinking, cooking, and washing) meet the ritual concerns of sacred life (the sanctity of water as divine purifier).

For Jnandev, the accessibility of this sacred site inheres in the faculty of hearing as an "entry" (*dvār*) for the *Bhagavad Gītā*'s wisdom; he is lauding the oral transmission of the *Bhagavad Gītā*'s message, and implying that this orality bypasses the barrier of literary technology. Jnandev is suggesting that one's ability to hear the *Bhagavad Gītā*, and in particular his paraphrase and commentary, makes of one's hearing, of one's self, a place where these "sacred rivers" meet; this is a statement that bears some similarity to Michael Warner's idea that a public is constituted by "mere attention."[44] The idea is that the primary mode of delivery for the *Bhagavad Gītā* through the *Jñāneśvarī* is a passively aural one, a mode of affect and emotion; this and other bhakti texts produce attentive publics of devotion, that is, listeners for whom barriers of reception are dismantled or minimized but for whom participation can be constituted merely by attentive listening.[45] Whether or not the text is preserved in writing, it reaches the greatest number of people (at least in Jnandev's age) through the aural sphere.

The next line appears to be an explicit recognition of the event of this text within the environment of literary vernacularization. As we have seen, Sanskrit literary power was of primary importance within the context of Yadava politics and society. Here, in the *Jñāneśvarī*, Sanskrit is portrayed as a man made levee that seeks to hold or contain knowledge, a barrier that isolates something like a "public good"—water being the metaphor here—of spiritual and philosophical knowledge. The *Jñāneśvarī* breaks the levee, the social boundaries of Sanskrit, in order to share the learning contained in one of its most vaunted texts, the *Bhagavad Gītā*, Jnandev tells us, and he draws our attention to the instrument of this access—Marathi. As the final line above makes clear, Jnandev invites anyone whomsoever to "bathe in the confluence" his *Jñāneśvarī* makes possible.

Here one finds not only a social ethical mandate toward the distribution of knowledge in a Marathi public sphere but also a critique of Sanskrit and Sanskritic learning itself. Implied in the passages reviewed is a challenge to the mediation of Sanskrit by restrictions determined by caste and gender. Yet Jnandev is not offering an assessment of society at large, but rather a challenge to caste- and gender-based restrictions on access to the *Bhagavad Gītā* preserved in Sanskrit, and he does so, in part, because he believes the *Bhagavad Gītā* itself, in Sanskrit, moves toward this goal for it is self-consciously a text for all humanity. A deliberate declaration of this vernacular manifesto is apparent in the various aims and hopes I have outlined, which Jnandev expresses in a medium that he considers new, though not unique. This declaration links a call for a new literary idiom to a liberal social ethics.

The Liberal *Gītā*

In the final chapter of the *Jñāneśvarī*, Jnandev explains that the *Bhagavad Gītā* is itself a distillation of very complicated ideas into a form that anyone can understand. This is a crucial point for Jnandev: his Marathi text extends the inherent ethics and implications of the Sanskrit *Bhagavad Gītā*. The *Bhagavad Gītā,* to Jnandev, is a socially liberal text.

> The person who hears, recites, or understands the Gītā will be given
>   nothing less than liberation (*moksha*).
> Just like a rich donor would never say to someone in need, "I have nothing to give." || Jn. 18.1673 ||[46]

> Therefore, whatever your desire may be, that desire [will be fulfilled]
>   solely by serving the *Gītā*.
> For what more could you draw from any other scripture? || Jn. 18.1674 ||

Thus the inscrutable words [of philosophy] were included and simplified
    in the Anusthtub meter [in the *Bhagavad Gītā*]
For the sake of women, low castes (*shudra*), and others. || Jn. 18.1678 ||

The authority of the *Jñāneśvarī* is fundamentally derived from the transference of the charisma and ethics of the Sanskrit *Bhagavad Gītā* to Marathi, to the *Jñāneśvarī* and, by extension, to a new field of Marathi discourse that should be open to all, that should be inherently public. The text explicitly enacts a key feature of vernacularization in this sense, for it invests the discursive power of the cosmopolitan language into the vernacular and, through the vernacular, to an audience that cannot be circumscribed by elite literary technologies, an audience contained within the quotidian. With all shifts of power, there is a shift also of the idioms of power, and the *Jñāneśvarī* uniquely makes this link, something we did not see with the literary materials of the Mahanubhavs, for example. If the idiom of power in the Mahanubhav literature we have examined is limited to authority within a small religious sect, the idiom of power in the *Jñāneśvarī* is bold and transparent, seeking a literary revolution in the vernacular explicitly understood not as a language of royal power but as the language of the common world, or at least *for* the common world. What happens when "women, low castes, and others" come to comprehend texts such as the *Bhagavad Gītā* is not elaborated, yet we can clearly see the connection Jnandev wishes to draw between caste, gender, and Sanskrit, as well as the ethics he sustains throughout this text that admonish the social restrictions placed around Sanskrit. At the same time, it is the inchoate social ethics of a Sanskrit text, the *Bhagavad Gītā*, that gives this vernacular text, the *Jñāneśvarī*, its own ethical force.

The most sustained and explicit critique of Sanskrit comes in the final chapter toward the very end of the *Bhagavad Gītā*. It is in response to verse 66 of chapter 18 of the *Bhagavad Gītā* that Jnandev makes plain his social critique of Sanskrit. Here is the *Bhagavad Gita*'s verse in chapter 18, translated beautifully by Laurie Patton, as are all the translations from the *Bhagavad Gītā* quoted in this book:

Letting go of all *dharmas*, take me alone as your place of rest,
And do not grieve, because I will free you from all evils. || BG 18.66 ||[47]

In response to this Sanskrit verse, Jnandev elaborates on the way in which the *Bhagavad Gītā* dispels all illusions and simply brings the reader or listener into an intimacy with Krishna. This notion of an intimacy with Krishna is vital to Jnandev's ethics of vernacularization. As I have mentioned earlier, the narrative and diegetic construction of the *Jñāneśvarī* imitates the intimate, yet overheard, dialogue between Krishna and Arjuna by reframing that dialogue in the *Jñāneśvarī* as a conversation between brothers as well as guru and student. Jnandev illustrates this intimacy by imagining an embrace between Krishna and Arjuna that occasions an emotional release in both figures, a catharsis that is a metaphor for the feelings one might have when hearing or reading the *Bhagavad Gītā*. Here, as everywhere else, the charismatic power of Krishna is indistinguishable from the charismatic power of his words in the *Bhagavad Gītā*. As a high emotional register attends this moment of intimacy in the text, it leads Jnandev to argue, in an emboldened voice, that the *Bhagavad Gītā* is a text that contains the entirety of the Vedas. For Jnandev, the Vedas stand as a sign of all that is wrong with Sanskrit exclusivity around caste and gender. Speaking as himself rather than in the voice of Krishna, Jnandev states his case:

> Thus Krishna disclosed the core concept (*mūḷasūtra*) of the Vedas through
>   the teachings of the *Gītā,*
> A text of singular purity to which everyone has a right. || Jn. 18.1416 ||

> How can it be possible to comprehend the *Gītā* as containing the essence
>   of the Vedas?
> It's a well-known theory, told before, but I will tell it. || Jn. 18.1417 ||

> The one whose exhalation gave birth to the sacred syllables of the Vedas,
> He, the Knower of Truth, through his conviction, spoke [the Vedas] from
>   his own mouth. || Jn. 18.1418 ||

> Therefore, I say it is right to consider the *Gītā* as the essence of the
>   Vedas . . . || Jn. 18.1419 ||

The "theory" (*upapattī*) here is that if Krishna is God, and the Vedas are the word of God, then the "song" of God is likewise the word of God, thus the *Bhagavad Gītā* is of the same stature as the Vedas and contains the same essence. Given that the *Bhagavad Gītā* comes after the Vedas, that it is in a sense more "modern" not just in time and language but in social impulse, then the *Bhagavad Gītā* must contain what came before it, that is, the Vedas. Furthermore, if what Jnandev accomplishes is a distillation of the meaning of the *Bhagavad Gītā* into Marathi, he has brought down to earth not only the sacred "Song of God" but the primordial Vedas themselves. What is perhaps more important than clarifying this point is to see how exactly Jnandev makes his case.

Jnandev uses a Sanskritic phrase to describe who has the right to read the *Bhagavad Gītā* in verse. The phrase, which I have translated as "a [thing of] singular purity to which everyone has a right" (*sarvādhikāraikapavitra*) suggests that everyone has access regardless of the person's social purity within the varna normative typology or systems of gender-purity inequity. This idea implies that the *Bhagavad Gītā* is a fundamentally different text from the Vedas because the *Bhagavad Gītā* is not restricted to certain kinds or classes of humans who possess specialized access or authority with regard to certain texts, nor is it a text restricted to a particular ritualistic function. Jnandev is pinpointing the issue of social purity in public contexts. This varna-normative typology, as we have seen, was a key feature of Hemadri's Sanskrit treatise, and a primary subject of the Brahminic ecumene of the Yadava century. Jnandev also appears to make this point with some humor by placing this statement within the context of a compound Sanskrit word, *tatpuruṣa*, a rather fancy verbal construction in a Marathi context.[48] The impression this set of verses gives is of Jnandev criticizing the superiority of the Vedas, from the point of their content and also of their orthodox elitism. Yet he does so as someone *on the inside,* as it were, someone who can read the Vedas and who has the linguistic ability to use Sanskrit even while writing in Marathi.[49]

This portion of Jnandev's commentary is followed by a succinct summary of the *Bhagavad Gītā*'s eighteen chapters, in which each is related to some aspect of the Vedic corpus in order to show that the *Bhagavad Gītā* has it all. Jnandev then returns to his critique of the Vedas, only this time with more force, as if emboldened by the preceding distillation and rationale:

Thus the holy book, the *Gītā,* contains the ocean of Samkhya philosophy.[50]
It is the Veda in essence, yet it is different. It is more liberal (*audārya*).
|| Jn. 18.1116 ||

The Veda contains great treasures, but there is no other quite as miserly.
For [the Veda] enters only the ears of the three castes [Brahmin, Kshatriya,
and Vaishya]. || Jn. 18.1447 ||

All other living beings also endure the suffering of the world, whether
they be women, low castes, or others (*strishudradika*).
They should no longer be denied access. || Jn. 18.1448 ||

Thus the way I see it, in order to correct this previous failing,
And to serve all people, the Vedas took the form of the *Gītā*. || Jn. 18.1449 ||

Not only can the *Gītā* saturate the mind through its meaning, but that
meaning can also be perceived by the ears through listening, and
meaning can dwell in the mouth through recitation || Jn. 18.1450 ||

By reading the *Gītā* in the company of the wise, [or] writing it out con-
tinuously as if writing a book. || Jn. 18.1451 ||

To those who act upon such intentions, [it is as if they have come upon] a
place opened in the public square (*cokhaṭā*) of *samsara*
That freely gives out the pure nourishment (*gavandi*)[51] of blissful libera-
tion (moksha). || Jn. 18.1452 ||

This is a significant critique Jnandev levels against the traditions that
uphold the exclusivity of the Vedas and all soteriological Sanskrit knowledge. The Vedas are miserly, elitist, and morally deficient (*uṇem*) if they
withhold their contents from the quotidian world, the *stri-shudra-adika*,
"women—low castes [Shudra]—others." The reason the Veda's elitism
represents a moral failing is, according to Jnandev, because all creatures
suffer and so all creatures equally require salvation, an ethics that may
owe something to Buddhism. The Vedas need to be corrected for this error
of social exclusion; they must "pay off" (*pheḍāveyā*) their moral debt to
humanity by taking the form of the *Bhagavad Gītā*. In contrast to the Vedas,
the *Bhagavad Gītā* is an emblem of generosity or "liberality." I translate this
term *audārya* as "liberal" in only the most basic sense, that is, of an idea
about social generosity that sees the individual as a figure of progressive
freedom in some domain, not just soteriological freedom, but social and

political freedom as well. By the logic of transference made clear in the text, all that Jnandev says of the *Bhagavad Gītā* is also to be said of his text, his *Jñāneśvarī*, a self-declared creation of social "liberality" around access to the salvational potential contained in the *Bhagavad Gītā*. As I will argue in the conclusion, this liberality, though perhaps confined to the salvational sphere, subsequently moves into the social sphere.

The final verse proposes an important metaphor that will surface again in chapter 7 of this volume. At the heart of the preservation of caste, along with endogamy, is the rule of commensality—the social mores that govern with whom one can and cannot eat because of varying levels of purity. We saw this issue highlighted in the *Līḷācaritra* with Chakradhar's early community of Mahanubhavs struggling to fully understand how to renounce the caste rules of commensality. Commensality is the quintessential encounter of caste in everyday life, the rules that govern the ordinary and essential act of eating socially. In this case, Jnandev likens his text to what is essentially a space free of any rule of commensality, an open banquet, a *gavandi*. In general, a gavandi is a service place set up to distribute free food, often as a charity; the related term in Sanskrit is *annachatra*, a "canopy" (*chatra*) under which there is "food" (*anna*). A gavandi is usually financed by a wealthy donor for the benefit of people to whom service rendered would accrue merit for the donor, such as holy men, Brahmins, or other high-culture figures, as well as the poor and needy—in particular, pilgrims on their way to a holy site. Jnandev's gavandi is "free," by which he means both free of cost and unrestricted in terms of caste access, as opposed to a free service of food that observed rules of caste purity by restricting access to certain castes, thus rendering it not "free" to many.[52] The metaphor directly communicates a challenge to caste through the rejection of commensality rules, making the gavandi free to anyone at all. Furthermore, Jnandev places this banquet in the town square, the meeting of "four corners," the chauhata, thus locating his divine meal within the public realm, at least in metaphor. Given his reference to the "City of Marathi," one can imagine he also means to include in his metaphor of the crossroads the very social nexus formed in colloquial language, the meeting place of many social groups that is Marathi itself. Both free, in terms of access, and public, in terms of location, Jnandev constructs his metaphor around the idea of open access to all, and this is the essence of his socially liberal perspective, a moral ideal that he adopts from his reading of the social ethics of the *Bhagavad Gītā*.

Jnandev also emphasizes the quotidian here in an important way. The location of the public square is described as samsara. This word samsara is rich with valences, and those valences track the distinctions I have drawn between cosmic and social dharma. Here, when Jnandev correlates samsara with the word moksha, the soteriological goal of Hinduism, he means samsara as "the cycle of rebirth" and, by extension, "suffering" because of that cycle. Liberation, or moksha, is the release from samsara. However, here another meaning of the word samsara is apparent, which is "of the world" and "secular life," and even "domestic duties."[53] In contemporary Marathi and Hindi, it means something like "the grind" in English, or even "the mundane": one finds a chain of stores in Maharashtra named Samsara that sells kitchenware, for example. The point is that Jnandev uses the word to mean both the cosmic release from cycles of rebirth as well as the quotidian world of the "everyday." Jnandev's urban, commonplace metaphor is highly conditioned by the transcendental and metaphysical. He is not proposing a real place in a real town, but a realm of the supernatural and supersocial expressed as a quotidian experience—he is again "superposing" a cosmic order over an ordinary thing. It is in this realm of the cosmic that all, regardless of caste or gender difference, should receive the *Bhagavad Gītā* and, by extension, the *Jñāneśvarī*. But it is in the realm of the quotidian that Jnandev places his own text. His work is not "the song of God" but the "the song of the people." In the next chapter we will explore *Jñāneśvarī* from another perspective by reading the influences and even intrusions of the quotidian into a text about transcendence and equal access to salvation.

Sonic Equality

And He said unto them, he that hath eares to heare, let him heare.
—*MARK* 4:9 (KING JAMES BIBLE)

Imagine how long your journey has been. Years have gone by and now you have grown old. You have lost much. Your husband, your first daughter, and your strength to work. Your son cares for you, and you are safe, but your days are slow watching the sun move across the sky. You wonder when it will all stop. You have sat for many hours in the evenings near the tree beside the temple and listened to a young man describe the sacred discussion between Krishna and Arjuna. Now the cycle of his story is almost complete. You decide to sit a little closer this time, toward the base of the tree, where the women gather who wear much more color-ful and finely stitched cloth than your plain white sari. You are timid, but you approach, so as better to hear the speaker.

If the *Līḷācaritra* appears as a response to the changing conditions of an older age, the *Jñāneśvarī* is a text seeking to condition and direct a new era. This era is imagined as transformative in the literary sphere, of sahitya, a sphere, as the term implies, that mingles literature, aesthetics, and social-ity. Jnandev envisions not merely an innovative literature but a set of social ethics for that literature derived from the core intention of the *Bhagavad Gītā*, an intention left unactualized in its medium, Sanskrit. He portrays an image of fresh gold mines of Marathi literature, and he positions his new text within the Yadava century's urban nexus through the metaphor of the crossroads, market and city. A public culture is imagined through the *Jñāneśvarī*, one with newly dismantled social boundaries to universal salva-tion. Jnandev's text proposes a worldview where all people, regardless of caste or gender difference, have equal access to the *Bhagavad Gītā*, but to what degree does the *Jñāneśvarī* both register and critique social inequity in other less soteriological and more mundane contexts? In other words, what is the social vision of this text that carries the momentum of literary vernacularization in the social relations of everyday life? Given the foundational place the *Jñāneśvarī* holds in the history of Marathi literature, and the social critique embedded within vernacularization, the question of the social vision of this text is vital.

This chapter explores the specific question of the social ethics of the *Jñāneśvarī* regarding the distinctions of caste and gender in Jnandev's world as emblematic of the ethics of vernacularization. We will examine this subject through the text's statements about social differences. We will pursue this question through an analysis of the very thing that makes this literary work so decidedly local and vernacular, which is Jnandev's use of the colloquial Marathi of his age to give his text the sense and sound of everyday life. As we will see, the radical nature of the *Jñāneśvarī*, its revolutionary potential, also draws it into the glacial flows of quotidian life, where the weight of normal, colloquial social practice slows the liberal visions Jnandev provides.

How is Jnandev's clear sentiment about access to salvation represented in the *Bhagavad Gītā* conveyed in other social realms, outside the salvational and theological? As we will see, several points in the *Jñāneśvarī* advocate the rejection of caste and gender distinctions in society at large. This is particularly clear in the first nine chapters, which is the first half of the text. However, the *Jñāneśvarī* also evinces implicit social inequities expressed through the use of the very colloquial Marathi that makes this text accessible to the general Marathi-speaking public of the thirteenth century. We will see an explicit rejection of social distinction set against a more restricted egalitarianism emerging from the colloquial registers of Marathi. I will argue that the very process of vernacularization, invested in everyday life, both seeks a capacious discursive field, yet is also tempered by the social mores of vernacular culture itself. This balance between heterodoxy and orthodoxy is the primary subject of what I describe as a nascent public sphere represented in the *Jñāneśvarī* and in the *Līḷācaritra*. Both texts register a sphere of public debate about social inequity, though the resolution to this subject remains the ongoing question of the quotidian revolution.

It is precisely in using colloquial Marathi, the language of a new public sphere, that the *Jñāneśvarī* presents many conventions of caste and gender inequity prevalent in everyday life as normative conventions. Like the Mahanubhavs who used Marathi to overcome social distinctions, the *Jñāneśvarī* uses Marathi to surmount the linguistic barriers of access to the *Bhagavad Gītā*. And just as the Mahanubhavs accommodated the social distinctions of everyday life outside their immediate circle of initiates, so too does the *Jñāneśvarī* reveal layers of accommodation with the world of common society. This is a position at odds with an idea that has often accompanied discussions of bhakti: that is, the notion that bhakti generally presents a politics of social equality.[1] There is no doubt that many "bhakti movements" in South Asia have presented this perspective. To a great degree, this was the fundamental point of view of the early Mahanubhavs, and in the century or two before, of the Virashaivas who flourished in Kannada-speaking regions south of the Yadava realm.[2] However, as we will see, bhakti, if the *Jñāneśvarī* represents this idea to a great degree, is a mode of religious expression and practice that is deeply invested in everyday life, and while it can provide models for social equality, it can also reinscribe the social mores of that quotidian world.

Just as the "caste question" animated public discourse in the colonial period and later,[3] one can also speak of a "caste question" posited throughout the *Jñāneśvarī*. We have seen this question asked and answered in the preceding three chapters of this book. The process of vernacularization contains a critique of caste and gender, if not explicitly so, then implied in the very course by which the interconnections of caste, gender, and language are broken through a shift from a language that came restricted to the sphere of the cosmopolis to a language that fills a region of everyday life. The terms Pollock uses—*literization* and *literarization*—signal this difference. Literization is not primarily a social issue, but a technical one—it names the rudiments of writing of a given language, which is entirely confined to an elite sphere. Literarization, however, is the process by which power, meaning, and social restriction are applied to the use of language, and this is regularly associated with things such as class, gender, region, but also—almost uniformly in South Asia—caste. Literarization is a social process, not a technical one, and a process, I have argued that exists at the nexus of the elite and the nonelite, the field of the everyday. In Maharashtra the *Jñāneśvarī* is remembered and extolled as a text that not only epitomized

Marathi as a literary language—that is, the quintessential moment of literarization in Marathi—but also did so by setting a particular social agenda. The text, as we saw, claims to break the levees of Sanskrit that contain the sacred flow of the *Bhagavad Gītā* and to put its essence into a language that is local and common, the *deshi* or "country" language, as Jnandev so often calls Marathi. This effort at marginalizing Sanskrit cannot be disassociated from an effort to adjust, if not dismantle, a key aspect of the interconnections of caste, gender, and language. In the process, the reduction of social distinction in one sphere influences and threatens other spheres. This is the kernel of the story of Chakradhar's trial, as we saw at the end of chapter 5: that his social egalitarianism, particularly around women, had threatened to alter a traditional way of life.

In this chapter, however, we will turn away from the question of vernacularization and literarization in the *Jñāneśvarī* and instead investigate directly the content of the *Jñāneśvarī* that addresses social difference in its many forms. I approach the text's treatment of social difference through a diachronic analysis of the text itself, following the flow of the *Jñāneśvarī* to see how and when social difference is discussed. A pattern is discernible: the first nine verses articulate a theology and ethics of transcendence by which social difference is erased within the cosmic sphere of dharma; the latter nine verses contain, through Jnandev's ample metaphorical troves, some of the kinds of caste and gender distinctions and hierarchies that lurk within the quotidian, colloquial Marathi of his age. I argue that we see an explicit critique of caste and gender asymmetries of power placed alongside colloquialisms of difference because vernacularization itself mediates social inequities through its valorization of the language and social sphere of everyday life. In other words, the ambivalence of the quotidian world informs the social politics of vernacularization itself.

The *Jñāneśvarī* as a whole—containing both an explicit theology of social equality and a subterranean discourse that displays the social inequity of the age—stands as emblematic of the quotidian revolution as a process that both accommodates everyday life at the core of public culture, yet also restricts that accommodation. Social change in the quotidian revolution is not a sudden charge of social revision but a slow process of progress and regress, moving ever closer toward the expansion of everyday life at the core of public culture. The process is made possible by the social conversation about inequity itself, a social debate at the core of an evolving public sphere.

In what follows I read the *Jñāneśvarī* as a commentary and a record of the process of vernacularization and its attendant politics. My analysis of the text is necessarily selective; I do not claim to represent the entirety of the text's meanings, particularly its theological meanings. In this sense, I read this text in a way that is different from how it is most commonly received, which is as a theological and scriptural text as well as a literary masterpiece of Marathi. Indeed, caste and gender equity are but two of the many discursive investments of the *Jñāneśvarī*, and may not even be among its most prominent for those who revere the text. In many conversations with devotees and spiritual teachers for whom the *Jñāneśvarī* is a subject of study or devotion, when I would say that my aim in studying the text was an exploration of debates around social inequity, I would be met with a quizzical expression. For many such interlocutors, this text unequivocally expresses social equality, but this subject is hardly the core message of the *Jñāneśvarī*. As some critics said of my book on the Marathi sant Namdev, I may here too bypass a reading of this text as theology for a reading of this text as social philosophy and even social history.[4] I can only say that a deep and vibrant theological literature surrounds this text, and it has not been my aim to add to this excellent work, a job for which I have quite inadequate skills. Instead, my goal is different: to see what the *Jñāneśvarī* can tell us about a momentous period of social and cultural change in the history of India and the world.

The *Jñāneśvarī* is a text, as it claims, which is exceedingly generous: it invites its readers and listeners to engage with its many meanings, confident that its overall message of social equality and humanism will be heard. Indeed, even in those quizzical encounters with theologians and spiritual teachers, I have found that each is characterized by a tremendous generosity toward me and my engagement with this text. And so I preface my reading of this text here with my deep respect for the *Jñāneśvarī*'s message and the legacy of Jnandev. My critique here is by no means a criticism of Jnandev or the *Jñāneśvarī*, or the many people who put their faith in this text and person. Quite on the contrary, it is out of a profound admiration for both the *Jñāneśvarī* and for the legacy of Jnandev, as well as the deep and rich history of meanings this text has produced, that I venture at all into an analysis of this essential and brilliant work of world religious literature.

The Cultural Politics of Transcendence

In some sense, caste is the very first issue raised in the *Bhagavad Gītā*. As Arjuna sees his armies arrayed against the forces of his cousins, he questions the nature of the war. He sees it for what it is: a moment when dharma is in decline, for only such a decline can account for the calamity on the battlefield that he now faces. The entire first chapter of the *Bhagavad Gītā* registers Arjuna's despondency at his predicament and the civil war that will ensue. Arjuna rationalizes that if kin begin to kill kin, then the very nature or dharma of the family will be destroyed. The *Bhagavad Gītā* records Arjuna's despondency as a series of likely results of the war's destruction of fundamental social norms:

> Son of Vrishni, when the absence of *dharma* has conquered, the women
>   of the family are defiled
> And caste-confusion is born in the corruption of women. || BG 1.41 ||[5]

Arjuna worries that the war he is about to wage will lead to the degradation of all social orders, and the structure of the family—which harbors the primary rules that govern caste through marriage—will be transgressed. This is the inauguration of a kind of "family values" motif within the *Bhagavad Gītā* that is translated and further highlighted in the *Jñāneśvarī*. As I have argued elsewhere, the Marathi Varkari tradition, of which Jnandev is regularly considered a primary member, evinces a very particular notion of family values, focused around a kind of Vaishnava family-oriented normalcy that has its own effect on the social practices that surround bhakti.[6] The first engagement with caste and gender—in the *Jñāneśvarī* and also in the *Bhagavad Gītā*—involves just such a debate about family values.

The last few lines of the first chapter of the *Jñāneśvarī* introduce the subject of caste explicitly through commentary on these verses from the *Bhagavad Gītā*. Jnandev's commentary follows the ideological sense of the Sanskrit text, suggesting that women bear the social dharmic burden of order within families and that their corruption is the corruption of the entire social system. Following verse 41 of the first chapter of the *Bhagavad Gītā,* Jnandev's commentary in Marathi reads:

When the high [*uttama*] enter into the families of the low [*adhamīṃ*],
  castes [varna] become mixed.
Thus caste rules [*jātidharma*] are turned upside down. || Jn. 1.249 ||

Great sin enters into such families
Just like a flock of crows freely descending upon food offered in the pub-
  lic square (*cohaṭā*). || Jn. 1.250 ||[7]

A curious feature of this metaphor is the way Jnandev elaborates the
meaning of this verse through reference to food, which, when discussing
caste, implies commensality, as we saw at the end of the last chapter and
throughout the *Līḷācaritra*. In the *Bhagavad Gītā*, Arjuna's anxiety is over
the question of women and procreation, and this is the focal point of the
degradation of caste. Yet Jnandev's first commentary on this verse shifts
the emphasis from women, marriage, and progeny—from endogamy—to
commensality in public, in the town square and market. The metaphor he
chooses compares the degradation of castes to a murder of crows descending upon a meal on a street corner, representing the deterioration of the
socially institutionalized system of commensality to an "uncivilized" ani-
mal-like order. As we saw in the previous chapter, and as we will see yet
again in what is to follow, food offered at the meeting place or market of
the town or village—the "four corners," as it were—is an enduring metaphor for Jnandev; it is also the location where Mahanubhavs would start
their quest for alms in a new village or town. Thus Jnandev links endogamy and commensality (which are not linked in the *Bhagavad Gītā* at this
point), bringing together two of the key features of jati in South Asia. But
we should note that Jnandev here is explaining Arjuna's statements, which
represent his confusion over the nature and morality of the war; Jnandev is
not yet expressing Krishna's teaching and corrective to Arjuna's confusion.
In other words, Jnandev is expressing a *misapprehension*; he is not reinforcing a caste prejudice, but he does so by tying together two key issues for
his audience, commensality and caste.

The next chapter of the *Bhagavad Gītā* contains Krishna's initial chastisement of Arjuna in which Krishna essentially tells him to do his caste
duty and to "act like a man" so to speak—that is, to behave like a warrior.
Krishna does not challenge Arjuna's vision of the chaos that will follow the

fratricide before them—for, as God, Krishna must know the disaster about to unfold—but instead Krishna reminds Arjuna that all warriors must do their duty because it is the right thing to do. Though bad things will come from the war, perhaps even the kind of intermingling of castes and loosening of gender restrictions that both Arjuna in the *Bhagavad Gītā* and Jnandev in the *Jñāneśvarī* decry, shunning one's dharma is a still greater evil.

It is in the third chapter of the *Bhagavad Gītā* that Krishna famously advises Arjuna: "Better one's own dharma, even if ineffective, than the dharma of another, practiced well."[8] Jnandev's commentary on this verse is presented through metaphor, and he again brings us back to commensality:

> Tell me: should a twice-born, even if he be poor, and the food be delicious
> Allow himself to be served in the home of a Shudra? || Jn. 3.216 ||[9]

The answer to this rhetorical question appears to be "no," a high-caste person should not dine in the home of a Shudra; this seems neither as a critique of the "twice-born" nor of the Shudra, but a simple statement about the norms of society in Jnandev's time. However, as I will point out in the conclusion, Jnandev is said to transgress just this social convention in his later hagiography—to dine in the homes and company of the "low castes"—even though this is not his own description of his life or activities in the *Jñāneśvarī*. As many scholars and commentators will explain, Jnandev, when he composes the *Jñāneśvarī*, is remembered to have not yet completed his social-spiritual journey. He has yet to meet all of his fellow bhaktas, many of whom are low castes, "Untouchables," and women, and all of whom will become his companions in hagiography, especially the Shudra tailor Namdev. The *Jñāneśvarī*, I have regularly been told by its admirers, represents a philosophical and theological ethics that Jnandev will realize fully through his later associations with the devotees of Vitthal; it is only through this fellowship that Jnandev becomes a full-fledged Varkari, but it is also through this social change within Jnandev's life that his social ethics comes to its fullest shape.

Caste is next invoked in the *Jñāneśvarī* in response to chapter 4, verse 13 of the *Bhagavad Gītā,* a verse that has received the attention of many commentators, especially political reformist thinkers of the modern period in India. This verse states in Sanskrit in Krishna's voice:

> The four castes were brought forth by me, distributing *guṇas* with
> actions;
> Although I am the Creator of this world, know me as the Imperishable
> One who does not act. || BG 4.13 ||[10]

Jnandev essentially paraphrases this verse for his listener. Yet he also introduces something missing from the *Bhagavad Gītā.* In the voice of Krishna, Jnandev says that these distinctions of caste are wrought "even though all are one."[11] Jnandev here is careful to remind his listeners that the question of caste is specifically one of the phenomenal world, and this is the point he believes Krishna is making when Krishna declares that he sets the conditions for caste in motion but he is not directly responsible for its effects. In the *Bhagavad Gītā,* caste is treated as both an important feature of human life and a secondary aspect of cosmic reality, a byproduct of the fact that the cosmos evolves from three essential elements (the basic ideas of Samkhya philosophy) and that these elements, of their own accord, form both the natural and social world. Krishna explains himself, and Jnandev replicates his answer: everything comes from Krishna in general, which is the essence of cosmic dharma, but the actual unfolding of the phenomenal world according to these immutable principles is a realm of shared responsibility, of social dharma. This latter realm is the sphere of action in the *Bhagavad Gītā,* the very reason Arjuna does not know what to do and why Krishna must convince him of the correct path. Caste, in the cosmic realm, is reduced to immutable traits or gunas inherent in all things and hence caste is just another by-product of cosmic order or, rather, of a kind of dharmic biology, the laws that govern the evolution of species. The *Bhagavad Gītā,* early on, sets these two conditional spheres in place, and this is the core of the *Jñāneśvarī*'s engagement with caste and gender in all its forms. Social difference and hierarchy are vital to the quotidian world, where everyday life choices either maintain or disrupt important social norms; at the same time, such social differences are utterly inconsequential in the cosmic reality that Krishna ultimately represents. This latter point is often expressed as the overall social message of the *Jñāneśvarī,* and it dovetails with Jnandev's received hagiography.

The dialectical meaning of dharma here—separated into cosmic and social forms—implies that social difference is ultimately something to transcend when and if a person renounces normal social life. But for those who remain within normal social life, transcendence is not advocated.

At the center of the ethical arguments of the *Jñāneśvarī* and the *Bhagavad Gītā*, then, rests a bifurcated cultural politics of transcendence, and this mirrors what we saw in the *Līḷācaritra*, where one set of rules applied to Mahanubhav initiates but another set applied to those who had not embarked on this path of transcendence and asceticism. Unlike the *Bhagavad Gītā*, the *Jñāneśvarī* is situated within quotidian social life played out as a conversation between two brothers; it is not a dialogue between "man" and "God" or even prince and charioteer, as is the *Bhagavad Gītā*, but rather between two men and overheard by an audience of "regular" people.[12] The *Jñāneśvarī* by design bridges the cosmic world of the *Bhagavad Gītā* and the quotidian world as well as the transcendence of social difference and its immanence in everyday life.

At many points in the *Bhagavad Gītā*, caste is a subject addressed by Krishna as a specific subject of transcendence. For example, one of the first explicit expressions of the elision of caste appears in chapter 5 of the *Bhagavad Gītā* when Krishna declares:

> The pandits see the same—in a Brahmin, gifted with knowledge and
> training,
> As in a cow, or in an elephant; as in a dog, or in a dog-cooker. || BG 5.18 ||[13]

This statement comes in the context of a discourse about renunciation and rejection of the fruits of action through detachment. The Sanskrit shloka juxtaposes, we can imagine, what would have been conceived of as two opposite ends of the social spectrum—a learned Brahmin and an "Untouchable" described euphemistically and derogatively as a "dog-cooker" (*śvapāka*), a common phrase of caste denigration in Sanskrit and other Indic languages.[14] The theological ethics of the verse is clear enough: a person who understands cosmic dharma renounces not only the fruits of his actions but also the superficialities of the quotidian world, seeing all beings as the same.

Jnandev reiterates and expands upon this proclamation of the *Bhagavad Gītā*:

> Then if a gnat and an elephant, or a dog-eating outcaste (*śvapaca*) and a
> high caste (*dvija*) [are not different]
> How could it still be that [we consider] someone as a stranger and
> another as an intimate? || Jn. 5.92 ||

Or a cow superior and a dog inferior?

How could this dream remain for people who are wide-awake?

How does one wake up from the dream that this is the case,

That the cow and dog [are different], that one is high and the other is
    low? || Jn. 5.93 ||[15]

If the experience of egoism remains, then one sees the world through
    [such] distinction (*bheda*).

But if [distinction] is not there at the beginning, then how can there be
    difference (*viṣama*)? || Jn. 5.94 ||

Jnandev is unequivocal here, as he is throughout the *Jñāneśvarī*: caste and gender distinctions, and all other social difference, are features of the phenomenal, quotidian world, but the cosmic reality underlying these distinctions supports no differences among living things. Here Jnandev draws out and restates the radical social politics of the *Bhagavad Gītā* with emphasis and poetic élan. Whatever aspects of everyday life and its social distinctions exist within the *Jñāneśvarī*, they must all be juxtaposed to such clear statements. Yet encoded within both the *Bhagavad Gītā*'s text and Jnandev's commentary is also a reification of the social distinctions erased in cosmic Truth. The social rank expressed here is dismissed as illusory, but it is nonetheless enumerated in both texts. In other words, the clear expression of hierarchy in the *Bhagavad Gītā* and the *Jñāneśvarī*, even if that hierarchy is rejected, still gives us some sense of the power of the social world to endure despite the theological and philosophical interventions of such passages.

It is in chapter 9 of the *Jñāneśvarī* that the theology and social politics of caste and gender transcendence are most clearly presented. This chapter of the *Bhagavad Gītā* discusses transcendence and devotion, emphasizing how all can approach Krishna as God because he transcends the phenomenal world. Thus, chapter 9 of the *Jñāneśvarī* epitomizes the distinction between a social dharma—the dharma of varna, jati, and the *aśrama* or "stages of life"—and a cosmic dharma that will be fully revealed when Krishna displays his cosmic form to Arjuna in the chapter 11 of the *Bhagavad Gītā*. Jnandev's commentary applies the philosophy of transcendence to social distinction, and it is here in chapter 9 that caste, as jati and varna, receives the greatest concentration of attention in the *Jñāneśvarī*.

Jnandev's commentary on caste in chapter 9 is occasioned by this verse from the *Bhagavad Gītā:*

When I dwell in human form, the confused ones have contempt for me
Not knowing my highest nature as the great lord of beings. || BG 9.11 ||[16]

Jnandev responds to this verse with several metaphors and explanations that further explicate the Sanskrit verse's apparent meaning: that only fools understand Krishna, or God, actually to be manifest with the mundane accoutrements of human life. In this discussion Jnandev reveals the repetitive poetics that are yet another signal of the orality and performativity of his text, and these particular passages are well known in the oral contexts of Marathi kirtan and pravacana. Jnandev expounds:

I, who have no name, am attributed names; I, who have no karma, am
    attributed karma.
I, who have no physical body, am attributed physicality (*dehadharma*).
    || Jn. 9.155 ||

Though I am shapeless, I am ascribed a shape; though I have no form, a
    form of me is adorned.
Though I am beyond all rituals and rites, they go on performing them.
    || Jn. 9.156 ||

I am without caste (varna), but am ascribed caste; I am without qualities
    (guna), but am ascribed qualities.
I am without feet, but shown with feet; I am without hands, but shown
    with hands. || Jn. 9.157||

The text continues this way, as Jnandev, in the voice of Krishna, elaborates that Krishna is not confined to the various physical and metaphysical qualities ascribed to him by his devotees. Krishna is without ears and eyes; without clan; without beauty, and so on. Jnandev compares all such perceptions to a person dreaming that they are in the midst of a forest, when actually they are asleep in their beds.[17] As he concludes this short section of his commentary, he summarizes:

Alas, [people] still ascribe to my Name the rules of nature (*prākṛta*) and of
social life (*manuṣyadharma*).
Yet their concept [of me] is the very opposite of true knowledge (*jñāna*).
|| Jn. 9.168 ||

The critique of caste—if we can call this a critique—begins in earnest in the
Bhagavad Gītā and in the *Jñāneśvarī* as an analysis of the Divine Self, of Krishna
in his cosmic form. The arguments that follow rest on the essential idea that
Krishna is beyond all social distinctions, and so these social distinctions are
of only fleeting, human value—they need to be transcended. Subsequently,
in response to verse eighteen in chapter 9 of the *Bhagavad Gītā,* in which
Krishna describes his nature as the seed (*bīja*) of the cosmic order and of universal creation, Jnandev provides these elaborations in the voice of Krishna:

I am there at the beginning of the universe as unmanifest desire and the
seed of thought;
And I am there at the end of time (*kalpāṃtī*), like a hidden treasure.
|| Jn. 9.291 ||

I shatter all Names and Forms; I dissolve caste distinction (*varṇavyaktī*).
I erase differences ascribed to birth-caste (jati); the distance between
such categories disappears. || Jn. 9.292 ||

Jnandev extends this theme in the subsequent commentary on this chapter, which explains through various metaphors and dialogic creations the
way in which Krishna removes the importance of social distinction through
his cosmic being. There is a particular emphasis on caste here, as a premier example of the "names and forms" Krishna dissolves. However, even
in this context of the transcendence of caste, Jnandev's commentary tends
to invoke specific features of the stereotypes of caste difference, which he
does in order to connect to his audience's understandings of social order in
everyday life. For example, the next time caste is mentioned by Jnandev is in
response to verse 30 of chapter 9 of the *Bhagavad Gītā,* which says in Sanskrit:

If the one who does evil honours me and not another,
That one is thought to be good. That one has begun in the right way.
|| BG 9.30 ||[18]

Jnandev paraphrases the verse in this way:

> Someone who worships me with great affection, such a person does not descend
> Back into another body, whatever their caste (jati) may be. || Jn. 9.411 ||

Though caste is not explicit in the Sanskrit verse, in Jnandev's commentary the implications of caste within the verse are highlighted. While the Sanskrit text juxtaposes two words—*sudurācā* or "a very wicked person," with *sādhu*, or "a virtuous person"—Jnandev, in his paraphrase, elaborates upon the word *sudurācā* by commenting upon jati or caste, an issue not explicit in the Sanskrit verse. The sense here is that anyone of any caste, *even a lowly caste*, will be saved. This interpretation of Jnandev's first line of commentary is common through the tertiary commentarial tradition on the *Jñāneśvarī*, that is, in such contexts as pravacana and literary commentarial contexts where scholars and lecturers (*pravacanakār*) often quote this line. Indeed, when I have asked *Jñāneśvarī* experts, kirtankars, and pravacanakars about caste, it is often this line that is invoked to elaborate Jnandev's position on the issue.[19] My point here, however, is the correlation that Jnandev appears to make, that the quality of *sudurācā*, of being "wicked," is a quality that people mistakenly relate to low-caste status. Jnandev is not declaring that low-caste people are "wicked"; he is stating that worshipping Krishna nullifies all such misconceptions. And, through this connection of quality and social position, Jnandev seizes an opportunity to critique a prejudice that may be lurking in the thoughts of his listeners. One gets the sense here that he is directing this correlation between the Sanskrit text and his Marathi commentary toward those individuals who may hold that an association exists between human value and caste status.

Jnandev concludes this section by introducing a new term to his text, the Sanskrit word *antyaja*, or "lowest born," a term often used to refer to Shudras, low castes, and "Untouchables."[20] The term is essentially one of comparison, with the "higher" born referring to the "twice-born" or *dvija*, signifying the first three varnas: Brahmin, Kshatriya, and Vaishya. As a comparative term, the meaning of *antyaja/antyā* is highly flexible. Jnandev declares in the voice of Krishna that all who approach Krishna with devotion will be saved, even if:

One's family may not be high born (*kula uttama*); one's birth (jati) might
be of the lowest order (*antyā*),[21] or one may even have had the bad
luck to possess the body of an animal. || Jn. 9.437 ||

This crescendo of references to caste is finally met by its engagement in
the same chapter of the *Bhagavad Gītā* in verse 32:

Son of Pritha [i.e., Arjuna], those who seek refuge in me, even those who
come from evil wombs,
Or women, Vaishyas, even Shudras, they, too, go on the highest path.
|| BG 9.32 ||[22]

Jnandev's commentary on this verse reiterates the nature of the various
sinful and lowly people who may yet approach Krishna.[23] As a way to illustrate the capacity of Krishna to accept devotees from all social worlds,
Jnandev highlights the story of Prahlad in the commentary he provides,
a demon who worshipped Vishnu, was persecuted for his faith, and is
often associated with low-caste bhakti figures, especially those who are
persecuted for their caste status or religious beliefs.[24] This devout demon
occasioned the necessity of an avatar of Vishnu, Narasimha, or the "man-
lion," who descended to Earth to save his devotee. Extolling the virtues of
Prahlad, Jnandev, in the voice of Krishna, says:

Therefore, family, jati, and varna, all these things are utterly inconsequential.
The only thing that matters, Arjuna, is me. || Jn. 9.452 ||

And four verses later, Jnandev states:

People are born with difference—Kshatriyas, Vaishyas, women, Shudras,
or lower castes (*antyādi*) and even others—up until that time that they
reach me. || Jn. 9.456 ||[25]

Then castes (jati) and egoism dissolve like a crystal of salt into the sea
When they have the experience of joining me. || Jn. 9.457 ||

In the voice of Krishna, Jnandev describes how all castes and all types
of people can come to him for refuge and are saved. Jnandev expands

the *Bhagavad Gītā*'s reference to "women, Vaishyas, and Shudras" to also include, on one end, Kshatriyas, and on another, "*antyā* and even others." This enumeration implies a Brahminic perspective, outlining a comprehensive survey of the non-Brahmin social category. But it also reveals a rejection of a Brahminic distinction of social being. Jnandev concludes by returning to rephrase the initial verse of the *Bhagavad Gītā* that inaugurated this portion of commentary:

> Therefore, Arjuna, whether Vaishya, Shudra, a woman, or of mixed caste
>   [lit. "womb of sin" or *pāpayonī*]
> All such people, if they come to me with devotion, can abide with me.
> || Jn. 9.470 ||

Jnandev's cosmic social ethics are clear, and it is also apparent how he derives these ethics from the *Bhagavad Gītā*. These verses typify the discourse about caste and gender most commonly associated with Jnandev in Marathi public culture, among devotees, and among most scholars of devotionalism in India in which Jnandev is considered a social reformer and a person who rejected differences of caste and gender in the sphere of bhakti. Jnandev believed social differences dissolve in Krishna, in the cosmic dharma, and therefore all social contexts collapse along the spiritual path of bhakti yoga. The concentration of such verses on caste and gender difference in chapter 9 tends to typify Jnandev's ethics of social distinction and his rejection of social inequities in the face of cosmic reality. My own experience is that scholars and devotees in India and elsewhere regularly invoke chapter 9 and these verses to establish Jnandev's social ethics, that is, to reveal Jnandev's highly inclusive social ethics and his rejection of casteism and sexism.

The penultimate verse of this chapter of the *Bhagavad Gītā* returns to the question of social difference; it follows the logic of verse 32, in which we are told that the lowest of castes, and women, can approach Krishna for salvation. In verse 33 of chapter 9 of the *Bhagavad Gītā,* Krishna says:

> How much more the pure Brahmins and the royal sages are devoted in
>   this way!
> When you have reached this unhappy realm, which perishes, become
>   devoted to me. || BG 9.33 ||[26]

Here Krishna reassures Arjuna that if lowly people as women, low castes, and "Untouchables" are saved, should they resort in bhakti to Krishna, then Arjuna has no need to worry about his own fate or that of his high-caste male fellows on the battlefield, all of whom are either "Brahmins" or "saintly kings." It is a moment for Krishna to appeal to Arjuna's "common sense," which braids social normativity and theological logic. However, in Jnandev's commentary on this verse he takes this opportunity to elaborate upon the glory of Brahmins in a fulsome, lengthy passage.[27] His laudatory language about Brahmins, presented in the midst of a theo-ethical explanation for why caste is ultimately irrelevant, is a peculiar intervention on Jnandev's part, though it does not depart from the general heterogeneous Brahminic tenor of the Sanskrit *Bhagavad Gītā* itself.[28] Yet it is also emblematic of the dual meanings of such reflection on the various social differences that are dissolved in cosmic reality: for, in enumerating all such differences that are transcended, we have a recital of exactly those social differences that make up mundane, everyday life. Jnandev's text, like the lives of the early Mahanbhavs recorded in the *Līḷācaritra*, must walk this line between a radical rejection of social difference and an accommodation of prevailing social norms. This line, I argue, is inherent in the ways in which the cosmic dharma of transcendence and essential unity of all things meets the dharma of complex social reality, the very problem at the heart of the *Bhagavad Gītā*'s narrative.

The idea that cosmic dharma transcends all social distinction is clear, yet so is the image of a world filled with social distinction. Up to this point, throughout the first half of the *Jñāneśvarī*, the cultural politics surrounding the transcendence of social distinction has involved recourse to arguments about cosmic dharma and the illusory nature of quotidian reality, even if similes drawn from everyday life have reinforced the power of this illusion of difference as it is expressed in the language of everyday life. Caste and gender are features of mundane existence, and those who can see beyond the mundane, to glimpse the cosmic, hold no such social distinctions in thought or practice. However, embedded in many of those passages just cited, and others throughout the text of both the *Bhagavad Gītā* and the *Jñāneśvarī*, is a paradox: while bhakti, utter devotion, provides a means to transcend social difference, it also simultaneously remains invested in normal quotidian life. Let us now turn to a discussion of how the tension between the cosmic and the quotidian unfolds in the politics of social difference, representing a sort of compromise between cosmic transcendence and the social mores of everyday life, mediate by the devotionalism at the core of both the *Bhagavad Gītā* and the *Jñāneśvarī*.

Social distinction and bhakti are intertwined in the *Jñāneśvarī*, both as a subject of critique and a subject of normative quotidian social order. Chapter 12 of the *Bhagavad Gītā* is chiefly concerned with the nature of bhakti. In general, ideas around devotion tend to proliferate in this latter portion of the *Bhagavad Gītā* as well as the *Jñāneśvarī*. In verses 6 to 7 in chapter 12 of the *Bhagavad Gītā,* Krishna describes the features of devotion that enable his devotees to fully reach him. These include surrendering the fruits of all actions to Krishna and being entirely absorbed in thinking of him. In response to these injunctions, Jnandev comments:

> Those of the way of bhakti (*bhaktipantha*) are the ones who come to me
>   [Krishna] happily
> And perform their caste duties completely and wholeheartedly.
> || Jn. 12.76 ||

This verse elaborates upon the *Bhagavad Gītā* by suggesting that if one simply maintains the status quo of social convention, that is, keeps to the quotidian social mores of their world, yet does so by surrendering all such action to Krishna, then people from all stations of life are equal before God because they are judged by their "faith" not by their "birth." In another sense, Jnandev is suggesting that, rather than be unhappy with one's station in life, if a person can surrender this disquiet and accept his or her lot in life by offering up the sum of one's actions in devotion to God, then he or she will be saved.

The sense here is that rejecting social distinctions in everyday life is something suitable only for those who have either understood the deep philosophical meanings of cosmic dharma (*jnana yoga*) or have undertaken the strenuous practices of renunciation while remaining in everyday life (*karma yoga*). However, for people who have done neither, or are not capable of either, the path of devotion (*bhakti yoga*) is the best option.

This passage links social distinction to bhakti explicitly and perhaps counterintuitively for some. It may seem ironic to a reader to see that it is precisely where we find an ample discourse that erases and undermines social distinction, in the field of bhakti, that we have a statement that seems to reinforce just those social distinctions, that appears to argue that caste distinction is an inherently good thing. Unlike the passages about caste and gender we have heard up to this point, which emphasized the illusory nature of social distinction, here, bhakti appears to enable caste and gender distinction and hierarchy or at least provide the means to abandon one's attachment to one's social status. Yet this moment is not ironic if one considers that, unlike the paths of jnana or "gnosis" and karma or "renunciation," the mode of bhakti is inherently social or, rather, public, as I have argued here and elsewhere. If bhakti is the way to worship your deity *socially,* then it is likely to be the place where there are the most accommodations to social normativity coupled with challenges to that normative order. If bhakti is a social and public thing, then the thorny problems of sociality and public culture will be nestled within a discourse on bhakti.

Since the path of devotion is situated within everyday life, renouncing the norms of everyday life, of caste and gender in particular, is not possible in some contexts—the *Līḷācaritra* gave us ample demonstration of this problem. In the *Jñāneśvarī* we find a response to verse 10 of chapter 12 of the *Bhagavad Gītā,* where Jnandev expands upon the idea that if one does not have the natural ability to pursue the path of knowledge or study (*abhyās*), then one has another option: simple devotion to Krishna. Again, in this context, social distinctions appear to endure, as Jnandev advises, in the voice of Krishna:

Do not cordon off your senses; don't cease your pleasures;
Do not curb your pride in your caste status (*svajātī*) || Jn. 12.115 ||

Here bhakti is not a yoga of the cosmic and transcendental, but the very human, practical, and ordinary and so perfectly suited for those who fully dwell within the realm of quotidian dharma. As the yoga or discipline best suited to the quotidian world, bhakti is also the path most likely to absorb one key feature of the quotidian world: social difference. And If this is the case—that the social vicissitudes of everyday life must become a theological and sociological problem in bhakti for these reasons—then it also follows that bhakti would be a premier subject of literary vernacularization. Bhakti, if it is a social form, as I have argued elsewhere, also mediates sociality itself.

The deep investment of vernacular bhakti in everyday life brings with it the imprint of ordinary social norms and hierarchies. After this particular discussion of bhakti and quotidian social mores, we have an interesting literary phenomenon: the noticeable rise in the text of Marathi colloquialisms that rely upon social difference for rhetorical effect. We have already seen some examples above, as we did in chapters 4 and 5. The *Jñāneśvarī* holds together the forces of its strident egalitarian theological ethics and its situation within a social world rife with distinction and difference. This is also why, though the *Jñāneśvarī* is filled with theology, philosophy, mythic stories, and humor, it is still considered primarily a bhakti text. I think this is so because its overarching construction is a social intervention: to bring the salvation of the *Bhagavad Gītā* to the common person. At the same time, it is not a text constructed from the rarefied nomenclature of high Sanskritic philosophy, but rather composed in the colloquial Marathi of the thirteenth century, in the language of a place and a time rife with social difference. A text of transcendence composed in the language of rich immanence—this is a discursive space tailor-made for social debate.

If we have seen, by and large, the rejection of caste and gender difference within the first half of the discursive frame of the *Jñāneśvarī*, it is in the latter half that social distinction is revealed implicitly in the colloquial Marathi Jnandev employs. And, in most cases, the use of these colloquial expressions of social inequality is metaphorical, in the service of explaining something other than social distinction. In the world of autochthonous language, high philosophy meets common idioms and a society's values are etched therein.

Colloquialisms of Difference

While one essential lesson of the *Jñāneśvarī* is that social distinction is irrelevant to the machinations of cosmic dharma, the text conveys this message in the language of social distinction itself, that is, the language of the everyday, the vernacular, that meeting place between "Marathi" and "Maharashtra" that the *Līḷācaritra* articulated. The very nature of a "vernacular" is distinction, to be a language with a culture distinct by region, primarily, as well as other locational factors. And Jnandev envisions a theological sphere that is egalitarian, yet he, like us, lives in a world that is not. And from this unequal social world he draws the material for the explanatory similes and scenarios that enliven his composition. The language of everyday life is the art of discourse in the *Jñāneśvarī,* and this choice of language—this full embrace of the vernacular as a language deeply situated in the particulars of place and time—displays many of the social preconceptions of Jnandev's age. I *do not* argue that what we see in Jnandev's language is *his* prejudice—we have already seen that he does not believe in the distinctions of caste and gender, and his later biography will bear this out in his public memory. Jnandev's position on social difference has been expressed very clearly in this chapter and in the preceding chapter of this book—he rejects caste and gender distinctions and is an advocate of social equity. What I will argue is that because Jnandev uses colloquial Marathi to express the salvational effects of the Sanskrit *Bhagavad Gītā,* some of the social inequity of his age is reflected in his medium. Jnandev calls upon Marathi colloquialisms in order to communicate his message to the general population and in this process, we can see the contours of the very social inequity that the early Mahanubhavs and Jnandev decry.

In chapter 13 of the *Jñāneśvarī,* caste is referenced through an interesting metaphor provided by Jnandev that draws from assumptions about social normalcy. Jnandev offers here a response to verse 8 of chapter 13 in the *Bhagavad Gītā,* where a rather fulsome list appears of positive attributes such as humility, nonviolence, simplicity, and so on.[29] Jnandev provides one of the longest commentarial passages of the *Jñāneśvarī* in elucidating this section. In response to the attribute of "cleanliness," and perhaps as a prelude to his discussion of the attribute of "steadfastness," Jnandev comments:

> Even if a man is walking along the road and meets a pure woman (*cokhī*),
>> or a Mahar [Untouchable] woman (Māhārī)
> He touches (*nātala*) neither, remaining steadfast in his attention.
>> || Jn. 13.478 ||

This passage is interesting for several reasons. The simplest reading is perhaps that a man of pure mind treats a high-caste woman and an "Untouchable" woman in the same way—he does not "touch," that is, disturb, either one. There is some reason to accept this interpretation, because the term juxtaposed to Māhārī is *cokhī* or pure, thus the dialogical translation is "pure one" versus "impure one" by implications of caste normativity.

Mahar, however, is not a word that means "impure" but rather is a jati name for an "Untouchable" caste. The word *Māhārī* simply means "a Mahar woman." On the other hand, *cokhī* is an adjectival noun and makes no reference to the name of a caste. Given that Jnandev is elaborating upon the idea of "cleanliness," one might expect that his invocation of the Mahar woman is meant to indicate a caste-based sense of impurity, thus signaling a particular reader or listener, one for whom contact with a Mahar woman would be considered impure. In other words, a "clean" man, a man of good manners, disturbs no woman, regardless of caste.

Some translators have associated the term *Māhārī* with the profession of prostitution,[30] even though neither Panse nor Velingakar in their glossaries of terms in the *Jñāneśvarī* give such a definition.[31] However, the term *prostitute* does not capture the social context revealed in this verse—the man touches neither woman, after all, meaning that another man might touch either. The verse may draw some of its power from the prevailing prejudice in the thirteenth century that low-caste or "Untouchable" women were sexually available. In other words, there is not an exchange of money for sex, as in prostitution, but rather the assumption that a Māhārī is simply available, for sex, labor, or other things.[32] This is not Jnandev's prejudice—this idea would be repugnant to his social ethics. But I do think he is drawing from a common linguistic trope of Marathi in his time, and in this context Māhārī may appear as a euphemism for a sexually available woman. The effect of the passage is to argue that a man who is steadfast does not find himself attracted to any type of woman at all, and so the simplest reading of this passage is the most general even if it conveys a very specific set of ideas about caste and gender.

Jnandev earlier seems to use the feminine form of the name of another "Untouchable" community in the region, the Mangs, in a verse of chapter 3 where he means to indicate something similar.

> [Desire (*kāma*) and anger (*kroda*)] have stripped peace of its goodness,
>> then dressed up Maya as a Mang woman (Māṇgi).
> Because of her [Maya], many holy men have been prone to pollution.
>> || Jn. 3.246 ||[33]

Here, as before, the feminine proper noun for a woman of an "Untouchable" caste, in this case the Mang caste, Māṇgi seems to be used as an index of something else, something negative, a disguise for the effects of "illusion" or Maya, the classic Indian philosophical idea that the phenomenal world hides the world of "ultimate truth" and often in a way that is filled with sense pleasure and distraction. Several scholars have translated the use of the proper noun *Māṅgi* to mean something like "prostitute" or "promiscuous," suggesting that Maya or the personification of "illusion" takes the form of a beguiling female who "corrupts" holy men, distracting them from their pursuit of ultimate reality.[34] The implication here is that a Māṅgi would distract a male's efforts at detachment and, importantly, celibacy. Caste, gender, and power are meld in such a colloquial use of Māṅgi, just as we have seen with Māhārī. Again, *I do not think that this is Jnandev's sentiment, but rather that of the colloquial Marathi of his age.* But I sense here a very particular challenge that is hardly directed at Mangs or "Untouchables." Instead, I get the impression that Jnandev is challenging *tantric* ascetics who use sex as part of their practice in which low-caste women often appear as essential. We saw a similar critique embedded in the story of Kamakhya's attempt to seduce Changadev retold very early in the *Līḷācaritra*. Both the early Mahanubhavs and Jnandev of the *Jñāneśvarī* are highly influenced by Natha yoga, yet both appear to reject tantric yoga in their time.

Throughout the *Jñāneśvarī* caste and gender differences sometimes appear as features of a literary trope, a way for Jnandev to express through metaphor some other theological or philosophical issue. In such cases, the language of the quotidian—as we have seen, for example—registers prevailing social norms. Just as Brahmins are sometimes conceived to be gluttonous, ritualistic automatons in the *Līḷācaritra*, the *Jñāneśvarī* also observes certain stereotypes about caste and gender. Although an exposition of that norm is not the point of Jnandev's analysis, yet we can look to such moments to recover the implications of language usage upon social normativity in Jnandev's age.

One such example can be drawn from chapter 15, which engages caste only once, with reference to the term *Chandal*, a word for a "fierce Untouchable" that we have seen before. The reference appears in Jnandev's elaboration of the second verse of this chapter of the *Bhagavad Gītā*, a verse that seeks to explain the cosmic evolution of the three primordial qualities (guna) of some Indian philosophy cosmology systems, such as Samkhya. The Sanskrit verse discusses how these gunas or qualities manifest in the phenomenal world through a metaphor of a tree sending branches of different qualities in many directions. In a portion of the text where Jnandev engages the guna or quality of *tamas* or "sloth," he offers these verses:

> The root of bad actions grows rapidly over and over
> And over and over, new roots spread widely. || Jn. 15.167 ||

> Then Chandals and other lowly people, such defective births [become]
>   many branches,
> And they form a thicket that lures those who have become lax in their
>   duties (*karmabhraṣṭa*). || Jn. 15.168 ||

The word Chandal, as we have seen, does not indicate an actual jati or varna, but appears to be—in Maharashtra of the thirteenth century—a term of abuse essentially meaning "outcaste" or someone who has strayed from social orthodoxy in some significant way. It is a term of abuse particularly among Brahmins, it seems, and so names a mythic or fictional "outcaste other" rather than an actual social group. The Chandal is often considered a kind of antipode to the "Brahmin" in a way that recalls the Buddhist injunction that all good people are "Brahmin" regardless, and indeed in spite of, their jati or varna.[35] Similarly, even Brahmins can be Chandals by action—as we have seen Prajnasagar and Mayata Hari point out in the *Līḷācaritra*. The term also indicates a general category of miscegenation and, by extension, of socially inappropriate intermixing. The idea here, of one bad action spawning others, is reminiscent of Arjuna's first challenge to Krishna, that with the onset of civil war other aspects of society will descend into chaos. Though a term embedded in the matrix of caste is used, it is a feature of the theoretical typologies of varna and not the social ethnology of jati that is marked. Instead, we have a claim that bad actions promote yet more bad actions. In a section of the text on "qualities," we must read this emphasis on how actions, compelled by one's social ontology, determine the future. There is here the "law of karma" at work, and in such cases arguments about caste are never far behind.

The echo of the Buddhist critique of caste as a result of action not birth is heard again in chapter 16 of the *Bhagavad Gītā*, a text well aware of its Buddhist antagonists. The first three verses of the *Bhagavad Gītā* in this chapter enumerate all the qualities of one born with a divine nature. These qualities include fearlessness, purity, wisdom, charity, self-restraint, and so on. The text does not ascribe these positive qualities to any particular varna. The fourth verse, however, describes negative traits and cautions:

Son of Pritha [Arjuna], fraud, insolence, and hostile conceit; anger, rough
  speech too, and ignorance
These are the traits of those born to the demonic condition. || BG 16.4 ||[36]

The set of three Sanskrit verses on the subject of the nature of good, plus one verse on the nature of the demonic, culminates in a fifth verse in which Krishna assures Arjuna that divine nature is the means of attaining "liberation" or moksha, whereas demonic nature is the cause of ensnarement in the world. Nowhere in these five Sanskrit verses of the *Bhagavad Gītā* is caste invoked explicitly, though the descriptions of those with a "divine" nature and those with a "demonic" nature have elsewhere been correlated to caste. Yet the absence of jati ascription is important, as it is with the designation Chandal, and this allows the *Bhagavad Gītā* its usual measure of hermeneutic possibilities.

In carrying the text's meaning into Marathi, Jnandev invokes both caste and gender. He states:

[In society] there is a boundary between Brahmins, who are placed in the
  first position, and women and others (*striyādika*) on the other side,
And in the middle is everyone else according to the person's rights.
  || Jn. 16.93 ||

Those religious practices (*devatādhāma*) that are of the highest devotional
  value[37]
They are the rituals enacted in orthodox ways. || Jn. 16.94 ||

Just as the twice-born perform the required six sacraments, just so the
  Shudra is expected to honor (*namaskārī*) the Brahmin
And thus both equally should receive the fruits of this offering (*yāgu*)
  || Jn. 16.95 ||

Coming toward the end of Jnandev's commentary on the *Bhagavad Gita* as a whole, this set of three verses serves as a summation for a general view of caste as the social order of dharma as opposed to its cosmic order. These passages suggest that caste serves to regulate society. Jnandev often reiterates that performing one's caste duties, with benevolence from all quarters, provides an ideal social dharmic scenario. This is an idea found regularly in dharmic texts for at least two thousand years, from its early articulations in the *Bhagavad Gītā* and Dharma Śāstra literature to the ideas of many of India's key nationalist leaders, including B. G. Tilak and M. K. Gandhi. It is an idea prominently expressed in the *Caturvarga Cintāmani* of Hemadri and, by extension, in the social science discourse of the Yadava century and the Brahminic ecumene. Caste is not exploitation, this point of view suggests, but social regulation. Higher castes, if they go outside the bounds of their own duties, exploit lower castes; and lower castes, if they refuse to undertake their traditional duties, disrupt social order. But if all castes benevolently undertake their prescribed duties, society is in harmonious and dharmic equilibrium. The word for this sense of collective social responsibility is distilled in the word *yāgu*, meaning "sacrifice" and it echoes the idea of an actual ritualistic sacrifice accruing benefit to the sacrificer or patron (very specifically the Vedic sacrifice, the pre-eminent activity of the ancient Brahmin). In this case the Brahmin and Shudra are considered "patrons" in the same sacrifice; they each have a role to play, and if both do their duties both receive the benefits of that sacrifice. Sacrifice here is a metaphor for a highly Brahminically oriented notion of society. Here the sacrifice itself is doing one's duty in the world, in quotidian life.

One can also see a particular hierarchy ascribed to this sacrifice. The Brahmin's duty is toward God and sacred rites; the Shudra's duty is toward the Brahmin. The duty of the Brahmin is otherworldly; the duty of the Shudra is this-worldly and circumscribed by sociality. The idea expressed here is as old as the "caste system" itself and is deeply embedded in the politics of social organization, from the family to the village to the town and city, and it undergirds practices like *jajmani* and *baluta*.[38] As we have seen throughout the text, this proclamation is a description of everyday life, not a prescription made by Jnandev. It is, after all, the *striyādika*—the "women and others"—for whom he has composed the *Jñāneśvarī*; Jnandev is unmistakeably their advocate. And yet we see this prevailing notion of caste normativity—so stridently rejected by modern activists and social critics, such as Ambedkar and Periyar and others—evince its deep roots here.

We should notice that Jnandev's commentary follows the idea of extrapolating the meaning of "sacrifice" from the context of the Vedic sacrifice very specifically, which is to say, of orthodox Brahminic worldviews. And we have already seen Jnandev's critique of the "miserly" and exclusive nature of the Vedas. It would be wrong to understand that Jnandev here is expressing his own views on the order of society, and yet we have through him a familiar idealization of Brahminic social normativity, just the kind of thing Chakradhar called *adhamatva* or "vileness" in the *Līḷācaritra*, a position Jnandev, in most parts of the *Jñāneśvarī* and certainly in his later hagiography, shares with Chakradhar. This passage powerfully reminds us of the prevailing social orthodoxies of Jnandev's age, even if it does not capture the capacious social ethics Jnandev asserts almost everywhere else in his text.

The final invocation of caste in chapter 16 of the *Jñāneśvarī* occurs at the beginning of a series of metaphors elaborating upon the second verse of this chapter of the *Bhagavad Gītā* and in particular expressing the sentiment of humility and shame. Jnandev discusses such sentiments as inherent in a king who experiences defeat or a proud person humbled by failure. Jnandev writes of something like shame:

Just as a renunciate would feel tremendous anxiety
If a group of Chandals came near with wine and women . . . || Jn. 16.175 ||

The example of the renunciate is interesting because he is supposed to be beyond all social difference; he is presumably one of the wise ones in Jnandev's elaboration of chapters 5 and 9, one who sees through the illusion of caste and gender difference, a person who has surpassed the veneer of social dharma. So why the anxiety when a group of Chandals comes by? And why the association of Chandals with "wine and women"?

This passage conveys a sense of the temptations of the phenomenal world and particularly its sensual pleasures. The association with the term Chandal implies an association with sexual availability and lax moral standards, the Chandal signaling the result of moral decrepitude. I think Jnandev's hypothetical renunciate here is embarrassed not simply because he has come upon Chandals with wine and women in tow, but because of the sexual improprieties that might occur to him, that might tempt him away from his resolutions as a renunciate. Furthermore, as we have seen, the term Chandal is typological, not ethnologically specific. In other words, a Chandal here could very well be a Brahmin—anyone who behaves in an antinomian way. One is reminded here of the novel *Saṃskāra* by U. R. Ananthamurthy (1979) where a Brahmin in a small village rejects the rules of caste—by eating meat (including the sacred fish from the temple's fish tank) and taking a low-caste woman as his partner—and upon his death a debate ensues about how to treat him, as a Brahmin or an outcaste, essentially a Chandal, and thus how to carry out his funeral rites.[39] The figure of the Chandal with "wine and women" is an abstract representation of the temptations that can unsettle quotidian social order, and it resonates with images of the antinomian Tantrika. The term *lāja*, used in the passage for "anxiety," is more apt to describe this sort of potential sentiment. As with the stories of a sage dreaming he has been born an "Untouchable," this story of a holy person accidentally encountering Chandals is ambivalent on questions of caste difference, allowing several interpretations, which the oral tradition of exposition, or pravacana, may liberally undertake. Of course, the force of the insult implies a pernicious casteism within Yadava society in general, but the power of the word here is metaphorical, even if likely directed at high- or middle-caste people.

Chapter 17 invokes caste in various metaphorical elaborations. This chapter of the *Bhagavad Gītā* involves a return to the discussion of how the three gunas or qualities mingle to create individual beings, which in turn can be classified according to a strict typology of essential difference. While this seems a natural place for a discussion of varna in particular to emerge, the text of the *Bhagavad Gītā* does not discuss varna or caste in any other way directly. But the three-plus-one division of society in the varna categories is implied throughout the text of the *Bhagavad Gītā.* This chapter also discusses sacrifice, food, and many other aspects of the social and phenomenal world, but caste is certainly an important subtext, especially in the first few Sanskrit verses. And Jnandev's interpretations of this section bear greatly on the question of caste in the text.

Chapter 17 of the *Bhagavad Gītā* begins with Arjuna asking if faith alone, aside from scriptural knowledge, is useful or sufficient along the path of dharma. Though Krishna's response simply details three types of faith, Jnandev's commentary enters a slightly different subject. Jnandev, in the voice of Krishna, describes how faith alone is insufficient; in addition, one must conform to social norms and customs and see that one's actions have repercussions:

> Don't hold to faith alone, O Arjuna, for does not a twice-born rubbing
>   elbows (*ghṛṣti*) with a lower caste (*antyaju*)
> Himself become a lower caste? || Jn. 17.51 ||

> Think about it: Would Ganga water be just as pure if poured from a liquor
>   bottle? || Jn. 17.52 ||

Jnandev's point here is that one cannot simply have faith, but one must also mind one's social interactions, for the phenomenal everyday world is also self-defining: you may possess an imperishable spirit, but in this quotidian world you are a particular kind of person. You must obey the rules of social dharma, otherwise suffer the effects. What is implied here is the transference of qualities through a system of purity that moves downward; what is stressed here is that a pure thing can become impure—though the converse, how an impure thing might be purified by association with purer objects, is not addressed. Though metaphors of caste and Ganga water are both used to express this point about "faith" in lieu of righteous action, the two features of this metaphorical passage are both meant to indicate something about "purity" in general within the social realm. The space for radical social action is the sphere of otherworldly salvation. And like Chakradhar among the Mahanubhavs, Jnandev carefully delineates the necessities of salvation and the necessities of common social interaction. As with other metaphors that invoke social order, this one gestures toward caste divisions of society based on birth, but also on actions.

The question of purity in the social and phenomenal world is a preoccupation of this chapter of the *Jñāneśvarī* and provides one further reference to caste. Verse 6 in chapter 17 of the *Bhagavad Gītā* discusses the "demonic" nature of people who senselessly torture their bodies through austerities or simply cause misery to themselves and thus the divine "Self" or atman—all of which appear as references to the kinds of tantric practices that both Jnandev and Chakradhar reject, hints at which we have seen above in at least two places. Jnandev adds that Krishna has mentioned these kinds of people so that the reader or listener can avoid them. This elaboration is given:

Just as a corpse must be placed outside the home, one should avoid
chit-chat with a lower caste (*antya*).[40]
Doesn't one wash one's hands when they are dirty? || Jn. 17.106 ||

The reference to both a corpse and an "Untouchable" conjures images of a severe left-handed tantra, where corpses, graveyards, and "Untouchables" are featured as essential elements of certain practices. However, these references are placed within quotidian life: the death of a family member or an encounter with a person of a lower caste out in public. Clearly, we have a point of view expressed from the Brahminic ecumene—from the cultural sphere of high-caste people—presented as a question of social propriety in Jnandev's quotidian world. Jnandev invokes the habitus of everyday life, noting that, just as one washes one's hands, one removes a corpse from one's home and avoids contact, even conversation, with "a lower caste." But this is the habitus of the high-caste world specifically. Since we know that Jnandev wants antyaja (as in "women, low castes, and others"), among others, to hear the *Jñāneśvarī*, this sort of statement may seem incongruous.

The sahitya, the literary sphere that Jnandev seeks to enter and expand, to make more public, is not fully participatory, which is, of course, the norm even today—the modern literary sphere, as the modern public sphere, is highly restrictive, though in principle both are open to be passively received. The metaphors of impurity here function in a public culture that shares an understanding of the underlining social dictates of "purity" as a physical substance, adhering in normal social circumstances, of which Jnandev's examples are illustrative. If the public sphere of modern secular democracies (like that of the U.S. or of India) tends to select participation by class,[41] then the emergent corollary of Jnandev's age is a sphere that selects by purity, in a sense, which is also a restriction by caste and gender. What this says about the relationship between "twice-born" and the "lower castes" is perhaps nothing more than what passed as social "common sense" in the Yadava century.

No mention of caste is made again in this chapter until Jnandev offers a commentary to verse 22 of chapter 17 of the *Bhagavad Gītā* toward the chapter's end. This is a verse that warns against giving alms to people who are not deserving and giving alms begrudgingly, both of which Krishna identifies as features of tamas, the guna associated with negativity. The corresponding set of verses in the *Jñāneśvarī* has served some historians and scholars as a snapshot of public life during the late Yadava period. Indeed, historians have mined the *Jñāneśvarī,* as well as the texts of the Mahanubhavs and songs associated with the earliest Varkari sant poets, for such portraits of everyday life from this period.

In this section Jnandev diegetically locates his listener within an urban area. We hear of money and goods given as "alms" in potentially iniquitous contexts to people of uncertain moral character, it seems: among bards, jugglers, prostitutes, gamblers, sorcerers, and barbarians (*mleccha*), particularly in town squares, military camps, and markets. Here is a translation of these verses in full:

> In the regions of the foreigners (*mleccha*),[42] in the mountains,
> In the tribal forests, in the military camps, and in the street-corner mar-
>   kets in town (*cohaṭā*) || Jn. 17.293 ||

> In all such locations, any time, day or night,
> You can find the magnificent plunder (*coriya*) of deception. || Jn. 17.294 ||

> Actors, bards, snake-charmers, prostitutes, and gamblers—
> They seduce as the very form of delusion. || Jn. 17.295 ||

> Beautiful dancing enhances [the delusion], a feast for the eyes,
> While songs of praise are whispered continuously into the ears.
> || Jn. 17.296 ||

> In addition to these trifles, floral fragrance wafts about,
> Then the specter of confusion appears. || Jn. 17.297 ||

> In this total conquest of the world there are great spoils,
> As if a Matang were giving away free food. || Jn. 17.297+ ||[43]

Jnandev draws us into his urban area by beginning with the space beyond the borders of Maharashtra, it seems, and his reference to the regions inhabited by Muslims may very well be the Ghurid line of northern India, which was then moving closer toward Maharashtra. The term here for "foreigner," *mleccha,* usually means "Muslim" and may suggest the emergent Sultanate power to the north of the Yadava realm, beyond the Vindhya Mountains, a natural barrier between northern India and western and southern India that would be crossed by Khilji's armies within a few years of the *Jñāneśvarī*'s date of composition. This passage invokes a geography of perceived sedition that draws us from the regions of "the foreigner" to the urban core of commerce and public society. The progression of that text's geography—from the mountains, to outlying tribal regions, to forests that surround an urban area, to military encampments that skirt a city, and then into the town core itself—all moves us deeper into urbanity. And so we arrive within the first verse at a familiar place: the town square market. We are then given a description of something like the "nightlife" or even the red-light district of such an urban area, a place filled with distractions, intoxicants, and moral dangers. While it is the urban that contains the allures Jnandev highlights here, urbanity or *nāgarapaṇe* is also invoked by him in more positive contexts—this may be his "City of Marathi," but dystopically represented. This passage seems to carry both a literal warning about the allures of the city, but also the heft of a metaphor about the kinds of illusory distractions that Jnandev has highlighted elsewhere. It is as if he wants his "City of Marathi" to challenge and reform the city he depicts here. Jnandev seems to emphasize that in these urban locations one loses one's sense of self and propriety in the context of what he calls "ill-gotten gains" and "spoils"—the services of pleasure and their exchange.

The rich metaphors Jnandev weaves here are aimed at making a point about giving money and goods for charity that follows the Sanskrit *Bhagavad Gītā* verse in arguing that charity given without the proper intention, without conscious discernment, is wrong. In this passage Jnandev warns that in the morally ambiguous places he describes one will be beguiled and compelled to give out money to those who do not deserve it. The recipients of charity here are not the needy or the spiritually heroic but another cast of characters entirely.

I am particularly interested in the verse that concludes this metaphorical section in the text. In this verse Jnandev epitomizes the "conquest of the world" by describing a Matang giving out free food for Brahmins, holy men, and the poor. The metaphor of a free public service of food is something we have seen before: we have noted the verse in chapter 18 of the *Jñāneśvarī* where Jnandev equates the benefits of reading the *Bhagavad Gītā* with those accruing to a wealthy person who freely distributes food to others.[44] The term in both contexts is the word gavandi. As mentioned earlier,

a gavandi is generally a good thing, an act of generosity. Indeed, this is
exactly how Jnandev uses the term in chapter 18, indicating that the *Bhagavad Gītā* is like a gavandi that gives out *brahman* or "The Universal Truth,"
freely and to all. However, here, one chapter earlier in the *Jñāneśvarī*, this
same metaphor of the gavandi typifies the very degradation of dharma.
How can we read this iteration of the metaphor of the gavandi?

Some scholars have appeared to relate the figure of the Matang here to
the idea of theft, choosing to interpret the final lines of the section as indicating that the Matang, like the other figures, seeks to "rob" someone of
something, making his gavandi an ironic one—not the distribution of free
nourishment but the acquisition of something ill-gotten.[45] This is likely a
reading of the word *coriya* to mean "theft." The interpretation of the word as
indicating "theft" may also be related to a historical prejudice about Matangs.
In the colonial period, British ethnology classified the Matang jati as a "Noti-
fied Caste," a caste the colonial government associated with criminality. This
was not merely the invention of the British, but was a long-standing prejudice. The caste designation Matang has conveyed some sense of suspected
"thief" in the modern reception of the *Jñāneśvarī*. For example, Dandekar,
in the glossary for the critical edition of the *Jñāneśvarī*, provides the definition of Matang not as a name of a jati but rather as *cora* or "thief."[46] Recall
how in chapter 4 a group of thieves offered to guide Chakradhar through
the "Untouchable" neighborhood because, they claimed, that neighborhood
was "full of thieves."[47] The association between low caste and theft seems
apparent. And so this verse is read by some to state that the height of moral
decrepitude is exemplified at the moment when a thief gives out food as
charity. Or, another way to put it: a Matang who freely distributes food is
somehow "robbing" the world of something—the Matang, giving away food,
is construed as a "thief." The "theft" in this sense, as Dandekar likely reads it,
involves the ritual impurity of food being distributed by an "Untouchable."

I do not think this reading is right, however. Given the great weight
Jnandev has placed on freely distributing the salvational words of the
Bhagavad Gītā to those who cannot access it, and especially to someone like
the Matang person mentioned here, the idea that the Matang would be a
thief seems to me contrary to Jnandev's ethics. I believe this passage communicates the negative inversion of the flow of benevolence, the result
of the "deception" or misapprehension of reality by those invested in the
sensual and quotidian world. A gavandi should serve those in need, not

the other way around. I think Jnandev is expressing the idea that it would be the opposite of charity to require that a figure of abjection in a world of caste inequity, here a Matang, be distributing free food to others. Such a sight would be one's indication that one inhabited a world of illusion and deception, an inversion of the generosity implied in the gavandi. The gavandi, recall, will become Jnandev's metaphor for the *Bhagavad Gītā*, rendered intelligible through the *Jñāneśvarī*, and thus a gift of "alms" to all people, but especially to "women, low castes, and others." The Matang is arguable the figure of Jnandev's ethical mission, of his gavandi through the *Jñāneśvarī*; the metaphor given here reverses this relationship.

If my reading is correct, then we can see this metaphor's position on caste distinction as a problem situated within the quotidian world. The urban descriptions here, the menu of sense pleasures of the city, are the locations of the everyday. It is in this context that Jnandev introduces his own text and his own social ethics, and he will also invoke the same metaphor of the gavandi in chapter 18,[48] as mentioned, but in a positive context. Here, in this inverted ethical world, Jnandev appears to express the vulnerability of the Matang, the way in which the quotidian world constructs the social relationships that have created "Untouchability" itself. The metaphor of a Matang giving away free food is an inversion of the egalitarian message of the text, but it is also a possibility in the sphere of the "ordinary" where action is determined by choice and decision, by discernment, the faculty Jnandev seeks to cultivate here in his listener.

The metaphor of a Matang giving out free food may have resonance with rules of commensality and perhaps even be a precursor to the problems of the "public restaurant," of not knowing who prepared one's food or how it was prepared. Yet this is not an indictment of the Matang, but of the society that inverts its proper ethics, a society in the midst of the "age of misfortune," the Kali Yuga, which is explicitly where Jnandev locates his text. And this critique of social ethics is the very reason for the *Jñāneśvarī* to exist. The Matang here is not a "thief"; rather, he has long been the victim of a theft—kept from the salvational message of the *Bhagavad Gītā*—and it is Jnandev's social ethics that returns to him his right to hear this text. While this passage, like others, has the effect of reminding the listener of the quotidian rules of social order, it also challenges an interpretation that might engender a new perspective. Jnandev's text, itself described as a gavandi in chapter 18 of the *Jñāneśvarī*, freely gives out "the bliss of liberation" to all within the world of samsara, of everyday life. In chapter 17 too we have samsara, but viewed through a different lens, configured as a world of dharmic dystopia. This passage, with its highly colloquial and detailed description of urban public pleasure, draws together several senses of the "vernacular": the particularities of place, language, and culture, but also of social practice gone wrong. Jnandev's unique challenge to this social inversion is apparent as the *Jñāneśvarī* comes to a close.

The *Jñāneśvarī*'s Last Words

The *Jñāneśvarī* concludes with two distinct parts: a penultimate section that contains a prayer for a "gift for grace," called the Pasāyadān, and finally a colophon.[49] The nine verses of the Pasāyadān are often extracted from the *Jñāneśvarī* as a kind of stand-alone "prayer," or "the gift of grace," the literal meaning of the word in Old Marathi.[50] Though this section says nothing explicitly about Marathi or social equality, it is often cited as a prime example of Jnandev's humanism tied to his literary effort and is for many Marathi speakers the original moment of Marathi humanism in general.[51] Often when I have raised the question of "caste" and "social justice" with *Jñāneśvarī* scholars and pravacanakars, they have invoked this section of the *Jñāneśvarī* as a representation of Jnandev's social egalitarianism as it relates to the rationale for the creation of the *Jñāneśvarī* in Marathi. Given how directly and consistently this penultimate section of the text is raised by people in discussion in public contexts, in writing and scholarship, and in the modern Indian public sphere in Marathi, I feel it contains a key sentiment relevant to our exploration of an emergent public debate about social justice as revealed in this text and time.

The Pasāyadān displays an ethics that we have seen in this chapter and the preceding one, a moral sentiment intimately tied to the use of Marathi as a language of public culture in the dissemination of spiritual, philosophical, and religious materials to a general population of listeners disenfranchised by the social restrictions in which they live. And so the Pasāyadān carries the weight of a primary statement of the overriding idealist and humanist impulse of the *Jñāneśvarī*. Many Maharashtrians, including those who may never have read or heard the *Jnanesvarī*, may know this prayer as a composition in its own right.[52] Indeed, the Pasāyadān is a central text of Maharashtrian identity itself. For example, the Pasāyadān (rather than the

Jñāneśvarī in its entirety) for decades has been on the standard syllabus of the Maharashtra State Board of Secondary and Higher Education.[53] Here is my rendering of it:

> "May God, the Universal Self, be satisfied by this offering of words
> And because of this satisfaction, may he bless me with the gift of his grace. || Jn. 18.1772 ||
>
> May the wicked drop their crooked acts and may they desire to keep good company.
> May a sense of friendship develop mutually among all beings. || Jn. 18.1773 ||
>
> May the darkness of sin be dispelled, and may we see the rise of personal responsibility (*svadharma*) in the world.
> May all living beings attain whatever they desire. || Jn. 18.1774 ||
>
> May the Lord's affection fall like a torrential rain
> And bring together all beings upon the earth in ceaseless company with auspicious souls || Jn. 18.1775 ||
>
> Who exist like a grove of wish-granting trees, like an array of wish-granting gems,
> With words like a sea of nectar. || Jn. 18.1776 ||
>
> Like unblemished moons, like suns that never burn away
> May those good people remain kin to all forever. || Jn. 18.1777 ||
>
> Throughout the three worlds, let there be complete happiness
> And may all perpetually praise the Ultimate Lord. || Jn. 18.1778 ||
>
> And may those who live according to this text [the *Bhagavad Gītā*] in this extraordinary world
> Have the same victorious dialogue [with God] that Arjuna had." || 18.1779 ||
>
> Then the Lord of the Universe [Nivritti] says, "This gift of grace will be given."
> Upon hearing this Jnandev was content. || 18.1780 ||

The last invocation reveals the capacious social ethics of vernacularization in the Pasāyadān and throughout the *Jñāneśvarī* and also highlights the prevailing cultural politics of such access within the time of the text's creation. Though, we are told, the "text" by which all should live is the *Bhagavad Gītā*, the medium through which all people might understand that text is the *Jñāneśvarī*. The "gift of grace" that Jnandev ultimately requests from his guru is the permission to complete and transmit the *Jñāneśvarī* in Marathi: the "gift of grace" is the *Jñāneśvarī* itself. This is a prayer for all people, but it is also a final request for the transference of charisma from the *Bhagavad Gītā* to the *Jñāneśvarī*, from Sanskrit to Marathi, a prayer for the power of the vernacular to transcend social boundaries. The echoes of a humanistic impulse are clear as Jnandev invokes a desire for the common, moral good of society, and the idea that enforcing this moral good is the individual duty of all. A prayer for a vernacular world of mutually intelligible debate about the common good ends the *Jñāneśvarī*.

With the Pasāyadān, the *Jñāneśvarī* reaches its narrative conclusion and closes the dialogic, diegetic frame of the text. What follows is the final portion of the text, the colophon, in the voice not of Jnandev but of Satchidananda, Jnandev's "scribe," who has written down Jnandev's oral literary performance, his hybrid of a granth or book and a kirtan or performance, literally, an oral-performative text. Here is the colophon:

In this age of strife and in the region of Maharashtra
    (*mahārāṣṭramaṇḍalīṃ*)
Along the southern bank of the Godavari River ‖ Jn. 18.1781 ‖

Purest in the world, eternal, like Varanasi,[54]
The lifeline of the Universe, the Goddess Shri Mahalasa, dwells.[55]
    ‖ Jn. 18.1782 ‖

[In Maharashtra], where all arts flourish, resides the descendant of the
    moon dynasty [i.e., the Yadavas],
Who rules justly, nourishing the land, [King] Shri Ramachandra, ‖ Jn. 18.1783 ‖

There too Jnandev, the disciple of Nivritti Natha, in the lineage of
    Mahesha [Shiva]
Ornamented the *Bhagavad Gītā* with Marathi. ‖ Jn. 18.1784 ‖

Thus, in the text of the [*Maha-*]*Bharata*, in the famous chapter called
  "Bhishma,"
A beautiful dialogue was held between Arjuna and Krishna. || Jn. 18.1785 ||

That dialogue is the essence of the Upanishads, which is the maternal
  home of all sciences (*śāstra*),
And which is like the lake [water] the Great Swans imbibe.[56] || Jn. 18.1786 ||

"Here, at the pinnacle of the *Bhagavad Gītā*, the Eighteenth Chapter is
  complete."
Thus says Jnandev, disciple of Nivritti. || Jn. 18.1787 ||

Again, and again, and again, may a wealth of merit from this book |
Bring all happiness to all beings. || Jn. 18.1788 ||

In Shake 1212 [1290 CE] Jnandev composed this commentary. |
Satchidananda Baba, with great reverence, was his scribe. || Jn. 18.1792 ||[57]

This colophon gives us important information. The exact details it provides, in terms of date, location, and personnel, serve to reinforce the
text's historicality, locality, and language—colophons like this one serve as
their own devices of vernacularization, of rooting a text in time and place.
Unlike the *Līḷācaritra*, which makes great efforts at self-referential historicity through its form of literary realism, the *Jñāneśvarī*'s only explicit historical anchor, other than the language of the text itself, is in this colophon.
This is a text that seeks to be philosophically enduring, conveying historical specificity as its conclusion.[58]

We hear the name and the praises of the Yadava king, Ramachandra, for
example, which gives us political historical time and political geography.
However, this does not indicate that Ramachandra actively supported the
production of this text, or was even aware of it. Rather, it was a matter
of social etiquette for an author to praise his ruler; I think the inclusion
of this "vote of thanks" represents that kind of literary decorum, but not
more than this. No stories accompany Jnandev that suggest he was either
persecuted by Ramachandra or supported by him, but simply that Jnandev
lived and composed during Ramachandra's reign. If we consider that
the story of Chakradhar's purported trial was known in Jnandev's time,

we might also imagine such a statement as a desire to register a gratitude that might inoculate one against the anger of a king. Whether or not Jnandev knew of Chakradhar is a topic too large to enter into here and one that has been examined by others.[59]

Politically, we can see these two texts as significantly different. Where the Mahanubhav texts reveal a religious sect extracting itself from political life—rejecting opportunities for royal largess, avoiding court figures, countermanding the orthodoxies of the Brahminic ecumene—we see in Jnandev's text a desire to praise or perhaps even placate the current Yadava ruler. While this does not imply any sort of support from the king, it does locate this text within the general field of conventional public culture rather than afoul of the normative social world of the Yadava century. Importantly, it links this message, passively, but attentively, to the political structure of the age, referring to itself—the *Jñāneśvarī*, that is—as within the ambit of the benevolence Ramachandra shows toward "art." The colophon indexes something like the gap that Habermas identifies as the space filled, in part, by the modern public sphere. The *Jñāneśvarī* intercedes between the "state"—the royal sovereign and his field of power—and the world of everyday life. This field of everyday life in the region of the Yadava dynasty is here referred to by the phrase *mahārāṣṭramaṇḍala*. We should read this term in relation to the invocation of Maharashtra in the *Līḷācaritra* (as a linguistic, cultural, and political region) and in the inscriptions studied in chapter 2 around the term *marāṭhe* (a community designation that combines the meanings of linguistic, cultural, and political region with the idea of devotion to Vitthal). Here we have a third, and unique, iteration. The geographic, political, and linguistic zone named Maharashtra is described as a *mandal*. This word indicates social organization primarily, but carries the sense of a familiar community. Though it can be used to designate geography, the sense here is not "territory," but a unit organized as a cohesive social entity, a social field.[60] The term indicates a community bounded by something more than terrain; it indicates a community unified by language.[61] The mandal is a linguistic and now literary sphere into which Jnandev speaks.

Immanuel Kant, some five hundred years later, will speak into the emergent public sphere of Prussia in his response to the question, "What is enlightenment?," and he will exhort his reader to "dare to think" but also "to obey." Here, similarly, Jnandev challenges his listener to dare to think beyond the orthodoxies of the Brahminic ecumene and even of normal everyday life; yet his obeisance to Ramachandra, like Kant's to Frederic the Great, also remains within the structures of social and political order. Like Kant, Jnandev seems to say that one must press at the boundaries of thought, but remain within the confines of normal social order. How can we describe Jnandev's radical ethics, confined as they are by the constraints of his quotidian world?

The field of the vernacular—if it is the field of the quotidian, as I have argued—always imports its cultural orientations into its representations of language, but also of images and in other forms. The vernacular sphere is already a field of context and uncertainty, and, as such, it is a field of constant social debate. In the *Jñāneśvarī*, vernacularization has a double valence: it is radical in challenging a perceived Sanskrit hegemony over a salvational text like the *Bhagavad Gītā*, and yet it must embrace the "ordinary" as it returns to the cultural and literary field of everyday life where social distinction is endemic and deeply rooted.

In discussions I have had with pravacankars and others who expound the *Jñāneśvarī*, the ultimate evidence of Jnandev's challenge to traditional social orders in society, and his apparently "anti-Brahminic" perspective, is exemplified by the simple fact that he took a sacred Sanskrit text—available only to those rare high-caste males who could read or understand Sanskrit—and transformed it into a literary work in Marathi for the benefit of all, irrespective of caste or gender. For them, whatever else Jnandev may say about caste or particular jatis in his text, whatever artifacts of colloquial Marathi of his age might indicate about social distinctions, the fact of the text itself is an indisputable witness to his egalitarian social ethics.

The reigning literary subject of the Yadava century, as we have seen, was Dharma Śāstra, orthodox Brahminic rules about correct social behavior and order. Even Hemadri, in his Sanskrit text about the correct order of society, his *Caturvarga Cintāmaṇi*, sought to supply a set of rules for the structure of everyday life that he expected would be enacted by women, low castes, and others. That is, like Jnandev, Hemadri also wrote a text "for the people," though in a language entirely inaccessible to that population.[62] To whatever degree the *Jñāneśvarī* is "conservative" or "radical" on the question of social distinction, the very fact that the text is on dharma, within a Brahminic ecumene obsessed with producing dharmic treatises, and yet not in Sanskrit, the lingua franca of such works in the period, is itself radical. Rather than take up a novel subject in an old language, Jnandev has taken up an old subject in a new one, and a politics must surround such a choice. Furthermore, Jnandev, as we have seen, describes his text as a dharma kirtan,[63] a public performance of dharma rather than a written "social science" text situated within the rarefied field of other such texts. How can we understand this ethical impulse that seeks to balance an unequivocal commitment to sharing a salvational message to all people with a careful modulation of the social effects of this idea?

I propose the concept of "sonic equality" as a description of the core of Jnandev's social ethics. Jnandev demands an unfettered field of sonic access to the *Bhagavad Gītā,* which requires both that the Sanskrit text be transferred to Marathi and that its meaning be explained in familiar, colloquial Marathi terms. At the same time, this text must be primarily oral or performative, though its preservation and perpetuation—clearly demonstrated by the scribe Satchidananda—requires also that it be written. Yet the medium of communication is clearly orality—the text should "enter the ears," as Jnandev informs us.

What is not fully present here is an unequivocal critique of all social inequity and an invitation to new social forms of organization. Though the *Līḷācaritra* does express this idea, it is also confined, in this case to the field of Mahanubhav initiates. In both the *Jñāneśvarī* and the *Līḷācaritra* we see social radicalism and social conservativism, a dialectic the texts try to balance. However, as we turn to the conclusion of this book we will see that the seed of sonic equality that is remembered, to be planted in the *Jñāneśvarī* by Jnandev, transforms into a discourse of social *equality* in the centuries after his life, when a set of sants and hagiographers will assume stewardship of Jnandev's public memory and portray him as a man who undergoes a significant social transformation, who comes to not only embrace but champion a full social egalitarianism. This portrayal of a shift from *sonic* equality to full *social* equality is premised on Jnandev's revolutionary act of vernacularization, his creation of the magisterial *Jñāneśvarī.* Though Jnandev does not fully dissolve the boundaries of social segregation in his text, he enables the vision of such a possibility by participating in a new discourse in Marathi about social critique. I see the rudimentary elements of a public debate about social equality emerge here in the swirl of this engagement, and there is no limit to the subjects it might embrace. Jnandev and the early Mahanubhavs are the progenitors of this humanist horizon and of the quotidian revolution as it slowly unfolds in the centuries to come.

The sonic equality of the *Jñāneśvarī* sits alongside the colloquialisms of inequality that populate the speech of thirteenth-century Marathi. On the one hand, we have a text that is marked by egalitarianism, constructed from the impulse for universal access, and dedicated to the spiritually disenfranchised. On the other hand, the text registers social distinction as a key feature of the aesthetic of the vernacular. The process of vernacularization limits egalitarian possibilities, even while it opens up other opportunities. The everyday is the place where patriarchy and casteism sit alongside the sonic equality that Jnandev champions and the seeds of social equality to come. A text that challenges social privilege and asymmetries of power is also a text that registers this inequity as normative. Vernacularization both confronts casteism and sexism in one realm and reinforces it another.

Here we see a cultural political process inherent in vernacularization, an unbounded dialectic of resolving difference and reproducing difference continuously along the plane of the everyday. This forms the very core of any public sphere, a field of debate in public contexts about vital social questions, about the "common good." Arriving at this common good, as the frog in the well discovered, is a halting path toward an uncertain goal. The quotidian revolution moves slowly because it contains within it both immanent critique and immanent contradiction. The debates of the public sphere usually contain some idea of a social world more capacious than the one in which the debate is occurring—in other words, by engendering a discussion of the future, the debate also precedes social change. This stimulates the effort to resolve difference in the context of the very distinction under debate, yet simultaneously compels new problems and sites of conflict to arise. This process of resolution of difference and the re-creation of it seems endemic to all public spheres of debate about the common good, new and old. I have read Jnandev's text in this midst of this enduring process as a conversation about the common good, about human worth and social justice sounded in the world of everyday life in the thirteenth century and still heard today, as urgently as ever.

Conclusion

The Vernacular Millennium and the Quotidian Revolution

This book has engaged a sliver of time from the thirteenth century to the first decade of the fourteenth century. In this brief era, historical memory places the composition of the *Līḷācaritra* in 1278 and the *Jñāneśvarī* in 1290. In part 1 I provided an overview of the cultural context for these two texts that helps to explain how and why they would emerge and become connected to the two figures—Chakradhar and Jnandev—who appear as the biographical metonyms of vernacularization in Marathi. I traced the outline of a public in Yadava-era inscriptions and the public memories of both figures within this context. Part 2 focused on Chakradhar, the early Mahanubhavs, and the *Līḷācaritra* primarily in order to understand how the lines of language, caste, gender, and everyday life merged and culminated in the composition of the *Līḷācaritra*. The text was concerned with historical accuracy in that it sought to portray the immediate past in as exact a way as possible through a kind of literary realism. Thus the text portrayed the proximate "prehistory" of vernacularization as a cultural form just before 1278. Part 3 accepted the *Jñāneśvarī* as a literary statement on the project of vernacularization that had passed its moment of origin, for this text looked forward to a "gold mine of literature" and a "City of Marathi" to come. As such, the *Jñāneśvarī* is a text situated at the precipice of the new vernacular millennium, rather than a text placed either before it or even during the historical shift to the literarization of Marathi.

My approach is to see how these two texts and contexts speak for a monumental shift in Indian culture. This is the "vernacular turn," on the one hand, and the period that represents the completion of that turn toward a new vernacular future, on the other. I have made this divide in order to highlight the historical self-consciousness of these texts and the agents of their creation. Vernacularization was not an inadvertent consequence of a kind of cultural ecological shift, but rather it was the result of a purposeful and self-aware critique of culture. I have located this power within the field of Marathi literary vernacularization in everyday life, a field deeply inflected by religion. My point is that vernacularization is a process of empowerment itself, but an empowerment that negotiated the mores of everyday life and, in the process, valorized the image of the "everyday." The driving core of vernacularization, I have argued, is the very quotidian social life it sought to emend. I have described the public debate about the common good that these texts represent as indicative of a nascent public sphere in Marathi.

As a way to close this book's argument about vernacularization and the quotidian world, we may briefly discuss the historical trajectories of the two major subjects we have studied. I would like to show how the groups that were shaped around Jnandev and Chakradhar engaged with Marathi public culture. A brief view of the very different routes taken in public culture by these two subjects in time demonstrates that vernacularization is a process that both deepened and expanded in the centuries after "the vernacular turn," and did so in ways that would not have been easy to predict in the thirteenth century. Yet the trajectories of these two subjects from the thirteenth century to the present display the force of vernacularization as a process that refigures the scope of the everyday at the core of public life.

Our two primary subjects evinced very different histories. As Jnandev and his text became absorbed into the largest devotional religion of the region, the Varkaris, the *Jñāneśvarī* and the public memory of Jnandev flourished over centuries at the heart of Marathi public culture. By contrast, the Mahanubhavs and the public memory of Chakradhar receded from the center of public culture through the centuries, while expanding to other areas of India, especially Punjab. The Mahanubhavs would return to the public sphere during the colonial period and after, when they became entangled in postcolonial political machinations. The quotidian revolution, like Raymond William's "long revolution,"[1] is a moniker for a process that circles back upon itself, time and again, and yet advances. It is a revolution not only in the sense of this circularity but also in the sense of change over time. It is not a rebellion, but the pressure for emendation and progression met by the glacial transformation of normative world views. Though the quotidian revolution may begin in the time of Jnandev and Chakradhar, it is a process inherent in the present.

The Vernacularization of Jnandev

In the decades and centuries just after the *Jñāneśvarī* is said to have been composed, Jnandev would ascend to the pinnacle of Marathi public culture as the harbinger of Marathi literature where he stands today as an emblem of the region's most enduring religious tradition, the Varkaris.[2] This was a significantly new trajectory in the public memory of Jnandev, for, as we have seen, there is no indication of devotion to the deity of the Varkaris within the *Jñāneśvarī*: no mention is made of Vitthal/Panduranga; nowhere do we hear of Pandharpur, the sacred site of the Varkaris, either. For devotion to Vitthal, we must turn to the songs or *abhangs* associated with Jnandev—on the authorship of which there is a long-standing debate that generally places their composition after the *Jñāneśvarī* was composed, perhaps by a few years or perhaps by centuries.[3] Although the details of this debate are not germane here, what is relevant to note is how the Varkari religion, and in particular its hagiographic tradition, came to remember the place of Jnandev within the ambit of the Varkari world, a pluralistic world of people from diverse castes, and even religions, as well as both sexes. From the normative Varkari point of view, the lack of any mention of Vitthal or Pandharpur, or other sants or figures, in key texts such as the *Jñāneśvarī* is explained by means of hagiography.

Jnandev tells us very little about himself in the *Jñāneśvarī*, as noted in chapter 3. We know that at the time of the *Jñāneśvarī*'s composition he lived in the town of Nevase, that his guru was his brother Nivritti, that he was a Natha, that he lived during the reign of Ramachandra, and that he composed the *Jñāneśvarī*. Together these give us a sense of when he might have lived and tells us a little about him. The text also allows us to assume that he was fluent in Sanskrit, that he was most probably a Brahmin, and that he was relatively young when he composed his text. The many stories we associate with Jnandev in hagiography are the result of later composers, and chief among them was the figure of Namdev (1270–1350), a Shudra tailor or Shimpi, a resident of Pandharpur and deep devotee of Vitthal.[4] Namdev and Jnandev are said to have been contemporaries, and it is Namdev who is said to have composed the first biographical texts we have for Jnandev. The essence of this biography is contained within three Marathi works called the "Ādi" or "Beginning," the "Tīrthāvaḷī" or "The Journey," and the "Samādhi" or "The Entombment."[5] The earliest manuscripts we have for these texts are from the middle of the sixteenth century, even though they are all attributed to the lifetime of Namdev. In other words, the biography of Jnandev by Namdev is remembered to have been composed either during the latter portion of Jnandev's brief life, in the period after he composed the *Jñāneśvarī*, or just after the life of Jnandev, or within two centuries of Jnandev's entombment. Put another way: Jnandev's biography is later than the *Jñāneśvarī*, and so it purports to record not only his early life but also events subsequent to the composition of the *Jñāneśvarī*.

The three compositions attributed to Namdev give us rich details about Jnandev's life, as well as the lives of his parents, grandparents, and siblings (brothers Nivritti and Sopan and sister Muktabai), details to which the *Jñāneśvarī* does not even allude. And in the latter two hagiographies—"The Journey" and the "The Entombment"—Namdev himself is present as a character, rendering these texts somewhere between biography and autobiography.

The "Ādi" begins with the story of Jnandev's parents and concludes as Jnandev completes his *Jñāneśvarī*.[6] Jnandev's father had renounced worldly life prematurely—while his children were still young, before his obligations to them and his wife were concluded. As a punishment to Jnandev's father, a Brahmin council in Paithan stripped them all—parents and children—of their caste status as Brahmins. In order to return to caste status, the council demanded that Jnandev's parents commit ritual suicide by jumping into a river—which they did. The council then required that the siblings appear before the tribunal in Paithan to demonstrate their Brahminic learning.

The "Ādi" appears aware of the intellectual and ethical progress of its subject. Nivritti and Jnandev debate the rationale for returning to caste status. Nivritti argues that there is no point in having their caste reinstated because they are beyond such distinctions of caste. Here is Nvritti's position expressed in the "Ādi," verse 890:

All the Brahmins said, "Go to Pratishthan. |
Bring back a certificate of purity, and we will reinstate your caste." || 1 ||

Nivritti replied, "But we don't belong to any caste, race, or legitimate
	family line. |
We're neither Kshatriyas, Vaishyas, Shudras, nor Brahmins.[7] || 2 ||

We're not Gods, demons, or ghosts. |
We're not holy men or devils. || 3 ||

What we are is indestructible, unmanifest, and ancient. |
By knowledge of the Self I have attained my desired form. || 4 ||

I am not of the five elements: water, fire, wind, sky, or earth. |
I am not a part of primordial nature. || 5 ||

I neither possess qualities, nor do I not possess qualities. |
I am not produced from the world of experience and sense." || 6 ||

Nivritti said, "Jnaneshwar, listen. |
This is my tradition." || 7 ||

Jnandev, however, is still the same person of the *Jñāneśvarī*, someone who
balances the demands of quotidian society with the transcendental truths
of the *Bhagavad Gītā*, someone willing to negotiate a common thing like
caste status with this august Brahmin council. And so Jnandev replies to
his brother (verse 891):

Jnandev said, "Contradicting Vedic laws is also our sin[8] |
Even if no distinction actually exists among individuals. || 1 ||

Violating such norms is a great sin |
So the Great Brahmin Lawgivers tell us. || 2 ||

People have individual responsibilities because of the different castes. |
Doing whatever is right for each person purifies that person. || 3 ||

Thus sants must also follow the rules of life. |
They should act as models for the behavior of others. || 4 ||

The family and filial rules must be safeguarded, |
And one must never act against these rules. || 5 ||

Though one may be pure in this life, |
It is still a sin to contradict scriptural authority." || 6 ||

Jnandev says, "Listen to me, Nivritti. |
This is the way prescribed in the sacred law books." || 7 ||

It is at the meeting of the council that we have perhaps the most famous story from Jnandev's life. This trial of Jnandev may have been inspired by the story of the trial of Chakradhar. They bear striking similarities and are located in the same place, Paithan. As the story goes, the council determines that nothing can be done for the children, and they recommend a life of abject devotion to God through bhakti. They imply that, as outcastes, this is the only option available to them. The children accept their fate, but the Brahmins are not yet done with them. When they learn of the lofty and peculiar names they each have,[9] the Brahmins laugh at them and poke fun at their august names. The Brahmins point out that names mean nothing, for nearby there is a buffalo also named Jnana, just like Jnandev. To this Jnandev says that he and the buffalo are indeed the same—not only do names not matter but form itself does not matter. The Brahmins are astounded at this precocious young man, and they dare Jnandev to cause the "dumb" animal to recite the Vedas. And this the buffalo does—with exemplary intonation, it is noted.[10] Jnandev's miracle reinforces the idea that a linguistic medium, Sanskrit in this case, should not stand in for soteriological, social, or theological value. The reader will hear echoes in this story of the rejection of Vedic authority and Sanskritic elitism that we saw displayed in the *Jñāneśvarī*. Figure C.1 provides an illustration of this episode from a late nineteenth century publication.

This point seems to mark Jnandev's turn toward embracing social equality. And this prepares Jnandev for a meeting with Namdev that will fully transform his social sphere. The "Ādi" ends as Jnandev completes his *Jñāneśvarī*, but before he has met Namdev and the many bhaktas who will fill his hagiography.

The "Tīrthāvaḷī" tells the story of how Jnandev, after composing the *Jñāneśvarī*, traveled to Pandharpur to meet Namdev because he had heard that Namdev represented the very best of bhakti—he was an exemplary bhakta. Jnandev's intention, we learn, was to convert Namdev to a *nirguni* or abstract, theological position, but Jnandev undertook this effort under the pretext of a pilgrimage to sacred sites of northern India. During their travels together, Namdev and Jnandev became intimate friends, but also strident debaters. The story culminates with an irony: it is Namdev who convinces Jnandev to accept a *saguni* or nonabstract devotionalism. It is this moment of "conversion" through conversation that, for Varkaris, marks the turning point of Jnandev's devotional attention toward Vitthal and Pandharpur, hence his inclusion within the genealogy of Varkari sants. The "Tīrthāvaḷī" is therefore not a story of pilgrimage but a story of a different journey: Jnandev's transition to Vitthal devotee and Varkari who visits Pandharpur, all compelled by the figure of Namdev and Jnandev's friendship with him.[11] The yearly Varkari pilgrimage marks this important story through ritual. It is usually the palanquin of Namdev that comes out to greet the palanquin of Jnandev when the procession of Varkaris arrive outside Pandharpur. That "reunion" is an explicit ritual memory of this story of Jnandev and Namdev's friendship and Jnandev's return to Pandharpur as a Vitthal devotee.

We also have here a turn toward an inclusive social ethics, for the "Tīrthāvaḷī," as a story of friendship between a Brahmin Sanskrit philosopher and an illiterate Shimpi or Shudra tailor, is also a metaphor for the elision of social difference. It is bhakti as spiritual force that draws Jnandev to Namdev, but it is bhakti as social force that pulls Jnandev into the orbit of an eclectic social world. Figure C.2 provides another illustration from the late-nineteenth-century *Bhaktavijay*, which shows Jnandev together with a socially heterogeneous group. From left to right, we see the low-caste sant Savata Mali, the "Untouchable" sant Kurmadas, the deity Krishna, Namdev, and finally Jnandev. Here we can grasp that Jnandev's sonic equality has transformed into a full-fledged social equality.

An important story accompanies the return of Jnandev and Namdev to Pandharpur in the "Tīrthāvaḷī"; indeed, the story is so important that it takes up half the text. Upon their return to Pandharpur, Vitthal insists that Namdev must perform the traditional rite that is incumbent upon someone who has completed a sacred pilgrimage: he must feed Brahmins.

FIGURE C.1. (*top*) Diptych showing scenes from the life of Jnandev, from a late nineteenth-century print-ed version of Mahipati's *Bhaktavijaya*. Author's collection

FIGURE C.2. (*bottom*) Illustration from a late nineteenth-century printed version of Mahipati's *Bhaktavi-jaya*, depicting Jnandev with sants Savata Mali, Kurmadas, and Namdev and the deity Krishna. Author's collection

Namdev makes all the preparations for this feast and invites his Pandharpur Brahmin guests. Jnandev is, of course, among them, and Vitthal too appears, taking a luminous human form. The Brahmins gathered assume that Vitthal—so radiant—must be a Brahmin like them, for why else would he be at this feast as an honored guest? However, when Vitthal sits down to dine with Namdev, the Brahmins become highly agitated and they question Vitthal, still thinking him to be one of them. They demand he do various acts of purification, and Vitthal complies with them all in a good-natured way (as did Jnandev and his family to the demands of the Brahmin council). Though this story is in part a "comedy of manners," it is also a critique of caste. It is a demonstration of another dual response to caste distinction in the vernacular context: resistance and accommodation at the same time. When the Brahmins eventually realize that they have been in the company not of a fellow Brahmin but of Vitthal himself, they plead for forgiveness, decry their ignorance and casteism, and ask that they forever remain in the company of Namdev.[12] This story carries many implications that we have seen already: associations with caste and commensality, assumptions about a person's caste status, and an accommodation to social norms even in the midst of a critique of those norms.

The final text, the "Samādhi," is a threnody or eulogy attributed to Namdev that recalls the moments leading up to Jnandev's self-entombment in Alandi. More so than the "Tīrthāvaḷī," the "Samādhi" also serves to solidify the deep connection between Namdev and Jnandev—the mutual bhakti they shared for the same deity and for each other. The text is a heartfelt farewell from Namdev, and all of Jnandev's companions, directed to Jnandev as he entombs himself. This final text fully situates Jnandev in an entire community of devotees, the early Varkaris, that included women, low castes, and "Untouchables" as well. On a visit to modern-day Alandi and to Jnandev's tomb, one meets with the stories of Jnandev's many friends, across the quotidian spectrum.

The stories that originate in these three texts attributed to Namdev come to populate the core ideas of Varkari hagiography and are canonized by the Varkari hagiographer Mahipati in the eighteenth century. Namdev's early biographies of Jnandev clearly resituate the saint, drawing Jnandev into a new social context with a renewed social ethics. What we see happening in the biographies of Jnandev attributed to Namdev is a vernacularization of Jnandev's legacy. Jnandev is reoriented within the world of everyday life. This draws in not only the saint and his public memory but also his text. Jnandev's high place in Marathi public culture is directly tied to his inclusion within the Varkari religion as one of its four key figures—along with Namdev, Eknath (sixteenth century), and Tukaram (seventeenth century). As for the *Jñāneśvarī*, by the time of Eknath the text is fully within the ambit of the Varkari world and entirely subsumed under devotion to Vitthal. As mentioned earlier, Eknath is said to have edited the *Jñāneśvarī* and refurbished the site of Jnandev's samādhi or entombment.[13] Here again is a process that brought Jnandev within the Varkari context through an association with Eknath. A century later, a female sant named Bahinabai—commonly considered a contemporary and devotee of Tukaram of the seventeenth century—famously uses the metaphor of a temple to describe the genealogy of the Varkari religion's key figures:

> By the grace of the saint [Tukaram] the building is complete.
> Jnandev laid the foundation and raised the temple frame.
> His servant Nama [Namdev] filled out the temple structure.
> Janardan's Eknath put up the column of the *Bhagavata*
> Singing *bhajan* at peace: Tukaram has become the pinnacle![14]

This passage "vernacularizes" Jnandev, as well as the other figures mentioned, through this grounding metaphor of place, a temple, an axis mundi, a key metaphor of location and institution. The aural temple of dharma, the dharma kirtan that Jnandev creates with the *Jñāneśvarī*, is here transposed into the new edifice of the Varkari religion itself. This metaphor is not random; the sense of structure and purposeful creation is, I think, intentional. I argued in *Religion and Public Memory* that around the figure of Namdev the collection of practices that make up bhakti (song-poems, performances, hagiography, pilgrimage, scholarship, expressions in multiple media, etc.) are not haphazard, but display a logic of remembrance and the craft of public presentation. People remember revered figures in social contexts *with a purpose*. The purpose we see in Namdev's hagiography of Jnandev is a vernacular reconfiguration of Jnandev that aligns the salvational politics of his text with the social politics of his remembrance. In saying this, I do not mean to reject the truth claims inherent in Namdev's biographies of Jnandev—in other words, I do not consider those texts "fictions." But I do think—fact or fiction—narratives have intentions and effects, and the intention and effect of Namdev's biographies of Jnandev were to bring his biography within the sphere of everyday life and transform his ethics of sonic equality into a display of social equality exemplified in the worlds of bhakti associated with the Varkaris.

Through the intermingling of hagiography and literature, Jnandev emerges from the thirteenth century as the figure we know today—Marathi literary innovator and social reformer who championed the plight of the "common man." Indeed, the place of Jnandev in Maharashtra's self-understanding is enormously significant. One of the most beloved films of Marathi cinema is the 1940 depiction of Jnandev's life, *Sant Dnyaneshwar*, made by the famous Prabhat Studios and directed by V. G. Damle and Sheikh Fattelal, who also made *Sant Tukaram* four years earlier. In figure C.3, we see a still of the scene where young Jnandev causes a buffalo to recite the Vedas.

Jnandev was not only a subject at the heart of Marathi public culture, as this film epitomizes, but he received particular attention as a figure

FIGURE C.3. Still from *Sant Dnyaneshwar* (1940) depicting the conclusion of the "Buffalo" scene.

of nationalist and subnationalist importance. A postage stamp issued by the Government of India memorialized the sant on the occasion of the seven hundredth anniversary of his entombment in 1997, for example (see figure C.4).

Like Jnandev, a host of other sants and devotional figures across Indian history have received such memorialization as heroes of "national integration" preceding Indian independence. However, Jnandev is perhaps unique in that the Government of India devoted a separate stamp to commemorating his *Jñāneśvarī* as well, as if to underscore that author and text are separable and follow their own trajectories and routes of vernacularization in history (see figure C.5).

In the seven centuries between the composition of the *Jñāneśvarī* and today, Jnandev and his public memory burgeon and become fixed within public culture. Jnandev and his *Jñāneśvarī* also come to flesh out a significant form in the emergent and later modern public sphere as a key referenent in the public construction of Marathi, Maharashtra,

FIGURE C.4. (*left*) Postage stamp issued by the Government of India in 1997 commemorating the seven hundredth death anniversary of Jnandev.

FIGURE C.5. (*right*) Postage stamp issued by the Government of India in 1990 commemorating the seven hundredth anniversary of the composition of the *Jñāneśvarī*.

and being Maharashtrian. The legacies I have briefly traced here—text, scholarship, film, stamps—all attest to how Jnandev and his text are not only embedded in the modern Marathi public sphere but are also iconic of some of its chief debates about caste, gender, social equality, and the past. A government-issued stamp that memorizes a text is a symbol that insists upon textuality within the field of the modern public. And it points toward a politics of social inclusion within a shared literary sphere. The process that drives these changes is the vernacularization of Jnandev and his public memory, and the effect of this vernacularization is to situate Jnandev in everyday life as a champion of the common person. We can see the rudiments of this idea in the *Jñāneśvarī*, but it is the force of vernacular culture that fully shapes the form of Jnandev we receive today. He is absorbed into a particular debate within the Marathi public sphere: about social equality, language, literature, and history. And Jnandev's genealogical relationship to this present moment is not simply the co-option of his legacy and literature over the last two centuries but reaches deeply into the inaugural moments of Marathi literary vernacularization itself.

My point in briefly recalling these hagiographic texts is to show the phenomenon of vernacularization at work in the years and centuries after Jnandev's purported life span. However, vernacularization here occurs primarily not as a literary intervention but rather as one within public memory in general. For what these three texts accomplish—and, indeed, what an association with Namdev also accomplishes—is the vernacularization of the figure of Jnandev. As the previous two chapters have shown, Jnandev is never displayed in social contexts with low castes or women within the diegesis of the *Jñāneśvarī*, and we have drawn several examples from the *Jñāneśvarī* that suggest such a free mingling of castes would not have been likely in the immediate ambit of Jnandev when the text was composed. His sonic equality directly speaks to and for the entire quotidian world. Yet in the years just after his life (or perhaps in his lifetime, depending on one's inclination toward textual evidence), Jnandev's sonic equality becomes fully realized in the social realm: Jnandev becomes *vernacularized,* and so does his ethics. The ethical world of sonic equality is transformed into an investment in the actual social milieu of everyday life, and an image of social equality arises at this confluence.

The Mahanubhavs in Modernity

The history of the Mahanubhav religion, the afterlife of the *Līḷācaritra*, and the public memory of Chakradhar all take a divergent path from that of Jnandev and his eponymous text. Where Jnandev and the *Jñāneśvarī* became central not only to the Varkari religion but also to the firmament of Marathi literature, culture, and the modern public sphere, the Mahanubhavs, Chakradhar, and the *Līḷācaritra* transitioned into less public realms in the centuries after the religion was founded. Though the religion remained in Maharashtra, it also moved to areas outside of Maharashtra, including Punjab, modern-day Pakistan, and modern-day Afghanistan. The Mahanubhavs did not become intimately intertwined with Marathi and Maharashtrian culture as was the case with Jnandev, his text, and his association with the Varkari religion. Instead, the Mahanubhavs retained their integrity in relative quietude.[15] As Amit Desai describes in his contemporary ethnographies of Mahanubhavs in rural Maharashtra, they exemplify a position of "marginality" in such areas even today, a position relevant to the asceticism the early Mahanubhav order taught.[16] To my knowledge, we have little record of the Mahanubhav religion, other than its own record, until the colonial period. But it is clear that the Mahanubhavs not only sustained their order, but grew greatly in the centuries that followed Chakradhar's departure from Maharashtra. The history of the Mahanubhav community after its foundation and up to the present is its own story of vernacularization. We should observe this history for its lessons about vernacularization and, in particular, the modern public sphere.

Shortly before Chakradhar's departure for northern India around 1273, as we saw, he ordered his followers to remain in Maharashtra. After the transition from the first generation of Mahanubhavs to subsequent generations, the locus of Chakradhar's followers grew more diffuse, with evidence of Mahanubhav communities in Gujarat, Rajasthan, and Punjab by the sixteenth century,[17] and even as far as Kabul in Afghanistan.[18] In Maharashtra over many centuries, Mahanubhavs appear to have moved out of large urban areas and into rural areas until the modern period. To my knowledge, no one has yet reconstructed the historical migration of Mahanubhav religious cultures throughout India, and this is not my goal here. As a religious community of lay people and ascetics who rejected the worlds of temple and court, their historical trace is confined to those few

Mahanubhav institutional contexts that retained archives and organizational memory. These texts largely ceased to record the religion's history, devoting ever more attention to theological matters. The literary realism of the *Līḷācaritra* and the *Smṛtisthaḷa* yielded to a literature of timeless theological commentary.

In the centuries after Chakradhar's life, the Mahanubhavs continued to produce texts—largely in Marathi and Sanskrit—that elaborated or commented primarily upon the *Līḷācaritra* or other core texts. We also find several genres of literature that are not idiosyncratic to the Mahanubhav sphere, especially commentaries on the *Bhagavad Gītā* (in Sanskrit and Marathi) and retellings of the marriage choice or *svayamvara* of Rukmini, Krishna's wife.[19] The extent of Mahanubhav literary production shows us that the group flourished (if literary production is a sign of flourishing) from the thirteenth century well into the mid-nineteenth century. In other words, we have an unbroken record of Mahanubhav literary production until the modern colonial period, which suggests the continuous existence of this group, as well as its spread to northern India, but its own history becomes obscured.

Despite this plethora of textual production and geographic diffusion, by the colonial period we find that the Mahanubhavs were largely unknown in the public sphere of western India, including in scholarship and other contexts in Marathi and English. They register hardly at all within the massive efforts of colonial ethnology, for example. The one exception is an entry in the colonial *Imperial Gazetteer of India* in 1887, and, to my knowledge, this is the only mention of the Mahanubhavs in any prominent government publication of the colonial period. My discussion of the Mahanubhav's entry into the modern Indian public sphere draws solely from publicly available documents *and relies on no informant input* or data other than publically available materials such as colonial publications, news media, and government documents.

Prompted by new data collected by the 1881 census that shows a population of Mahanubhavs in Maharashtra, the 1887 *Gazetteer* provides an entry for the religion that displays a curious mixture of historical confusion and ethnographic observation about the Mahanubhavs. In a section of the *Gazetteer* on the district of Ritpur (Riddhapur), William Wilson Hunter refers to the Mahanubhavs as "Manbhau" and states that the religious community derived its name from "Mang-Bhau" or "the Brothers of the Mangs," a title

Hunter said was applied to the sect because of the fact that their purported founder, one Kishen Bhat, had married a Matang or Mang woman, that is, a woman of an "Untouchable" jati.[20] No mention is made of any text, such as the *Līḷācaritra*, much less do we hear of Chakradhar or any other key figure. Hunter places the origin of the "Manbhaus" in the middle of the fourteenth century, and Kishen Bhat is described as the "spiritual advisor of a Raja who ruled at Paithan."

The reader will see that some of what Hunter reports echoes what we know of the Mahanubhavs from other sources: a kind of qualified monotheism, the worship of Krishna, rejection of the "ties of caste and religion," a life of asceticism, etc. Yet we also hear of a mysterious "magic cap" that would make Kishen Bhat appear in the likeness of Krishna! What this report of 1887 makes clear is that although the Mahanubhavs existed at this point in Maharashtra and are registered in the ethnological surveillance of the colonial state in this one instance, they remained opaque in the view of colonial-era scholarship and in Indian public media. The confabulation Hunter's report gives us—the odd reconfiguration of the Mahanubhav name, mixing perhaps the title *bhaṭa* or Brahmin with the name Krishna, the invention of a magic cap, and so on—shows but the shadows of an awareness of the Mahanubhavs in the former heartland of their community, Riddhapur in Maharashtra.

The report does give us interesting demographic data culled from the 1881 census, however. The census reported 4,111 "Manbhaus" in Berar— 2,193 men and 1,918 women—a majority of whom reported their occupation as "beggar," by which we must assume they declared to inquisitive colonial officials that they were initiated mendicants.[21] Of those few who reported an occupation, the list included moneylending, agricultural labor, carpentry, and textile work, suggesting that the Mahanubhav order was confined to no single caste or occupation. The community comprised both those who were integrated within the political economy and culture of the region and others who retained their ascetic orders, as is the case today. The Mahanubhavs continued to straddle the space between everyday life and the renunciation of everyday life during the period of Hunter's report, it seems.

In part, the reason for this striking ignorance about the Mahanubhavs among colonial-era experts in ethnology, history, and literature is the fact that for centuries the Mahanubhavs had preserved their texts in a secret cipher (*lipi*) and kept the history and practices of their religion a secret from non-Mahanubhavs, that is, from the general public.[22] The rationale for this seclusion is not clear as we have no firsthand statement by any Mahanubhav figure, to my knowledge, that addresses either the use of the cipher or the sense of persecution that might have compelled the Mahanubhavs to resort to such secretive measures. In the *Gazetteer* of 1887, Hunter tells us that the "Manbhaus" were persecuted because their "doctrines repudiated a multiplicity of gods" and that the "hatred and contempt" endured by the religion "arose from . . . [the group's] endeavors to restore the monotheistic principle of Brahmanism as taught in the Vedas." However, in the correction to this entry in volume 21 of the *Gazetteer* in 1908, we learn instead that the entire "Mang-brother" appellation was an "absurd Brahminic derivation," which has the disingenuous effect of exculpating Hunter but also drawing out the colonial suspicion of the Brahmin *pandit*.[23] What changed between these two entries in the *Gazetteer* with two very different conclusions, particularly regarding "Brahminism"?

In the *Times of India*, the "paper of record" during this period, on Friday, November 15, 1907, the famous Indian scholar R. G. Bhandarkar composed a critical intervention regarding the public's knowledge of the Mahanubhavs.[24] In a short piece titled "The Manbhav Sect: The Gazetteer Trips," Bhandarkar sought to correct Hunter's statements in the *Gazetteer* of 1887 about the Mahanubhavs because "two learned mahants or spiritual heads of the sect" from Ludhiana (contemporary Indian Punjab) and Peshawar (contemporary Pakistan) had approached him with evidence of their history.[25] It is largely in response to Bhandarkar that the *Gazetteer* retracted and corrected its previous text.

Following Bhandarkar's article an argument emerged that claimed that opposition from Brahminic authorities had pushed Mahanubhavs out of mainstream Maharashtrian public culture and toward the fringes of society, and this had also compelled them to transcribe their texts in lipi as a means of avoiding perceived Brahminic surveillance. The source for this idea is composite. The story of the *Līḷācaritra*, as outlined in chapters 4 and 5, does suggest that while most of the Mahanubhavs, including Chakradhar, were Brahmins, a significant opposition to the Mahanubhavs was mounted at the nexus of the state and the Brahminic ecumene in the Yadava era. Similarly, it would appear that a majority of the Mahanubhav texts from the thirteenth to the nineteenth century were composed by

Brahmins—judging from the samples given in Raeside's bibliography of Mahanubhav literature.[26] Yet we notice that non-Brahmin names (i.e., those that do not contain common markers such as *vyāsa* or *bhaṭa* or some variation) appear to increase in number as we move closer to the modern era. One can imagine that the "Mang-bhau" ("Brothers of the Mangs") appellation also registers a social reality and a social ethics—for Chakradhar taught exactly such "brotherhood" within the social ethics of his community.

We may speculate based on this admittedly light archive that Brahminic involvement in the Mahanubhav religion declined over time in Maharashtra. Today most Mahanubhavs I have met are not Brahmins, but (in Maharashtra in any case) belong to one of the many Maratha jatis. Yet we can also see the same familiar fuzziness with regard to the role of Brahmins and "Brahminism" in the public and private affairs of the Mahanubhav religion. In the first *Gazetteer* article, it is a return to a pure "Brahminic" monotheism of the Vedas that is cited as the source of conflict for the Mahanubhavs, perhaps evincing the influence of socio-religious movements of the colonial era, such as the Arya Samaj. And in the second issue of the *Gazetteer* it is implied that Brahmins were at the heart of "maligning" the Mahanubhav religion. This odd contradiction reveals much misunderstanding. But it does appear that the representation of Brahmins within the religion of the Mahanubhavs declined in leadership contexts in any case. This is likely the result of the fact that Mahanubhavs are not an endogamous group; they usually marry people by the rules of caste endogamy within their given region rather than choose other Mahanubhavs for marriage. Caste endogamy, in this case, is perhaps perceived as contrary to the social egalitarianism of the religion itself. Yet this reduction in the representation of Brahmins within this religious order does not indicate a conflict, to my mind.

The Mahanubhav religion's reentry into public culture in western India bears echoes of the purported trial of Chakradhar, a trial based on processes of vernacularization located through the vicissitudes of everyday life and presented within public culture. Here we see this within the modern public sphere, itself epitomized by the *Times of India* and the *Gazetteer* as the palimpsests of our inquiry. The Brahminic ecumene's supposed persecution of Chakradhar becomes a story of a general Brahminic persecution of Mahanubhavs. And the resonance with the trial and narrative movements of the *Līḷācaritra* around gender, caste, and society return us to one of the key problems of vernacularization—the accommodation of "everyday life" at the core of public culture. The Mahanubhavs had removed their literary and historical record from the public field, even while they continued to live in and alongside the flow of everyday life, both as "householders" and as ascetics.

The theme of a trial would continue in this modern record of the Mahanubhavs. By the early 1980s, court cases and political controversy would envelop the reentry of the Mahanubhavs into Indian public life. V. B. Kolte was an eminent scholar of Marathi literature and history and especially of the Mahanubhavs. His work on the *Līḷācaritra* in 1978 and on the early history of the Mahanubhavs became the subject of legal, political, and civil action. In the district court of Amravati in January 1982, the Association (Mandal) of Mahanubhavs in Nagpur filed a civil suit against Kolte and the Government of Maharashtra, which had published his edition of the *Līḷācaritra*, in an effort to suspend the publication of Kolte's edition. The petition was rejected, as was another petition in October of that year.[27] The story of this conflict is an important instance of the complex negotiations of the quotidian revolution in public culture and the public sphere of Indian democracy.

The nature of the allegations against Kolte's work by the Nagpur Mandal involved the inclusion of stories from the life of Chakradhar that they believed were either spurious or defamatory. In particular, they claimed that including certain lilas would create "hatred between the Hindu and Mahanubhav religions."[28] They argued that Kolte's work, especially his critical edition of the *Līḷācaritra* published by the Government of Maharashtra, contravened the protections of section 295a of the Indian Penal Code, which protects Indian citizens from "deliberate and malicious acts intended to outrage religious feelings of any class by insulting its religion or religious beliefs." In other words, the Nagpur Mandal feared that the *Līḷācaritra* would insult some Hindus, and, given that Kolte had edited the *Līḷācaritra* and the Government of Maharashtra had published the text, Kolte and the government were liable for any potential defamation. The particular fear of the Nagpur group of Mahanubhavs involved a certain lila within the *Līḷācaritra* that I need not repeat here. They worried that the publication of this lila would inflame Hindu anger in some general sense.

A third attempt to halt the government's publication of Kolte's *Līḷācaritra*, spearheaded by the Nagpur Mandal, was initiated on November 29, 1991.

This time the government agreed, but then lifted the ban on May 6, 1992, only to reinstate it again in August.[29] Two years later, in 1994, a political figure of India's primary "Hindu Nationalist" political party, the Bharatiya Janata Party (BJP), renewed calls for action, this time against Professor Kolte himself, then an eighty-seven-year-old retiree.[30] Kolte defended himself in all these cases by arguing that the offending lilas were not endorsed by him; rather he merely had transcribed whatever lilas he found in old manuscripts given to him by, among others, Mahanubhavs who had held those texts for hundreds of years, albeit in relative secrecy.[31]

Yet the more significant contest appeared to take place within the community of Mahanubhavs. While the Nagpur Mandal had initiated a decade of legal and political efforts to oppose Kolte's work, simultaneously other key leaders of the Mahanubhavs defended Kolte and advocated for his text. In particular, a key scholar and *mahant* of the Mahanubhav order, according to the *Times of India*, declared that "the move of the government [to withhold publication of Kolte's *Līḷācaritra*] was politically motivated" and that "all the allegations made by the Nagpur Mandal were baseless."[32] This debate, playing out in the public sphere in the early 1990s, was both between Mahanubhavs and a sense of a general "Hindu" community and also within the Mahanubhav order itself.

I should strenuously state here that I take no position on this issue whatsoever and endeavor to relay only details available in the public record. Indeed, whatever one's position on this issue or on the larger question of the effectiveness of a penal code such as the one invoked by the Nagpur Mandal (and many other groups before and after), this legal and public tussle over the place and pronouncements of the Mahanubhavs highlights a key feature of vernacularization, as I have described it in this book.

As we have seen, the first small group of Mahanubhavs that surrounded Chakradhar did not agree on everything—they debated and struggled with one another and with their founder. We see in the Nagpur Mandal's complaint some remnant of Chakradhar's injunctions to his followers to respect the cultures in which they exist—to minimize offense and discord, even while remaining true to their own egalitarian ethos. The fault lines between a life in public and the private vows of Mahanubhavs were issues ever present in the foundation of the community, and these struggles appear to have endured. And in Nagaraja's reactions to the Nagpur Mandal's efforts, we hear not only a countervailing voice but also the direct outcome of the egalitarianism of the Mahanubhavs—a world conditioned by debate rather than orthodoxy, a key feature, at least in principle, of any configuration of the public sphere. In both cases, contemporary Mahanubhavs remained attentive to their founder's ethics and inspiration.

Last Thoughts

What does the history of vernacularization in Marathi social worlds tell us about the processes of vernacularization today? The force of vernacularization—of drawing subjects into the gravitational pull of "everyday life"—exerted its power over the last seven hundred years in many ways, exemplifying the glacial shift of the quotidian revolution into the present. Just as the vernacular turn may engender a nascent Marathi public sphere in thirteenth-century in India, the central function of vernacularization continues to craft the content and character of the ongoing and vibrant modern public sphere today. India's current public sphere, especially as it intersects with politics, remains deeply invested in representing "everyday life" and "the common man." Such processes continue to define the vernacularization of democracy in contemporary India, registered as ever more minute accommodations of the "ordinary" by vested political and social interests.

For scholars who explore the contemporary life of Indian politics, the deepening of the core of political participation is much more than the localizing or regionalizing of a political idiom—like changing the name of a city from Bombay to Mumbai, as happened in 1995. Instead, this vernacularization is rooted in the valorization of the "common man," a stock figure at the core of the contemporary political sphere in India. The rise of the political Aam Aadmi Party—the "Common Man Party"—is but one recent, though crucial, example. The longest-running political cartoon in the *Times of India,* drawn daily by R. K. Laxman (1921–2015) from 1951 until shortly before his death, follows the bewilderment of the "common man" as he encounters the enigmas of Indian politics and the Indian state. And in Maharashtra, in particular, all political parties vie to represent the "Marathi *māṇūs,*" the Marathi man.[33] The common person (configured variously by class, gender, and region) remains at the heart of the discourse of Indian democracy, represented anew each election cycle.

In this book I have argued that the process of vernacularization, the quotidian revolution, has distinct social and political origins in any given context, yet it has no distinct concluding point—it is a process begun but not finished. What Christophe Jaffrelot has eloquently called "India's silent revolution" is part of the long process I have outlined here, though marked in the modern period by recourse to the democratic power of majoritarian politics.[34] We can trace its historical origins to particular places, times, and languages in South Asia, but we should also attend to forces enacted upon public culture that are self-replicating and perpetual. There is no doubt that the process of vernacularization in many parts of South Asia drew from the elite literary and royal spheres of the older cosmopolitan world, embodied in Sanskrit literary theory and text. However, this book has sought to show that this location for vernacularization was joined by another: in Maharashtra—as perhaps in most linguistic regions of the subcontinent—the process of vernacularization mediated between the royal-elite and the quotidian, and between institutional religion and religious innovation, by occupying, at least discursively, the position of the "everyday." Regardless of the location from which it is inaugurated or the direction from which it arrives, I argue that all processes of vernacularization share that same epicenter in the discourse of everyday life. In contemporary India, vernacularization continues to thrive in the interstices of state and society, of the secular and sacred, all focused upon the vast sphere of everyday life that has a renewed political valence in the context of a secular democracy of voters and individual rights.

We have also seen in this study that vernacularization retains ambivalence at its core. The valorized quotidian field at the center of public culture uses the idioms of the common world, which are themselves encoded with social difference. This results in a vacillation embedded in the process of vernacularization, what I have described as an unbounded dialectic of resolving difference and reproducing difference continuously. I think of this process as definitive of cultural politics or perhaps all politics—all negotiations of power and its distribution. Studies of contemporary Indian political culture evince this sense of politics, at the intersection of vernacular culture, as a dialectical system of resolving and reproducing difference simultaneously. Hansen describes this as "a generative and destructive process, questioning hierarchies and certitudes, while producing undecidability . . . at the heart of the social world."[35] Similarly, in Partha Chatterjee's examination of political culture, he finds that the politics of the governed, of those situated within the nonelite spheres of everyday life, forms a field of resistance that must negotiate the legal and nonlegal, the state and civil society, the promise of representation and the realities of elite politics.[36] Vernacularization reveals this process at its core, both in the thirteenth century and in the twenty-first century. Seen this way, vernacularization is perhaps a fundamental aspect of social life itself, involving human culture at is most creative and daring, yet displaying humanity in all its normal, quotidian glory. This is the ethics of Chakradhar and Jnandev that demands our attention, even in the present. They stand as witnesses to the turbulence of change and the enduring hope for a more egalitarian future.

Notes

Preface: The Shape of the Book

1. Mahanubhavs do not believe Chakradhar died, but rather departed Maharashtra in 1273. I use the dates 1194–1273 to mark the time Chakradhar lived among his followers in Maharashtra.
2. Many of Jnandev's followers do not believe he died but rather is still entombed in Alandi.
3. See the introduction for my rationale for this statement.

Introduction: The Argument of the Book

1. See Povinelli 2006.
2. Pollock 2006.
3. I am inspired here by Gramsci's idea of a passive revolution. Gramsci, however, uses the term in a very modernist, capitalist context, and with less emphasis on everyday life, but more emphasis on ordinary social structures, such as education, organized religion, and media.
4. See Novetzke forthcoming.
5. This is the most common title given to this text, a text that otherwise contains no title. Other titles include the *Bhavarthadīpīka* and the *Jñānadevī*. I refer to this figure as Jnandev since this is the name used in the *Jñāneśvarī* to designate its author. Jnaneshwar a later name applied to this *sant*.
6. Pollock 2006:283.
7. Ibid., 4–6. My thanks to Sheldon Pollock, who gave critical advice on aspects of this book, particularly in relation to theorizing vernacularization, gender, and public culture.

8. Ibid., 283.

9. Pollock in Eisenstadt, Schluchter, and Wittrock 2001:41–74. For Pollock's fullest treatment of this subject, see Pollock 2006.

10. Pollock 2006:6.

11. Ibid.

12. Ibid., 22.

13. Ibid., 7.

14. Pollock engages with caste in his book, but caste does not form a central problematic in his analysis. Gender is not a subject Pollock engages, in part because of the nature of his field of exploration, a field dominated by high-caste men (though not necessarily Brahmins, as he points out). European studies of vernacularization do emphasize gender, however. I thank Pollock for pointing this out to me.

15. Pollock shares this view. See Pollock 2006:12, 204–22, 397–409.

16. Hansen 1999:9. See also Hansen 1996, and Chatterjee 2011. The intimate connection between vernacular culture and everyday life is apparent in studies well outside South Asia. See for example Abrahams 2005 and Lefebvre 1991 [1947].

17. Hansen 2001:69.

18. Ibid., 68.

19. Ibid., 87. See Hansen's engaging examination of the "ordinary" as a process of "othering," which he traces from Hegel to Kojève to Lacan and Žižek (ibid., 197–98). I should note here I am making no connection or asserting no relationship between Bal Thackeray or other contemporary political figures and either Jnandev or Chakradhar.

20. Michelutti 2007. See also Michelutti 2008.

21. Flueckiger 2006:xi.

22. Ibid., 14–15. See also the work of DeNapoli 2014. In the context of gender and public performance, we see something like the opposite of "vernacularization" as the investment of everyday life within public culture with the erasure of the devadāsī from the history of Indian classical dance. See the excellent work of Soneji 2012.

23. Mir 2010:120, 182. For Telugu and the situated nature of language in everyday life transformed in political power in the contemporary period, see Mitchell 2009. See also Mantena 2013.

24. See Jalal 2000.

25. Pandian 2009:16, 105 and Daniel 1987. See Prasad 2007.

26. Birla in Pandian and Ali 2010:86.

27. Mahadevan 2015.

28. See, for example, Abrahams 2005. I would note, however, that the *everyday* is a keyword not restricted to the "vernacular" but also employed by scholars to study the "cosmopolitan" as well. See a wonderful example in the work of Bayat 2008.

29. Taylor 2007.
30. De Certeau 1984. See in particular his discussion of "strategy" and "tactic" (ibid., xix). As I am not engaging the "philosophical psychology" of "everyday life," I have avoided engaging the prominent statements on this idea by Freud or Lacan, which are all taken up by de Certeau.
31. Scott 1985; Chatterjee 2004, 2011. Chatterjee does not invoke de Certeau and does not use his terminology; indeed, Chatterjee emphasizes how certain efforts deemed "illegal" by the state represent "strategies" by the governed to affect political society.
32. Guha in Guha and Spivak 1988:40.
33. De Certeau 1984:xix.
34. See Gadkari 1996:180. Gadkari cites the *Bhāgavata*, the *Devī Purāṇa*, the *Narasiṃha Purāṇa*, and also the *Mahābhārata*.
35. For example, Dandekar 1963:18:1448.
36. This leaves aside the fact that Sanskrit is not uniform over region, but varies region by region, as does English, though it is largely intelligible to anyone who knows Sanskrit in general; this is essential to Pollock's idea of the cosmopolis, that the diversity of region, though present and registered in Sanskrit, is yet overcome by an overall symmetry of grammar and vocabulary. See his engagement with this idea in Pollock 2006:39ff.
37. Pollock 2003:4.
38. See King 1999.
39. See Pollock 1998:29ff and Pollock 2006:423–36.
40. Pollock 1998:31.
41. Pollock 2006:429–30.
42. Ibid., 5, 432ff, and 434.
43. See ibid., 330–79, and Pollock 1998:30–31.
44. Pollock 2006:479.
45. Ibid., 382.
46. For examples of this complexity, see Wentworth 2011 for Tamil and Busch 2011a for Hindi/Urdu. See also Busch 2011b:7–9 and Behl, Weightman, and Pandey 2000 and Behl and Doniger 2012. For Punjabi, see Harpreet Singh's recent dissertation, Singh 2013. My thanks to Allison Busch and Whitney Cox for a discussion of this subject.
47. See also Nagaraj 2003.
48. My thanks to Whitney Cox for this challenging observation and for discussing much of this book and giving valuable feedback.
49. See Novetzke 2008b.
50. Hawley 2015. My thanks to Jack Hawley for extensive comments on chapters 1, 2, and 3 of the book.
51. In using this term, I take inspiration from the work of Bourdieu's *Distinction* (1984 [1979]), but I am not restricting the use of this term to the

social frames Bourdieu employs. For more Bourdieun appropriations, see chapter 3.

52. See Thapar 2003 and Doniger 2009.

53. The key modern scholarship on caste would include the work of Louis Dumont, M. N. Srinivas, Bernard Cohn, Nicholas B. Dirks, and Susan Bayly. A wonderful survey begins Guha's recent book (Guha 2013), and I would recommend Roberts 2008 and Das 2001.

54. Cohn 1971, 1987, 1996; Dirks 1987, 2001.

55. Srinivas 1994. For the view that ritual purity ordered the caste system, see Dumont 1980.

56. Monier-Williams, Leumann, and Cappeller 1899:418 (column 1).

57. For theories about the historical emergence of jati, see the work of Burton Stein, D. D. Kosambi, and Romila Thapar.

58. Examples would include the Jat caste, which is found in northern India among Sikhs, Hindus, and Muslims; or the Chamar caste, which is found throughout central, western, and northern India, across religious, regional, and linguistic divides. See Rawat 2011.

59. National Sample Survey Organization 2001.

60. See Guha 2013.

61. For example, the first censuses conducted in India under colonial rule in the early nineteenth century began by enumerating varna and only later came to recognize the far more detailed and quotidian designations of jati.

62. For more on the issue of "Untouchability" in the Laws of Manu, see *The Laws of Manu*, translated by Wendy Doniger (1991) and Olivelle and Olivelle 2004.

63. See, as representative, B. R. Ambedkar's *The Annihilation of Caste* (2014 [1936]) and "Manu and the Shudras," online resource at http://www.ambedkar.org /ambcd/57.%20Manu%20and%20the%20Shudras.htm (accessed on April 13, 2014). See Rao 2009. Occasionally I use "Untouchable" not to deemphasize the reality of the social stigma forced on such individuals and communities but rather to respect that people described with this term may not themselves accept it.

64. See Patrick Olivelle's discussion of this issue in Olivelle and Olivelle 2004: xvii–xviii.

65. For example, see Ghurye 1961 and Gupta 1991 and 2004.

66. For studies that have observed the intersection of caste and gender, see, for example, Marglin 1985 and Rege 2006. The key origin for this critique is Ambedkar, contained in a graduate student paper he wrote when at Columbia University in 1916.

67. See Patton 2005 and Laurie Patton's forthcoming "Grandmother Language: Women and Sanskrit in Maharashtra and Beyond." See also the ongoing work of Ute Huesken.

68. Even a cursory look at the most recent censuses of India indicates that the population of women, low-caste men, and men of scheduled castes and tribal castes constitutes a vast majority of India's contemporary population. Taken as a designation of India's population, the phrase "women, low castes, and others" would describe approximately 91 percent of the total population. Seen conversely, those that are not "women, low castes, and others" would constitute a mere 9 percent at best. For a very helpful table on these demographic statistics, see Jaffrelot 2003:323 (table 9.5), which is based on the statistics used by the Mandal Commission Report of 1980. It is likely that the percentage of "women, low castes, and others" will significantly increase when the results of the recently completed socioeconomic and caste census are fully released.
69. Viswanath 2014:190ff.
70. I quote here from one of my anonymous reviewers, an exemplary critic of my work who forced me to adopt and display a far more self-conscious use of such theoretical terminology. I thank the reviewer for this invaluable critique.
71. Personal communication, November 2, 2014.
72. Spivak 1988:314.
73. I will leave aside here the debate around the public sphere and the "private" nature of civil society. This debate does seem uniquely germane to the modern state, rules of property, the twilight of feudalism, and the emergence of liberal democracy in the West. For a brilliant critique of Habermas in relation to the liberal subject, see Povinelli 2006.
74. Habermas 1989:52.
75. Novetzke 2007b and 2008b.
76. My formulation of a public here, and elsewhere, emerges from my reading of the work of Michael Warner (2002).
77. Warner 2002:87ff.
78. Habermas 1989:xviii and xvi, 50.
79. I am not alone in situating the origins of a given public sphere before modernity. See the volume edited by Emden and Midgley (2012). Also see Melve (2007), who situates an emergent public sphere in Europe to the eleventh century around the investiture controversy between the Catholic Church and the monarchies of Europe. Abu-Lughod (1991) speaks of "public debt" and "public trade," but not a public sphere. However, her work suggests the kinds of rationalized economic social systems that Habermas identifies as essential to the emergent public sphere in Europe, what Abu-Lughod calls "the world system" of the mid-thirteenth century onward.
80. Talal Asad's critical interventions in the field of religious studies and definitions of religion might also apply to the field of the study of public spheres. See Asad 1993.

81. Observing Habermas's insistence on "communicative rationality" and a "reasoning public" introduces another feature of a public sphere in general which is active in the thirteenth-century materials of this book (1989:50). This is the way in which a public sphere not only expands the scope of debate within society but also restricts that scope in formalistic ways. Habermas, for example, traces the rise and decline of the public sphere in Europe, noting how it grew more "public" with increased rights of social access and enfranchisement in Europe and America, and how it declined and took on the form of a "spectacle" in the mass media of the 1960s and later. The world of late capitalism and high global consumerism saw the decline of the public sphere, according to Habermas, for in part it came with a decline in rational argument in public, which, we might note, is also when the public sphere became far more capacious and ecumenical (ibid., 141ff).

82. Taylor 2004:83, 86.

83. I have referred to this specific phenomenon as "the Brahmin double" and traced its use. See Novetzke 2011.

84. For more on other studies of the history of the public sphere outside Europe, see Koo 2007. My thanks to Clark Sorenson for this reference.

85. Orsini 2009; Rajagopal 2009; Wakankar 2010; Bhargava and Reifeld 2005; and Naregal 2001.

86. See Rudolph and Rudolph 2006, especially chapter 4, "The Coffee House and the Ashram Revisited," 140–76, and note the discussion of Habermas and critics on pages 144–49.

87. Appadurai and Breckenridge 1988; Breckenridge 1995; Haynes 1991; Frietag 1989; Hardgrove 2004; Yandell and Paul 2000; and my own work, Novetzke 2007b and 2008b. See also a special issue of South Asia dedicated to the idea of the public in modern South Asia, Ingram, Scott, and SherAli Tareen 2015.

88. Bayly 1996:180–211 and Agarwal 2009, especially Chapter 2; see also Sen 2005.

89. However, Pollock, perhaps rightly, dismisses Habermas as offering "little in the way of a convincing account of the nature of the 'premodern,' at least in the case of South Asia" (Pollock 2006:8).

90. Here I take particular inspiration from the work of Janet L. Abu-Lughod and her book *Before European Hegemony* (1991), a study of the thirteenth-century world economy.

1. The Yadava Century

1. The first attestation of this term *marathe* as a self-designation by the Yadavas occurs in an inscription, discussed in chapter 2, attributed to the reign of Ramachandra or Singhana III, the last inscription of the Yadavas offering a gift to the Pandharpur temple, dated to 1311 CE. See PMKL 37. The word does not mean "Maharashtra," which occurs

much earlier as a name for the region; and the word does not indicate the Maratha caste/jati either. Instead, the word means "belonging to Maharashtra," as Feldhaus and Tulpule gloss the word, but it implies the confluence of language, religion, culture, and place, as we will see below. See Feldhaus and Tulpule 1999:533. For the place name *Maharashtra* in the *Līḷācaritra*, see LC-U 536–37. For the same place name in the *Jñāneśvarī*, see Jn. 18.1781.

2. See Palshikar 2007.
3. See Keluskar 1921. Jijabai's royal blood also complicated the alliance between Jijabai and Shahji. For a study of the intersections of memory and history in Maratha historiography, see Deshpande 2007.
4. Ali 2004:2.
5. Many historians, such as Satish Sharma, Romila Thapar, D. D. Kosambi, Irfan Habib, and others, heuristically use the term *state* in their work on medieval India. This use of the idea of the state is often related to Marxist and materialist analysis associated with feudalism, "oriental despostism," and "the Asiatic mode of production."
6. Most commonly associated with Aidan Southall and Burton Stein.
7. Inden 1985:159–79 and Inden 1990.
8. Ali 2004:7.
9. See Kulke 1995:16.
10. Pollock 2006:420.
11. See Mitchell 1999 and Abrams 1988.
12. Ali 2004:3.
13. See Cohen and Arato 1992 for an excellent study of the many permutations of the concept of "civil society" and its relationship to the state, economy, and private sphere.
14. While I also consider the systems of village governance—such as *jajmāni* and *balutedāri*—to constitute a stratum of the state, or the "substate," these highly localized governmental systems tend to collapse the broader distinctions between state and civil society at such microlevels.
15. See Chatterjee 2004:4, 39 for the "elite" nature of civil society as opposed to the "politics of the governed." See also Chatterjee 2001, especially page 173.
16. See Habermas 1989.
17. We come close with Partha Chatterjee's compelling engagements with the idea and function of civil society in postcolonial India, but here too it is an "institution of modern associational life originating in Western societies" and so ill-fitting the "politics of the governed" in postcolonial India. See Chatterjee 2001:172–73.
18. I borrow this term from the exemplary work of Rosalind O'Hanlon, though I apply it to a context several centuries earlier, but in a direct genealogical relationship to her subject. See O'Hanlon 2011.

19. The earliest inscription to mention the Yadava line yet to be found is from 1000 CE, though other sources, including later Yadava genealogies, place the origin of the dynasty in the ninth century.

20. Kapstein 2002:158.

21. Though Hemadri, the commander of the Yadava army who also served as minister and chief archivist, records that Mahadev retreated because "he refrained from killing a woman," the *Pratāpacaritramu* of the late sixteenth century from the Telugu region of the Kakatiya dynasty, instead recalls a resounding defeat of Mahadev in which he paid a a high ransom for his life. While Hemadri valorizes his king as "the one who roars at the Hoysalas," the Hoysalas record Mahadev sneaking from the battlefield at night to return to his territory. See Verma 1970:132–33.

22. An inscription from Purushottampuri tells us of the plot to enter the court in the guise of female dancers (see *Epigraphia Indica* [1939]: 199), and the *Līḷācaritra* tells us of the eye-gouging (LC-P 476).

23. Ramachandra is the last true sovereign of the Yadava Empire. Upon his death in 1311, and the death of his successor, Singhana III (who mounted a short-lived rebellion), the Yadava territory became entirely subsumed under the Delhi Sultanate and Devgiri was renamed Daulatabad.

24. One may find references attributing the first Marathi literary creation to the state-sponsored philosopher Mukundaraja of the mid-twelfth century, but these are now discounted by scholars, as discussed in chapter 2.

25. I mark the end of this "golden age" at the year 1294 when Alauddin Khilji captured Devgiri, the Yadava capital, and essentially made the Yadavas a vassal state to the Delhi Sultanate. However, the Yadava reign continued for another eighteen years perhaps. In 1311 we have the last inscription issued under the sovereignty of the Yadava state, a donation of funds to the Pandharpur temple and Vitthal's devotees there. The Yadava dynasty was entirely absorbed into the Delhi Sultanate in 1317.

26. As we will see in chapters 4 and 5, Islam is already present and routinized in the culture of the Yadava era in the form of mosques, according to the *Līḷācaritra*.

27. See Joshi 1951, 1952; Ritti 1973:21–27, for the contours of the Kannada origin of the Yadavas; Murthy 1971 also finds that "Karnataka" is the likely origin of the Yadavas. See also Ranade 2009. The claim that the Yadavas are of "Maratha" origin has been made by George Moraes, V. K. Rajwade, C. V. Vaidya, A. S. Altekar, D. R. Bhandkarkar, J. D. M. Derrett, D. B. Mokashi, and others. I will not enter this debate here, however, though I will point out that the *Smṛtisthaḷa,* attributed to the fourteenth century, calls the Yadava rule *marhāṭe,* as do inscriptions from the time period, suggesting that if the Yadavas did not begin with an identification with Marathi, they certainly ended that way. See Deshpande 1969:26 (chapter 86).

28. See Doniger 1981:I.54.6, I.108.7, X.62.10. For the various names the Yadavas used for themselves, see Verma 1970:1–7; Ritti 1973:21–25.
29. Michelutti 2008; J. N. Singh Yadav has published at least four books detailing these claims. In addition, see Khedkar 1959.
30. For the latter, see Talbot 2001:51, who points out that they also have claimed Kshatriya status in some inscriptions.
31. For Maharashtra, see, for example, Bapat 1998 and O'Hanlon 2010b.
32. Kosambi 1961:214.
33. Hemadri, in the *Caturvarga Cintāmaṇi* uses this title for the dynasty (see Murthy 1971:22). Sevuna is usually how other polities referred to this dynasty as well.
34. See Dhavalikar 1972, especially 25–26 and 29–30.
35. See Murthy 1971:10 and Ranade 2009:32.
36. Pollock 2006:4ff.
37. See Tulpule 1979:312–13. It is uncertain how long Marathi, or some early form of it, has been a spoken language. Marathi is an Indo-European language that shows the influence of Sanskrit as well as Maharashtri Apabhramsha, but is heavily influenced by South Indian Dravidian languages, especially Tamil and Kannada. Some recent scholarship has suggested that traces of Marathi exist in inscriptions and texts from the time of Ashoka or even earlier. Throughout the centuries of the language's existence, it has gathered vocabulary and sounds from various other languages, including, importantly, Persian, Arabic, and English.
38. The primary source here, and in general, for Marathi inscriptions is the collection edited by Tulpule 1963 (PMKL).
39. A debate on which inscription in Marathi is actually the "first" continues without resolution. See Dhavalikar 1972 for more on this. See also B. Deshpande 2002:9–21. Deshpande argues that the inscriptions in Shravanabelgol are the oldest instances of full Marathi inscription (a sentence rather than simply a word or phrase), which he dates to 983 CE.
40. PMKL 1.
41. PMKL 2.
42. PMKL 4.
43. Evidence for the use of modi, however, exists only from the sixteenth century onward. See Guha 2010; also Deshpande 2016.
44. See Guha 2010 and Deshpande 2014.
45. Some Marathi epigraphs are in modi as well as Kannada script, though these all date from the sixteenth century or later. See Dhavalikar 1972:30. For the argument that Marathi was the state language of the Yadavas, see Bhave 1963 [1898]:24ff; see also Deshpande 1979:69. Guha 2010 argues against this position, and I think he is right.
46. The *Caturvarga Cintāmaṇi* has been printed several times. See Dixit 1902, 1903.

47. A survey of any history of the Yadava period will make this point clear. Indeed, some works rely entirely on such texts, particularly the literature of the Mahanubhavs. For example, a study such as Babras 1996, on the social life of women in the Yadava period, is based almost entirely on Mahanubhav texts, for there are few other sources that would be useful in such a historiography. See also Sontheimer 1982.

48. There is a long history of contention around the caste status of Kayasthas relative to Brahmins and Kshatriyas in the varna typology. For more on this see O'Hanlon 2010a, b; O'Hanlon and Minkowski 2008; see also Ranade 2009:120–21, and chapter 2, this volume.

49. PMKL 34.

50. For more on the anxieties of Brahminhood in the premodern period, see O'Hanlon's many essays, especially O'Hanlon 2014; see also Novetzke 2011 for the idea of a "Brahmin Double."

51. See the Bendigere plates in *Indian Antiquary* (Fleet and Temple [1885]:74) for a list of twenty-four gotra distinctions. Panse discusses the variety of Brahmin jatis and occupations during the Yadava period; see Panse 1963:106–14. See also O'Hanlon 2013 and 2014.

52. Verma discusses a fascinating set of epigraphical materials that describe the origin of the Kayastha communities from the varnas of Brahmin, Kshatriya, and Shudra. See Verma 1970:230. See Mulay 1972: 300ff for a discussion of Kayastha names in inscriptions of the Deccan.

53. For studies of this process from the seventeenth century in Marathi contexts, see O'Hanlon 2010a, b.

54. See Ramanujan 1973 and Narayana Rao and Roghair 1990. As we will see in chapters 4 and 5, Basava is often connected to Chakradhar and Jnandev through a common Shaiva Natha genealogy.

55. LC-P 72.

56. See Tulpule 1963:95ff.

57. PMKL 2.

58. PMKL 1; see figure 2.1.

59. Amba Jogai contains several inscriptions, the oldest from 1144 CE by the Mysore Hoysalas, in 1188 CE, as well as from 1228–1229 CE and in 1240 CE, the latter all under the Yadavas. See PMKL 5, 23, 25, 67. Kholeshwar's donations are from 1228 (PMKL 23) and 1240 (PMKL 25). The former, a gift to a Brahmin temple, is notable in part for it mentions that it is written in the "Maharashtra language" (*mahārāṣṭra bhāṣaya . . . likhyate*). The latter endows a temple in a *brahmanapuri* in the name of his daughter, Lakshmi.

60. Master 1957.

61. The remaining two comprise a record of some financial cost sharing between two villages and a curse—very common in Marathi—that threatens

dire consequences to anyone who contravenes the inscription, which is in Sanskrit, to which the Marathi curse is appended.

62. From PMKL 17, dated to 1189 CE to PMKL 51, dated to 1311 CE. While inscriptions from the reigns of Singhana and Krishna number six and four, respectively, under Ramachandra's reign, the number of Marathi inscriptions rises to around fourteen.

63. The exceptions being PMKL 19, 20, 22, 28, 32, 33, 36, 38.

64. These are PMKL 18, 20, 21, 23, 24, 25, 26, 27, 29, 31, 37, 41, 45, 48, 50.

65. These are PMKL 30, 40, 42, 43, 44, 47. PMKL 35 is likely a gift to a Brahmin adviser to Ramachandra, a Shivadeva Pandit, but this does not seem to be a gift given in relation to a traditional caste-based endeavor.

66. See Tulpule 1963:95ff; Verma 1970:231ff; Panse 1963:111ff; Ranade 2009:112ff; Ritti 1973:248; Babras 1996:49; Mulay 1972. See also Mulay's extensive list of names and suffixes for Brahmin donees (Mulay 1972:243, 267–80, 290–92).

67. See Bapat 1993 and 1998, and chapter 3. See also LC-U 288 where Chakradhar tells a Gurav that, in the absence of Brahmins in his village, the Gurav should become a "leader" (*agraṇīyā*).

68. PMKL 27. See PMKL 46, which may indicate a gift to a trusted minister of Ramachandra who may be a Gurav.

69. See PMKL 21, 23, 27, 70.

70. The term *sattra* is from the Sanskrit *chatra,* "canopy," and often refers to a charity distribution of food, as noted earlier. However, the term is also used to describe a boarding house for traveling Brahmins, particular who are on pilgrimage or undertaking religious service.

71. Altekar 1960:562.

72. See Panse 1963:102ff; Apte 1972:30–35. See also Verma 1970:262–63, 297. The fact that Dharma Śāstra eclipsed all other literary endeavors of the age may be suggestive. As Romila Thapar says of the original creation of this literary canon on social orthodoxy, "The severity of the Dharma-Shastras was doubtless a commentary arising from the insecurity of the orthodox in an age of flux." Thapar 2003:279. While Thapar is discussing a period around the beginning of the first millennium CE, we might assume that the recurring dominance of this literary genre within the restricted literary sphere of Sanskrit in the Yadava century implies just such a rising "insecurity" within an orthodox Sanskritic establishment.

73. These exceptions would include the works of mathematics and astrology ascribed to the famous scholar Bhaskaracharya (1114–1185), as well as work attributed to his father, son, and grandson. A work on music, the *Saṅgītaratnākara,* attributed to Sarangadeva at the court of Simhana, and the *Suktimuktāvali,* an anthology of Sanskrit verses by a Brahmin minister Jalhana (c. 1250) also stand out, as does the *Harilīla* attributed to Bopadeva.

74. See Dandekar 1972.

75. Guha 2010.

76. Dandekar 1972:30–31, 55.

77. Murthy, for example, refers to Hemadri's *Caturvarga Cintāmaṇi* this way: "Hemadri, the champion of Brahminism tried to check the rebellion against the caste system and other orthodox social practices" by compiling his text (Murthy 1971:167). My thanks to Jason Schwartz for helpful conversations on this subject.

78. Altekar 1960:565.

79. The appendix was perhaps added after Hemadri finished his text. See Kane 1930:355.

80. For the text of the dynastic eulogy (*prashasti*) contained in the *Vratakhaṇḍa*, in particular, see Bhandarkar 1957:152–63.

81. Mukherjee 1998:133, 205.

82. See Verma 1970:226–31.

83. Narasimhachar 1923 (illus. 59).

84. *Epigraphia Indica* 1939: 208; Verma 1970:226.

85. Ritti 1973:213.

86. Verma 1970: 295–96.

87. See Deshpande 1935.

88. Bhave's point about evidence for the existence of Marathi genres of oral, and perhaps even written, literature is a point I accept, as do other scholars (see Tulpule 1979, for example). My key contention is that this does not add up to proof of royal patronage of Marathi literature.

89. Doniger 1991:xxiii. Patrick Olivelle in his introduction calls the mythical figure of Manu a "learned Brahmin from somewhere in northern India." See Olivelle and Olivelle 2004:xxii.

90. See Dumont 1980:71–72.

91. See, for example, Heesterman 1985; Hocart 1950; Dirks 1987. In addition to stabilizing the political sphere in a given region, Brahmins served other more "magical" purposes. See Inden 1990; White 2009.

92. The Peshwa position passed through hereditary lines from Balaji Vishwanath in 1713 to Bajirao II in 1818. Though Chitpavan Brahmins had achieved sovereignty through their roles as prime ministers (*peśawā*) to the early Maratha kings, they were regularly reviled by their Brahmin brethren of a different jati, the Deshastha Brahmins, in part because the Deshasthas felt that Chitpavans functioned in a nonbrahminic capacity; they did not act like Brahmins. Despite this, the records of the Peshwa period clearly show steady beneficence toward religious, educational, literary, ritualistic, and monastic activities undertaken by Deshastha Brahmins during their reign.

93. Pollock 2006:183.

94. This practice would change in later centuries, but in the Yadava period it was the norm. See Ranade 2009:66ff. In general, the Kulkarni is beneath

the Patil. And the Patil answers to the Deshmukh. In the thirteenth century it appears that almost all Kulkarnis were Brahmins, where as Patils and Deskhmukhs were often not Brahmins. This association is not necessarily true in the present.

95. For a useful survey of this literature, see Champakalakshmi 2001. The function of temple donations and donations of land to Brahmins in other contexts as a way to connect and normalize geopolitical spheres has been specifically noted by Stein 1980; Appadurai and Breckenridge 1976 (see especially p. 25); and Talbot 2001 and (especially relevant) 1991. These analyses have tended to emphasize property and resource revenue, which is correct; my argument is that "soft power" through the stabilization of the state rule of property and markets was vital as well. This also aligns with the other major use of land grants, clearing and extending territory into undomesticated areas.

2. Traces of a Medieval Public

1. Pollock 2006:3.
2. In Bappabhatti's *Tārāyaṇa*, attributed to the late eighth century, with attestation first in the thirteenth century, comes a story of a Jain monk (Bappabhatti) who met his future patron, Amma Nagavaloka, while the latter was trying to read out a Sanskrit *prashasti* on the wall of a temple. See Bhayani 1987:3. My thanks to Andrew Ollett for this reference.
3. Pollock 2006:3.
4. For examples in Sanskrit and Telugu, see Reddy and Natarajan 2011.
5. PMKL 5.
6. PMKL 13.
7. PMKL 18.
8. PMKL 45.
9. Pollock cites the first "workly text" of Marathi to be the inscription of Brahmadevarane, attributed to 1305 CE (Pollock 2006:324–25). However, I think the curse inscription in Marathi is a better example and certainly no less "expressive" or imaginative. For the sense of a workly text in Pollock's usage, see ibid., 3, 25. For the idea of the "speech act" the original text would be Austin 1962.
10. The phrase in Marathi is often: *jo lopi tehacie maye gādhau jhave*. Rendered in colloquial English, it says, "anyone who contravenes this donation, a donkey will fuck his mother." For multiple instances, see PMKL 40, 41, 43, 44, 46 (pp. 76, 84, 216, 226, 300, 305, 362). Notably, stating that someone's mother will have sex with a donkey is still a mainstay of Marathi profanity. Interestingly, the donkey curse was not nearly as popular in the neighboring region of Andhra Pradesh at around the same time. See Reddy and Natarajan 2011.

11. For the Shilaharas, see PMKL 14 (1184 CE) and 16 (1187 CE); for the Yadavas under Ramachandra, see PMKL 40 (1289 CE) and 43 (1298 CE); for the Bahmani Sultanate under Firoz Shah, see PMKL 57 (1398 CE); and for the Vijaynagar Empire under Harihara see PMKL 58 (1402 CE) and under Devaraya see PMKL 69 (1408 CE). The curse outside of the Yadava period and political territory might be in any language. For example, a Persian inscription at Masur, Maharashtra, from 1472 CE (Hijri 850) records the curse and also carries the illustration of the curse. My thanks for this reference to Sumit Guha, who notes a translation of this Persian inscription in the India Office Library (manuscript no. D.14).

12. From the Marathi word *gaḍagaḷa*, a stone or piece of rock, or a roughly hewn stone object.

13. Tulpule, in PMKL, describes three subsets of the donkey curse: 1. stones where the visual and literary curse are present; 2. stones where only the visual image is present; 3. stones with only the text of the curse. See Tulpule 1963:58. Here I take the stones as a whole, all three types, as a single set conveying the same message.

14. PMKL 14.

15. PMKL, 14, lines 15–16 (p. 76).

16. More are discovered regularly. See a note on the discovery of four more gadhegal in the Raigad District of Maharashtra in 2012. See Dalal, Kale, and Poojari 2015.

17. For the Marathi texts of these stones, see PMKL 1, 3, 41.

18. Dalal, Kale, and Poojari 2015.

19. In the examples given by Reddy and Natarajan (2011) we find that most curses ward off challenges to Brahmin endowments in the Andhra context as well, and often violence to or the killing of Brahmins is a sin equated with taking away a Brahmin's endowment.

20. See Verma 1970:248–50.

21. Dr. Kurush Dalal of the Center for Extra Mural Studies at Mumbai University has conducted extensive fieldwork on this subject, and I am indebted to his research here.

22. Dhere 1990:126–28.

23. Dalal, Kale, and Poojari 2015. See also Johari 2015.

24. The evil eye literature is far too voluminous to cite here. A great place to start is Alan Dundes's "Wet and Dry: The Evil Eye" (Dundes 1981b). For South India in particular, see the work of Melanie Dean (2011).

25. Many other examples could be cited. Common sights in India are a chili and lime strung together and hung on vehicles (rickshaws, cars, buses, trucks, etc.) or outside shops; pumpkins absorbing the evil eye effects outside houses; a black shoe dangling from a vehicle's bumper (or a painted depiction of one on the bumper); and the ubiquitous warnings on "goods

carriers" (trucks) in India that read, for example, "you with the evil eye, your face will be blackened!" (*burī nazarwāle tere muh kālā*) or "evil eye: keep your distance!" (*chaśm-e-badadūr*). For a wonderful book that, in part, engages visual evil eye prophylaxis on ornately decorated Pakistani goods carriers, see Elias 2011.

26. Evidence from the *Līḷācaritra* suggests that the evil eye was a common belief system during the time of its composition. See LC-P 315.

27. A common profanity in Marathi transfers the gadhegal into the present: *tujhyā āīlā gāḍhav lāgel,* "a donkey will have your mother." For examples of jokes about mothers and donkeys, see Siegel 1987. Interestingly, Siegel's only citation for a joke involving donkeys having sex with mothers is in relationship to Kayasthas, the usual scribes of inscriptions. See ibid., 161. The *Pañcatantra* "fables" of medieval India are replete with the figure of the donkey as fool. And for an example of a mother joke in the Bible, see 2 Kings 9:22. For donkey humor in the Bible see Numbers 22:27–30.

28. Dean 2013:188. Dean shows that in contemporary Tamil Nadu the object of "conspicuous consumption," such as a new mobile phone, can become what she calls a "commodity prophylactic," an ironic use of one kind of object of envy to deflect the evil eye from another object. See also Osella and Osella 1999 and 2000.

29. Warner 2002:87ff.

30. Steinmetz 1999:70.

31. Ironically, we have greater public expressions and support for Marathi outside the Yadava arena than within. As Tulpule notes, the Hoysalas established a "college" for the study of Marathi, it seems, while nothing like it existed in under Yadava rule. For the Hoysalas, perhaps knowing Marathi was a matter of "national security," as with today's Title VI centers for area studies in the U.S. See Tulpule 1979:313.

32. See, for example, Deshpande and Rajadhyaksha 1988:7; Deshpande 1993:117.

33. Karve 1969:56.

34. For details on this history, see Tulpule's introduction to *Mahārāṣtra Sāraswat*'s fifth edition, published with Tulpule's editorial oversight (Bhave 1963 [1898]).

35. Bhave 1963 [1898]:24. See the discussion of this text in Pollock 2006:184ff.

36. LC-P 61. See also Sontheimer in Sontheimer and Aithal 1982:351ff.

37. The refusal of bhakti figures, as well as famous poets and authors, to accept the funds of kings is a common trope in Indian literary history. Tukaram famously refuses the gifts of Shivaji, for example.

38. Bhave 1963:26.

39. See Tulpule 1979:316 for a thorough discussion of this issue, where he revises his position on this text from previous scholarly work (Tulpule 1960:1).

40. See, for example Ranade 2009:5, 217.

41. See PMKL 18 for a Marathi inscription from Jaitrapala regarding land attached to a Brahmin agrahara. No mention is made of any gifts for Mukundaraja or any other literary figure.

42. This argument is made by S. G. Tulpule for example. See Tulpule 1979:428, "The history of royal patronage offered to Marathi authors dates back to the time of Narendra, the early Mahanubhav poet, who had refused to receive it from Ramadev Yadava out of self-respect." See also ibid., 338–39. Bhave also engages this text and situates it within the sphere of Yadava patronage (Bhave 1963:94ff). Interestingly, Tulpule does not repeat this claim in his massive work in Marathi, *Marāṭhī Vāṅgmaya Itihāsa* (Tulpule 1984). In this work, he makes a series of associations—the support for Pandharpur by the Yadavas, the fact that during the Yadava reign the Mahanubhavs and Jnandev, or as he says, the Varkaris, arise, etc., all this he says makes the Yadavas special to the "Marathi people" (27). So, while Tulpule doesn't make a claim in this work for courtly patronage, he does suggest that Yadavas created the environment that made vernacularization possible, a position with which I entirely agree.

43. See Raeside 1960:494.

44. See *Smṛtisthaḷa,* chapter 113, in Feldhaus and Tulpule 1992:104–5.

45. *Smṛtisthaḷa,* chapter 113, in Deshpande 1969:37. Apparently rejecting royal patronage is a common trope in the biographies of poets (devotional and secular), especially of northern India. My thanks to Jack Hawley, Heidi Pauwels, and Allison Busch for pointing this out to me. On *kavikula* see Busch 2011.

46. There are several Mahanubhav composers about whom claims are made of royal patronage during the very end of the Yadava era or later. The most prominent of them was Bhaskara Bhatta Borikar (c. 1313). Kolte and others claim he was patronized by the Yadava court, though there is no evidence from the Yadava court to this effect; in any case, he comes three decades after composition of the *Līḷācaritra* and *Jñāneśvarī,* and his compositions are attributed to a period when the Yadava court is essentially dissembled and under the control of the Delhi Sultanate. See Tulpule 1979:338. See also Kolte 1935, 1984:239–41.

47. See, for example, my discussion of such encounters between Namdev and kings or sultans in Novetzke 2008b:162ff.

48. Or perhaps even more broadly—*kavikula* may indicate a kind of poetic guild or even jati with some resonance across South Asia, much like the term *Kayastha* registered the community of writers. See Busch 2011:188ff.

49. Though the word *abhang* usually means "unbroken" or "steady" and often names a verse form that will be popularized by Namdev, here, in relation to the word *grantha,* I read the word as it is read by Tulpule and Feldhaus in their dictionary of Old Marathi, where they cite the *Līḷācaritra,* LC-U 402 and this verse in the *Smṛtisthaḷa* as well. See Feldhaus and Tulpule 1999:23.

50. See PMKL 17, 34 (which consists of seven inscriptions), and 51.

51. The closest we come is PMKL 51, an inscription of 1311 CE that refers to a devotee of *marathe*. This word, however, likely indicates the "Maratha" region, that is, Maharashtra, and does not refer to support for Marathi as such. See Tulpule's discussion of this word in Tulpule 1979:259.

52. See Dhere 2011 [1984]:234ff.

53. See Novetzke 2008b.

54. Ibid.

55. On the abhangs, see Kiehnle 1997. Some scholars note that the word vari appears in the *Jñāneśvarī*. However, when it appears, it does not suggest pilgrimage to Pandharpur, much less the Varkari religion. Though Tulpule and Feldhaus in the *Dictionary of Old Marathi* cite the *Jñāneśvarī* (Jn. 18.67) as referring to "the regular practice of going on a pilgrimage," they do not indicate that this means the pilgrimage to Pandharpur. All other citations for vari simply mean "a turn," which is also what I think it means in Jn 18.67. See Tulpule and Feldhaus 1999:643.

56. As I point out in *Religion and Public Memory* (Novetzke 2008b:35–73), this lack of mention of the early Varkari sants or of Pandharpur and Vitthal by Jnandev in the *Jñāneśvarī* is explained by Varkaris simply by pointing out that he had yet to meet Namdev, who is the catalyst for Jnandev's turn toward Varkari faith.

57. See ibid.

58. Ibid., 43.

59. The Pandharpur Temple has a number of inscriptions in Sanskrit and Kannada as well, such as the inscriptions of 1237 and 1270 in Sanskrit. Inscriptions in several languages continue well into the nineteenth century.

60. PMKL 17. The last line is not legible, but the last word, *karma*, is, so I have guessed here at the meaning. I thank Shobha Kale for enormously helpful discussions of this and all other translations of inscriptions.

61. PMKL 17; See Tulpule 1963:87. This term, *devaparivār*, can also sometimes refer to the "holy retinue," that is, God and his or her "family." But I do not think this is the meaning in this case.

62. PMKL 17, lines 8–9.

63. Deleury 1960:193.

64. Novetzke 2007b and 2008b.

65. Hawley 2015.

66. PMKL 34. Most of the inscriptions' given funds were intended to support a weekly or monthly gift of an item, such as flowers or food for devotees, etc. This set of inscriptions is a major source for Marathi historiography in this period.

67. PMKL 34, line 32, pillar 1.

68. PMKL 34, line 2. The very last line is hard to read. It says something like, "In the land of the day . . . in the land of the night . . . the temple . . ." It could refer to places, or times of day, but I believe it refers to "eternity."

My thanks to Whitney Cox, who helped me translate the Sanskrit portion of this text. Errors of translation are, however, mine alone.

69. PMKL 34, line 3.

70. PMKL 34, line 31.

71. See the possible exception of the Shilahara inscription in Parel of 1184 CE mentioned earlier. Line 18 of the inscription may contain the sequential letters *bhakt*.

72. As noted earlier, the Hoysalas and many others also gave funds to the Vitthal Temple in Pandharpur.

73. Full access to the Pandharpur Temple for all castes was the political project of Maharashtrian Brahmin social activist and Gandhian P. S. Sane or Sane Guruji (1899–1950). In May 1947 he began a fast unto death to open the temple to all worshippers including "Untouchables," which succeeded in its object.

74. The Yadava dynastic line formally ended in 1317.

75. We have the name of Keshavadeva. Tulpule states that this was likely issued in the time of Singhana III's rule by the waning Yadava court. See Tulpule 1963:83, 258.

76. See Dhere 1984 for a discussion of these inscriptions in relation to Vitthal.

77. This refers to the figure named Keshavadeva.

78. The term here is *pañcaguṇa* or "the five elements/qualities" and refers to five common implements of ritual worship or puja that match to the five elements of space, air, fire, water, and earth.

79. PMKL 51, lines 1–4, 7, 10–12.

80. See Novetzke in Beck 2005.

81. Pollock notes that in 779, in Udddyotanasuri's *Kuvalayamālā*, *marahaṭṭhe* is attested in a mimetic representation. See Pollock 2006:96, and *n*53.

82. Karve 1962.

3. The Biography of Literary Vernacularization

1. Foucault 2003:390.

2. Sangari 1990:1464. I am particularly thankful to Kumkum Sangari for conversations on this topic. I am also thankful to the participants of the Yale Conference on Gurus, organized by Srilata Raman, in 2014. Critical advice from Srilata Raman, Phyllis Granoff, Vasudha Dalmia, Heidi Pauwels, Adheesh Sathaye, Martin Fuchs, Smriti Srinivas, Amanda Lucia, and Nikhil Govind was especially useful.

3. I used the term *venture spiritualist* earlier and *spiritual innovator* here in a way that echoes the idea of the "portfolio capitalist" proposed by Subrahmanyam and Bayly 1988. However, there are significantly differences in that the spiritual innovator may intersect with forms of capital, but such figures appear to trade in the symbolic capital of a given cultural field.

4. The Chakradhar essentially exits human history with his departure "north" in 1273. By placing this date here I do not mean to assert that Chakradhar died, which is something his followers believe has not yet happened.

5. Secondarily, we have the *Smṛtisthaḷa* (c. early fourteenth century), a biography of Bhatobas, the first leader of the Mahanubhavs after Chakradhar's death, attributed to several contributors. And we have the *Sūtrapāṭha* (c. 1290 CE). See the discussion by Feldhaus and Tulpule 1992:56–59. In addition, there is the *Ṛddhipurlīḷā* (a biography of Gundam Raul, a precursor to Chakradhar) attributed to Mhaibhat as well (c. 1287 CE). In English, for the *Smṛtisthaḷa* see Feldhaus and Tulpule 1992; for the *Sūtrapāṭha* see Feldhaus 1983; for the *Ṛddhipurlīḷā* see Feldhaus 1984. The *Līḷācaritra* is not readily accessible in an English version, though a translation, tuned to the desires of the Mahanubhavs, was made by E. R. Jadhav in 2009. A scholarly English translation of the *Līḷācaritra* is underway by Anne Feldhaus in the Murthy Classical Library Series at Harvard University Press.

6. LC-P 1.

7. LC-P 1. For more on Dattatreya, see Rigopoulos 1998.

8. LC-P 2, 15, 16–17. The *Smṛtisthaḷa* records the date of death of Gundam Raul as 1286–87 CE (*Smṛtisthaḷa* 5). The date of Chakradhar's "departure" is 1273 CE (*Smṛtisthaḷa* 1). No date of life or death is given for Changadev, but we can assume a date of death approximate to 1210 CE, according to the logic of the Mahanubhav texts. See Feldhaus and Tulpule 1992:4.

9. Much like the Catholic trinity, the Mahanubhavs have no problem reconciling their five Krishnas with a single overarching deity.

10. The term *lila* is common in hagiography as a description of episodes from the life of a sacred figure. For an excellent examination of the historiographic function of *lilas*, see the dissertation of Shruti Patel, "At Play with History," Department of History, University of Washington, forthcoming in 2016.

11. LC-P, 2. See also Rigopoulus 1998.

12. See Feldhaus 1984.

13. LC-P 15.

14. The figure of this fierce yogini, Kamakhya (here Kamaksha), is common in yoga and tantra lore as a stand-in for the powerful yogini. See Carl Ernst in White 2011.134. See also David Gordon White's *Kiss of the Yogini* (2003), where Kamakhya is not only a yogini but also a place (a town), a Goddess, a *pīṭha*, a *cakra*, etc. See his chapter, "The Place of Love."

15. LC-P 16.

16. Dhere 1977 has argued that Haripal/Chakradhar is the same person as Harinatha, the purported guru of Mukundaraj. I do not find this argument convincing, however. For more on this, see ibid., 246–86.

17. Verma 1970:75.

18. This character trait is perhaps an echo of a similar problem faced by one of the heroes of the *Mahābhārata*, the Pandava prince Yudhishthira.

19. LC-P, 17–18.

20. For example, in my own previous work (Novetzke 2011:237) I described Chakradhar's caste as "Deshastha Brahmin," a not uncommon assumption given the founding of this sect in Paithan, a major center for Deshastha Brahmin activities. See Dhere 1977:279. Indeed, some Deshastha Brahmins claim Chakradhar as their own. However, it is highly likely that I was incorrect, and the discussion that follows is also an attempt to clarify this important question.

21. See Feldhaus and Tulpule 1992:26*n*47, where they state that he "probably was not [a Brahmin]," but see also Feldhaus 2003:257*n*14. My thanks to Anne Feldhaus for conversations on this subject, even though we may not agree. Though Tulpule 1979:316 says that Chakradhar was from a family of "royal ministers," he does not mention his caste; in the *Old Marathi Dictionary*, edited by Tulpule and Feldhaus, they cite the passage in which Chakradhar calls himself a "Lād Samaka," glossing this phrase as indicating "a member of a particular subcaste of Brahmanas" (Tulpule and Feldhaus 1999:607). Suman Belvalkar in *Līḷācaritratīl Samājikdarśan* refers to Chakradhar as a Lad Brahmin (2009:139, 144). In *Mahārāṣṭra Sāraswat*, Bhave refers to Chakradhar as a "Samavedi Brahmin" (1963 [1898]:46). Dhere says that Chakradhar was remembered as a "Sāmavedi Lād Brahmin" (1977:279), though he also argues that Chakradhar is Harinath, preceptor to Mukundaraj, thus a Maharashtrian Brahmin (see ibid., chapters 11–12 for more on this). The Marathi *Encyclopedia of the Lives of Medieval Figures* or *Madhyāyugina Caritrakoś*, edited by Siddheshwarashastri Chitrava, states that Chakradhar's father's caste was that of the "Sāmavedi Lād Brahmins" (1937:350). Nene appears to accept that Chakradhar was a Lad Samaka Brahmin, though he usually referred to Chakradhar simply as a *prādhanaputra*, the son of a minister (1954 [1936]:10, 23). Kolte, curiously, never addresses the question of Chakradhar's caste, to my knowledge; nor does Tulpule in his edition of the *Līḷācaritra*. Sontheimer, in his work on this text, also does not mention Chakradhar's caste (Sontheimer and Aithal 1982). Ritti, representing a South Indian view of the Yadava century, calls Chakradhar a "Gujarati Brahman" (1973:295). In Gujarati historiography, Chakradhar is remembered to be a Gujarati Lad Brahmin as well as the son of a royal minister; see Bogilal Sandesara's work in the section on "*Dharmasampradāyo*" (religious sects) in Parikh and Shastri 1976:362–75. My thanks to Neelima Shukla-Bhatt for this reference. On the other hand, the most recent study of the Mahanubhavs, an excellent work undertaken by Rigopolous, states that Chakradhar was "a Kshatriya" (2011:47).

22. P. Nagpure, a Mahanubhav and a lay scholar who has edited the *Līḷācaritra,*
states that Chakradhar was a Kshatriya. See Nagpure 2004:41–42. On the
other hand, B. G. Jadhav, another Mahanubhav lay scholar of the *Līḷācaritra,*
states that Chakradhar was a Brahmin, though he explains the "kingly"
aspects of Chakradhar's life as Haripal by presenting Haripal's father as
a regent who ruled Broach for a short interim, thus technically a king
or raja for some period of time. See Jadhav 2009:34. I have found no evidence to support the idea that Vishaldev, the father of Haripal, served as a
regent king, though this may have been the case. The current holder of the
Namdev Chair of Marathi Studies in the Marathi Department of Pune
University, Dr. Avinash Awalgaonkar, describes Chakradhar as a Brahmin
who came from a family of royal ministers and military leaders (interview
with Dr Awalgaonkar, Pune University, July 17, 2013). This is a sentiment I
heard echoed by contemporary Mahanubhavs who insisted that Chakradhar
was a Brahmin, often making this point by comparing him to Jnandev in particular (interview with Mahanubhavs at Mahanubhav Ashram and Krishna
Mandir, Sangvi, Pune, June 17, 2013).
23. LC-U 516. See also *Sūtrapāṭha* 11:a61 in Feldhaus 1983 and chapter 281 in the
Ṛddhipurlīḷā, edited and translated by Feldhaus (Feldhaus 1984:147).
24. LC-P 20.
25. A neuter noun ending in short *a,* like the word *rāja* adds an *anusvār* along
with a long *e* sound in its plural form. Hence this is not the plural form of
rāja. In any case, there is no direct correlation between the word *rāja* and
a given varna or jati. Kings could be of any jati, including those associated
with varnas other than Kshatriya. In other words, one can be a *rāja* but also
be, by varna or jati, a Brahmin, for example.
26. Tulpule and Feldhaus 1999:588. The Khategram inscription is dated to
1348 CE. See PMKL 53.
27. LC-P 32.
28. Feldhaus and Tulpule define this term as a "particular subcaste of Brahmanas"
in the *Old Marathi Dictionary* and cite this passage of the *Līḷācaritra* as proof
(1999:607).
29. See Joshi 1974:346. See the *Indian Cultural Dictionary* (*Bhāratīya Saṃskṛtikoś*),
which makes this clear (ibid.). Under *lāda* we find two different caste
groups. The first is from Karnataka, the Lads who are traders and claim
Kshatriya status (ibid., 348). The second entry is for the Lad Brahmins or
Latyayan Brahmins of Gujarat, reciters of the *Sāma Veda,* the caste most
likely associated with Chakradhar here (ibid., 346–48). In addition, we are
told that among both "Brahmins and Marathas" there are subcastes who
call themselves "Lād" in reference to their region of origin (ibid., 351).
One often finds in Maharashtra that Lad Brahmins are considered the
same as, or similar to, Saraswat Brahmins, which is perhaps because of

their "foreign" origin: Saraswats are generally from the coastal region of Maharashtra, Goa, and Karnataka (and often speak Konkani as a mother tongue); Lads are from Gujarat.

30. LC-U 150.

31. See LC-P 466, 470, for example.

32. LC-P 117–18.

33. LC-P 19–20.

34. LC-P 20.

35. Tulpule and Nene divide the *Līḷācaritra* into three parts, but Kolte does not believe the *ekāṃka* (first, "solo" part) is a separate portion. See Kolte 1978:62–63.

36. Primarily a Natha yogi named Muktabai and a man named Bolha Baria (LC-P 22–24). The Muktabai of the *Līḷācaritra* is not the Muktabai who is said to have been Jnandev's sister. For more, see Dhere 1977:117–36.

37. See LC-P 26, where he is called Mallinatha. Chakradhar also shows he is well versed in the lore of the Nathas. See LC-P 198 for a story he tells of Adinath. The Nathas were, and are, a ubiquitous sect of tantric yogis, as well as householder yogis, from the medieval period. Most of the early Varkari sants are considered Nathas (like Jnandev and Namdev).

38. This is not the first time Chakradhar has devotees however. The initial period of his solo wandering is filled with encounters and people who care for him along the way. Perhaps the most significant figure in this period is Bhandarekar, a Kanava Brahmin who is said to have served Chakradhar for sixteen years, and whom Chakradhar comforts at the time of his death (LC-P 46–51). Toward the end of the *Līḷācaritra*, as Chakradhar is selecting the figures that will continue his teachings after his departure, he recalls Bhandarekar, who he claims was superior in intelligence and devotion to Mhaibhat, Chakradhar's follower and author of the *Līḷācaritra* (LC-U 591).

39. LC-P 105. In the LC edited by Tulpule, this marks the end of the section he calls "Ekāṃka" or "Solitary Chapter." For the distinction between this first period and the next, see Kolte 1978:62–63.

40. We will see that several people comment on Chakradhar's excellent Marathi in the *Līḷācaritra*.

41. Nagadev was initially a devotee of Dados, an associate of Chakradhar (LC-P 239). At several points, Bhatobas's mercenary occupation and skills are displayed. For the best example, see LC-U 534, where he disarms several soldiers barehanded, takes their weapons, and chases them away. His ability to swear is also revealed here. He insults the soldier who returns to beg for their swords back. He yells to the soldier, "Next thing, I'll take your wife!"

42. See LC-P 299, where he shows up a *rājguru* or teacher of warfare, as the guru is instructing his students. Chakradhar apparently knows a particularly advanced technique that easily defeats the guru in swordplay. But Chakradhar refuses to teach the technique to the guru because it would

mean the guru would better equip his students to kill, and responsibility
for those future deaths would rest in part with Chakradhar.

43. The Brahmin-warrior hybrid is another trait shared with Basava. See
Narayana Rao and Roghair 2014 [1990].

44. LC-U 534–36.

45. The tribunal and witnesses are described in the text in this way:
"Hemadpandit, Sarangpandit, Mayata Hari, Prajnasagar [were there];
the major leaders of the village, the Mahajan, scholars, historians,
holymen, students, Jain ascetics, members of the Natha sect all assembled" (LC-U 536). Prajnasagar is also a sympathetic interlocutor with
Chakradhar in several lilas. For example, see LC-U 516.

46. LC-U 436. Some manuscripts describe his "ears" being amputated, others a
"limb." Many followers reject the veracity of these stories.

47. LC-U 550.

48. LC-U 585ff.

49. LC-U 613.

50. LC-U 603. Kolte notes that this lila is not in the oldest layer of the textual
history of the *Līlācaritra*. Cf. LC-U 182, that suggests Islam is already a living
religion in the region before the arrival of Khilji and his armies.

51. LC-U 637ff, LC-U 641. Kolte carefully notes variations in this lila, as well
as its representations in manuscripts. He attests that this lila is in the
oldest manuscript he consulted (manuscript "A" of 1554 CE) as well as five
others. Again, this is a story disputed by some Mahanubhavs. I include it
here, along with some other disputed lilas, not as a statement of fact, or an
endorsement of veracity, but because of the apparent prevalence within
the received textual archive of the Mahanubhavs in general of these lilas.

52. LC-U 643.

53. LC-U 644–45.

54. LC-U 644–45.

55. For more on Namdev, see Novetzke 2008b; Callewaert and Lāṭha 1989; and
Novetzke 2012.

56. See discussions of these texts in Novetzke 2008b.

57. Some scholars will place his birth at 1275 CE, and in Apegav, near Aurangabad,
rather than in Alandi. See Tulpule 1979:330 for more references on this debate.

58. For example, Jn. 18:1448.

59. I am grateful to Seth Powell, who pointed out the explicit references to
haṭhayoga in this text. See Jn. 6:192–210 for a clear mention of hathayoga
positions and in particular the three *bandhas* (*mūla, jālandhara,* and
uḍḍiyāna). Powell feels this may constitute one of the earliest references to
the three *bandhas* of hathayoga (personal communication, May 15, 2015).
See also the work of James Mallinson (2014), especially 232ff.

60. See Jn. 18:1784.

61. For a succinct review of the Varkari religion, see Keune and Novetzke 2011.
62. Many examples exist in South Asia, and many within the sphere of bhakti. Paradigms for such figures that bear a close relationship to both Jnandev and Chakradhar exist within the Lingayat or Virashaiva religion, at least a century older than the subjects discussed here, located in northern Karnataka, bordering the Yadava realm (125 km from Pandharpur, 420 km from Devgiri). For example, a key figure is Basava (c. 1134–1196 CE) who bears remarkable similarities to Chakradhar and Jnandev—like these two, Basava is remembered to have been a Brahmin and an itinerary mendicant; all three preached a radical rejection of caste for their followers, yet this radicalism was constrained in many ways; all three circulated around the temple cultures of their region (though Basava, famously, rejected the temple as the locus of religiosity). All three are considered within the sphere of the Shaiva yogi, particularly in relationship to Natha yogic practice. Basava also differs from Chakradhar in that Basava is attributed actual poetic compositions called *vacanas*, and these "utterances" differ from Jnandev's *Jñāneśvarī* in their brevity, simplicity, and affect of spontaneity. See Ramanujan 1973 for more on Basava and other Virashaiva figures, as well as Narayana Rao and Roghair 2014 [1990]. Many scholars have discussed the connection between the Virashaivas and the religious worlds and figures of thirteenth-century Maharashtra. See Panse 1963:136–40. The most extended scholarly engagement is by R. C. Dhere who has traced several lines of connection among Shaiva Natha figures linking Allam Prabhu (c. twelfth century), another Lingayat and contemporary of Basava, with figures like Visoba Khechar, the early Mahanubhavs, and the early Varkaris, including Jnandev, all of whom were Nathas, it seems. See Dhere 1977:94–136, chapters 4–5, in particular. See also Dhere 1991.
63. I take inspiration here from Ritu Birla's idea of the "vernacular capitalist" in colonial India. See Birla 2010. However, where vernacular capitalists in colonial modernity unified modern capitalism with older networks of caste and kinship, I argue that the spiritual innovator of medieval India forged past and through these alliances of caste and kinship.
64. See *The Theory of Social and Economic Organization* (Weber and Parsons 1947).
65. My thanks to Martin Fuchs for several conversations about his own idea of "relationality" here.
66. Bourdieu 1994:30.
67. Bourdieu 1984:30.
68. All references and phrases cited are from ibid., 29–110.
69. Ibid., 29.
70. See Bourdieu 1986.
71. See Rotman (forthcoming).
72. A form of this same argument has been made by Jayant Lele in his essay (Lele 1981a), and also by Sontheimer (1982:331–32).

4. The Vernacular Moment

1. See Feldhaus and Tulpule 1992.
2. Deshpande 1969:1–2.
3. Such as Bhandarekar, Bhatobas, Mhaibhat, Nathoba, Sarang Pandit, Lukhadeoba, Nathoba, Janopadhye, Upadhye, Indrabhat, Markand, Pathak, Damba, Padmanabhisan, Ekaisa, Umaisa, Daimba, Ausa, Abaisa, Sadhe, Baisa, Mahadaisa, Lakhubaisa, Demaisa.
4. Novetzke 2011.
5. LC-P 314, LC-U 120.
6. LC-P 332.
7. For a useful list of castes identified in the *Līḷācaritra*, see Belvalkar 2009:145. For Gondhols, for instance, see LC-U 103.
8. LC-U 497.
9. LC-P 84.
10. LC-P 474.
11. As we have seen, Changadev, according to the *Līḷācaritra*, departs his body and his soul animates Chakradhar.
12. LC-P 5.
13. This kind of motif is common in northern India, where it is often referred to as *bhojanabhaṭa*, feeding the Brahmins. My thanks to Jack Hawley for this reference.
14. LC-P 12.
15. In Andhra Pradesh, today, Teli is considered an "OBC" or "Other Backward Class" rather than an SC or "Scheduled Caste," which likely implies that Telis were considered Shudra, not Vaishya. In a later lila, Chakradhar again dines at the home of a Teli in Maharashtra, LC-P 34.
16. As earlier mentioned, Gundam Raul, along with Changadev Raul and Chakradhar, is considered a living incarnation of Krishna in the age of the early Mahanubhavs.
17. LC-P 39.
18. LC-P 41.
19. LC-P 27. The text uses the term *camākara* as well as *camār*. See Rawat 2011 for a convincing challenge to the historical association between Chamars and leatherwork in North India.
20. There is a complicated politics of marriage here and elsewhere in the text. Chakradhar himself has already left his first wife; he will shortly marry again, and also leave that wife for he is devoted to the life of the renunciate. Here, we should note, it is the wife who leaves the husband.
21. The term used here is *nibandha*, a kind of "digest" of Dharma Śāstra legal codes.
22. Sontheimer (Sontheimer and Aithal 1982:338) reads the end of this passage to mean that the villagers prostrated themselves before Chakradhar and

made their declaration. However, the text appears to state that Chakradhar, by this time, had left the region. Furthermore, the townspeople had not harassed Chakradhar but the Chambhar man; thus the apology would not make as much sense if directed at Chakradhar. Curiously, the lila ends with Mahadaisa asking Chakradhar what happened to the man after that, and Chakradhar replies, "Woman, his family line came to an end." The term used, *nirvāṃśa*, may be a corruption of a form of *nirvāṇa*, or "extinguishment" as in spiritual liberation, but the text is unclear. Of course, the reference to the end of his genetic line may also simply be a testament to the fact that he became a renunciate (and a divorcee as well).

23. In American English *uppity* bears racial connotations, as it was a term used by white people to describe African Americans who displayed class distinction normally reserved for the white middle and upper classes. I use it here to signal a similar judgment expressed by the figures in this story toward the Chambhar man.

24. The term is *khelane* to play or pretend. This word perhaps resonates with the very term for each of the episodes of Chakradhar's life as the word *lila* also means "play" and is a particular form of divine action attributed to Krishna.

25. A similar story appears in the biography of Gundam Raul, with a Matang or Mang, in this case, and the punishment is not death but being tied to a tree. See Feldhaus 1984:69 (chapter 73).

26. I note in another work that this is actually a very common phenomenon, particularly in Maharashtrian public culture over the centuries. See Novetzke 2011.

27. The text often interchanges the jati names Mahar, Mang, and Matang, on the one hand, and Chambhar and Chamar, on the other.

28. LC-P 86.

29. LC-P 100. This, like many other instances, shows the humor evident in the *Līḷācaritra*.

30. LC-U 552.

31. LC-U 14, 82, 245.

32. In LC-U 99 she angers Chakradhar by employing a Brahmin to perform Brahminic ancestor worship for her; also, she is the daughter-in-law of Upasani, a particularly obstinate and orthodox Brahmin associated with Chakradhar. See LC-U 120.

33. LC-P: 459.

34. One *liṅga* represents the Koli, one represents the Gauli, and the liṅga in the middle Shiva who brings them together. The text also makes clear that the Koli "is an avatar of Shiva" and the Gauli "is the human soul."

35. See LC-U 508 and the next chapter for another story that makes this point.

36. For just one example, the earlier-mentioned movement led by Sane Guruji to open the Pandharpur Vitthal Temple to "Untouchables" in 1947. Many more examples could be cited.

37. LC-U 384. This story reminds us of Chakradhar's willingness to enter the home of Dados shortly after the death of Dados's father, a time when the home would be considered "polluted." See LC-P 84.

38. LC-U 102.

39. LC-U 159.

40. See Nene 1954:132 (lila 240).

41. We might notice, however, that Chakradhar himself regularly visits the homes of Brahmins—the *Līḷācaritra* records far more offerings of food by Brahmins to Chakradhar than by all other castes combined. Chakradhar is beyond caste distinction, the text implies, and so from whom he receives food is irrelevant in a social sense.

42. LC-U 288.

43. LC-U 288. It may have been convention in thirteenth-century Marathi to refer to Guravs as rana. See LC-P 67ff and Kolte's gloss of *rana* (1978:908). Also see PMKL 46, in which the term *rana* may be applied to a Gurav temple priest.

44. The story of Chakradhar's second marriage to a woman belonging to a Huda or horse-trader jati of Andhra (LC-P 39) is perhaps another example, but the nature of Chakradhar's caste status vis-à-vis his divine status would complicate a simple reading of this moment as inter-caste marriage. And in any case, the father of the bride appears to think that his family and Chakradhar are of the same caste, or at least compatible.

45. This is a practice not uncommon today in India, that is, feeding Brahmins with the hope of achieving some other aim in life.

46. For a description of begging practices among the Mahanubhavs, see Feldhaus and Tulpule 1992:17–18.

47. LC-P 223. The reference to Dharma Śāstra is to chapter 2, verse 185 of the Laws of Manu. See Doniger and Smith 1992:36 and Olivelle and Olivelle 2004:104. My thanks to Don Davis and Patrick Olivelle who located this passage in the Pañcārthabhāṣya on the Pāśupatasūtra (1, 9, 279.1) and in the *Mitākṣarā* of Vijñāneśvara, a twelfth-century commentary on the *Yājñavalkyasmṛti* (verse 1.29). It may occur elsewhere.

48. See Belvalkar 2009:142 for this citation.

49. LC-U 152. It is interesting to note that the sign Sadhe believes indicates that this is a Brahmin's home is a Tulsi plant at the entrance to the home. However, Chakradhar reminds her that there is a grocer in Devgiri to whom they regularly go for alms, and he has a Tulsi plant as well. This suggests that to determine a person's caste by such signs and indications is not an easy thing, even in rather small regional settings, then or now.

50. LC-U 78. See also *Sūtrapāṭha* 13:106–8 in Feldhaus 1983:203.

51. LC-U 78.

52. In some texts, this is *adhama*, "vile."

53. LC-U 398. Here the word *adharmatva* is replaced by *adhamatva* or "vileness."

54. A story that bears some echo with the narrative plot of the *Bhagavad Gītā*, where Arjuna seeks to surrender his weapons rather than fight his family and teachers, but is ultimately convinced that there is nowhere he can hide from his own dharma as a warrior. Here, however, the lesson is not "do one's duty," but that there is no escape from the "ultimate reality" that practicing caste distinction accrues karma and delays ultimate salvation.

55. LC-U 245.

56. A reference here, again, to being a Dhora, as mentioned earlier.

57. This is a reference to Markand's propensity to lie about things. See LC-U 37–38 for the story referenced here.

58. From the *Sutta Nipāta* 1.7; see Chalmers 1932:116–42.

59. LC-U 158.

60. It is ambivalent because this is a story of the triumph of romance, perhaps, but the loss of social connection.

61. Note that the term in the text is *māhārī*, which may also mean "prostitute" through a conventional ethnic slur common in thirteenth-century Marathi. Unlike the previous story, this story is not about love but seduction. The story implies that a Mahar woman seduced a Brahmin man and forced him to do "wrong" things as a result. It is thus also perhaps a story that carries the valences of a caste prejudice—that Mahar women are like prostitutes and are seductive (which will recur in the *Jñāneśvarī*)—and that sex in general will distract the mendicant in unfortunate ways. I do not attribute this prejudice to Chakradhar, however, who is clearly an opponent of such prejudices. My note here is meant to help the reader understand the colloquial resonance of this term in this context.

62. LC-U 493.

63. LC-U 494.

64. LC-U 72.

65. The man calls himself a *bāhirilupāīku*, which may mean a "foreign soldier" but could also mean a soldier who stands guard outside the village. It may also indicate a "soldier for hire," a soldier of the bazaar. This may also be a play on words, for he is a soldier standing "outside," both outside the temple and outside normative Hindu society.

66. See the biography of Gundam Raul, chapter 6, where Sadhe accepts water from a Kunbi because it has been purified and made prasad by Gundam's touch. Feldhaus 1984:47.

67. LC-P 470.

68. One reason he may be uncertain about Chakradhar's caste is that Mahadaisa's former guru, Ramdev or Dados, was likely a Gurav or a person of mixed-caste background.

69. Guha 2013.

70. This is also a point Sontheimer (1982) makes very well.
71. See Feldhaus 1982.
72. This assumption is buttressed by the many travelogues left by Islamic scholar-travelers, such as that of Ibn Khurdadba (c. tenth century), Al Beruni (c. eleventh century), or Al Idrisi (eleventh–twelfth century) that describe caste difference and rivalry within Indian society.
73. This is made clear by the works of Jyotiba Phule or B. R. Ambedkar, for example, that target "Brahminism" as the chief driving force of caste oppression. However, see Ambedkar's fascinating statement that aligns the interest of Brahmins with Dalits (former "Untouchables") against their mutual rivalry with Marathas. See Ambedkar 1955:34.
74. See Guha 2013.
75. This was noted by Ambedkar, for example, when he compared the persecution of Brahmins as a minority in villages, after Gandhi's assassination, to that of Schedule Castes regularly. See Ambedkar 1955. Intermediary, powerful castes, such as the Marathas, are called "dominant castes" by Srinivas (1994).
76. For example, see Sharma 1978:115.
77. See O'Hanlon 2010b.
78. See Verma 1970:230–31.
79. See Kaminsky and Long 2011:403–4. However, there are many origin stories for Kayasthas.
80. The largest caste group of Kayasthas in Maharashtra is the Chandraseniya Kayastha Prabhu (CKP) community. Some CKPs are active in politics in contemporary India; perhaps the most famous CKP family in India today is that of the late Shiv Sena leader Bal Keshav Thackeray.
81. PMKL 34.
82. LC-P: 119.
83. *Smṛtisthaḷa* 193 in Feldhaus and Tulpule 1992:131.
84. The most prominent male Brahmin member of the Mahanubhav community, Bhatobas, was a soldier, not a scholar.
85. LC-P: 72. This lila is also mentioned in chapter 1. Sontheimer engages this story as well (Sontheimer and Aithal 1982:342ff), however, he attributes it to the Uttarārdha section.
86. Bapat 1998. See LC-U 288 where Chakradhar tells a Gurav that, since there are few Brahmins in his village, the Gurav should assume leadership in the village, which appears to mean both ritual and sociopolitical leadership. This suggests a high degree of contact and interchangeability between Brahmins and Guravs, but also a hierarchy, at least from Chakradhar's perspective and that of his Brahmin followers.
87. Bapat 1998:67.
88. Bapat 1993.

89. As noted in chapter 2, I do not consider temples to be public spaces in anything like the way we conceive of public space in modern liberal theory. However, the temple is a place where multiple social groups would meet, though many were of course excluded, as noted.

90. See PMKL 27.

91. LC-P 314. Chakradhar teases Dados, who may have been a Gurav, about his proclivity for worldly pleasures rather than the hard life of the renunciate in the hills. As an example of such worldly pleasures, Chakradhar suggests Dados will forego the beautiful austerities of the hills for the culinary pleasures of the agraharas along the banks of the Godavari River.

92. LC-U 127. See Nene 1954 [1936]:57 (Uttarārdha 91). See also a discussion of this by Belvalkar 2009:141–42.

93. LC-P 251.

94. The Godavari River is said to have been formed when the Rishi Gautama killed a cow. For more on this, see Feldhaus 1995:46.

95. LC-P 137.

96. LC-U 277ff.

97. Kolte (as well as Sontheimer and Aithal 1982:354) reads gujarā or "Gujarati" for Gurav here, though he gives gurav as the variant reading (Kolte 1978:514). I think that Gurav is the right reading, as referring to the man as a Gujarati makes little sense here in terms of the various abusive terms and social issues the text invokes. Also, the only other time we encounter a Gujarati person in the *Līḷācaritra,* Chakradhar speaks to him in Gujarati. Given that this doesn't happen here (and no comment is made about this shared connection), it does not seem that the lila itself suggests the person is a Gujarati.

98. LC-P 82ff. The first figure Kolte introduces in his survey of the "Family of Chakradhar" in his biography of Chakradhar is Dados. See Kolte 1952:66.

99. See Tulpule and Feldhaus 1999:124, where the Marathi gloss for this word is both *pūjārī* and Gurav.

100. Dados is described as an autodidact with imperfect knowledge (see Kolte 1952:66), and this suggests to me that he did not receive classical "Brahminical" training and so is not a Brahmin. His mother's name is Ranaisa (see LC-U 428, and also LC-U 256, where most texts call her his student), and, as we have seen, the designation *Rana* may have been a conventional way to refer to Guravs; see LC-U 288, as well as LC-P 82, and Kolte's gloss of *rana* (1978:908), suggesting that Ramdev/Dados's mother was a Gurav. Despite all this, it is perplexing that someone who belongs to a caste of Shaiva temple caretakers would name their son after a Vaishnava deity, e.g., Ram (as in Ramdev), and I see nowhere that Chakradhar refers to Dados/Ramdev as Rana. It is possible that the complexity around Dados/Ramdev's caste is the result of an intercaste marriage between a Brahmin Vaishnava father and a Shaiva Gurav mother (Ranaisa), and this too

might account for some of the social insults Dados faces. If Dados is a Gurav, tracking his relationship to Chakradhar and other Brahmin Mahanubhavs adds to our understanding of conflict between Brahmins and Guravs in the Yadava century. If he is not a Gurav, he is still a temple caretaker not entirely accepted in the sphere of Brahminic varna. But, as I said previously, it is my sense that Dados is a Gurav. My thanks to Anne Feldhaus—who is very skeptical of my claim here—for an extensive discussion of this and many other issues in this book. The hypothesis that Dados was a Gurav is mine alone.

101. LC-U 1ff.

102. It may not be strange for Brahmins to take a non-Brahmin as their guru, given that the very caste (jati, varna) designation of Chakradhar is unclear, yet all his followers are Brahmins. However, as I have argued in the introduction, I think Chakradhar was likely understood to be a Brahmin, even though the *Līlācaritra* leaves this vital question vague. We might also note that the inscriptional record discussed in chapter 1 shows that Guravs often were placed alongside Brahmins as recipients of state gifts, suggesting a high-caste status.

103. See LC-U 518–519. Chakradhar calls Dados here a *kumahātma,* a "false Mahatma" because of his jealously and accusation that Chakradhar has stolen his followers. These two lilas record a potent "war of words" between Dados and Chakradhar; Chakradhar does not take Dados's insults "lying down," as it were, but retaliates. Note that R. C. Dhere believes that Dados was the preceptor of Mukundaraj, thus linking Chakradhar and Mukundaraj. See Dhere 1977:246–86.

104. *Smṛtisthaḷa* 221 in Feldhaus and Tulpule 1992:140.

105. LC-P 453.

106. LC-U 406.

107. LC-U 424.

108. See PMKL 17, 34 (which consists of seven inscriptions), and 51.

109. In subsequent years, the Pandharpur Temple would also receive state support from the Marathas, the Peshwas, the administration of the Bombay presidency, and the postcolonial Bombay state and later the state of Maharashtra. While I know of no direct evidence that suggests state support for the Pandharpur Temple under the Bahmani or Bijapuri Sultanates, Pandharpur, the Varkari religion, and the temple itself flourished and grew from 1300 to 1700 CE, indicating at least benign regard. As Richard Eaton notes, the Pandharpur Temple was both important enough to be a target of Afzal Khan's destructive tendencies in 1659, in an effort to intimidate Shivaji (see Eaton 1978:183–85 and Gordon 1993:67), as well as vital enough to general "Maharashtrians" that many Hindu figures defected from the service of Adil Ali Shah II and Sikandar Adil Shah in subsequent years because of such acts against the temple (Eaton 1978:287).

110. See Narayana Rao and Roghair 2014 [1990] and Ramanujan 1973.

111. Lorenzen 1972.

5. The Mahanubhav Ethic

1. See Raeside 1960.

2. Jnandev, however, did not write down his *Jñāneśvarī* either; it was transcribed in situ by a figure named in the text as Satchidananda Baba. However, the transcription is understood to be word for word, a dictation, and thus there is some rationale in this sense in calling Jnandev the "author" of the *Jñāneśvarī*.

3. My thanks to Whitney Cox for this formulation.

4. See *Sūtrapāṭha* 12:27 in Feldhaus 1983:200. The translation of this *sutra* is by Anne Feldhaus.

5. For more on the bakhar genre, see Guha 2004.

6. For example Narayana Rao, Shulman, and Subrahmanyam 2001; Pollock 1989. See also a special issue of *History and Theory* that engaged this book and this debate (Pollock 2007; Chekuri 2007; Mantena 2007; and Narayana Rao, Shulman, and Subrahmanyam 2007). I have also extensively engaged this subject in Novetzke 2008b as well as 2007a and 2006.

7. A valuable resource for the historical artifacts contained in the *Līḷācaritra* is the work of Suman Belvalkar (2009).

8. For example, the *Līḷācaritra* spares no detail in recalling Chakradhar's gambling problem, as Haripal, but even after receiving the soul of Changadev (LC-P 18), or the fact that he left not one wife but two wives behind (LC-P 19, 32). The text even records his remorse and guilt at having left his first wife and son (LC-U 150). We also have numerous stories of Chakradhar as a highly competitive person, many moments when he challenges his followers to competitions of strength, especially with Bhatobas, who Chakradhar goads into a coconut-breaking contest and a stone-throwing contest (LC-U 225, 226), as well as a banana-eating contest (LC-U 239). In one case Chakradhar goes so far as to defeat even a young girl at a game, causing her to cry (LC-U 391, 403, 404, especially 407 and 408).

9. Ali 2013:241.

10. Ibid., 257.

11. Ibid., 239.

12. See Deshpande 1979 and 1993. We may add "Hindu" here as well, at some points in history, as both Jainism and Buddhism originally used a language other than Sanskrit, though both returned to the use of Sanskrit, along with other languages as well. Also note the fact that the lingua franca of the male Brahminic world is Sanskrit, even in very practical contexts, is

conveyed in a story from the life of Gundam Raul when a Tamil Brahmin visits him. Since no one can speak Tamil, Mhaibhat must speak to him in Sanskrit. See Feldhaus 1984:148.

13. See Deshpande's taxonomy drawn from the work of Rajashekhara, the *Kāvyamimāṃsa* of c. 900 CE (1993:28).

14. For more on this linguistic history of Marathi, see Tulpule 1979:311–12; Bloch and Chanana 1970.

15. See Nicholson 2010.

16. Deshpande 1979:58.

17. My point here in drawing in Buddhism and Jainism is not to argue that these are "Brahminic" but rather than they participate in the same discursive world as "Brahminic Hinduism." See, for example, Arnold 2005.

18. The origin of the *ovi* in "women's work songs" may be apocryphal, and it does not seem that the *Jñāneśvari* understands its metric medium to be such. However, as I will note in the next chapter, the author of the *Jñāneśvari* sought to reach "women, Shudras, and others" and so the use of a simple, popular, "folk" poetic meter is a strategy certainly connected to reaching women, among others. For the gendered source of the ovi as "women's work song" see the *Manasollasa* by Someshwar, cited by Feldhaus, Atkar, and Zagade 2014:7n10; see also Tulpule 1979:451.

19. Vitthal is often also referred to as "Mother Vitthal" or Vitthai.

20. Though some have speculated that Muktabai here is the sister of Jnandev, who goes by this name as well, there is no reason in the text to accept this correlation. Even the diegetic logic of the text would make it hard to accept, since the Muktabai here is described as very old when Chakradhar meets her early in his own life. Given Chakradhar's purported floruit, this would make Muktabai around eighty years older than her brother Jnandev. The story referred to here is LC-P 23.

21. See Kolte's discussion of this in his introduction to the *Līḷācaritra* (Kolte 1978:69).

22. See discussion in Feldhaus and Tulpule 1992:56–59. Like them, I use V. N. Deshpande's 1939 edition of the *Smṛtisthaḷa* in this book. Translations are mine unless otherwise noted.

23. Feldhaus and Tulpule 1992:4.

24. Based on Raeside 1960.

25. As the conclusion will note, over the centuries, after the foundation of the Mahanubhav religion, fewer and fewer Brahmins become Mahanubhavs, until we find, in the modern period, almost no Brahmin Mahanubhavs in Maharashtra.

26. Feldhaus and Tulpule 1992:26.

27. See ibid., 26–29 for several episodes.

28. See *Smṛtisthaḷa* 118, ibid., 107.

29. In addition, the text displays figures like Kavishvarbas, Pandit, and Lakshmidharbhat using Sanskrit. See *Smṛtisthaḷa* 20, 116, 119–21, 202, 204 (ibid., 75, 106–7, 108, 134, 135–36).

30. *Smṛtisthaḷa* 88, ibid., 94; see also ibid., 29.

31. *Smṛtisthaḷa* 14, ibid., 73. See also moments when Sanskrit is used to win arguments with opponents of the Mahanubhavs, as in *Smṛtisthaḷa* 116, ibid., 106–7.

32. *Smṛtisthaḷa* 15, 73. At another point in the *Smṛtisthaḷa* we hear that women "cannot retain a whole sermon" and so they must be instructed in a way different from men (ibid., 126 [*Smṛtisthaḷa* 171]). This passage is odd considering that fact that it appears as if women, such as Hiraisa and Mahadaisa, were understood to have the best memories of all the followers; Hiraisa, for example, is said to have memorized the entire *Līḷācaritra* and thus saved the "text" from extinction when all copies were lost in the early thirteenth century. On Hiraisa and the edition attributed to her, see Kolte 1978:69.

33. *Smṛtisthaḷa* 66 (ibid., 87–88). See also Feldhaus 2003:191ff.

34. Ibid., 29 and *Smṛtisthaḷa* 66 (ibid., 87–88, 157, and note 118).

35. Ibid., 75 (*Smṛtisthaḷa* 20), and note 48 (*Smṛtisthaḷa* 154).

36. Feldhaus 2003. Though Chakradhar, early in the *Līḷācaritra*, does travel south of Maharashtra, most of the narrative takes place in Maharashtra.

37. The primary lila imparting the general set of rules (dharma) for the order after Chakradhar's "absence" (*asannidhāna*) is LC-U 585.

38. See Feldhaus 1983:200 in *Sūtrapāṭha* 12:22–256. See also a discussion of the essence of these passages in Feldhaus 2003:183ff.

39. Feldhaus 2003:188ff.

40. It is worth noting that Kannada words are replete in both the *Līḷācaritra* and in the *Jñāneśvarī*, though the language of both texts is unmistakably Marathi.

41. There are several times in the *Līḷācaritra* when we are reminded of this. Feldhaus cites a lila in which Chakradhar's facility with Marathi is complimented (2003:187), which is also in LC-U 133. At another point, Chakradhar meets a trader from Gujarat and speaks in Gujarati with him, which the lila reports made Chakradhar very happy (see LC-U 453). In another episode, in order to avoid meeting the Yadava king Mahadev, Chakradhar took on the dress and turban of a Gujarati and spoke in Gujarati (which is transcribed in the text itself) in order to fool a messenger of the king (see LC-P 237), as we will see in this chapter. At another point, LC-U 479, Mahadaisa compliments Chakradhar's eyes and asks if all Gujaratis have lovely eyes. He says, "Gujarat means 'the light of the eyes.'" I have found no other references to the word *Gujarat* having this meaning, and, of course, it is possible that Chakradhar is simply making a joke.

42. Feldhaus 2003:192.

43. See ibid., 185, 188, 191–92.

44. For example, according to the diegesis of the text, the passage on the for-
    malization of rules after Chakradhar's departure (LC-U 585) occurs after
    Chakradhar's trial (LC-U 536).
45. Feldhaus 2003:193.
46. See Weber 1963 [1922].
47. See Feldhaus 2003:186.
48. This description is all the more peculiar when, as we'll see in more detail
    later, Chakradhar appears to be the subject of persecution from the
    Yadava state in some (disputed) lilas, and hence his followers are perhaps
    in jeopardy as well. Furthermore, at least twice Chakradhar describes
    the arrival of the Sultanate armies, suggesting they will bring with them
    murder, rape, mutilation, and slavery (ibid., 193). See also LC-U 182. It is
    interesting to note that he makes his comment while visiting a *madrassa*,
    attesting to the presence of Islam as a religion in civil society before the
    arrival of the Delhi Sultanate armies, circa early twelfth century. See also
    LC-U 603.
49. These are apparently understood by Chakradhar to be typical Shudra or
    Gopal names of three boys and three girls, but may reflect names he has
    heard. See LC-P 53 for the first instance of these boys' names.
50. The name Prajnasagar is common among learned Jain ascetics as well, thus
    he may have been a Jain ascetic and not a Brahmin scholar. The text is not
    clear, though the nature of his questions to Chakradhar suggest a shared
    religious context around questions of the self or soul that appear endemic
    to Hinduism, not Jainism.
51. LC-U 484.
52. LC-U 516. See also chapter 281 in the *Ṛddhipurlīlā*, edited and translated by
    Feldhaus (Feldhaus 1984:147). This same question will be asked of Chakradhar
    at his purported trial, at which Prajnasagar is present.
53. LC-U 516 and *Sūtrapāṭha* 11:a61 in Feldhaus 1983:199. This passage echoes
    several similar statements in a variety of texts. For example, it sounds quite
    similar to a passage of the "Adi" attributed to Namdev. See the Namdev
    Gatha abhang 809, verse 2 in Kavitkar et al. 1970. There is also a parallel in
    chapter 4, verse 13 of the *Bhagavad Gītā* where Krishna states that though
    he has created the four varnas, he is not defined by them. Another state-
    ment, very similar to the one made here by Chakradhar, is attributed to the
    Buddha in the *Sutta Nipāta*. See Chalmers 1932:455, 456. I'm sure there are
    many more examples.
54. See Feldhaus 1984:147–48 (chapter 281).
55. I say "perhaps" here because in Gundam Raul's biography the Dravidian
    Brahmin is quoted as speaking Marathi, not in Sanskrit, and he questions
    Gundam Raul in Marathi. See Kulkarni 1980:75 (chapter 281).
56. See LC-U 536–37.

57. For the *Bhagavad Gītā* reference, see BG 4.13. This ambivalence is perhaps reflected in Prajnasagar's own response to the persecution of Chakradhar, as Prajnasagar flees the land that witnessed that persecution, emulating, in at least one way, the migration of Chakradhar himself from his homeland, "Maharashtra," to a foreign land.

58. LC-U 133ff.

59. For example, LC-U 228.

60. LC-U 133.

61. This appears to occur in LC-U 567 onward.

62. LC-U 228.

63. See LC-P 444, LC-U 171.

64. One such figure is Dados, or Ramdev, apparently a Gurav or Kathiya, a Shaiva temple priest and caretaker.

65. They are Krishna (r. 1247–1261), Mahadev (r. 1261–1271), and Ramachandra (r. 1271–1311).

66. Here, for example, there is some conformity with Habermas's idea that the public sphere mediates between the state and "the public" (especially represented by civil society).

67. LC-P: 61. This is a passage cited by Bhave in his work and recounted in chapter 2. Dados also learns of Chakradhar from a Gurav friend (see LC-P 82).

68. It is worth noting here that much later Chakradhar will command his followers to "avoid financial transactions" (LC-U 585).

69. See Hira Lal 1916:141 (inscription 196).

70. LC-P 74ff.

71. LC-P 115ff.

72. LC-P 116.

73. LC-P 203.

74. LC-P 210.

75. LC-P 225ff.

76. In the text, Chakradhar's name is given as "Shri Changadev Raul Gosavi."

77. LC-P 227–8.

78. Many figures of state and civil society, as well as fairly ordinary figures, either are portrayed as on the verge of renouncing their secular power in order to follow Chakradhar, as when one of Ramachandra's cavalry officers is so beguiled by Chakradhar that he wanders the countryside praising Chakradhar and considering renunciation (LC-U 76).

79. LC-P 237.

80. LC-P 203.

81. LC-P 476.

82. We might note here again that Chakradhar also tells his followers to say in Maharashtra (LC-U 585). While Chakradhar's order to his followers does not appear to be directed toward remaining in a politically stable region, if we

read that passage along with the one upbraiding Indrabhata, we get something like a declaration that Maharashtra, and the Yadava dynasty, maintain a stable political sphere, which I have argued in chapter 1 to be the case.

83. LC-U 182; see the variant recensions given by Kolte (1978).

84. LC-U 603. It should be noted again that this lila as well as the previous one are not universally represented in the manuscripts consulted by Kolte and in all likelihood are later additions.

85. See Feldhaus and Tulpule 1992:94 (chapter 86). We can imagine that the episode being related is the capture of Ramachandra by Malik Kafur in 1307. Note here that Bhatobas refers to the rule of the Yadavas as marhāṭe or Maratha rule. In chapters 83–85, preceding this passage, we hear of "Turks" invading the region of the Yadavas. From the description and issues around the lifespan of Bhatobas, this is likely not a description of the invasion of 1310 by the Khilji Sultan's armies led by Malik Kafur, when Ramachandra in fact aided them as they passed through the Yadava territories on their way to attack the kingdom of the Hoysalas. Nor is it likely a reference to the attack of 1307, when Ramachandra was briefly apprehended and brought to Delhi, for reasons, in part, that Feldhaus and Tulpule mention relating to the dates of Bhatobas (see ibid., 156n135). Instead, this is likely a reference to the expeditionary forays of 1294, as Feldhaus and Tulpule suggest.

86. LC-U 327. See the next lila for another such incident surrounding meals. Regarding the depiction of Brahmins, such representations are common in Sanskrit contexts with the figure of the *vidūṣak* or "fool" who is often a Brahmin, and this is carried out throughout Marathi literature, especially in hagiography and folk theater (*tamāśā*). It must be noted that I say this without the intention to insult Brahmins, only to point out the trope and its relevance here.

87. LC-U 332.

88. This is also the rationale, more or less, that leads Dados to struggle with his devotion to Chakradhar.

89. See Tulpule 1967 (part 2):174.

90. LC-U 464.

91. LC-U 465.

92. See LC-U 476ff.

93. LC-U 585.

94. See LC-U 552, 564–67, 575, 585, 587, 591, 595ff.

95. See LC-U 509. We might note that this story comes after a rather infamous story, likely interpolated into the text, in which "Vitthal" is described as a cattle thief. In a certain way, both stories appear to insult two social groups: the followers of Vitthal, on the one hand, and the sympathizers with the social structures Hemadri represents, on the other.

96. LC-U 534.

97. The word here is *Ganga,* but the Godavari is implied.

98. Hemadri.

99. A "great soul" or a great renunciate. This is a common word among spiritualists and gurus of all sorts in this period. At one point Chakradhar mocks Dados by calling him a "ku-mahātma" a "false Mahatma." At other times, he extorts his followers to "act like Mahatmas." The word seems to have carried a far more quotidian connotation in the thirteenth century than it does now in the post-Gandhi world.

100. Holy men who consume only milk.

101. This number "eighteen" may indicate that all the important families, or representatives of the important castes of the village, were represented, meaning the entire community was represented. My thanks to Sumit Guha and Anne Feldhaus for clarify on this reference.

102. This figure of speech indicates to "stomach" something, to bear something offensive in silence, or simply to keep silent. Chakradhar is saying that they are not the kind of people to keep quiet because they have already made up their minds.

103. A Sanskritic word for an "Untouchable" that we have seen before.

104. LC-U 536. This means they cut off his nose. In different versions of the story other forms of mutilation are recounted. I should emphasize that many Mahanubhavs reject the veracity of this story.

105. These "judges" are all Brahmins, suggesting that Chakradhar was tried by a jury of his peers, in a sense, yet a further indication that Chakradhar was understood to be a Brahmin.

106. The tribunal here may have been following something akin to the orthodox prescriptions found in the Laws of Manu, where, "if a men persist in seeking intimate contact with other men's wives," a ruler may "cut off his nose," among other punishments. Of course, the lilas that tell us this story do not impute to Chakradhar any such wrongdoing. See the Laws of Manu, chapter 8:352 and commentary in Doniger 1991:189 and Olivelle and Olivelle 2004:321 (reference to note from verse 352) and 146 (verse 155).

107. This is despite the fact that Jains, Hindus, and Buddhists have long accepted women into monastic contexts.

108. Sontheimer and Aithal 1982:357.

109. I am citing here the Sixth Amendment of the U.S. Constitution. For the correlate rule in the *Laws of Manu* see chapter 8, verses 14–16 and Olivelle and Olivelle 2004:168.

110. My thanks to Steven Lindquist for advice on the etymology of this term.

111. Several scholars, such as S. V. Ketkar, have suggested that the "original" meaning of the title *Maharashtra* indicated the *Rashtra* or country of the "Mahars," and here we see a play with this very etymology, though intended

in this case to be an insult. The most common reading of the meaning of the region's name is "the Great" (*mahā*) "nation" (*rāṣṭra*).
112. LC-U 550.
113. See LC-U 552, 564–67, 575, 585, 587, 591, 595ff.
114. LC-U 603.
115. LC-U 648.
116. LC-P 137.
117. It is worth reiterating here that one of the largest populations of Mahanubhavs in India is in Punjab.
118. LC-U 639ff.

6. A Vernacular Manifesto

1. See in particular Tulpule's discussion of this in Tulpule 1984:18, 496–564 and Tulpule 1979:334. One might argue that Mahadaisa's *Dhavale* is the first explicitly literary text of Marathi as it likely came before the *Jñāneśvarī*. But undoubtedly the *Jñāneśvarī* in popular culture and usually in historical work is considered the first work of Marathi literature that is self-consciously literary.
2. See Davis 2014. I have provided here an admittedly unsophisticated survey of the *Mahābhārata* and the *Bhagavad Gītā* to serve as a necessary preamble to the *Jñāneśvarī*. My aim is not a comprehensive survey of these two texts, of course.
3. See Laurie Patton's introduction (*The Bhagavad Gita* 2008:vii–xxxv).
4. For a recent study of this problem in Indian thought, see Gurcharan Das's *The Difficulty of Being Good* (Das 2010).
5. See Karve 1969; González Reimann 2002.
6. For a great introduction to this concept see Raghavan and Dandekar 1958.
7. See Raeside 1960:479–80, 482, text nos. 102–14, 130, 133. Interestingly, the Krishna Mandir maintained by the Mahanubhavs in Sanghvi, Pune, has the entire *Bhagavad Gītā* in Sanskrit written along the inner temple walls. When I asked about this—and why it is in Sanskrit not Marathi—they told me that the Mahanubhavs have a long tradition of *Bhagavad Gītā* commentary, predating the *Jñāneśvarī* and that they preserve the Sanskrit because this was the language in which Krishna spoke, thus reiterating the logic of the use of Marathi in the *Līḷācaritra* as the language that Chakradhar spoke.
8. As mentioned, the colophon (likely composed by the scribe of the *Jñāneśvarī*, Sachidananda Baba, and not attributed to Jnandev directly) does mention the Yadava king Ramachandra and Yadava rule, but not Hemadri.
9. See Novetzke 2009.
10. Dandekar 1953.

11. Rajwade 1909. See also Milind Wakankar's discussion of Rajwade and the *Jñāneśvarī* in Wakankar 2010.

12. Several attempts have been made to create a critical edition of the *Jñāneśvarī*, yet no such edition exists, to date. The scholar S. N. Banhatti began such a project, and made significant progress, but was not able to complete the work before his death. In the reading of the *Jñāneśvarī* that is contained in this book, and for all references elsewhere, I have generally followed the semicritical edition by V. Dandekar et al., published by the Maharashtra State Government Press in 1963. The editors have essentially followed the Rajwade text, checked against the Sakhare text, and combined variants of nine other texts. Where I have differed from either the Marathi or the Sanskrit reading given by Dandekar et al. I have noted such divergence. In many cases, I have followed the more popular version of the text, and the one used by the Varkaris, which Dandekar himself used when, seven years earlier, he wrote his *Sārtha Jñāneśvarī* or his own commentary on the *Jñāneśvarī* (Dandekar 1953). I have used Dandekar's semicritical edition as my standard because it represents the meeting of scholarship and devotional use and thus is a sort of ecumenical text across devotional and scholarly lines. Since my goal in this chapter of the book is not to find the oldest version of the *Jñāneśvarī*, nor to read the text through its most critical distillation, I have selected a way in between these extremes. The reader, luckily, has available a plethora of other texts, readings, and studies of the *Jñāneśvarī* with which to adjust or challenge my readings here.

13. See Kiehnle 1997 (no. 1):41–42. See also Joshi 1955:105, 126–27.

14. Pollock 2006:26, 318–29.

15. See Jn. 18.1448, 1678.

16. Examples are found throughout. For one set of examples, see Jn. 18.1754, 1759, 1770.

17. Jn. 18.1771. For more on kirtan, see Novetzke 2008b and Schultz 2013.

18. To my knowledge, the term *pravacana* never appears in the *Jñāneśvarī*, though it is ubiquitously associated with the oral and written hermeneutics of the text.

19. See Novetzke 2008b, chapter 3.

20. The issues involving authorship and bhakti materials (which are not unique to bhakti or even to India) have been described best by Hawley (1988). See also my essay "Divining an Author" (Novetzke 2003).

21. There is a popular story associated with Satchidananda that describes how Jnandev raised him from the dead and brought him back to life.

22. There is perhaps the valence of caste here, for the person who overhears and narrates the *Bhagavad Gītā* within the *Mahābhārata*, is the figure of Sanjaya, a Suta or "bard" by caste, and not a Brahmin like Vyasa. Presumably, Jnandev could identify with either, but chooses, explicitly, to identify with Vyasa.

23. Jn. 13.1158.

24. Jn. 1.67. Jnandev has a fondness for this metaphor, which he reuses in Jn. 9.9.

25. Text is *lemkurūvāca* (Jn. 9.19) and *gītā niṣkapaṭa māe* (Jn. 18.1761).

26. He calls his audience his "wealthy parents" or *māhyerem śrīmamtem*, thus also gendering himself as female, a bride who has returned to her *māher* or natal home and will be protected and pampered (Jn. 9.3). He compares his text to the lisping or limping of a child just learning to talk or walk and wishes for same reaction of parental delight (Jn. 9.6). He notes how a father will feed his child from his own plate (Jn. 9.15) and how a mother cow's udder fills with milk when the calf suckles (9.18). Many of these metaphors are paraphrased at the end of chapter 15 (Jn. 15.464).

27. Jn. 12.18, 18.28.

28. Jnandev refers to his work as *sahitya* or literature throughout the *Jñāneśvarī*. For example, see Jn. 6.13, where he says his coming chapter is "beautiful literature" (*sāhityāciyāarh baravā*).

29. See Tulpule 1979:314–15 for some mention of such texts.

30. Pollock 2006:27.

31. The most common script of Sanskrit, devanāgarī or "the divine [script] of the city," is also the script of the *Jñāneśvarī*.

32. See Pollock 2006, chapters 3 and 12 in particular.

33. In contemporary Marathi, chauhata becomes *cavāṭhā,* and means "out in the open" or "in public," often implying areas of demotic congress—the "street," as it were—and a similar meaning is at work here as well; see Jn. 18.1452, for example.

34. See the geography of the Mahanubhavs that lays out clearly the networks of public importance in the Yadava era through references in the *Līḷācaritra* and subsequently in the *Sthānapothī* that record Chakradhar's peregrinations.

35. Prasad 2007:12.

36. He calls Marathi both *marhātā/marhātī* and *marhāṭhī,* typical spellings of the language, as well as simply *deśī,* "of the land," the local language.

37. References are Jn. 6.14, 7.201, and 7.204.

38. See, for example, Pollock's engagement with a text attributed to the king Bhoja (r. 1011–55), the *Śriṇgāraprakāśa* or "Light on Passion" that seeks to "construct a cosmopolitan literary system" highlighting the *rasa* of *śriṇgāra* as a premier subject of courtly Sanskrit literature (Pollock 2006:105ff and appendix A.I). See also Cox 2012. My thanks to Whitney Cox for his insights on this subject.

39. References are Jn. 18.1695 and 10.47.

40. Note also that the *Bhagavad Gītā* contains no internal iteration of a self-reflexive gendered quality, quite unlike the *Jñāneśvarī*. Jnandev here is not describing the *Bhagavad Gītā* as feminine—his metaphor links the *Bhagavad Gītā* and his text explicitly.

41. References are Jn. 9.23, 18.1687, 18.1784. The gender of this text as well as the *Bhagavad Gītā* itself as feminine is common. Indeed, Jnandev genders himself this way, referring, as we have seen, to his audience as his parental home or *māher*, which literally refers to the home of a bride as opposed to a groom. This, too, is quite common—the Varkari sants regularly call Pandharpur their *māher*. Furthermore, Jnandev is commonly called *māuli* or mother.

42. It is hard to convey Jnandev's metaphor here. The "two rivers" through Jnandev's metaphors here are the Ganga and Yamuna, as well as the rasas of peace or *śānta* and amazement or *adbhū*, and so he means both "rivers" and the emotions of rasas.

43. See Kama Maclean's book (2008) on the Kumbha Mela for a historical analysis of the status and growth of the festival, particularly in the colonial period.

44. Warner 2002:87ff.

45. See Novetzke 2007b, 2008b.

46. I follow the variant reading here, represented in a majority of the manuscripts consulted by the editorial committee.

47. Patton 2008:202.

48. My thanks to Whitney Cox for advice on this compound word.

49. As we will see in the conclusion, in hagiographical accounts that follow the composition of the *Jñāneśvarī,* attributed to the sant Namdev in the fourteenth century, there will be a popular story circulated about Jnandev that he causes a buffalo to recite the Vedas before a bewildered Brahmin tribunal.

50. *Samkhya* or "enumeration" is a philosophical system, usually associated with Shaivism and with Shaiva yoga, that is dualistic and engages the idea of "creation" through an enumeration of the various elements that make up the cosmos, such as the male and female elements of Purusha and Prakriti, and the "qualities" or gunas. This would have been philosophical orthodoxy for Natha yogis, as Jnandev and Nivritti are claimed to be.

51. A *gavandi* is synonymous with an *annachhatra,* that is, a "food shelter." See the discussion in chapter 7, this volume.

52. Even today, such practices are not uncommon, as when some tea sellers might keep one set of glasses for low castes or "Untouchables" and another for middle- and high-caste customers.

53. See Feldhaus and Tulpule 1999:725 for citations for samsara carrying these meanings in both the *Jñāneśvarī* and *Rūkmiṇī Svāyaṃvara* attributed to the early Mahanubhav poet Narendra.

7. Sonic Equality

1. A classic statement is by V. Raghavan in his *Great Integrators* address on All India Radio (see Raghavan 1966). From scholars, see, for example, Lorenzen

1995 and recently Wakankar 2010. For a deep engagement and overview of Raghavan and this idea in general, see Hawley 2015.

2. See Ramanujan 1973 and Nagaraj 2003. As Nagaraj in particular points out, the Virashaiva position on social inequality underwent a significant transformation in the "routinization" of that religious tradition, accommodating itself to quotidian society to a great degree.

3. See Rao 2009.

4. See, for example, Deshmukh 2009. The book is Novetzke 2008.

5. Patton 2008:14.

6. See Novetzke 2005.

7. This appears to refer to the custom of a married man offering food to crows at a crossroads before he eats, as a part of funeral rites. See Joshi 1974.

8. Patton 2008:45.

9. Jnandev's metaphors are very broad and plentiful, as when he comments on this same verse, "Even if one's wife is ugly, it is still virtuous to enjoy [married life] with her." See Jn. 3.219.

10. Patton 2008:52.

11. Jn. 4.79, "*etha eka ci hem dhanuṣapāṇī*," "Even though [they are] one, Arjuna . . ."

12. I say this knowing that the position of Krishna as a deity or a human is ambiguous in the *Mahābhārata*, but it is not ambiguous in the *Bhagavad Gītā*, where *bhagavad/bhagavat* clearly refers to Krishna.

13. Patton 2008:66.

14. This is a reference to the idea that only a very lowly caste would eat dog meat.

15. Here "cow" and "dog" likely serve as metaphors for Brahmin and "Untouchable."

16. Patton 2008:104. This is a continuation, perhaps, of the metaphor used in chapter 5, this volume.

17. Jn. 9.158.

18. Patton 2008:109.

19. For scholarly attention to this line and what it implies about the historical conditions of Jnandev's time, see Verma 1970:326n2, for example.

20. This word also appears as *antyā*, "the last," but carries the same meaning. See Velingakar 1959:5. See also B. R. Ambedkar's *The Untouchables* (Ambedkar 1969 [1948]:142–45) for a discussion of this term.

21. Again, Dandekar gives *antyā* or "last" here rather than *antyaja*, but I use the more common reading here. Usually, in the Rajwade/Dandekar edition, we find *antyaja* given as *antyā*, but the meaning is the same in any case, at least according to R. N. Velingakar in the *Jñāneśvarīcem Śabda-Bhāṇḍār* (Velingakar 1959:5). Also see Monier-Williams 1899:43 (column 3, line 8355).

22. Patton 2008:109.

23. Why Vaishyas—one of the three "twice-born" varna groups—are included here is a subject for another time, but for a lucid and succinct discussion of this fascinating issue, see Gokhale 1977. My thanks to Andy Rotman for this reference. See also a more quotidian engagement with this idea in Roy 2014.

24. Lorenzen 1996.

25. Here again Dandekar gives *antyā* rather than *antyaja*, but the meaning is the same.

26. Patton 2008:110.

27. See Jn. 9.471–79. Jnandev appears unique in this approach, as early Sanskrit commentators do not appear to take this as an opportunity to extol the virtues of Brahmins, but simply explain Krishna's rationale, as I noted previously.

28. As noted earlier, the *Bhagavad Gītā* is perhaps a kind of "centrist" Brahminic Hindu response to the social and theological challenges of Buddhism.

29. This is verse 7 in the Sākhare edition (1955), Dandekar's commentarial edition, as well as several others. However, the Rajwade/Dandekar critical edition corresponds to the verse number usually found in the *Bhagavad Gītā*.

30. Several translators of the *Jñāneśvarī* have assumed this indicates sexual desire. See, for example, M. R. Yardi's translation of this line (1991:346), or that of R. K. Bhagwat (1979:373), or that of Manu Subedar (1941:199). Others simply ignore the literal meaning of this verse, as in the translation by P. S. Rahalkar, who finds that it is the "street" that does not differentiate between a pure or impure woman (2011:409), or the translation by R. S. Lokapur (1997).

31. This is an old association, but it is not one I am suggesting has any truth to it. It seems clear that prostitution was not limited to a caste, etc., and certainly this is not true of Mahar women. See, for example, Phadke 1984:148–54, translated by Rege 2006:42. For more on this, see Jogdand 1995:220. See also Verma 1970:243, where he discusses this and similar terms for prostitute in the *Jñāneśvarī*. For contemporary explorations of the connections between caste and prostitution, see Shah 2014.

32. I thank Hemant Apte for elaborating this position.

33. Compare this verse with verse Jn. 10.41 discussed in the previous chapter, where Jnandev has claimed that his Marathi paraphrase and commentary on the *Bhagavad Gītā* will reverse this imbalance, where *śānta* will win over *śṛṅgāra,* the latter used here in its verbal form to mean "being dressed up."

34. Jnandev refers to prostitution, as opposed to sexual availability, euphemistically in other places and with no reference to caste, further suggesting that this is not his meaning. For example, in Jn. 18.794 where Jnandev refers to "a wife from the market," a *bhetihāṭicem kalatra,* who is explicitly a prostitute but without caste designation. Other translators of the *Jñāneśvarī* have rendered the word *māṇgī* as "whore" (such as Yardi 1991:71). Pradhan translates *māṇgī* as "low born" (1967:98), whereas Lokapur appears to understand the word to mean "treacherous" (1995:163). Kripananda and

Subedar leave the word out of their translations. Feldhaus and Tulpule cite this passage for their definition of *māṇgī*, and they describe the term very clearly as "a woman of the Manga caste" (1999:540), as does Velingakar in his word index of the *Jñāneśvarī* (1959:400).

35. See the last of the twenty-six chapters of the *Dhammapada*, especially verse 393, where birth is rejected as a condition for Brahminhood. See Muller 1881:90.

36. Patton 2008:170.

37. Rajwade/Dandekar read here *devatādhama* or "the abode of the Gods" rather than *devatadharma*, "the law of the Gods." I prefer the latter reading, which is present in six of the ten manuscripts consulted and is the most common reading in general.

38. See Guha 2013.

39. See Ananthamurthy 1979.

40. I read *bhakhaṇe* here as *bhakaṇe*.

41. Habermas makes this point himself by declaring the public sphere to be "bourgeois" (Habermas 1989), and his many critics further hone the class exclusivity of the public sphere. See Chatterjee 2004 for a different formulation of the idea that the public sphere, or here civil society, is not directly accessed by "the governed."

42. This term likely means "Muslim" here, and the presence of Islam is attested in the *Līḷācaritra*, as we saw.

43. In the *Jñāneśvarī*, and in other contexts in Marathi, the two jati names, Mang and Matang, are interchangeable. This verse is not given in the Rajwade/Dandekar edition as the standard, though it is in almost all other versions and used by Dandekar in his commentary. The editors note that this verse is present in six of the ten manuscripts consulted. I have included it here for these reasons—as it appears to be the standard reading, and the Rajwade manuscript provides a deviation from the standard. I have given it this number, "17.297+", though in the Sakhare and Dandekar editions it is 17.299 and in the Rajwade/Dandekar edition it has no number but is mentioned only in the apparatus. The verse is popularly known, however. For example, I believe it is the inspiration for a well-known *lāvaṇī* by the Marathi balladeer of colonial Bombay, Patthe Bapurao Kulkarni (1868–1941) and his song, "Mumbāī cī *lāvaṇī*" or "The Ballad of Bombay," composed around 1910. Indeed, there are several other such ballads about Bombay by earlier composers that all seem to mimic Jnandev's verses here.

44. Jn. 18.1452.

45. See translations of Yardi (1991:504) and Lokapur (1995:1332), for example, where they read *coriya* as "theft" and "stolen money."

46. See the appendix "Śabdakoś" in Dandekar 1963:112. This gloss is also given by Velingakar 1959:406. However, M. G. Panse in the *Index: Verborum of Jnaneshvari* (1953) does not contain this gloss in English

47. LC-P:100.

48. This metaphor appears in one other place in the *Jñāneśvarī*, which is in
Jn. 13.230. In this verse Jnandev discusses extreme ideas of *ahiṃsa* or "nonviolence." He seeks to point out that to kill an animal in order to extract
some "medicine" from its bodily fluids is immoral—Jnandev appears to be
an animal rights advocate of the thirteenth century. Elaborating upon what
he sees as hypocrisy, he says, "It is like tearing down homes to build man-
sions and temples. It is like giving out free food (gavandi) that is the product
of rapacious business practices." Notwithstanding his advocacy of ahimsa,
however, Jnandev criticizes the extreme Jain practice of starving oneself
to death as a means to avoid causing harm to other creatures (Jn. 13.236).

49. Some versions of the *Jñāneśvarī* will include yet one more colophon, this
one attributed to the sixteenth-century sant Eknath, in which he describes
his efforts at creating a critical edition of the *Jñāneśvarī*. I have not included
this here, however.

50. Probably this word is derived from the Sanskrit compound *prasāda-dāna*,
the "gift" or *dāna* of "grace" or *prasāda*. It may also be derived from *pasā*,
meaning "a hand held out to receive an offering." See Tulpule and Feldhaus
1999:416 for these possibilities. Whatever the origin of the word, the meaning is clear: "the gift of grace," a phrase that implies a plea for protection.
The Pasāyadān runs from Jn. 18.1772 to 1880.

51. See my essay, Novetzke 2008a.

52. Many people now in their fifties to seventies recall having learned this
"prayer" in elementary school in Maharashtra and it is recited still today in
private schools in Pune and elsewhere from elementary school to college.

53. See the 2012 syllabus here: https://www.mahahsscboard.maharashtra.gov
.in/sscsyllabus.pdf (accessed on February 11, 2016).

54. Literally, "an area of five leagues," or *paṃcakrośakṣetra,* which is likely
another name for Varanasi. See Monier-Williams, Leumann, and Cappeller
1899:575 (col. 3).

55. Mahalasa is a Goddess of the region of Newase and elsewhere around the
Deccan coast and plateau. She is considered an avatar of Vishnu and is widely
revered. Uniquely, she wears a sacred thread, usually reserved for Brahmin
males. She is also associated with Shiva, Parvati, and the worship of Khan-
doba (associated with Shiva), to whom she is sometimes married. There may
be a resonance here between the fact that she wears a sacred thread, and the
term used to describe her, which is *jīvanasūtra*, the "thread of life."

56. This is a reference to the (real and mythical) Lake Manasa or Manasasar-
ovar near Lhasa, in the Tibetan Himalaya. It is considered to be a sacred
lake representing the stillness and transcendence of the mind (*manas*)
through meditation and yoga. On the lake swim swans (*haṃsa*), which are
mythologically referred to as Paramahamsa or Supreme Swans, which

represent, similarly, a high level of spiritual attainment for individuals. The metaphor here suggests that the *Bhagavad Gītā* is like that sacred symbolic lake on which these mythical swans swim, i.e., the *Bhagavad Gītā* contains the kernels of "enlightenment."

57. Verses 1789–91 are in Sanskrit and reproduce the concluding verses of the eighteenth chapter of the *Bhagavad Gītā*.

58. For a rationale for the incompatibility of "philosophy" and "history" in classical Indian texts, see Pollock 1989.

59. See Kolte 1978:74–75 and especially Dhere 1977:287–304. Dhere speculates that the Natha connection between Chakradhar and Jnandev may have a geographical location in the town of Trimbak at the Tribakeshwar Temple there.

60. Today, Maharashtra language and culture organizations outside India call themselves Maharashtra Mandals, as do other language-cultural organizations.

61. The contemporary social organization for Marathi-speakers in the diaspora in the U.S., for example, is called the Marathi Mandal.

62. My thanks to Jason Schwartz for pointing this out to me.

63. Jn. 18.1771.

Conclusion

1. Williams 1961.

2. For a fuller treatment of this subject, see Novetzke (forthcoming).

3. For a succinct review of this debate in English, see Kiehnle 1997:2–6.

4. See Novetzke 2008b.

5. For details on these texts, their dates, and variants, see ibid.

6. Portions of this conclusion are also to be found in Novetzke (forthcoming).

7. This is a common formulation made by Brahmins who disavow caste. Chakradhar makes this statement about himself on several occasions. See *Sūtrapāṭha* 11:a61 in Feldhaus 1983:199. This passage echoes a statement attributed to the Buddha in the *Sutta Nipāta*. See Chalmers 1932:455, 456.

8. That is, the sins of Jnandev's father are inherited by Jnandev and his siblings.

9. Jnandev means "Lord of Wisdom"; Sopan means "Steps to Heaven"; Nivritti means "Cessation"; Mukta means "Liberation."

10. Of course, there are multiple variations on this story, but the outline is the same. See Mahipati's version (Abbott and Godbole 1982 [1933]), which is an almost word-for-word reiteration of Namdev's version, but with commentarial and aesthetic flourishes; see also the film version, *Sant Dnyaneshwar* (1940).

11. Subsequently, many songs or abhangs will appear that bear Jnandev's name and convey Vitthal bhakti. See Kiehnle 1997 for an analysis of these songs and some of the debate that surrounds the identity of their author(s).

12. See Kavitkar et al. 1970, abhang 958

13. See Novetzke 2009.

14. See Zelliot 1987:92.

15. Raeside 1976.

16. Desai 2010:314. I would note, however, that it is likely Mahanubhavs have participated in urban social life from the moment of their origin—and today, of course, there are many Mahanubhavs among the urban and global classes of the world, in India and outside. They are far from an obscure group, but have many followers, in many areas of life, all over the world.

17. See Raeside 1960:465. The northern Mahanubhav tradition seemed both highly routinized and connected with its "parent" organizations in Maharashtra. We see evidence of this from an article in the newspaper *Tribune*, published from Lahore, where, on February 2, 1915, under "local and provinicial" news, page 5, it notes "Another Punjabi Vidya Sagar" and a correspondent writes: "Pandit Range Raj Shastri R. P. Mahanubhava (Lahori) has been granted the title of 'Vidya Sagar' by the 'Virat Doshi Mahanubhava Vidya Mandal, Amraoti.'"

18. See Frowde 1908:302 and Bhandarkar 1907.

19. See Raeside 1960. His introduction to this bibliography gives valuable details about the textual history of the Mahanubhavs and in particular its discovery in modern scholarship.

20. Hunter 1887:58. One can find the *Gazetteer*'s (still incorrect) correction of its previous erroneous entry in Frowde 1908:301–2; however, "Kishan Bhat" is still ascribed as the originator of the Mahanubhavs. Kishen Bhat is not a name or title represented in the *Līlācaritra* or the *Smṛtisthaḷa*, to my knowledge. However, the *Gazetteer*, vol. 21, in its "correction," states that among the Mahanubhav sects one "Matangapatta . . . [was] confined to Mahars and Mangs, which is said to have been founded by one Krishnabhatta, about whom is told the legend of an amour with a Mang woman. This sect is still represented in Ahmadnagar District" (ibid., 302). This they appear to take from Bhandarkar (1907), who gives a more fulsome description of this Kishan Bhat and his alleged associations with the Mahanubhavs.

21. In the 1901 census, however, the total number of people who self-reported as "Mahanubhav" dropped to 2,566 (Frowde 1908:302). In 1881, the total population of Berar was 2.7 million, and in 1901, 2.8 million. See Dyson 1989.

22. Raeside 1970:328 notes that the invention of lipi is attributed to Ravalovyasa in 1335 CE, but the earliest references to lipi are a century later.

23. Frowde 1908:302.

24. V. L. Bhave, in *Mahārāṣṭra Sāraswat*, is likewise a figure who corrects the historical record regarding the Mahanubhavs, though the first full edition of his text doesn't appear until 1919 (technically edition number two, but the first complete edition), though his "monthly" (*māsik*) articles were

published as a compendium in 1899. I have not been able to verify whether his essays on the Mahanubhavs appeared in this 1899 publication or only in the 1919 publication.

25. Bhandarkar 1907:7.
26. Raeside 1970.
27. Unhale 1992:6.
28. Ibid.
29. "Book Stayed" (1992).
30. "BJP Calls for Action Against Writer" (1994).
31. Ibid.
32. Unhale 1992:6.
33. Hansen 2001:7. While not about the figure of the *Marathi māṇūs* in politics, there are multiple studies that examine the Marathi "everyday" figure, man and woman. See, for example, Eaton 2005, in particular his use of Tukaram's life (ibid., 129–54) and Feldhaus 1995.
34. See Jaffrelot 2003.
35. Hansen 1999:18; see also ibid., 25, 28.
36. See Chatterjee 2004:39–41.

Glossary

ABHANG (*abhaṅga*): Marathi [M], literally [lit.] "unbroken"; a verse form used for devotional songs in Marathi from the earliest period onward. The abhang is often considered a form of the ovi.

ADVAITA: Sanskrit [Skt], lit. "nondual"; in Sanskritic philosophy, one of the most influential schools of thought that argues there is no distinction between God and human souls.

AGRAHARA (*agrahāra*): Skt, a donation of land, usually to a Brahmin, and often given by a figure of state, such as a king, minister, or general.

ANTYAJA: Skt, lit. "lowest born"; in Sanskrit, this term sometimes means Shudra and sometimes means "Untouchable," but it is a comparative term primarily, not a designation of actual caste status. The term is used this way in Marathi as well, usually juxtaposed to *dvija* or "twice-born."

APABRAMSHA (*apabhraṃśa*): Skt, "deviation" or "corruption," a term in Sanskrit for languages other than Sanskrit in northern India, from approximately the sixth century to the thirteenth century, the precursors to medieval and modern languages such as Hindavi.

ATMAN (*ātman*): Skt, "the self" or "the soul."

AVATAR (*avatāra*): Skt, incarnation, often associated with Vishnu and his various incarnations that include Narasimha, Rama, and Krishna.

BAKHAR: M, lit. "chronicle"; an offical, state record-keeping form in prose used in Marathi from the fifteenth century onward. Considered a "historical" record.

BALUTA (*balutā*): M, a system of hereditary occupation, property rights, governmental and ritual entitlement within a small region, such as a village, often determined by, or intersecting with, both varna and jati. A cognate of the *jajmani* system.

BHAGAT: Skt, M, etc., lit. "a devotee," related to bhakta and bhakti.

BHAKTA: Skt, usually lit. "one who exemplifies bhakti," but also lit. "distributed, divided, loved" as well as "cooked" as in food or a meal; a term that generally denotes someone who is devoted to something in ways that conform to the general idea of bhakti.

BHAKTI: Skt, lit. "distribution, division, belonging to, attachment, devotion"; usually glossed as "devotion"; implies both a devotion to one's deity and a devotion to a community or public.

BHANITA (*bhaṇitā*): Skt, lit. "spoken" but also "relation" and "description"; the name of the line in Indian (Sanskrit and regional-language) poetry and song, usually ultimate or penultimate, that signifies the purported author's name.

BRAHMAN (*brahman*): Skt, the "absolute."

BRAHMANAPURI (*brāhmaṇapurī*): Skt, lit. "a Brahmin's town," a town, the revenue of which is taxable for the maintenance of a Brahmin, a family of Brahmins, a group of Brahmins, or a Brahminic endeavor such as a temple, monastery, or other organization.

BRAHMANATVA (*brāhmaṇatva*): Skt, M, lit. "Brahminness," the quality of being a Brahmin by caste and action. Often used interchangeably in Mahanubhav texts with *brahmanya*.

BRAHMANYA (*brāhmaṇya/brāhmaṇya*): Skt, M, lit. "Brahminness," the quality of being a Brahmin by caste and action. Often used interchangeably in Mahanubhav texts with *brahmanatva*.

BRAHMIN (*brāhmaṇa*): Skt, lit. "the one who calls out"; the first of the four varna categories; often translated as "priest"; as a professional designation, the term implies a ritual officiant, a scholar or other literate and lettered person, a temple overseer, and so on.

CHAMAR (*cāmār*): M, the name of an "Untouchable" jati in Maharashtra and elsewhere. Also spelled Chamhar (*cāmhār*) and Chambhar (*cāmbhār*) in Marathi.

CHANDAL (*caṇḍāla*): Skt, lit. "fierce, angry ones"; a classical Sanskrit word for "Untouchables" and outcastes in general.

CHARITRA (*caritra*): Skt, lit. "comportment, exploits"; usually glossed as "biography."

CHAUHATA (*cauhaṭā*): a public square and/or market. Also sometimes rendered *chaurasta* (*caurāsta*), where the "four roads" meet.

DANA (*dāna*): Skt, "gift," a donation.

DARSHAN (*darśan*): Skt, lit. "view"; two key meanings are indicated by this term: 1. viewing a diety, sacred person, or sacred object in Hinduism; 2. a term used in the sense of a "school of thought" or "point of view" differentiating the six classical Indian philosophical systems.

DESHI (*deśī*): Skt, lit. "of the land/region"; a reference to a regional language, a vernacular; in the Marathi context, a reference to Marathi.

DESHMUKH (*deśmukh*): M, the hereditary office of a regional leader.

DEVANAGARI (*devanāgarī*): Skt, the name for the script most commonly associated with Sanskrit and some other Indian langauges, such as Marathi and Hindi.

DHARMA: Skt, lit. "that which is held together, maintained, made firm"; a key concept in Hinduism, Buddhism, Jainism, and Sikhism that is variously translated by terms ranging from "law, practice, duty, justice" to "way" and "religion," the latter particularly since the nineteenth century. Its antonym is *adharma.*

DHARMA ŚĀSTRA: Skt, "social science," texts and essays on the proper order of society.

DVIJA: Skt, lit. "twice-born"; refers to the first of the four varna groups, who have engaged in the sacred thread ceremony and received a "second birth" through that ritual. The *dvija varna* groups are Brahmin, Kshatriya, and Vaishya.

"EKĀMKA": M, lit., "alone," sometimes refers to the first division of the *Līḷācaritra* containing all stories of Chakradhar and others leading up to the point at which one of Chakradhar's key devotees, Baisa, joins the Mahanubhav order and is initiated.

GADHEGAL (*gāḍhegāl*): M, "donkey stone" or "donkey curse." Refers to both the image of the donkey curse and the verbal formula etched in stone.

GAVANDI (*gavāṃdī*): M, a public and free service of food offered by a benefactor for the benefit of strangers, usually people engaged in some religious merit-accruing activity, such as a pilgrimage. Similar to the Sanskrit *annachhatra* or "food pavilion."

GOSAVI (*gosāvī*): M, a derivation of Skt *gosvamin*, lit. "master of cows"; an honorary title given to spiritual masters or deified people, usually within the sphere of Vaishnavism and Krishna worship; a common title for Chakradhar in the *Līḷācaritra* and other Mahanubhav texts.

GOTRA (*gotra*): Skt, "clan," usually a patrilineal genealogy. For some Brahmin communities, *gotra* refers to a genealogy in relationship to a key ancestor, perhaps of the mythic seven sages.

GRANTH: Skt, lit. "tying together"; refers both to 1. a book and 2. a composition.

GUNA (*guṇa*): Skt, lit. "a quality or characteristic." See *saguna* and *nirguna.*

GURAV: M, a non-Brahmin temple priest and caretaker; often considered a jati in Maharashtra and elsewhere.

GURU (*gurū*): Skt, teacher.

JAJMANI (*jajmānī*): M, derivation of Skt *yajamāna* or "patron"; indicates a hereditary system of relations among jati groups in a community, such as a village, often determining economic, social, and religious benefits and responsibilities.

JATI (*jāti*): Skt and M, lit. "birth"; refers to the cross-religious divisions of Indian society that name any of thousands of "castes" usually associated with a particular form of traditional labor, region, and/or other charateristic idiosyncratically related to an ethnos, e.g., Shimpi as the jati title for the Maharashtrian tailor caste or Deshastha as a jati of a Maharashtrian Brahmin caste. In the most general sense, jati governs rules of endogamy and commensality. This term is related to, but not synonymous with, varna, another term often glossed as "caste." See under *varna.*

JIVA (*jīva*): Skt, "life soul," a living being.

JNANA YOGA (*jñāna yoga*): Skt, lit. "the discipline [*yoga*] of knowledge [*jnana*]"; one of the three *yogas* of the Bhagavad Gītā, juxtaposed with the discipline of action (karma) and devotion (bhakti).

KARMA: Skt, lit. "action"; used in multiple ways in Hinduism, Buddhism, and Jainism primarily; sometimes indicates a kind of accumulated record of activities in one's life; sometimes indicates "destiny"; sometimes juxtaposed to other modes of soteriology, the other yogas of the *Bhagavad Gītā*.

KAVYA (*kāvya*): Skt, "poetic," refers to literary style and aesthetics, usually associated with Sanskrit.

KAYASTHA (*kāyastha*): Skt and M: a general class, and sometimes a caste (jati), of professional scribes and writers. In general Kayasthas are considered "high-caste" in Maharashtra.

KIRTAN (*kīrtan*): Skt, M, Hindi, etc., lit. "to recite, to glorify"; a public performance genre in India among Hindus and Sikhs primarily, kirtan takes multiple forms in different regions. In Marathi, kirtan is a mixed form of song, dance, theater, exposition, music, and so on, in a fairly structured format. A performer of kirtan is called a *kīrtankār*.

KSHATRIYA (*kṣatriya*): Skt, approximate literal meaning is "ruler" or "warrior," likely related to *kṣetra*, "the field" or "field of battle" as in Kurukshetra, the hoary battlefield of the war depicted in the *Mahābhārata*; the second of the four castes in the varna hierarchy.

KULA (Skt *kula*; M *kuḷa*): family, group, tribe, association.

KULKARNI (*kuḷakaraṇi*): M, village accountant.

LILA (Skt, *līlā*; M *līḷā*): lit. "play"; primarily refers to both the "playful" actions of Krishna and Rama, that is, their life stories, and the telling of those stories in the context of a "play"; also a term to refer to particular stories or events in the lives of Chakradhar, Changadeva, and Gundam Raul in Mahanubhav texts and in particular the *Līḷācaritra*.

LINGA (*liṅga*): Skt, lit. "a mark or sign"; a metonymic representation of Shiva, sometimes resembling or in the form of a phallus, and often coupled with a *yoni*, lit. "womb, uterus, source." A central feature of Shaiva worship.

LIPI (*lipī, lipi*): M, "writing," refers to orthographic practice, and in particular, the "secret" orthography of the early Mahanubhavs called *sakaḷa lipī*.

MADRASSA (*madrassa*): Persian, "school," usually a school of Islamic learning.

MAHAJAN (*mahājana*): M, "the great people," usually refers to village leaders and elders; can also sometimes indicate Brahmins in particular.

MAHANUBHAV (*mahānubhāva*): M, the name of a religious community centered around forms of Krishna that arose in the thirteenth century in Maharashtra.

MAHAR (*mahār*): M, the name of a jati considered by some to be "Untouchable," primarily in Maharashtra; the largest jati of "Untouchables" in Maharashtra;

a *mahārvāḍā* or "Mahar neighborhood" is an area of town with a concentration of Mahar inhabitants.

MAHATMA (*mahātmā*): Skt, "great soul," an honorific, appears in thirteenth-century Marathi as a term for a holy person, somewhat like "Baba" in contemporary contexts in India.

MANDAL (*maṇḍala*): M, "a circle," a social group, a geopolitical region (province).

MANDIR: Skt, lit. "home"; usually indicates a Hindu or Jain temple.

MARATHE/MARATHA (*marāṭhe/marāṭha*): M, a term that indicates the region and culture associated with "Maharashtra." In the thirteenth century this term did not connote a caste group, Maratha, as it does now.

MATANG/MANG (*mātaṅga* [*mātāṅga*]/*māṅg*): M, the name of a jati considered by some to be "Untouchable," primarily in Maharashtra.

MATHA (*maṭha*): Skt, lit. "a dwelling"; usually glossed as a type of Hindu monastery, often run by and for Brahmins or high castes in the Yadava century.

MAYA (*māyā*): Skt, lit. "illusion"; an epistemological idea in several Indic philosophies and religions that posits the phenomenal world is an illusion; also means simply the phenomenal world without the connotation of an illusion.

MELA (*meḷā*): Skt, lit. "a meeting"; refers to a gathering or confluence of any kind; in the context of Hinduism, usually indicates a public gathering at a holy or pilgrimage site at a particularly auspicious time.

MLECCHA (*mlecha*): M, foreigner, usually refers to Muslims.

MODI (*moḍī*): M, refers to a calligraphic script commonly in use by scribes in Marathi.

MOKSHA (*mokṣa*): Skt, lit. "release"; in Hinduism, the freedom of the self (*ātman, jīva,* etc.) from the cycle of rebirth (*saṃsāra*).

NATHA (*nātha*): Skt, the general designation for a variety of Shaiva religious communities throughout India who practice various forms of yoga and meditation in an attempt to generate superhuman powers and immortality. All the major early figures of Marathi bhakti are remembered to have been Nathas, including Chakradhar and Jnandev.

NAYAK (*nāyaka*): Skt, M, Hindi, etc, lit. "a leader"; in Mahanubhav contexts a term and sometimes a name that often indicates Brahmin caste status; also a term for the male protagonist of a drama; also, a designation for the leader of a militia.

NIBANDHA (*nibandha*): Skt, "a treatise," an essay on a topic, often refers to essays on social science (*dharma shastra*).

NIRGUNA (*nirguṇa*): Skt, lit. "having no [*nir*] characteristics [*guṇa*]"; in the context of bhakti and its performative and devotional practices, refers to the worship of a nonanthropomorphic deity, often associated with monotheism, nondualism (*advaita*), and antagonism toward the depiction of deities, pilgrimage, external worship, etc.; often associated with meditative disciplines and especially with mantra practices.

OVI (*ovī*): M, a poetic metrical form, the two most common of which are the *grānthik* or "literary" form, usually recited rather than sung, made of three lines of equal length and one of half the length of the previous three, the form preserved in the *Jñāneśvarī*; and the *kaṇṭhastha* or "voice" ("oral") form, usually song, which conforms to the meter of the abhang in general. May derive from *ovaṇe*, to "thread, stitch, sew," but also "to sow" and to pound, as in pound wheat; sometimes associated with "women's work songs," though this connection seems highly conjectural, yet common in Marathi cultural memory.

PRADHAN (*pradhān*): Skt, lit. "chief"; a royal minister, usually of a "high caste" but theoretically of any caste, gender, or religion.

PRAKRIT (*prākṛta*): Skt, a term used to name several different languages derived from, or in genealogical relationship to, Sanskrit, and often inflected by gender, region, caste, or other social marker. The term implies a relationship to "nature" as a feminine-gender concept.

PRASAD (*prasad*): Skt, lit. "favor, grace"; refers to an item given to a deity or holy person that is returned to the giver and usually distributed as a "blessing."

PRASHASTI (*praśasti*): Skt, lit. "public praise"; often used to refer to those portions of inscriptions or texts that praise a benefactor, king, or other significant figure.

PRAVACANA (*pravacana*): Skt, lit. "exposition"; a lecture, usually a public lecture, on any subject, though in Marathi this term is often used to refer to a lecture on the *Jñāneśvarī*. Someone who gives a *pravacana* is called a *pravacanakār*.

PUJA (*pūjā*): Skt, lit. "worship"; the ritual actions and implements invovled in Hindu veneration of a deity or divine figure; can take place anywhere, in a temple, a home, or any location deemed "sacred."

PURANA (*purāṇa*): Skt, lit., "of the old,"; myth, legend, classical stories, past events; can refer to a collection of general mythological texts of the ancient, classical, and medieval periods, and are often morality tales.

"PŪRVĀRDHA" (*pūrvārdha*): Skt, lit. "the first half"; the first of the two parts of the *Līḷācaritra*, usually marked from the beginning of collected memories about Chakradhar, Changadev, and Gundam Raul to the period just before Bhatobas becomes a devotee of Chakradhar. In some versions of the *Līḷācaritra*, the "Pūrvārdha" is also distinguished from an earlier period, called the "Ekāṃka," by the point at which one of Chakradhar's key devotees, Baisa, joins the Mahanubhav order and is initiated.

RAJE (*rāje*): M, "of the royal court"; in Old Marathi the term means political rule or political administration, referring to the "offices" of the royal court.

RAJYA (*rājya*): Skt, "royal." A term that designates the functions, actions, theories, and aesthetics of kingship.

RANA (*rāṇā*): Skt, M, "king"; often used in the *Līḷācaritra* by Chakradhar to refer to Guravs.

RASA (*rasa*): Skt, "juice," taste, flavor, aesthetic.

RASHTRA (*rāṣṭra*): Skt, M, "country, land, region."

SABHA (*sabhā*): Skt, "company, assembly," a group convened to judge something, most often used in connection to Brahmin assemblies; often implies a public assembly.

SADHU (*sādhu*): Skt, lit. "one who is unimpeded," "straight"; a Hindu holy renunciate.

SAGUNA (*saguṇa*): Skt, lit. "with [*sa*] characteristics [*guna*]"; in the context of bhakti and its performative and devotional practices, refers to the worship of a describable, often anthropomorphic, deity. Regularly embraces the depiction, in physical and literary form, of deities, their mythology, modes of worshipping them, etc. Often involves described relationships between devotees and deities in human ways, i.e., the love of a mother for a child, of a lover for another lover, etc.

SAHITYA (*sāhitya*): Skt, lit. "association, society, harmony"; usually refers to "literature" of high aesthetic merit.

SAMADHI: Skt, lit. "put together, union"; several meanings, including 1. a state of deep meditation; 2. a tomb or other memorial containing a holy person, usually a yogi; 3. a text that tells the story of the last days of life of a particular figure, usually a holy figure. In this book, *samadhi* refers to one of three key biographical texts attributed to the Marathi *sant* Namdev about Jnandev; a deep meditative state that Jnandev is said to undertake, as described by Namdev; and the physical location and memorial where Jnandev is said to still reside in the deep state of *samadhi* (meditation).

SAMKHYA (*samkhya*): Skt, lit. "counting, reckoning"; a philosophical system in Hinduism, usually associated with Shaivism and with Shaiva yoga that is dualistic and engages the idea of "creation" through an enumeration of the various elements that make up the cosmos, such as the male and female elements of Purusha and Prakriti and the many "qualities" or gunas.

SAMSARA (*saṃsāra*): Skt, lit. "going around"; the state and conditions of metempsychosis or transmigration in Hinduism, Buddhism, and Jainism. Often synonymous with mundane and "everyday" life.

SANNYASA (*sannyāsa*): Skt, lit. "abandonment"; refers to the act of renouncing social life. Someone who does this is called a *sannyasi*.

SANT: Skt, lit. "a good person"; in Maharashtra the term indicates any of the religiously accomplished figures associated with the Varkari lineage or other bhakti groups and does not pertain to *nirguna bhakti* especially; often glossed as "saint" or "saint-poet," the latter conveying that fact that many sants are attributed song-poems (abhang, ovi, etc.).

SHAIVA (*śaiva*): Skt, lit. "belonging to Shiva"; a designation for a person, place, or thing associated with Shiva, especially related to the worship of Shiva; often used to refer to those individuals and communities that worship Shiva in some form.

SHAKA (*śaka*): Skt (M *śake*), one of two main ways of measuring the passing of years in India associated with Hinduism; the second is the Vikram year. The *shaka* year begins its count in 78 CE. *Shaka* is sometimes referred to as the *śālivāhan* year after the king Shalivahan, and the year begins its count from Shalivahan's defeat of the king Vikramaditya (after whom the Vikram year is named).

SHASTRA (*śāstra*): Skt, lit. "command, instruction"; generally a "science" or knowledge system, or a text that details a knowledge system. Often this term indicates Dharma Śāstra texts, especially the *Laws of Manu*.

SHIMPI (*śimpī*): M, lit. "tailor"; a caste (jati) name in Maharashtra; Namdev's caste in Maharashtra.

SHLOKA (*śloka*): Skt, a type of verse, usually a couplet with sixteen syllables; most often in Sanskrit, but also in Marathi, Hindi, and other languages.

SHRI (*śrī*): Skt, lit. "light, luster, auspiciousness"; one name for Lakshmi, the consort of Vishnu, and in particular Lakshmi as depicted in the Shri Rangam Temple in Tiruchirappalli, Tamil Nadu; a prefix term to denote auspiciousness, as for a name, place, text, etc.

SHUDRA (*śūdra*): Skt, the fourth of the fourfold varna hierarchy.

SMRITISTHALA (*smṛtisthaḷa*): Skt, lit. "the place [*sthala*] of memory [*smriti*]"; a memorial; textually, a series of memories or recollections, especially among the Mahanubhavs.

STRISHUDRADIKA/STRISHUDRADI (*Strīśudrādika/ Strīśudrādi*): Skt, M, lit., "women, Shudras, and others."

SUTRA (*sūtra*): Skt, "thread," refers to technical literature on a given subject, usually made up of aphorisms.

TANTRA (*tantra*): Skt, "a weave," refers to a set of practices sometimes associated with yoga and intended for specific benefits.

TIRTHA (*tīrtha*): Skt, "a ford," a crossing place along a river, refers to pilgrimage places.

"UTTARĀRDHA" (*uttarārdha*): Skt, lit. "the Last Half"; the second of the two portions of the *Līḷācaritra*, usually marked by the time when Bhatobas becomes a devotee of Chakradhar.

VACANA: Skt, "a speech," sometimes refers to the utterances of particular sant figures, especially Vira Shaivas composing in Kannada.

VAISHNAVA (*vaiṣṇava*): Skt, lit. "belonging to Vishnu"; a designation for a person, place, or thing associated with Vishnu, especially related to the worship of Vishnu or associated forms and deities, such as Krishna and Rama; often used to refer to those individuals and communities that worship Vishnu in some form.

VAISHYA (*vaiśya*): Skt, lit. "the one who dwells; inhabitant; home owner"; the third of the four varna groups; often translated as "merchant"; traditionally associated with "trade."

VARKARI (*vārkarī*): M, lit. "the ones who do [*karī*] the pilgrimage/rounds [*vār*]": the title of the pilgrims who go to Pandharpur to visit the temple of Vitthal on a yearly or twice-yearly basis; the largest devotional or bhakti group of Maharashtra, the Varkaris, of which Jnandev, Namdev, Eknath, and Tukaram are the chief sants.

VARNA (*varṇa*): Skt, lit. "appearance, color": the theoretical socioreligious heirarchy of classes or "castes" enumerated in the Vedas and legal texts (Dharma Śāstra), and elsewhere, consisting of four ranked parts: Brahmins, Kshatriyas, Vaishyas, and Shudras.

VARNASHRAMADHARMA (*varṇāśramadharma*): Skt, the orthodox Hindu social theory that prescribes duties and stages (*ashrama*) in life according to caste (varna), gender, and age. Traditionally, there are four stages encumbent upon high castes or "twice-born" *dvija*, which are those of the celebate student or *brahmacārya*, the householder or *gṛhastha*, the "forest-dweller" or *vanaprastha*, and *saṃnyāsa* or "renunciate."

VITTHAL (*viṭhṭhala*): M, the deity who is the principle object of devotion in Pandharpur and to Varkaris; also commonly called Viṭhobā and Pāṇḍuraṇga.

VRATA (*vrata*): Skt, "a vow."

YOGA (*yoga*): Skt, "discipline," a set of physical, mental, psychic, and mystical practices oriented toward some end or goal.

YUGA: Skt, lit. "a yoke"; refers to an age within mythic world time in Hinduism.

Bibliography

Abbott, Justin E., and Narhar R. Godbole, trans. 1982 [1933]. *Stories of Indian Saints: English Translation of Mahipati's Marathi Bhaktavijaya*. Delhi: Motilal Banarsidass.

Abrahams, Roger D. 2005. *Everyday Life: A Poetics of Vernacular Practices*. Philadelphia: University of Pennsylvania Press.

Abrams, Philip. 1988. "Notes on the Difficulty of Studying the State." *Journal of Historical Sociology* 1, no. 1 (March): 58–89.

Abu-Lughod, Janet L. 1991. *Before European Hegemony: The World System A.D., 1250-1350*. New York: Oxford University Press.

Agarwal, Purushottam. 2009. *Akath Kahani Prem ki: Kabir ki Kavita aur unka Samay*. New Delhi: Rajkamal Prakashan.

Ali, Daud. 2004. *Courtly Culture and Political Life in Early Medieval India*. Cambridge: Cambridge University Press.

——. 2013. "Temporality, Narration and the Problem of History: A View from Western India c. 1100-1400." *Indian Economic and Social History Review* 50, no. 2: 237–59.

Altekar, A. S. 1960. "Part VIII: The Yadavas of Seunadesha." In Ghulam Yazdani, *The Early History of the Deccan*, parts 7–11, 515–74. London: Oxford University Press.

Ambedkar, B. R. 1955. *Thoughts on Linguistic States*. Mumbai: Anand Sahitya Sadan.

——. 1969 [1948]. *The Untouchables*. Shravasti: Bharatiya Bauddha Shiksha Parishad.

——. 2014 [1936]. *The Annihilation of Caste: The Annotated Critical Edition*. Mumbai: Navayana.

Ananthamurthy, U. R. 1979. *Samskara*. Trans. A. K. Ramanujan. Delhi: Oxford University Press.

Appadurai, Arjun, and Carol Breckenridge. 1976. "The South Indian Temple." *Contributions to Indian Sociology*. 10, no. 2: 187–211.

——. 1988. "Why Public Culture?" *Public Culture* 1, no. 1: 5–9.

Apte, P. P. 1972. "Dharmashastra and Arthashastra." In Ramchandra Narayan Dandekar, ed., *Sanskrit and Maharashtra: A Symposium,* 30–35. Poona: University of Poona.

Arnold, Dan. 2005. *Buddhists, Brahmins, and Belief.* New York: Columbia University Press.

Asad, Talal. 1993. *Genealogies of Religion: Discipline and Reasons of Power in Christianity and Islam.* Baltimore: Johns Hopkins University Press.

Austin, J. L. 1962. *How to Do Things with Words.* Cambridge: Harvard University Press.

Babras, Vijaya G. 1996. *The Position of Women During the Yadava Period: 1000 A.D. to 1350 A.D.* Bombay: Himalaya.

Bapat, J. B. 1993. "The Gurav Temple Priests of Maharashtra." *South Asia* 16, no. 1: 79–100.

——. 1998. "A Jatipurana (Clan-History Myth) of the Gurav Temple Priests of Maharashtra." *Asian Studies Review* 22, no. 1: 63–78.

Bayat, A. 2008. "Everyday Cosmopolitanism." *ISIM Review* 22, no. 1: 5.

Bayly, C. A. 1996. *Empire and Information: Intelligence Gathering and Social Communication in India, 1780-1870.* Cambridge: Cambridge University Press.

Beck, Guy L., ed. 2005. *Alternative Krishnas: Regional and Vernacular Variations on a Hindu Deity.* Albany: State University of New York Press.

Behl, Aditya, S. C. R. Weightman, and Shyam Manohar Pandey [Mañjhana]. 2000. *Madhumālatī: An Indian Sufi Romance.* Oxford: Oxford University Press.

Behl, Aditya, and Wendy Doniger. 2012. *Love's Subtle Magic: An Indian Islamic Literary Tradition, 1379-1545.* New York: Oxford University Press.

Belvalkar, Suman. 2009. *Līḷācaritratīl Samājdarśan.* Mumbai: Popular.

The Bhagavad Gita. 2008. Trans. Laurie L. Patton. London: Penguin.

Bhagavan, M., and A. Feldhaus eds. 2008. *Speaking Truth to Power: Religion, Caste, and the Subaltern Question in India.* Delhi: Oxford University Press.

Bhagwat, R. K., trans. 1979. *Sri Jnanadeva's Bhāvārtha Dīpikā: Otherwise Known as Jnaneshwari.* Madras: Samata.

Bhandarkar. R. G. 1907. "The Manbhav Sect: The Gazetteer Trips. Section: Latest Telegrams." *Times of India,* November 15, 7.

——. 1957. *Early History of the Dekkan.* Calcutta: Susil Gupta.

Bhargava, Rajeev, and Helmut Reifeld. 2005. *Civil Society, Public Sphere, and Citizenship: Dialogues and Perceptions.* New Delhi: Sage.

Bhave, V. L. 1963 [1898]. *Mahārāṣṭra Sāraswat.* Ed. S. G. Tulpule. Mumbai. Popular.

Bhayani, H. C., ed. 1987. *Tarayana: An Anthology of Bappabhatti's Prakrit Gathas.* Ahmadabad: Prakrit Text Society.

Birla, Ritu. 2010. "Vernacular Capitalists and the Modern Subject in India: Law, Cultural Politics, and Market Ethics." In Anand Pandian and Daud Ali, *Ethical Life in South Asia,* 617–26. Bloomington: Indiana University Press.

"BJP Calls for Action Against Writer." 1994. *Times of India,* September 9, 10.

Bloch, Jules, and Dev Raj Chanana. 1970. *The Formation of the Marāṭhī Language.* Delhi: Motilal Banarsidass.

"Book Stayed." 1992. *Times of India,* October 10, 16.

Bourdieu, Pierre. 1984 [1979]. *Distinction: A Social Critique of the Judgment of Taste.* Cambridge: Harvard University Press.

——. 1986. "The Forms of Capital." In John G. Richardson, ed., *Handbook of Theory and Research for the Sociology of Education,* 241–58. New York: Greenwood.

——. 1994. *The Field of Cultural Production.* New York: Columbia University Press.

Breckenridge, C. 1995. *Consuming Modernity: Public Culture in a South Asian World.* Minneapolis: University of Minnesota Press.

Bronner, Yigal, Whitney Cox, and Lawrence McCrea, eds. 2011. *South Asian Texts in History: Critical Engagements with Sheldon Pollock.* Ann Arbor: Association for Asian Studies.

Busch, Allison. 2011a. "Hindi Literary Beginnings." In Yigal Bronner, Whitney Cox, and Lawrence McCrea, eds., *South Asian Texts in History: Critical Engagements with Sheldon Pollock,* 203–28. Ann Arbor: Association for Asian Studies.

——. 2011b. *Poetry of Kings: The Classical Hindi Literature of Mughal India.* New York: Oxford University Press.

Callewaert, Winand M., and Mukunda Lāṭha. 1989. *The Hindī Songs of Nāmdev.* Leuven: Departement Oriëntalistiek.

Cantlie, Audrey, and Richard Burghart, eds. 1985. *Indian Religion.* London: Curzon.

Certeau, Michel de. 1984. Steven Rendall, trans. *The Practice of Everyday Life.* Berkeley: University of California Press.

Chalmers, Robert. 1932. *Buddha's Teachings: Being the Sutta-nipāta or Discourse-Collection.* Cambridge: Harvard University Press.

Champakalakshmi, R. 2001. "Reappraisal of a Brahmanical Institution: The Brahmadeya and Its Ramification in Early Medieval South India." In K. Hall, ed., *Structure and Society in Early South India: Essays in Honour of Noboru Karashima,* 59–84. New Delhi: Oxford University Press.

Chatterjee, Partha. 2001. "On Civil and Political Society in Postcolonial Democracies." In S. Kaviraj and S. Khilnani, eds., *Civil Society: History and Possibilities,* 165–78. Cambridge: Cambridge University Press.

——. 2004. *The Politics of the Governed: Reflections on Popular Politics in Most of the World.* New York: Columbia University Press.

——. 2011. *Lineages of Political Society: Studies in Postcolonial Democracy.* New York: Columbia University Press.

Chatterjee, Partha, Tapati Guha-Thakurta, and Bodhisattva Kar, eds. 2014. *New Cultural Histories of India: Materiality and Practices.* Delhi: Oxford University Press.

Chekuri, Christopher. 2007. "Textures of Time: Writing Politics Back Into History." *History and Theory* 46, no. 3: 384–95.

Chitrava, S., ed. 1937. *Madhyayugini Citrakoś.* Pune: Bharatiya Chitrakosha Mandal.

Cohen, Jean L., and Andrew Arato. 1992. *Civil Society and Political Theory*. Cambridge: MIT Press.

Cohn, Bernard S. 1971. *India: the Social Anthropology of a Civilization*. Englewood Cliffs, NJ: Prentice-Hall.

——. 1987. *An Anthropologist Among the Historians and Other Essays*. Delhi: Oxford University Press.

——. 1996. *Colonialism and Its Forms of Knowledge: the British in India*. Princeton: Princeton University Press.

Cox W. 2012. "Bhoja's Alternate Universe." *Journal of the Royal Asiatic Society* 22, no. 1: 57–72.

Dalal, K. F., S. Kale, and R. Poojari. 2015. "Four Gadhegals Discovered in District Raigad, Maharashtra." *Ancient Asia* 6, no. 1, DOI: http://dx.doi.org/10.5334/aa.12320 (accessed March 16, 2015).

Dandekar, Ramchandra Narayan, ed. 1972. *Sanskrit and Maharashtra: A Symposium*. Poona: University of Poona.

Dandekar, S. V. 1953. *Sārtha Jñāneśvarī*. Pune: Prasada.

Dandekar. S. V., B. M. Khuperkar, N. R. Phatak, A. K. Priyolkar, and R. N. Velingkar, eds. 1963. *Śrī Jñāneśvarī*. Mumbai: Government Central Press.

Daniel, Valentine. 1987. *Fluid Signs*. Berkeley: University of California Press.

Darity, William S. Jr., ed. 2008. *International Encyclopedia of the Social Sciences*. 2d ed. New York: Macmillan.

Das, Gurcharan. 2010. *The Difficulty of Being Good: On the Subtle Art of Dharma*. New York: Oxford University Press.

Das, Veena. 2001. "Caste." In Neil J. Smelser and Paul B. Baltes, eds., *International Encyclopedia of the Social and Behavioral Sciences*, 1529–32. Amsterdam: Elsevier.

Davis, Richard. 2014. *The Bhagavad Gita: A Biography*. Princeton: Princeton University Press.

Dean, Melanie. 2011. "From Darshan to Tirushti: 'Evil Eye' and the Politics of Visibility in Contemporary South India." Ph.D. diss., University of Pennsylvania.

——. 2013. "From 'Evil Eye' Anxiety to the Desirability of Envy: Status, Consumption, and the Politics of Visibility in Urban South India." *Contributions to Indian Sociology* 47, no. 2 (June 2013):185–216.

De Bary, William Theodore. 1958. *Sources of Indian Tradition*. New York: Columbia University Press.

Deleury, G. A. 1960. *The Cult of Vithoba*. Pune: Deccan College.

Denapoli, Antoinette. 2014. *Real Sadhus Sing to God: Gender, Asceticism, and Vernacular Religion in Rajasthan*. New York: Oxford University Press.

Desai, A. 2008. "Subaltern Vegetarianism: Witchcraft, Embodiment and Sociality in Central India." *South Asia: Journal of South Asian Studies* 31, no. 1: 96–117.

——. 2009. "Anti-'anti-witchcraft' and the Maoist Insurgency in Rural Maharashtra, India." *Dialectical Anthropology* 33, nos. 3/4: 423–39.

——. 2010. "Dilemmas of Devotion: Religious Transformation and Agency in Hindu India." *Journal of the Royal Anthropological Institute* 16, no. 2: 313–29.

Deshmukh, Madhuri. 2009. Review in H-Asia (October). URL: https://networks .h-net.org/node/22055/reviews/22150/deshmukh-novetzke-religion-and-public-memory-cultural-history-saint (accessed August 20, 2015).

Deshpande, Brahmanand. 2002. *Studies in Epigraphy*, vol. 1. Aurangabad: Kailsah.

Deshpande, Madhav. 1979. *Sociolinguistic Attitudes in India*. Ann Arbor: Karoma.

——. 1993. *Sanskrit and Prakrit, Sociolinguistic Issues*. Delhi: Motilal Banarsidass.

Deshpande, Prachi. 2007. *Creative Pasts: Historical Memory and Identity in Western India, 1700–1960*. New York: Columbia University Press.

——. 2014. "Scripting the Cultural History of Language: Modi in the Colonial Archive." In Partha Chatterjee, Tapati Guha-Thakurta, and Bodhisattva Kar, eds., *New Cultural Histories of India: Materiality and Practices*. Delhi: Oxford University Press.

——. 2016. "Shuddhalekhan: Orthography, Community, and the Marathi Public Sphere. *Economic and Political Weekly* 50, no. 6 (February 6): 72–82.

Deshpande, K., and M. V. Rajadhyaksha. 1988. *A History of Marathi Literature*. New Delhi: Sahitya Akademi.

Deshpande, V. N. 1935. *Mahādamba: Adhyā Marāṭhī Kaviyātrī* [Mahadambha: The First Marathi Poetess]. Pune: Continental.

——, ed. 1969. *Smṛtisthaḷa*. Pune: Venus.

De Souza, J. P., and C. M. Kulkarni, eds. 1972. *Historiography in Indian Languages; Dr. G. M. Moraes Felicitation Volume*. Delhi: Oriental.

Dhavalikar, M. K. 1972. "Epigraphical Sources in Marathi." In J. P. De Souza and C. M. Kulkarni, *Historiography in Indian Languages; Dr. G. M. Moraes Felicitation Volume*. Delhi: Oriental. 24–33,

Dhere R. C. 1977. *Chakrapāṇi*. Pune: Vivekarma.

——. 1984. *Śrī Vitthal: Ak Mahasamanvay*. Pune: Anjali.

——. 1990. *Lok Sahitya-Śodh aṇi Samīkṣa*. Pune: Shrividya.

——. 1991. *Prācīn Marāṭhī Vāṇgmay*. Pune: Anjali.

——. 2011 [1984]. *The Rise of a Folk God: Viṭṭhal of Pandharpur*. Trans. Anne Feldhaus. New York: Oxford University Press.

Dirks, Nicholas B. 1987. *The Hollow Crown*. Cambridge: Cambridge University Press.

——. 2001. *Castes of Mind: Colonialism and the Making of Modern India*. Princeton: Princeton University Press.

Dixit, S. A., ed. 1902. *Caturvarga Cintāmani* [Hemadri], vol. 1. Benares: Prabhakari.

——. 1903. *Caturvarga Cintāmani* [Hemadri], vol. 2. Benares: Prabhakari.

Doniger, Wendy, ed. and trans. 1981. *The Rig Veda: An Anthology. One Hundred and Eight Hymns, Selected, Translated, and Annotated*. Harmondsworth: Penguin.

——. 2009. *The Hindus: An Alternative History*. New York: Penguin.

Doniger, Wendy, and Brian K. Smith, trans. 1992. *The Laws of Manu*. London: Penguin.

Dumont, Louis. 1980. *Homo Hierarchicus.* Chicago: University of Chicago Press.

Dundes, Alan, ed. 1981a. *The Evil Eye: A Folklore Casebook.* New York: Garland.

——. 1981b. "Wet and Dry: The Evil Eye." In Alan Dundes, ed., *The Evil Eye: A Folklore Casebook,* 257–312. New York: Garland.

Dyson, T. 1989. The Population History of Berar since 1881 and Its Potential Wider Significance. *The Indian Economic and Social History Review* 26, no. 2: 167–201.

Eaton, Richard Maxwell. 1978. *Sufis of Bijapur, 1300–1700: Social Roles of Sufis in Medieval India.* Princeton: Princeton University Press.

——. 2005. *A Social History of the Deccan, 1300–1761: Eight Indian Lives.* Cambridge: Cambridge University Press.

Eisenstadt, S. N., Wolfgang Schluchter, and Björn Wittrock. 2001. *Public Spheres and Collective Identities.* New Brunswick, NJ: Transaction.

Elias, Jamal. 2011. *On Wings of Diesel.* London: Oneworld.

Emden, C., and David R. Midgley. 2012. *Changing Perceptions of the Public Sphere.* New York: Berghahn.

Epigraphia Indica, vol. 25. 1939. New Delhi: Director General, Archaelogical Survey of India.

Feldhaus, Anne. 1982. "God and Madman: Gundam Raul." *Bulletin of the School of Oriental and African Studies, University of London* 45, no. 1: 74–83.

——. 1983. *The Religious System of the Mahānubhāva sect [The Mahānubhāva Sūtrapāṭha].* New Delhi: Manohar.

——. 1984. *The Deeds of God in Ṛddhipur.* New York: Oxford University Press.

——. 1995. *Water and Womanhood: Religious Meanings of Rivers in Maharashtra.* New York: Oxford University Press.

——. 1996. *Images of Women in Maharashtrian Literature and Religion.* Albany: State University of New York Press.

——. 2003. *Connected Places.* New York: Palgrave Macmillan.

Feldhaus, Anne, and S. G. Tulpule. 1992. *In the Absence of God: The Early Years of an Indian Sect: A Translation of "Smṛtisthaḷ," with an Introduction.* Honolulu: University of Hawaii Press.

——. 1999. *A Dictionary of Old Marathi.* Mumbai: Popular.

Feldhaus, A., R. Atkar, and R. Zagade. 2014. *Say to the Sun, "Don't Rise," and to the Moon, "Don't Set": Two Oral Narratives from the Countryside of Maharashtra.* New York: Oxford University Press.

Fleet, J. F., and R. C. Temple, eds. 1885. *Indian Antiquary,* vol. 14. Bombay: Popular.

Flueckiger, Joyce Burkhalter. 2006. *In Amma's Healing Room: Gender and Vernacular Islam in South India.* Bloomington: Indiana University Press.

Foucault, Michel. 2003. "What Is an Author?" In Paul Rabinow and Nikolas Rose, eds., *The Essential Foucault,* 377–92. New York: New Press.

Freitag, Sandria. 1989. *Collective Action and Community.* Berkeley: University of California Press.

Freud, Sigmund. 1962 [1930]. *Civilization and Its Discontents.* New York: Norton.

——. 1989 [1927]. *The Future of an Illusion.* New York: Norton.

Freud, Sigmund, and James Strachey. 1989 [1901]. *The Psychopathology of Everyday Life.* New York: Norton.

Frowde, H. 1908. *The Imperial Gazetteer of India*, vol. 21. Oxford: Clarendon.

Gadkari, Jayant. 1996. *Society and Religion.* Bombay: Popular Prakashan.

Ghurye, G. S. 1961. *Caste, Class, and Occupation.* Bombay: Popular Book Depot.

Gokhale, Balkrishna Govind. 1977. "The Merchant in Ancient India." *Journal of the American Oriental Society* 97, no. 2: 125–30.

González Reimann, Luis. 2002. *The Mahabharata and the Yugas: India's Great Epic Poem and the Hindu System of World Ages.* New York: Peter Lang.

Gordon, Stewart. 1993. *The Marathas, 1600–1818.* Cambridge: Cambridge University Press.

Guha, Ranajit, and Gayatri Chakravorty Spivak, eds. 1988. *Selected Subaltern Studies.* New York: Oxford University Press.

Guha, Sumit. 2004. "Speaking Historically: The Changing Voices of Historical Narration in Western India, 1400–1900." *American Historical Review* 109, no. 4: 1084–103.

——. 2010. "Serving the Barbarian to Preserve the Dharma." *Indian Economic and Social History Review* 47, no. 4: 497–525.

——. 2013. *Beyond Caste: Identity and Power in South Asia, Past and Present.* Leiden: Brill.

Gupta, Dipankar. 1991. *Social Stratification.* New Delhi: Oxford University Press.

——. 2004. *Caste in Question: Identity or Hierarchy?* New Delhi: Sage.

Habermas, Jürgen. 1974. "The Public Sphere: An Encyclopedia Article" [1964]. *New German Critique,* no. 3: 49–55.

——. 1989. *The Structural Transformation of the Public Sphere: An Inquiry Into a Category of Bourgeois Society.* Cambridge: MIT Press.

——. 2010. "Leadership and *Leitkultur.*" *New York Times,* October 28. http://www .nytimes.com/2010/10/29/opinion/29Habermas.html (accessed February13, 2016).

Hall, Kenneth R., ed. 2001. *Structure and Society in Early South India: Essays in Honour of Noboru Karashima.* New Delhi: Oxford University Press.

Hansen, Thomas B. 1996. "The Vernacularization of Hindutva: BJP and Shiv Sena in Rural Maharashtra." *Contributions to Indian Sociology* 30, no. 2: 177–214.

——. 1999. *The Saffron Wave: Democracy and Hindu Nationalism in Modern India.* Princeton: Princeton University Press.

——. 2001. *Wages of Violence: Naming and Identity in Postcolonial Bombay.* Princeton: Princeton University Press.

Hardgrove, Anne. 2004. *Community and Public Culture: The Marwaris in Calcutta.* New York: Columbia University Press.

Hawley, John Stratton. 1988. "Author and Authority in the Bhakti Poetry of North India." *Journal of Asian Studies* 47, no. 2: 269–90.

——. 2015. *A Storm of Songs: India and the Idea of the Bhakti Movement.* Cambridge: Harvard University Press.

Haynes, D. E. 1991. *Rhetoric and Ritual in Colonial India.* Berkeley: University of California Press.

Heesterman, J. C. 1985. *The Inner Conflict of Tradition.* Chicago: University of Chicago Press.

Hira Lal, Rai Bahadur. 1916. *Descriptive Lists of Inscriptions in the Central Provinces and Berar.* Nagpur: Printed at the Government Press.

Hocart, A. M. 1950. *Caste: A Comparative study.* London: Methuen.

Hunter, W. W. 1887. *The Imperial Gazetteer of India,* vol. 12. London: Trubner.

Inden, Ronald B. 1985. "Lordship and Caste in Hindu Discourse." Audrey Cantlie and Richard Burghart, eds., *Indian Religion,* 159–79. London: Curzon.

——. 1990. *Imagining India.* Oxford: Blackwell.

Ingram, Brannon D., J. Barton Scott, and SherAli Tareen, eds. 2015. "Imagining the Public in Modern South Asia." Special issue. *South Asia: Journal of South Asian Studies* 38, no. 3.

Jacobsen, K. A., ed. 2011. *Brill Encyclopedia of Hinduism,* vol. 3. Leiden: Brill.

——. 2012. *Brill Encyclopedia of Hinduism,* vol. 4. Leiden: Brill.

Jadhav, B. G., ed. and trans. 2009. *Leelacharitra.* Domegram: Raul.

Jaffrelot, C. 2003. *India's Silent Revolution.* New York: Columbia University Press.

Jalal, A. 2000. *Self and Sovereignty: Individual and Community in South Asian Islam Since 1850.* London: Routledge.

Jogdand, Prahlad Gangaram. 1995. *Dalit Women in India: Issues and Perspective.* New Delhi: Gyan.

Johari, Aarefa. 2015. "Revealed: The Secret of the 'Ass-Curse' Stones Scattered Across Maharashtra." *Scroll.in,* http://scroll.in/article/684926/revealed-the-secret -of-the-ass-curse-stones-scattered-across-maharashtra (accessed March 31, 2015).

Joshi, M. 1974. *Bhāratīya Saṃskṛti Koś.* Pune: Bharatiya Sanskriti Kosh Mandal.

Joshi, N. G. 1955. *Marāṭhī Candoracana.* Baroda: Layadristya Punarvicar.

Joshi, S. B. 1951. "Etymology of Place-Names Patti-Hatti, Some Observations on the History of Maharashtra and Karnataka." *Annals of the Bhadarkar Oriental Research Institute* 32:41–456.

——. 1952. *Marhāṭi Saṃskṛti: Kahi Samasya.* Pune: Antar Bharati.

Kaminsky, Arnold P., and Roger D. Long. 2011. *India Today: An Encyclopedia of Life in the Republic.* Santa Barbara: ABC-CLIO.

Kane, Pandurang Vaman. 1930. *History of Dharmashastra.* Pune: Bhandarkar Oriental Research Institute.

Kapstein, Ethan. 2002. "Two Dismal Sciences Are Better Than One." *International Security* 27, no. 3: 158–87.

Karve, Irawati Karmarkar. 1962. "On the Road: A Maharashtrian Pilgrimage." *Journal of Asian Studies* 22, no. 1 (November): 13–29.

——. 1969. *Yuganta, the End of an Epoch.* Pune: Deshmukh.

Kaviraj, S., and S. Khilnani, eds. 2001. *Civil Society: History and Possibilities.* Cambridge: Cambridge University Press.

Kavitkar, G. V., D. Kir, H. Inamdar, N. Relekar, and N. Mirajkar. 1970. *Śrī Nāmdev Gāthā.* Bombay: Government of Bombay Press.

Keluskar, K. A. 1921. *The Life of Shivaji Maharaj: Founder of the Maratha Empire.* Bombay: Manoranjan.

Keune, Jon, and Christian Lee Novetzke. 2011. "Varkaris." In K. A. Jacobsen, ed., *Brill Encyclopedia of Hinduism,* 3:617–26. Leiden: Brill.

Khedkar, V. K. 1959. *The Divine Heritage of the Yadavas.* Allahabad: Parmanand.

Kiehnle, Catharina. 1997. *Jñāndev Studies 1–3,* 48, nos. 1–2. Stuttgart: Franz Steiner.

King, Richard. 1999. *Orientalism and Religion.* New York: Routledge.

Kolte, V. B. 1935. *Bhāskarabhaṭṭa Borīkara caritra va kāvyavivecana.* Amarāvatī: Vidarbha.

——. 1952. *Śrī Cakradhar Caritra.* Malakapur: Aruna.

——, ed. 1978. *Mhāiṁbhaṭ saṅkalit Śrīchakradhar Līḷācharitra.* Mumbai: Maharashtra Rajya Sahitya Samskriti Mandal.

——. 1984. *Mahānubhāv Saṃśodhan,* vol. 2. Malakapur: Aruna.

Koo, Jeong-Woo. 2007. "The Origins of the Public Sphere and Civil Society." *Social Science History* 31, no. 3: 381–409.

Kosambi, D. D. 1961. "Social and Economic Aspects of the *Bhagavad Gītā.*" *Journal of the Economic and Social History of the Orient* 4, no. 2: 198–224.

Kulkarni, V. D. 1980. *Śrī Govindaprabhu Caritra.* Pune: Venus.

Kulke, H., ed. 1995. *The State in India, 1000–1700.* Delhi: Oxford University Press.

Lacan, Jacques. 1977. *Écrits: a selection.* New York: Norton.

LC-P, see Kolte's *Līḷācaritra* (Kolte 1978), Pūrvārdha verses.

LC-U, see Kolte's *Līḷācaritra* (Kolte 1978), Uttarārdha verses.

Lefebvre, Henri. 1991 [1947]. *Critique of Everyday Life.* London: Verso.

Lele, Jayant, ed. 1981a. "Community, Discourse, and Critique in Jnaneshwar." In Jayant Lele, *Tradition and Modernity in Bhakti Movements,* 104–12. Leiden: Brill.

——, ed. 1981b. *Tradition and Modernity in Bhakti Movements.* Leiden: Brill.

Lokapur, R. S. 1995. *The Jñāneśwarī: Text as Adopted by V. K. Rajwade.* Belgaum: Impressions.

Lorenzen, David N. 1972. *The Kāpālikas and Kālāmukhas: Two Lost Śaivite Sects.* Berkeley: University of California Press.

——, ed. 1995. *Bhakti Religion in North India: Community Identity and Political Action.* Albany: State University of New York Press.

——. 1996. *Praises to a Formless God: Nirguṇī Texts from North India.* Albany: State University of New York Press.

Maclean, Kama. 2008. *Pilgrimage and Power: The Kumbh Mela in Allahabad, 1765–2001.* New York: Oxford University Press.

Mahadevan, Sudhir. 2015. "A Very Old Machine: The Many Origins of the Cinam in India." Albany: State University of New York Press.

Mallinson, James. 2014. "Hatha Yoga's Philosophy: A Fortuitous Union of Non-Dualities." *Journal of Indian Philosophy* 42, no. 1: 225–47.

Mantena, Rama. 2007. "Textures of Time: The Question of History in Precoloinal India." *History and Theory* 46, no. 3: 396–408.

——. 2013. "Vernacular Publics and Political Modernity: Language and Progress in Colonial South India." *Modern Asian Studies* 47, no. 5: 1678–705.

Marglin, Frédérique. 1985. *Wives of the God-King: The Rituals of the Devadasis of Puri.* Delhi: Oxford University Press.

Master, Alfred. 1957. "Some Marathi Inscriptions, A.D. 1060–1300." *Bulletin of the School of Oriental and African Studies, University of London* 20, no. 1/3: 417–35.

Melve, L. 2007. *Inventing the Public Sphere: The Public Debate During the Investiture Contest (c. 1030–1122).* Leiden: Brill.

Michelutti, Lucia. 2007. "The Vernacularization of Democracy: Political Participation and Popular Politics in North India." *Journal of the Royal Anthropological Institute* 13:639–656.

——. 2008. *The Vernacularisation of Democracy: Politics, Caste, and Religion in India.* New Delhi: Routledge.

Mir, Farina. 2010. *The Social Space of Language Vernacular Culture in British Colonial Punjab.* Berkeley: University of California Press.

Mitchell, Lisa. 2009. *Language, Emotion, and Politics in South India: The Making of a Mother Tongue.* Bloomington: Indiana University Press.

Mitchell, Timothy. 1999. "Society, Economy, and the State Effect." In G. Steinmetz, ed., *State/Culture: State-Formation After the Cultural Turn.* Ithaca: Cornell University Press.

Monier-Williams, Monier. 1899. *A Sanskrit-English Dictionary Etymologically and Philologically Arranged with Special Reference to Cognate Indo-European Languages.* Oxford: Clarendon.

Mukherjee, S. 1998. *A Dictionary of Indian Literature.* Hyderabad: Orient Longman.

Mulay, Sumati. 1972. *Studies in the Historical and Cultural Geography and Ethnography of the Deccan, Based Entirely on the Inscriptions of the Deccan from the 1st–13th century A.D.* Pune: Deccan College, Postgraduate and Research Institute.

Muller, Max. 1881. *The Dhammapada.* Oxford: Clarendon.

Murthy, A. V. N. 1971. *The Yadavas: the Sevunas of Devagiri.* Mysore: Rao and Raghavan.

Nagaraj, D. R. 2003. "Critical Tensions in the History of Kannada Literary Culture." In Sheldon Pollock, ed., *Literary Cultures in History: Reconstructions from South Asia,* 323–82. Berkeley: University of California Press.

Nagpure, P., ed. 2004. *Līḷācaritra.* Amravati: Omkar.

Narasimhachar, R., ed. 1923. *Epigraphia Carnatica,* vol. 2. Bangalore: Mysore Government Central Press.

Narayana Rao, Velcheru, and Gene H. Roghair. 2014 [1990]. *Śiva's Warriors: The Basava Purāṇa of Pālkuriki Somanātha*. Princeton: Princeton University Press.

Narayana Rao, Velcheru, David Dean Shulman, and Sanjay Subrahmanyam. 2001. *Textures of Time: Writing History in South India, 1600–1800*. Delhi: Permanent Black.

——. 2007. "Textures of Time: A Pragmatic Response." *History and Theory* 46, no. 3: 409–27.

Naregal, Veena. 2001. *Language Politics, Elites, and the Public Sphere*. New Delhi: Permanent Black.

National Sample Survey Organisation. 2001. *1999–2000: NSS 55th round, July 1999–June 2000*. New Delhi: National Sample Survey Organisation, Ministry of Statistics and Programme Implementation, Government of India.

Nelson, Cary, and Lawrence Grossberg, eds. 1988. *Marxism and the Interpretation of Culture*. Urbana: University of Illinois Press.

Nene, H. N., ed. 1954 [1936]. *Līḷācaritra*. 3d ed. Nagpur: Narayana.

Nicholson, A. 2010. *Unifying Hinduism: Philosophy and Identity in Indian Intellectual History*. New York: Columbia University Press.

Novetzke, Christian Lee. 2003. "Divining an Author: The Idea of Authorship in an Indian Religious Tradition." *History of Religions* 42, no. 3: 213–42.

——. 2005. "A Family Affair." In Guy L. Beck, ed., *Alternative Krishnas: Regional and Vernacular Variations on a Hindu Deity*, 113–38. Albany: State University of New York Press.

——. 2006. "The Subaltern Numen: Making History in the Name of God." *History of Religions* vol. 46, no. 2: 99–126.

——. 2007a. "The Theographic and the Historiographic in an Indian Sacred Life Story." *Sikh Formations* 3, no. 2: 169–84.

——. 2007b. "Bhakti and Its Public." *International Journal of Hindu Studies* 11, no. 3 (December): 255–72.

——. 2008a. "Humanism, Religion, and the Nation: Sant Namdev as a *Mānavatāvādin*." In M. Bhagavan and A. Feldhaus, eds., *Speaking Truth to Power: Religion, Caste, and the Subaltern Question in India*, 30–46. Delhi: Oxford University Press.

——. 2008b. *Religion and Public Memory: A Cultural History of Saint Namdev in India*. New York: Columbia University Press.

——. 2009. "History, Memory, and Other Matters of Life and Death." In K. Pemberton and M. Nijhawan, eds., *Shared Idioms, Sacred Symbols*, 212–32. New York: Routledge.

——. 2011. "The Brahman Double. The Brahminical Construction of Anti-Brahminism and Anti-Caste Sentiment in the Religious Culture of Pre-Colonial Maharashtra." *South Asia History and Culture* 2, no. 2: 232–52.

——. 2012. "Namdev." In K. A. Jacobsen, ed., *Brill's Encyclopedia of Hinduism*, 4:296–302. Leiden: Brill.

——. Forthcoming. "Vernacularizing Jnandev: Hagiography and the Process of Vernacularization." *International Journal of Hindu Studies*.

O'Hanlon, P., and D. Washbrook, eds. 2011. *Religious Cultures in Early Modern India*. London: Routledge.

O'Hanlon, Rosalind. 2010a. "Letters Home: Banaras Pandits and the Maratha Regions in Early Modern India." *Modern Asian Studies* 44, no. 2: 201–40.

——. 2010b. "The Social Worth of Scribes." *Indian Economic and Social History Review* 47, no. 4: 563–95.

——. 2011. "Speaking from Shiva's Temple: Banaras Scholar Households and the Brahman 'Ecumene' of Mughal India." In P. O'Hanlon and D. Washbrook, eds., *Religious Cultures in Early Modern India,* 121–45. London: Routledge.

——. 2013. "Contested Conjunctures: Brahman Communities and 'Early Modernity' in India." *American Historical Review* 118, no. 3: 765–87.

——. 2014. *At the Edges of Empire: Essays in Social and Intellectual History of India*. New Delhi: Permanent Black.

——. 2015. "Discourses of Caste Over the Longue Duree." *South Asia History and Culture* 6, no. 1: 102–29.—

O'Hanlon, Rosalind, and Christopher Minkowski. 2008. "What Makes People Who They Are? Pandit Networks and the Problem of Livelihoods in Early Modern Western India." *Indian Economic and Social History Review* 45, no. 3: 381–416.

Olivelle, Patrick, and Suman Olivelle, trans. 2004. *Manu's Code of Law: A Critical Edition and Translation of the Manava-Dharmasastra*. Oxford: Oxford University Press.

Orsini, Francesca. 2009. *The Hindi Public Sphere, 1920–1940: Language and Literature in the Age of Nationalism*. New Delhi: Oxford University Press.

Osella, Fillippo, and Caroline Osella. 1999. "From Transience to Immanence: Consumption, Life-Cycle, and Social Mobility in Kerala, South India. *Modern Asian Studies* 33, no. 4: 989–1020.

——. 2000. *Social Mobility in Kerala: Modernity and Identity in Conflict*. London: Pluto.

Palshikar, Shreeyash. 2007. "Breaking Bombay, Making Maharashtra." Ph.D. diss., University of Chicago.

Pandian, Anand. 2009. *Crooked Stalks*. Durham: Duke University Press.

Pandian, Anand, and Daud Ali. 2010. *Ethical Life in South Asia*. Bloomington: Indiana University Press.

Panse, Murlidhar Gajanan. 1953. *Linguistic Peculiarities of Jñāneśvarī*. Pune: Deccan College Postgraduate and Research Institute.

——. 1963. *Yādavakālīna Mahārāṣṭra*. Mumbai: Mumbai Marāṭhī grantha Saṅgrahālaya.

Parikh, R. C., and H. G. Shastri, eds. 1976. *Gujarāt no Rājakīya aṇe Saṃskṛtik Itihās* (*The Political and Cultural History of Gujarat*), vol. 4. Ahmedabad: B. J. Vidyabhavan.

Patton, Laurie L. 2005. "Can Women Be Priests? Brief Notes Toward an Argument from the Ancient Hindu World." *Journal of Hindu-Christian Studies* 18, no. 1: 17–21.

——, trans. 2008. *The Bhagavad Gita*. London: Penguin.

——. Forthcoming. "Grandmother Language: Women and Sanskrit in Maharashtra and Beyond."

Pemberton, K., and M. Nijhawan, eds. 2009. *Shared Idioms, Sacred Symbols*. New York: Routledge.

Phadke, Y. D., ed. 1984. *Dinkarrao Javalkar Samāgra Vāṇgmay*. Pune: Mahatma Jotirao Phule Smata Pratishthan.

Pollock, Sheldon. 1989. "Mimamsa and the Problem of History in Traditional India." *Journal of the American Oriental Society* 109, no. 4: 603–10.

——. 1998. "The Cosmopolitan Vernacular." *Journal of Asian Studies* 57, no. 1: 6–37.

——, ed. 2003. *Literary Cultures in History: Reconstructions from South Asia*. Berkeley: University of California Press.

——. 2006. *The Language of the Gods in the World of Men: Sanskrit, Culture, and Power in Premodern India*. Berkeley: University of California Press.

——. 2007. "Textures of Time: Pretextures of Time." *History and Theory* 46, no. 3: 366–83.

Povinelli, Elizabeth. 2006. *The Empire of Love*. Durham: Duke University Press.

Pradhan, V. G., trans. 1967. *Jnaneshwari*, vol. 1. Ed. H. M. Lambert. London: Allen and Unwin.

——. 1969. *Jnaneshwari*, vol. 2. Ed. H. M. Lambert. London: Allen and Unwin.

Prasad, Leela. 2007. *Poetics of Conduct: Oral Narrative and Moral Being in a South Indian Town*. New York: Columbia University Press.

Rabinow, Paul, and Nikolas Rose, eds. 2003. *The Essential Foucault*. New York: New Press.

Raeside, I. M. P. 1960. "A Bibliographical Index of Mahānubhāva Works in Marathi." *Bulletin of the School of Oriental and African Studies, University of London* 23, no. 3: 464–507.

——. 1970. "The Mahānubhāva Sakaḷa Lipī." *Bulletin of the School of Oriental and African Studies* 33, no. 2: 328–34.

——. 1976. "The Mahanubhavs." *Bulletin of the School of Oriental and African Studies* 39, no. 3: 585–600.

——. 1988. "Investigating Mahanubhava Practice and Beliefs." *Man* 23, no. 3: 561–62.

Raghavan, V. 1966. *The Great Integrators: The Saint-Singers of India*. [Delhi]: Publications Division, Ministry of Information and Broadcasting.

Raghavan, V., and R. N. Dandekar. 1958. "The Hindu Way of Life." In William Theodore de Bary, ed., *Sources of Indian Tradition*, 201–380. New York: Columbia University Press.

Rahalkar, P. S., trans. 2011. *Jnyaneshwari: An English Translation*. London: Usha P. Rahalkar.

Rajwade, V. K., ed. 1909. *Śrī Jñāneśvarī*. Dhule: Atmaram.

Rajagopal, Arvind, ed. 2009. *The Indian Public Sphere: Readings in Media History*. New Delhi: Oxford University Press.

Ramanujan, A. K. 1973. *Speaking of Śiva*. Harmondsworth: Penguin.

Ranade, Anuradha K. 2009. *Socio-economic Life of Maharashtra. 1100–1600 A.D.* New Delhi: Serials.

Rao, Anupama. 2009. *The Caste Question: Dalits and the Politics of Modern India.* Berkeley: University of California Press

Rawat, Ramnarayan S. 2011. *Reconsidering Untouchability: Chamars and Dalit History in North India.* Bloomington: Indiana University Press.

Reddy, B. R. C., and R. Natarajan. 2011. "Social History Through Inscriptions." *Indian Historical Review* 38, no. 1: 51–64.

Rege, Sharmila. 2006. *Writing Caste, Writing Gender: Reading Dalit Women's Testimonies.* New Delhi: Zubaan.

Richardson, John G., ed. 1986. *Handbook of Theory and Research for the Sociology of Education.* New York: Greenwood.

Rigopoulos, Antonio. 1998. *Dattātreya: The Immortal Guru, Yogin, and Avatāra: A Study of the Tranformative and Inclusive Character of a Multi-faceted Hindu Deity.* Albany: State University of New York Press.

——. 2011. *The Mahānubhāvs.* London: Anthem.

Ritti, Shrinivas. 1973. *The Seunas: The Yadavas of Devagiri.* Dharwar: Department of Ancient Indian History and Epigraphy, Karnatak University.

Roberts, Nathaniel. 2008. "Caste, Anthropology of." In William S. Darity Jr., ed., *International Encyclopedia of the Social Sciences,* 461–63. 2d ed. New York: Macmillan.

Rotman, Andy. Forthcoming. "Bazaar Religion: Marketing and Moral Economics in Modern India." Cambridge: Harvard University Press.

Roy, Arundhati. 2014. "The Doctor and the Saint." *Caravan,* March 1, http://caravanmagazine.in/reportage/doctor-and-saint (accessed March 20, 2014).

Rudolph, Lloyd, and Susanne Hoeber Rudolph. 2006. *Postmodern Gandhi and Other Essays.* Chicago: University of Chicago Press.

Sakhare, N., with K. Bhiḍe, eds. 1955. *Sānvaya va sārtha Śrīmadbhagavadagīte saha Jñāneśvarī.* Pune: Bikshu Kṛshṇānanda Sarasvatī.

Sanderson, Alexis. 2013. "The Impact of Inscriptions on the Interpretation of Early Shaiva Literature." *Indo-Iranian Journal* 56:211–44.

Sangari, Kumkum. 1990. "Mirabai and the Spiritual Economy of Bhakti." *Economic and Political Weekly* 25, no. 27 (July 7): 1464–75.

Sant Dnyaneshwar. 1940. Prabhat Film Company, Pune. Directors V. G. Damle and Sheikh Fattelal. Marathi. 139 minutes.

Schomer, Karine, and W. H. McLeod. 1987. *The Sants: Studies in a Devotional Tradition of India.* Berkeley: Berkeley Religious Studies Series.

Schultz, Anna C. 2013. *Singing a Hindu Nation: Marathi Devotional Performance and Nationalism.* New York: Oxford University Press.

Scott, James. 1985. *Weapons of the Weak: Everyday Forms of Peasant Resistance.* New Haven: Yale University Press.

Sen, Amartya. 2005. *The Argumentative Indian: Writings on Indian History, Culture, and Identity.* New York: Farrar, Straus and Giroux.

Shah, A. M. 1998. *The Family in India: Critical Essays.* New Delhi: Orient Longman.

Shah, Svati Pragna. 2014. *Street Corner Secrets: Sex, Work, and Migration in the City of Mumbai.* Durham: Duke University Press.

Sharma, Tej Ram. 1978. *Personal and Geographical Names in the Gupta Empire.* New Delhi: Concept.

Siegel, Lee. 1987. *Laughing Matters.* Chicago: University of Chicago Press.

Singh, Harpreet. 2013. "Religious Identity and the Vernacularization of Literary Cultures of the Panjab, 1500–1700." PhD diss., Harvard University.

Smelser, Neil J., and Paul B. Baltes, eds. 2001. *International Encyclopedia of the Social and Behavioral Sciences.* Amsterdam: Elsevier.

Soneji, Davesh. 2012. *Unfinished Gestures.* Chicago: University of Chicago Press.

Sontheimer, G. S. 1982. "God, Dharma and Society in the Yadava Kingdom of Devagiri According to the Lilacharitra of Chakradhar." In G. S. Sontheimer and P. K. Aithal, eds., *Indology and Law,* 329–58. Wiesbaden: Franz Steiner.

Sontheimer, G. S., and P. K. Aithal, eds. 1982. *Indology and Law.* Wiesbaden: Franz Steiner.

Spivak, Gayatri Chakravorty. 1988. "Can the Subaltern Speak?" In Cary Nelson and Lawrence Grossberg, eds., *Marxism and the Interpretation of Culture,* 271–313. Urbana: University of Illinois Press.

Srinivas, M. N. 1994. *The Dominant Caste and Other Essays.* Delhi: Oxford University Press.

Stein, Burton. 1960. "The Economic Function of a Medieval South Indian Temple." *Journal of Asian Studies* 19, no. 2: 163–76.

——. 1980. *Peasant, State, and Society in Medieval South India.* Delhi: Oxford University Press.

Steinmetz, G., ed. 1999. *State/Culture: State-Formation After the Cultural Turn.* Ithaca: Cornell University Press.

Subedar, M. 1945. *Gita Explained.* 3d ed. Bombay: Manu Subedar.

Subrahmanyam, S., and C. A. Bayly. 1988. "Portfolio Capitalists and Early Modern India." *Indian Economic and Social History Review* 25, no. 4: 401–24.

Talbot, Cynthia. 1991. "Temples, Donors, and Gifts: Patterns of Patronage in Thirteenth-Century South India." *Journal of Asian Studies* 50, no. 2: 308–40.

——. 2001. *Precolonial India in Practice: Society, Region, and Identity in Medieval Andhra.* Oxford: Oxford University Press.

Taylor, Charles. 2004. *Modern Social Imaginaries.* Durham: Duke University Press.

——. 2007. *A Secular Age.* Cambridge: Belknap.

Thapar, Romila. 2003. *Early India: From the Origins to AD 1300.* Berkeley: University of California Press.

Thavare, G. M. 1940. *Śrī Cakradhar va Mahānubhāva.* Pune: Adyatmik Sahitya Prasashan.

Tulpule, S. G. 1960. *An Old Marathi reader.* Pune: Venus.

——. 1963. *Prācīn Marāṭhī Korīv Lekha.* Pune: Pune University.

——, ed. 1964. *Līlācaritra: Ekāṃka.* Nagpur: Suvichar.

——, ed. 1966. *Līḷācaritra: Pūrvārdha,* parts 1 and 2. Nagpur: Suvichar.

——, ed. 1967. *Līḷācaritra: Uttarārdha,* parts 1 and 2. Nagpur: Suvichar.

——. 1979. *Classical Marathi Literature.* Wiesbaden: Otto Harrassowitz.

——. 1984. *Marāṭhī Vaṇgmayaca Itihāsa,* vol. 1. Pune: Maharashtra Sahitya Parishad.

Tulpule, S. G., and Anne Feldhaus. 1999. *A Dictionary of Old Marathi.* Mumbai: Popular.

Unhale, Sanjeev. 1992. "Ban on Biography Under Fire." *Times of India,* October 8, 6.

Velingakar, R. N. 1959. *Jñāneśvarīceṃ Śabda-Bhāṇḍār.* Mumbai: Marathi Sanshodhan Mandal.

Verma, Onkar Prasad. 1970. *The Yādavas and Their Times.* Nagpur: Vidarbha Samshodhan Mandal.

Viswanath, Rupa. 2014. *The Pariah Problem: Caste, Religion, and the Social in Modern India.* New York: Columbia University Press.

Wakankar, Milind. 2010. *Subalternity and Religion: The Prehistory of Dalit Empowerment in South Asia.* Abingdon: Routledge.

Warner, Michael. 2002. *Publics and Counterpublics.* New York: Zone.

Weber, Max. 1963 [1922]. *The Sociology of Religion.* Boston: Beacon.

Weber, Max, and Talcott Parsons. 1947. *The Theory of Social and Economic Organization.* New York: Free Press.

Wentworth, Blake. 2011. "Insiders, Outsiders, and the Tamil Tongue." In Yigal Bronner, Whitney Cox, and Lawrence McCrea, eds., *South Asian Texts in History: Critical Engagements with Sheldon Pollock,* 153–76. Ann Arbor: Association for Asian Studies.

White, David Gordon 2003. *Kiss of the Yoginī: "Tantric Sex" in Its South Asian Contexts.* Chicago: University of Chicago Press.

——. 2009. *Sinister Yogis.* Chicago: University of Chicago Press.

——, ed. 2011. *Yoga in Practice.* Princeton: Princeton University Press.

Williams, Raymond. 1961. *The Long Revolution.* London: Chatto and Windus.

Yandell, Keith E., and John. J. Paul, ed. 2000. *Religion and Public Culture.* Surrey: Curzon.

Yardi, M. R., trans. 1991. *Shri Jnanadeva's Bhāvārtha Dīpikā: Popularly Known as Jnaneshwari.* Pune: Bharatiya Vidya Bhavan.

Yazdani, Ghulam. 1960. *The Early History of the Deccan,* parts 7–11. London: Oxford University Press.

Zelliot, Eleanor. 1987. "Eknath's Bharude: The Sant as a Link Between Cultures." In Karine Schomer and W. H. McLeod, *The Sants: Studies in a Devotional Tradition of India,* 91–109. Berkeley: Berkeley Religious Studies Series.

Index

offerings to, 143; food offerings to Chakradhar by, 335*n*41; Gurav relations with, 162–67, 337*n*86; jatis, 133; Jnandev on, 259; Kayastha rivalries with, 158–62; kings relation to, 69–70; Kshatriya support of, 68–69; lineages of, 163; literary forms and, 56; as Mahanubhavs, 302, 341*n*25; maintaining power among, 58–59; power in Yadava century, 57; social capital of literacy and, 67–73; social stability created by, 70–71; as sovereigns, 69; temple economy and, 162–63; valorization of, 66–67; Yadava support of, 44, 61, 156

Breckenridge, Carol, 34, 71

Buddhism, 15; *Bhagavad Gītā* responding to, 266; caste critique of, 266; languages used in, 178; Sanskrit use by, 340*n*12

Camus, Albert, 9

Capitalist networks, 12

Caste, 19–26; action and, 266; in *Bhagavad Gītā*, 251, 270; bhakti and, 261; British romanticization of, 21; Buddhist critique of, 266; of Chakradhar, 108–9; commensality and, 143, 241; degradation of, 248–49; dharma and, 251, 268; dharma and pride in, 145–46; endogamy and, 143; family values and, 248; food and privilege of, 150; gender and, 25–26; inequities in, 245; of Jnandev, 115, 117; Jnandev on, 253–56; *Jñāneśvarī* and, 248–59; karma and, 266; Krishna on, 251, 252; language and, 189, 191; linguistic differences and, 138–39; of Mahanubhavs, 143–45, 160; phenomenal world and, 251, 253;

physical separation of, 138; Pollock and, 310*n*14; power alignments and, 156; pride in, 145–46, 148–49; purity and, 143; signs of, 335*n*49; social regulation through, 268; terminology, 21–25; transcendence and, 252, 255; trial of Chakradhar and, 207, 208, 209; typologies of, 158; vernacularization and critique of, 27; women and, 263–64; worshipping Krishna and, 256–59

Caste politics, 156–69

Caste prejudice, 151–53

Caste rivalries, 156–57

Caturvarga Cintāmaṇi (Hemadri), 55, 64–66, 134, 268, 282

Censuses, 313*n*68; Mahanubhav population, 299; varna and jati in, 312*n*61

Chakradhar, ix–xii, xiv, 3, 4, 9, 14, 19, 89; on begging, 143–47, 149–50; Bhatobas challenged by, 192–93; biographical sources, 105–6; birth of, 108; Brahminic ecumene and, 44, 46, 57, 193; caste and gender critiques and, 26; caste of, 108–9, 153–54, 328*n*20–22, 339*n*102; competitiveness, 340*n*8; cultural capital transferred by, 57; cultural politics taught by, 149, 187–93; departure from Maharashtra, 113–14, 203, 210, 298, 309*n*1, 327*n*4; devotees of, 330*n*38; figures resembling, 332*n*62; food offerings to, 335*n*41; gambling problem, 109–10, 340*n*8; gender distinction rejected by, 140; Gundam Raul and, 110; Guravs and, 163; as historical figure, 103–4; innovations of, 126; instruction to stay in Maharashtra, 185–86, 203, 209, 344*n*82; Islam and, 199–200, 209–10, 343*n*48; Jnandev

and, 259–60; vernacularization
  and, 284
Curses, donkey, 78–86, *81*

Dados, 134, 148, 164–66, 194, 338*n*91,
  338*n*100; Chakradhar mocking,
  339*n*103, 346*n*99
Daimba, 133
Dakhala, 163
Dako, 142
Dalit, 24
Damle, V. G., 294
Dandekar, S. V., 221, 275
Dean, Melanie, 84
de Certeau, Michel, 13
Delhi Sultanate, 48, 97, 113, 199,
  316*n*23, 316*n*24
Demati, 203–4, 206
Democracy, vernacularization of,
  10–11
Demonic nature, 267, 271
Desai, Amit, 298
Deshastha Brahmins, 320*n*92, 328*n*20
Deshi, 25
Deshpande, Madhav, 178
Devanagari, 55
Devotionalism, 16, 17, 259–60, 291
Dharma, 23, 229; *Bhagavad Gītā* and,
  217–19; caste and, 251, 268; caste
  pride and, 145–46; commensality
  and, 250; cosmic and social forms,
  251–52, 253; debate and, 218;
  decline of, 248; faith and, 270–71;
  in *Jñāneśvarī*, 217; Krishna on, 250;
  social distinction and cosmic,
  259–60
Dharma kirtan, 283
Dharma Śāstra, 23, 24, 25, 55;
  commentaries on, 63–64;
  dominance of, 319*n*72; kingship
  and, 69–71; as social science,
  217–18; Yadava patronage and, 123

Dhere, R. C., 82, 91
Dictionary of Old Marathi (Feldhaus and
  Tulpule), 109
Divine nature, 267
Donative inscriptions, 59, 61
Doniger, Wendy, 69
Donkey curse, 78–86, *81*
Dridhaparahara, 47
Dumont, Louis, 69
Dvāpar yuga, 216
Dvija, 23

Eaton, Richard, 339*n*109
Egalitarianism, xiv, 262, 276
Eknath, 221, 222, 294
Elites, 8–9; as Mahanubhav, 9; Marathi
  and, 9; Sanskrit and, 8, 119;
  strategy as world of, 13
Elitism: Brahminic, 133; Jnandev
  rejection of, 119; of Vedas, 240
Endogamy, 143, 241; commensality
  and, 249
Ethics: of *Jñāneśvarī*, 237, 277; of
  vernacularization, 238. *See also*
  Social ethics
Everyday life, 13, 105; habitus of, 272;
  Jñāneśvarī interceding in, 281
Evil eye, 82–84, 322*n*25
Exogamy, 143, 148

Faith and dharma, 270–71
Family values, 248
Fattelal (Sheikh), 294
Feldhaus, Anne, 109, 180, 181, 184–86,
  190
Five Krishnas, 107
Flueckiger, Joyce, 11–12
Food: Brahmins offering, to
  Chakradhar, 335*n*41; caste privilege
  and, 150; Mahanubhav practices
  and, 143–44
Forward castes, 23

Inscriptions: Akshi, 79–80, *81*; *bhakti* in, 96–97; curses on, 78; donative, 59, 61; Marathi, 54–55, 59, 75–77, 317*n*39; as public performance, 75–77; Sanskrit, 59; Tulpule collection of, 59–60

Islam, 316*n*26; Chakradhar and, 199–200, 209–10, 343*n*48; Jnandev and, 273

Jaffrelot, Christophe, 306

Jainism, 15; Sanskrit use by, 340*n*12

Jains, languages of, 178

Jaitugi, 48

Jajmani system, 157

Jalhana, 66–67

Jati, 21, 25; Brahmin, 133; caste rivalries and, 156–57; censuses and, 312*n*61; cultural meanings of, 22; defining, 22; literary form and, 56; as social ontology, 25; Untouchability and, 24, 133

Jijabai, 40

Jñānayoga, 219

Jnandev, ix–xi, xiv, 3, 9, 14, 15, 309*n*2, 340*n*2; access to salvation and, xiv, 244, 275–76; on *ahiṃsa*, 354*n*48; on *Bhagavad Gītā* as liberal text, 236–42; *Bhagavad Gītā* study by, 117, 118; biographical sources, 105–6, 114–15, 287–88; Brahminic ecumene and, 44, 46, 57; on Brahmins, 259; on caste, 253–56; caste and gender critiques and, 26; caste of, 115, 117; caste stripped from, 288–90; Chakradhar and, 280–81; commensality and, 241; cultural capital transferred by, 57; cultural politics of, 120; elitism rejected by, 119; ethics of vernacularization, 238; on faith, 270–71; figures resembling, 332*n*62; "four corners"

metaphor, 241, 249; as historical figure, 103–4; humanism of, 277; innovations of, 126; Islam and, 273; language choice as social statement by, 282; life of, 114–20; as literary innovator, 122–23; on Marathi, 229–34; Marathi literature and, 214, 243, 282; Muktabai and, 341*n*20; Namdev meeting, 291, 293; Namdev writings about, 288–91, 293–95; nationalist and subnationalist importance, 296; as node of orientation, 105; oral literary tradition and, 77; political stability enabling, 71; postage stamp memorializing, 296, *296*; presentation of *Jñāneśvarī*, 225–26; as primary voice of *Jñāneśvarī*, 223; principle of negativity and, 33; on prostitution, 352*n*34; public culture imagined by, 243; public memory of, 40, 286; Ramachandra and, 86; Sanskrit scholarship by, 117; self-deprecation by, 227; self-entombment of, 293; Shudras and, 250; social critique of, 220; social equality and, 290; social ethics of, 258, 264, 283; social politics of, 115–16; tomb of, 221; transcription of, 340*n*2; translation of salvational discourses and, 25; urban area descriptions by, 273–74; Varkaris and, 92–93, 119, 291, 293, 298; Vedas critique of, 238–40; vernacularization and, 72; vernacularization of, 287–97; on worship of Krishna, 256–57

Jñāneśvarī, ix, x, xii–xiv, 26, 28, 40, 46; aural literature and, 68; authorial voice of, 223–24; authority of, 237; *Bhagavad Gītā* and, 222–23; bhakti in, 219, 260; as bhakti text, 262;

Kirtan, 224, 226
Kishen Bhat, 356n20
Knowledge/power dialectic, 7
Koli, 157
Kolte, V. B., 303–4
Kosambi, D. D., 51
Kothaloba, 160
Krishna, xii–xiii, 51–52, 88, 225, 291,
    300; in *Bhagavad Gītā*, 215–16,
    225; *Bhagavad Gītā* connecting
    to, 238; on caste, 251, 252; caste
    and worshipping, 256–59; on
    dharma, 250; on faith, 270; Gurav
    worship of, 163; in *Jñāneśvarī*,
    223; Mahanubhav worship of,
    107; as seed of cosmic order, 255;
    Untouchables worshipping, 258–
    59; women worshipping, 258–59
Krishna (Yadava), 48–49, 66, 194;
    Chakradhar meeting with, 87
Krishna Mandir, 347n7
Kshatriyas, x, 23, 24, 329n22;
    Brahmins supported by, 68–69;
    Kayasthas and, 158, 159
Kulke, Hermann, 41
Kurmadas, 291

Lāda, 329n29
Lad Brahmins, 329n29
Lads, 329n29
Lake Manasa, 354n56
Lakhubaisa, 165
Lakshmidharba, 183
Language: Brahminic ecumene
    opinions of, 179; caste and, 189,
    191; Chakradhar comfort with,
    187–88, 342n41; cultural politics
    and, 187–93, 213; of difference,
    Jñāneśvarī and, 262–77; gender
    and, 179; Jains use of, 178; Jnandev
    choice of, as social statement,
    202; *Jñāneśvarī* choice of, 263;

landscapes of, 50–57; Mahanubhav
    debate of choice of, 181; Prakrit,
    177–78, 230; symbolic capital
    signaled through, 77; trial of
    Chakradhar and, 208; vernacular,
    5–6, 76; vernacularization and
    promotion of, 7; within Yadava
    territory, 50. *See also* Marathi;
    Sanskrit
*Language of the Gods in the World of Men,
    The* (Pollock), 6
Languages: *Apabhraṃsha*, 177;
    Buddhism use of, 178
Laws of Manu, 23, 346n106
Laxman, R. K., 305
Lele, Jayant, 21
Liberalism, 2
Līḷācaritra, ix, x, xi–xii, xiv, 40, 46, 48;
    authors of, 172; *bakhar* and, 68;
    as biography, 173; Brahminism
    critiqued by, 132–42; caste rivalries
    in, 157; Chakradhar as prime agent
    of, 172; Chakradhar biographical
    information and, 106; Chakradhar
    meeting with Krishna (Yadava),
    87; Chakradhar vernacularized
    in, 183–87; composition of, 4;
    contemporary literature and,
    68; as cultural history, 55–56;
    cultural politics represented in,
    131–32; geographical attention
    in, 184; Gurav-Brahmin rivalry
    in, 162–67; historical context in,
    220; as historical literary realism,
    xi, 173–75; instruction to stay in
    Maharashtra in, 185–86; Kolte
    work on, 303–4; literary Marathi
    emergence and, 50, 160; literary
    realism in, 173, 187; Mahanubhav
    writing about, 299; on Marathi
    and gender, 179–80; Marathi as
    practical choice for, 213; physical

Līḷācaritra (*continued*)
    separation of castes in, 138; social
inequity critique in, 142; social
radicalism and conservatism in,
283; trial of Chakradhar in, 201–10;
Untouchables in, 136–38; on use of
Marathi, 175; writing of, 114, 171

Linguistic nationalism, 74

Literacy, 59; aural, 76–77; Brahminic
ecumene and, 72, 122; Chakradhar
position on, 160–61; oral, 76–77,
230, 235; Sanskrit and, 72; social
capital and, 67–73, 123; social
justice and, 161–62; social value
of, 161; written, 230; Yadava
patronage and, 122

Literarization, 6, 53, 68, 230; *Jñāneśvarī
and*, 230; of Marathi, 68, 170–71,
245–46; space for, 170–71

Literary culture, 16

Literary Cultures in History (Pollock), 16

Literary economy, 157, 168; Brahmin-
Kayastha conflict and, 160

Literary field, 122

Literary innovation, 122–23

Literary Marathi: emergence of, 160;
historical material in, 55

Literary public, vernacular, 229–36

Literary realism, 173; historical, xi,
173–75; vernacularization and, 187

Literization, 6, 53, 245

Lorenzen, David, 21

Lukhadeoba, 134

Mahābhārata, 15, 51, 216–17; Ganesh as
scribe of, 225

Mahadaisa, 148–49, 153–54, 164,
165–66, 198

Mahadashram, 195–96, 201–2

Mahadev, 48, 62, 66, 194, 195, 196–98,
316n21

Mahadevan, Sudhir, 12

Mahajana, 62

Maha Kumbha Mela, 234, 235

Mahalasa, 354n55

Mahanubhavs, ix, xi–xii, 14; *Bhagavad
Gītā* commentary by, 220, 347n7;
Brahminism as social affliction for,
155; Brahmins and, 302, 341n25;
caste and gender critiques and, 26;
caste status of, 143–45, 160; census
information, 299; commentary
writings, 299; Dados and, 164–66;
disagreement among, 304; elites
as, 9; food and, 143–44; formation
of, 4; geography and, 184; Guravs
and, 164; Krishna worshipped
by, 107; language choice debate
among, 181; legal actions by,
303–4; as literary community, 172;
literary production by, 172, 299;
lives of leaders recorded by, 89; in
Maharashtra, 298; Marathi used
by, 110–12, 169, 175–76, 181–83,
185, 245; in modernity, 298–305;
numbers of, 356n21; political
stability enabling, 71; public
culture and, 286, 302–3; royal
patronage of composers, 324n46;
Sanskrit texts by, 180, 181–82;
social critique of early, 142–55;
social equality and, 201; social
ethics of egalitarianism among,
xiv; spread of, 298; suffering and,
186; temples deemphasized by, 167;
women and, 179–80; Yadava state
animosity with, 113

Maharashtra, 39, 314n1; census
information, 299; Chakradhar
departure from, 113–14, 203, 298;
Chakradhar instruction to stay in,
185–86, 203, 209; Mahanubhavs in,
298; as *mandal*, 281; Mayata Hari
leaving, 208–9; Pasāyadān and

identity in, 277–78; Prajnasagar
leaving, 208; vernacularization of, ix
Maharashtra State Gazetteer, 86
Maharashtri, 177
Mahārāṣtra Sāraswat (Bhave), 86
Māhārī, 263–64, 336*n*61
Mahipati, 293
Mānasollāsa (Someshwar III), 87
Maṇatu, 12
"Manbhaus," 299–301
"Manbhav Sect: The Gazetteer Trips,
The" (Bhandarkar), 301
Mandal, 281
Mandal Commission Report of 1980,
23, 313*n*68
Mang, 299–300
Māngi, 264–65
Manu Smriti, 156
Manusmṛti, 69
Maratha Confederacy, 69
Marathe, 314*n*1
Marathi: Chakradhar use of,
110–12, 185; donkey curse in,
79; emergence of literary, 2;
inequity framed by use of, 244–45;
influences on, 317*n*37; Jnandev
comparing to Sanskrit, 232–33;
Jnandev on, 229–34; *Jñāneśvarī* and,
222, 229–33; literarization of, 68,
170–71, 245–46; Mahanubhav use
of, 110–12, 169, 175–76, 181–83,
185, 245; as outside control of
Brahminic ecumene, 208; as
practical choice, 213; as Prakrit
language, 230; profanity, 321*n*10,
323*n*27; public around, 29; public
culture, 29, 286; social difference
and colloquialisms in, 262–77;
taxonomies of Sanskrit and, 176–
83; transfer of symbolic capital to,
170–71; vernacularization of, x, xi,
17–18; vernacularizing Chakradhar

through, 183–87; vernacular
literary turn, 5; women and, 207;
Yadava attitudes toward, 74–75;
Yadava court and, 9
Marathi humanism, 277
Marathi inscriptions, 54–55, 59,
317*n*39; as public performance,
75–77
Marathi literarization, 68, 245–46;
space for, 170–71
Marathi literature: appearance
of, 39; aural, 68; emergence of,
50; Jnandev and, 214, 243, 282;
Jñāneśvarī as first work of, 214–15;
Pandharpur and, 166–67; social
space of, 3; vernacularization
preconditions, 101; Vitthal and,
166–67; widened social field of, 26;
in Yadava century, 39; Yadava state
and patronage of, 86–91
Markand, 146
Market economies, public spheres
and, 71
Marriage, 108, 109, 333*n*20, 335*n*44
Master, Alfred, 59
Matangs, 152, 274–76, 300
Mayata Hari, 205–9, 266
Medieval Marathi public, 100–102
Mhaibhat/Mhaimbhat, 107, 114, 160,
171, 172, 182–83, 209; Chakradhar
debating, 191–92
Michelutti, Lucia, 11
Mir, Farina, 12
Mitchell, Timothy, 42
Modi, 54–55
Mudha Aditi temple, 205
Muktabai, 115, 341*n*20
Mukundaraja, 88
Muslims. *See* Islam

Nagadev, 112, 330*n*41
Nagaraj, D. R., 18

Prahlad, 257

Prajnasagar, 189–91, 205–8, 266

Prakrit languages, 177–78; Marathi
as, 230

Prasad, 153

Prasad, Leela, 12, 231

Pravacana, 222, 226

Prayag, 234, 235

Principle of negativity, 33

Prostitution, 264, 352n34

Public: attention constituting, 235;
bhakti, 91–100, 166; *bhakti* creating,
20; Chakradhar minimizing offense
to, 153–54; defining, 28–29; fear of,
78–86; *Jñāneśvarī* directed towards,
231; medieval Marathi, 100–102;
public sphere distinguished from,
32; public sphere mediating state
and, 344n66; vernacular literary,
229–36

Public culture: decentralization
of, 168; defining, 29; Jnandev
imagining, 243; *Jñāneśvarī* and, 243,
281, 287; Mahanubhavs and, 286,
302–3; Marathi, 29, 286; social and
political ecology of, 46; Varkaris
and, 286

Public performance: gender and,
310n22; inscriptions as, 75–77; in
Yadava century, 44

Public realm, 12

Public religiosity, 170

Public sphere, 26–35, 313n73; civil
society and, 43; defining, 27–28;
Habermas on, 30, 71, 313n79,
314n81; Kant on, 281; market
economies and, 71; origins of,
313n79; principle of negativity
and, 33; public distinguished from,
32; purity and selection by, 272;
rationality and, 31–32; scope of
societal debates and, 314n81; state

and public mediated by, 344n66;
structural transformation of, 32

Pundalik, 98

Purana literature, 15, 159

Purity, 143, 153; commensality and,
241; public sphere selection by,
272; social, 239

Purushottama, 66, 70

Purva Mimamsa, 58, 65

Qissa, 12

Quotidian: defining, 13; defining space
of, 9–10; power and, 15

Quotidian revolution, xiv, 284, 286,
305–6

Radical ascetics, 169

Raeside, Ian, 180

Rajashekhar, 178

Rājataraṅgiṇī, 175

Rajwade, V. K., 221

Rajya, 7–8

Ramachandra, 48–50, 64, 66, 198,
200, 280, 281; Bhatobas on,
199–200; capture of, 199, 345n85;
Chakradhar and, 199–200; donation
to Vitthal temple at Pandharpur,
95–96; donkey curse during reign
of, 80; Jnandev and, 86; Marathi
patronage by, 87

Ramdrana, 194, 197

Rashtrakutas, 47

Rationality, 31–32

Ratnamāla, 181, 183

Ravidasis, 24

Religion: agrahara and, 62; bifurcation
of, 18–19; cultural inequality in,
3; power and, 7; routinization of
charisma in, 186; vernacularization
and, 16–17

Religiosity, public, 170

Renunciates, 143, 269

caste rivalries and, 156; center
of power moved by, 167–68; of
Chakradhar, 183–87; Chakradhar
and, 72; critique of caste and
gender and, 27; cultural fissures
in, 156; cultural politics and, 284;
defining, 6, 7, 10; of democracy,
10–11; in everyday life, 2; gender
and, 310n14; history of power
and, 7–8; of Jnandev, 287–97;
Jnandev and, 72; Jnandev ethics
of, 238; lessons of history of,
305; literary, 40; literary realism
and, 187; of Maharashtra, ix; of
Marathi, x, xi, 17–18; Marathi
literature, 101; of non-language
expressive idioms, 6; of political
idioms, 11; power displayed
through, 6–7; primary driver of,
34; promotion of language and,
7; religion and, 16–17; in royal
courts, 2, 7; situating, 7; social
equality and, 283; social ethics of,
279; social inequality and, 15–16;
social inequity mediated by, 246;
sociopolitical order and, 45–46,
46; time periods and, 6; topos of
everyday life and, 105; transfer of
authority through, 237; written
records and, 6; Yadava dynasty
and, 40
Vernacular language, 5–6; sphere
of, 76
Vernacular literary public, 229–36
Vernacular polity, 42, 50, 52
Vernacular turn, 2–4, 5, 286
Village governance, systems of,
315n14
Vīragal (hero stones), 82
Virashaivas, 18
Vishnu, 257
Vishwanath, Balaji, 320n92

Viswanath, Rupa, 26
Vitthal, 52, 88, 187, 222, 291, 293;
devotion to, in Pandharpur,
91–100; *Jñāneśvarī* and, 294;
Marathi literature and, 166–67
Vitthal Temple, 75, 91, 166–67; growth
of, 97; Ramachandra donation to,
95–96
Vivekasindhu (Mukundaraja), 88
Vritti, 61
Vyasa, 225, 234

Waghmare, Sudhir, 12
Wakandar, Milind, 33
Warner, Michael, 28, 33, 85, 235
Western Chalukyas, 47
William, Raymond, 286
Women: caste and, 263–64; instruction
of, 206–7, 342n32; Mahanubhavs
and, 179–80; Marathi and, 207;
memories of, 342n32; Sanskrit and,
176–77, 182; as Shudras, 25; social
order and, 248; Untouchable, 264;
worshipping Krishna, 258–59
Written literacy, 230
Written records, vernacularization
and, 6

Yadava century, 13, 14; Brahmin
power in, 57; golden age of, 50, 56,
316n24; historical materials from,
55; *Jñāneśvarī* place within, 281;
Marathi literature in, 39; public
sphere in, 44; Sanskrit literary
power in, 235; Sanskrit literary
production in, 63; social and
political ecology in, 46; stability
of, 71
Yadava dynasty, ix–x, 39, 47–50;
attitudes towards Marathi of,
74–75; Brahminic ecumene and,
70–71; Kayastha patronage by, 156;